和月伸宏

NOBUHIRO WATSUKI

~~~ERRY BLOSSOMS ~~ THE SPRING

~~~ SPRING ('99) IT WILL BE FIVE YEARS ~~ THE START OF *RURO-KEN*. WOW, ~~T A SURPRISE.

IN THE SPRING FIVE YEARS AGO, WHEN THIS NEWCOMER (WHO DIDN'T KNOW HIS RIGHT FROM HIS LEFT) GOT ARTISTICALLY STUCK, HE WOULD GO TO SEE THE EVENING BLOSSOMS AT A NEARBY KINDER-GARTEN. HE LIFTED HIS SPIRITS BY SAYING TO HIMSELF, "FLOWERS BLOSSOM, AND BLOSSOMS SHED!"

WHEN I THINK BACK NOW, IT WAS SO STUPID.

BUT EVEN AFTER FIVE YEARS, I STILL THINK, "FLOWERS BLOSSOM, AND BLOS-SOMS SHED!"

Rurouni Kenshin, which has found fans not only in Japan but around the world, first made its appearance in 1992, as an original short story in *Weekly Shonen Jump Special*. Later rewritten and published as a regular, continuing *Jump* series in 1994, *Rurouni Kenshin* ended serialization in 1999 but continued in popularity, as evidenced by the 2000 publication of *Yahiko no Sakabatô* ("Yahiko's Reversed-Edge Sword") in *Weekly Shonen Jump*. His most current work, *Buso Renkin* ("Armored Alchemist"), began publication in June 2003, also in *Jump*.

RUROUNI KENSHIN
VOL. 25: THE TRUTH
The SHONEN JUMP Manga Edition

STORY AND ART BY
NOBUHIRO WATSUKI

English Adaptation/Pancha Diaz
Translation/Kenichiro Yagi
Touch-Up Art & Lettering/Steve Dutro
Design/Matt Hinrichs
Editor/Kit Fox

Managing Editor/Elizabeth Kawasaki
Director of Production/Noboru Watanabe
Vice President of Publishing/Alvin Lu
Vice President & Editor in Chief/Yumi Hoashi
Sr. Director of Acquisitions/Rika Inouye
Vice President of Sales & Marketing/Liza Coppola
Publisher/Hyoe Narita

Printed in the U.S.A.

Published by VIZ Media, LLC
P.O. Box 77010
San Francisco, CA 94107

SHONEN JUMP Manga Edition
10 9 8 7 6 5 4 3 2 1
First printing, April 2006

www.viz.com

THE WORLD'S
MOST POPULAR MANGA

www.shonenjump.com

SHONEN JUMP MANGA

Rurouni Kenshin™

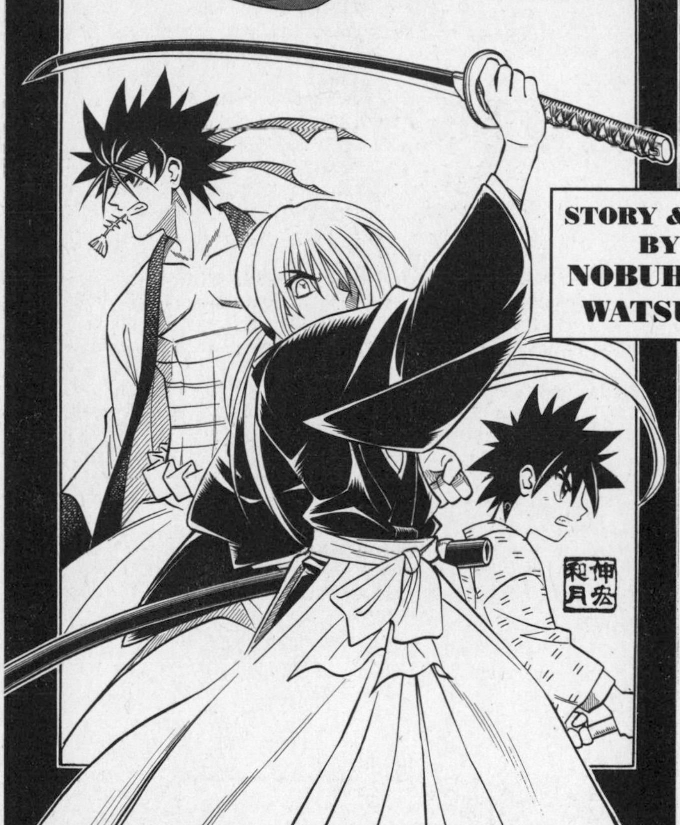
伸宏
和月

STORY & ART
BY
NOBUHIRO
WATSUKI

MEIJI SWORDSMAN ROMANTIC STORY

Vol. 25: THE TRUTH

CAST

緋村剣心（人斬り抜刀斎）

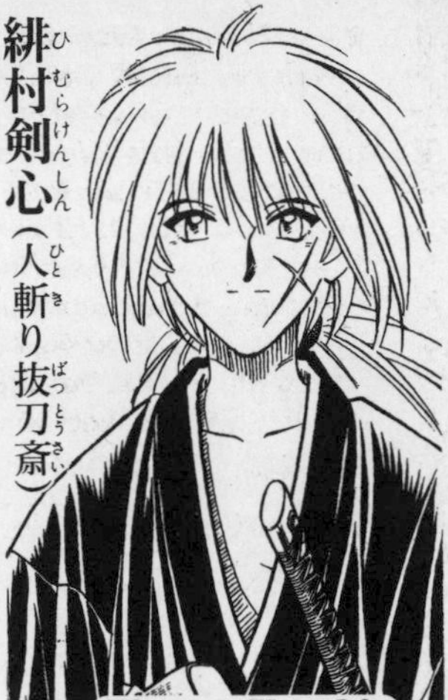

Himura Kenshin (Hitokiri Battōsai)

雪代縁

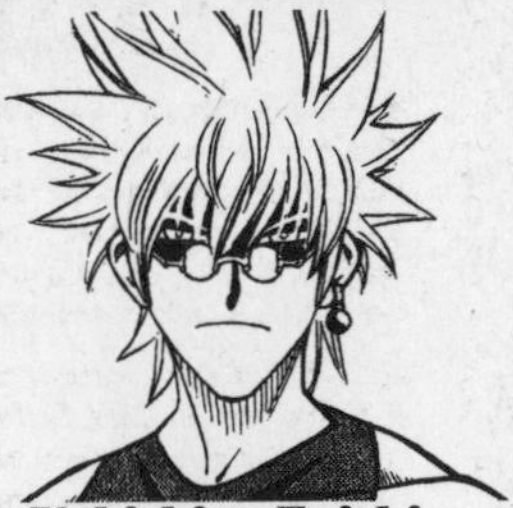

Yukishiro Enishi

斎藤一

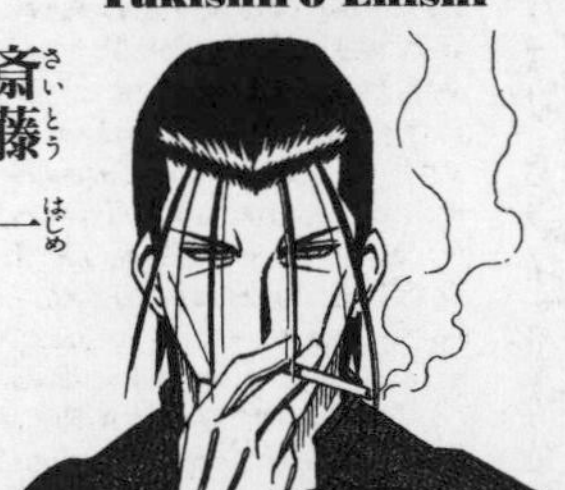

Saitō Hajime

明神弥彦

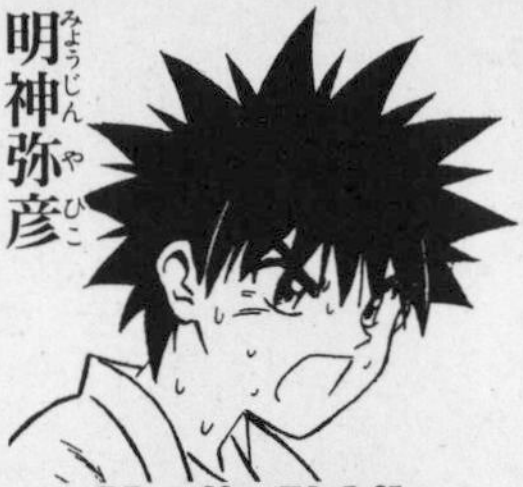

Myōjin Yahiko

三条燕

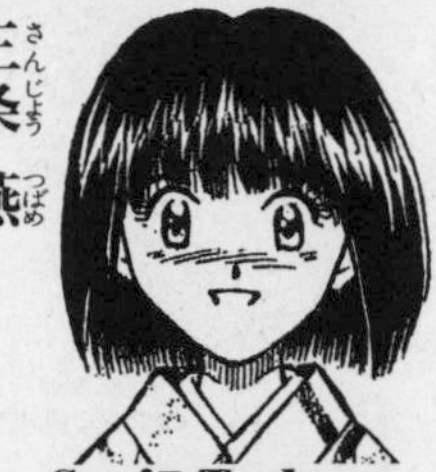

Sanjō Tsubame

神谷薫

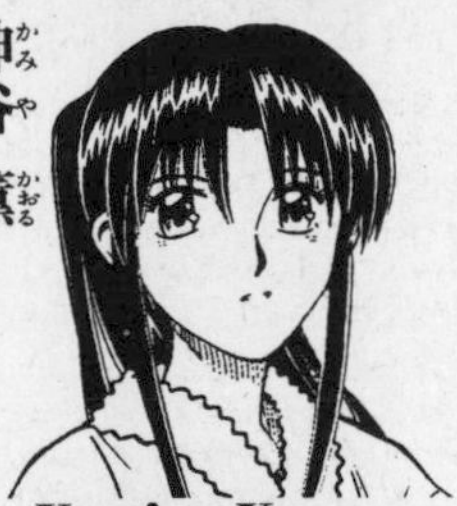

Kamiya Kaoru

四乃森蒼紫

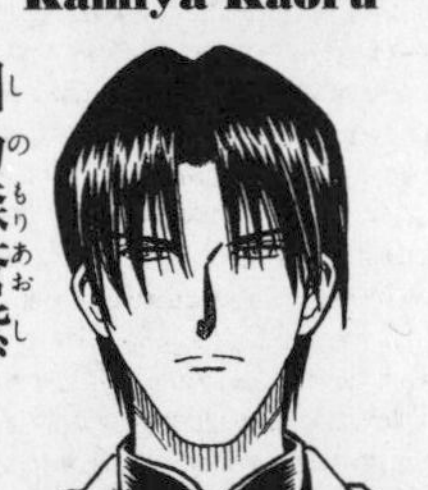

Shinomori Aoshi

るろうに剣心

和月伸宏

Once he was *hitokiri*, an assassin, called Battōsai. His name was legend among the pro-Imperialist or "patriot" warriors who launched the Meiji Era. Now, Himura Kenshin is *rurouni*, a wanderer, and carries a reversed-edge *sakabatō* blade, vowing to never kill another soul.

オイボレ

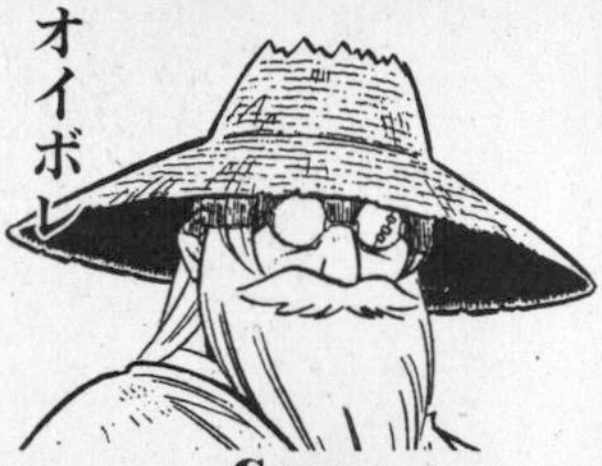

Geezer

鯨波兵庫(くじらなみひょうご)

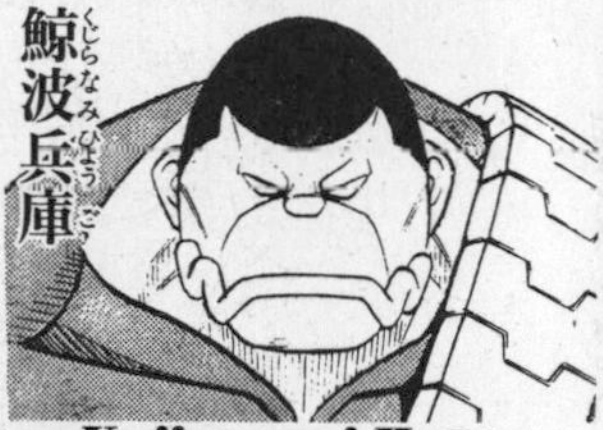

Kujiranami Hyōgo

THUS FAR

Those with grudges against Battōsai have gathered to take their revenge. To make matters worse, Kenshin finds out that the mastermind of this new attack is Enishi, the brother of Kenshin's deceased wife Tomoe—who died at Kenshin's own hand. And yet Kenshin decides to fight in order to protect the present, and begins by telling his friends of his past.

Enishi and his crew appear midair above Kamiya Dojo in hot air balloons, but Enishi's true intention is to take away the person most important to Kenshin, thereby casting him into a living hell. Enishi murders Kaoru and flees with Gein while the four other attackers are arrested. Kenshin blames himself for being unable to protect the person dearest to him and exiles himself to the "Fallen Village," where those who have given up on life gather. Aoshi and Misao arrive from Kyoto and are told the dreadful news. But Aoshi is suspicious of the circumstances of Kaoru's death and exhumes her grave. Upon examining the body, it becomes evident that it is a "corpse doll" created by Gein. Kaoru is alive—captive on an isolated island in the Tokyo bay that is used by Enishi's organization as a relay point for their weapons trade. Yahiko and Misao begin searching for Enishi's hideout in the Arakawa estuary while Aoshi lays a trap in the graveyard, defeating Gein when he comes to retrieve his "corpse doll." Aoshi then heads to the Tokyo hideout with Saitō, but...

CONTENTS

RUROUNI KENSHIN

Meiji Swordsman Romantic Story

BOOK TWENTY-FIVE: THE TRUTH

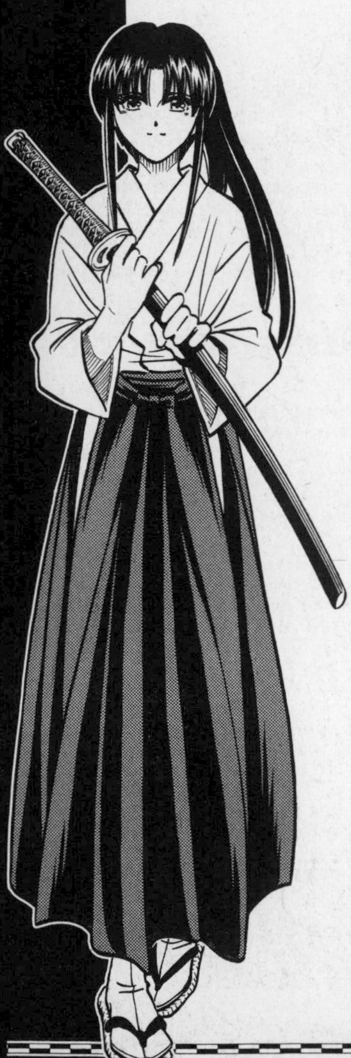

Act 218 Madness Released

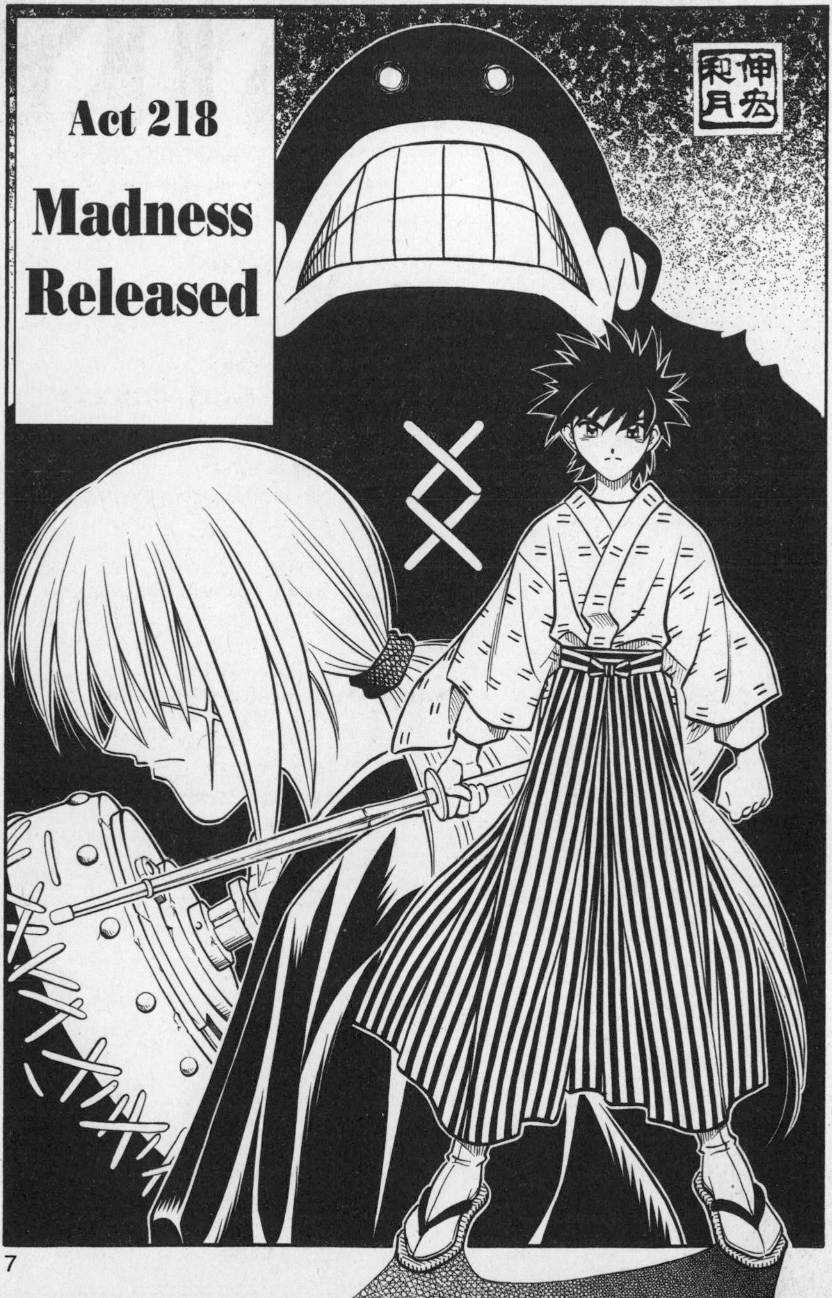

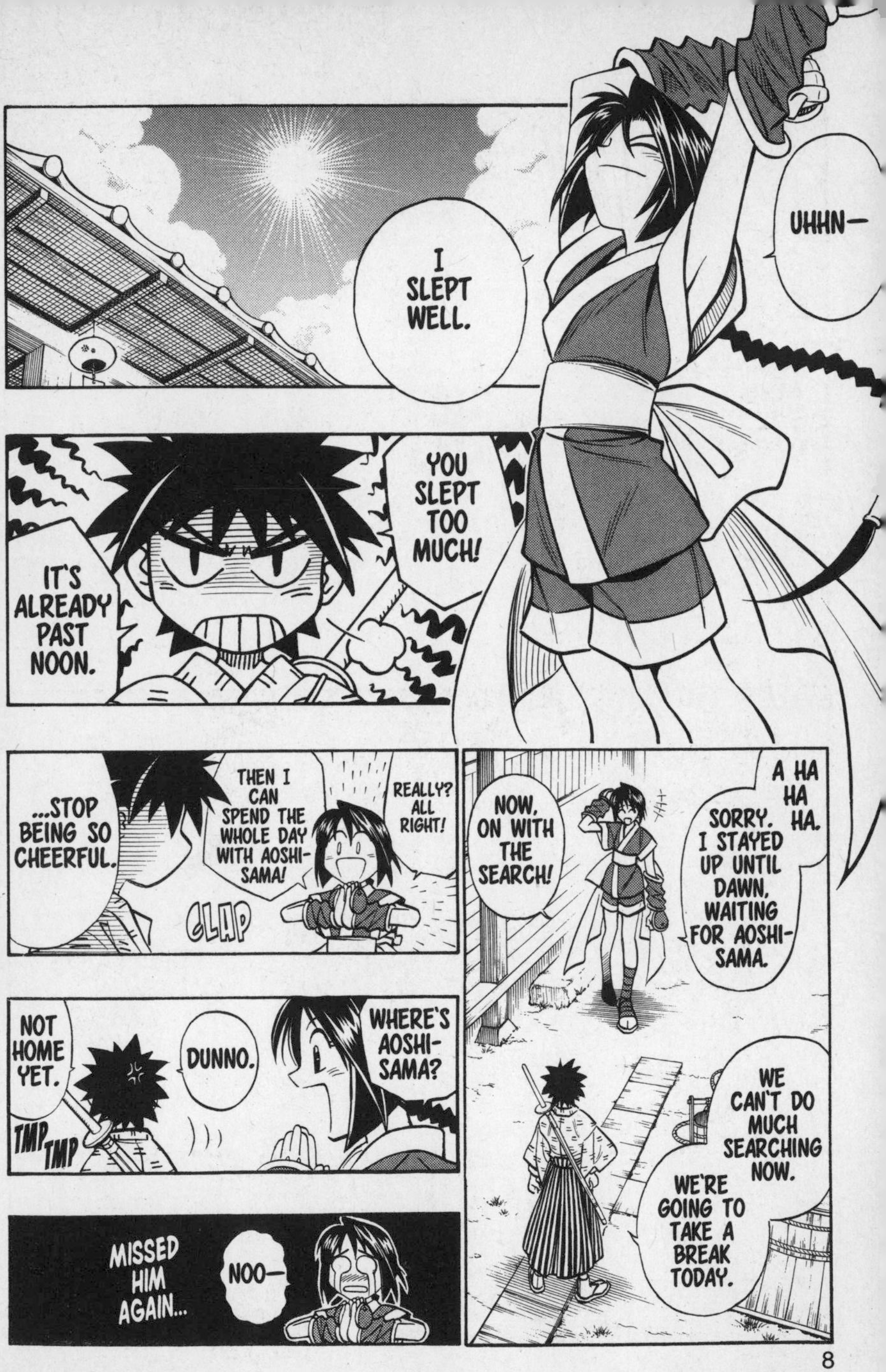
UHHN—
I SLEPT WELL.
YOU SLEPT TOO MUCH!
IT'S ALREADY PAST NOON.
A HA HA HA.
SORRY. I STAYED UP UNTIL DAWN, WAITING FOR AOSHI-SAMA.
NOW, ON WITH THE SEARCH!
WE CAN'T DO MUCH SEARCHING NOW.
WE'RE GOING TO TAKE A BREAK TODAY.
REALLY? ALL RIGHT!
THEN I CAN SPEND THE WHOLE DAY WITH AOSHI-SAMA!
CLAP
...STOP BEING SO CHEERFUL.
WHERE'S AOSHI-SAMA?
DUNNO.
NOT HOME YET.
TMP TMP
NOO—
MISSED HIM AGAIN...

READ THIS WAY

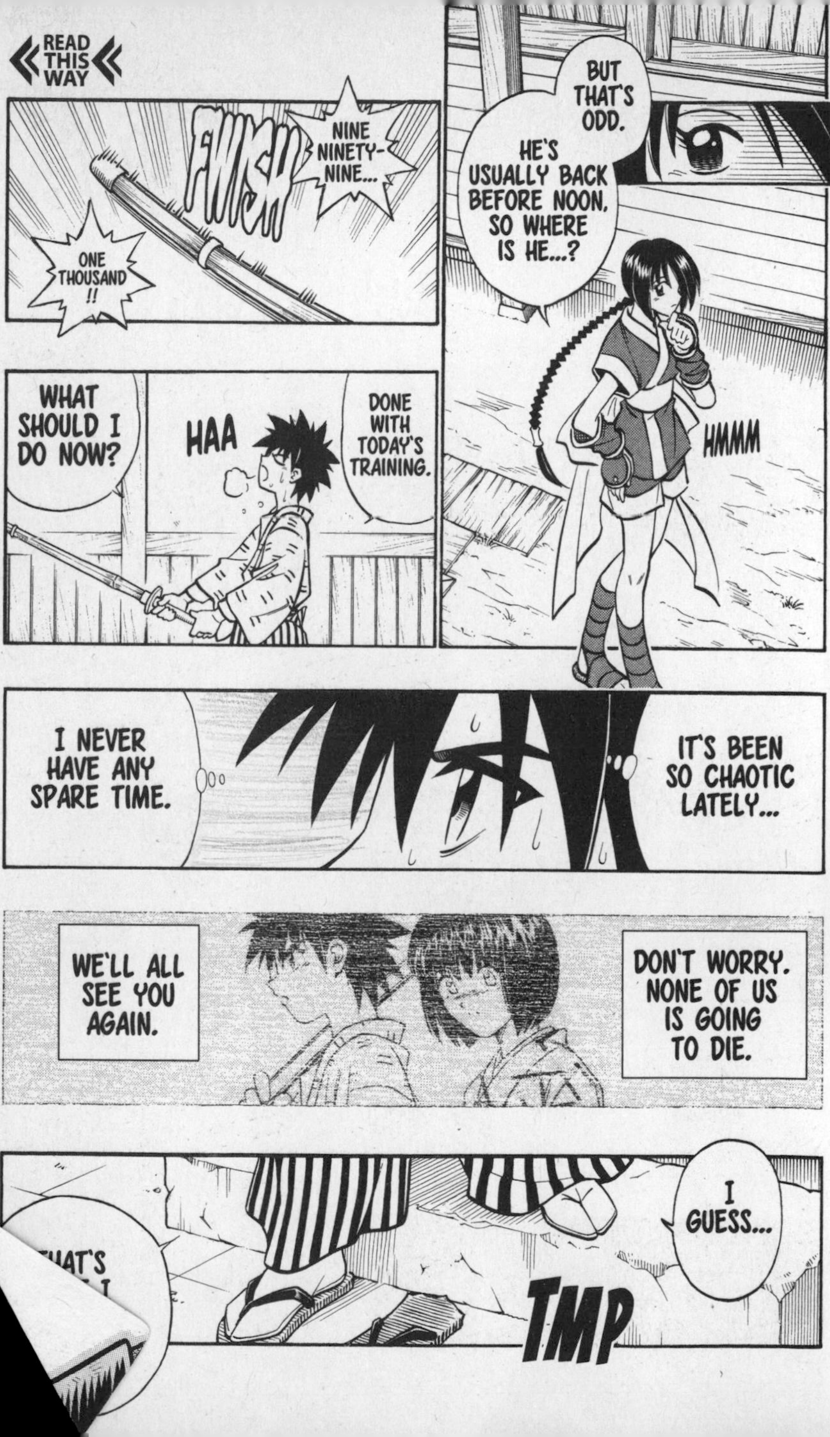
BUT THAT'S ODD.
HE'S USUALLY BACK BEFORE NOON, SO WHERE IS HE...?
HMMM
NINE NINETY-NINE...
FWISH
ONE THOUSAND !!
DONE WITH TODAY'S TRAINING.
HAA
WHAT SHOULD I DO NOW?
IT'S BEEN SO CHAOTIC LATELY...
I NEVER HAVE ANY SPARE TIME.
DON'T WORRY. NONE OF US IS GOING TO DIE.
WE'LL ALL SEE YOU AGAIN.
I GUESS...
TMP

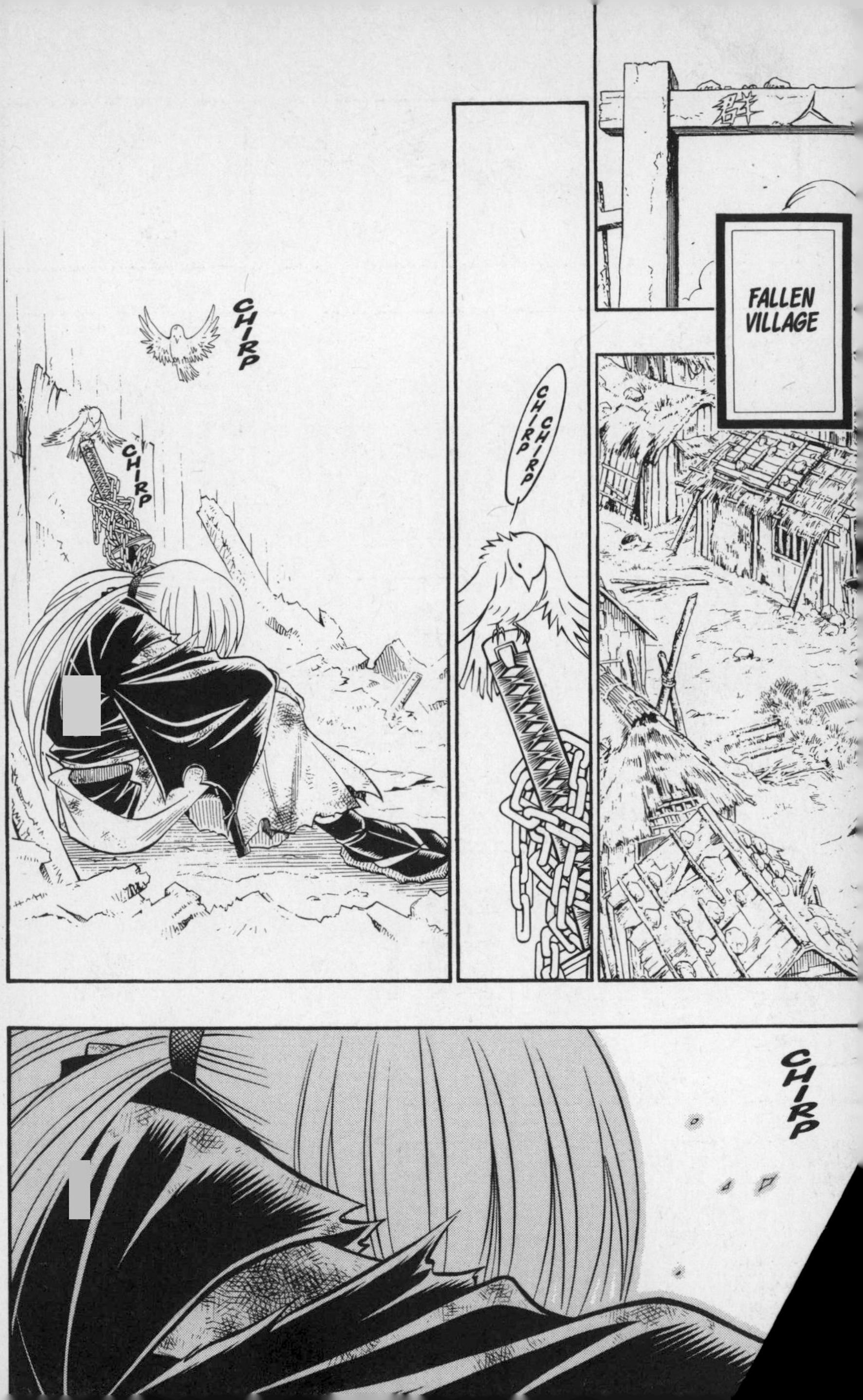
FALLEN VILLAGE
CHIRP CHIRP
CHIRP
CHIRP
CHIRP

READ THIS WAY

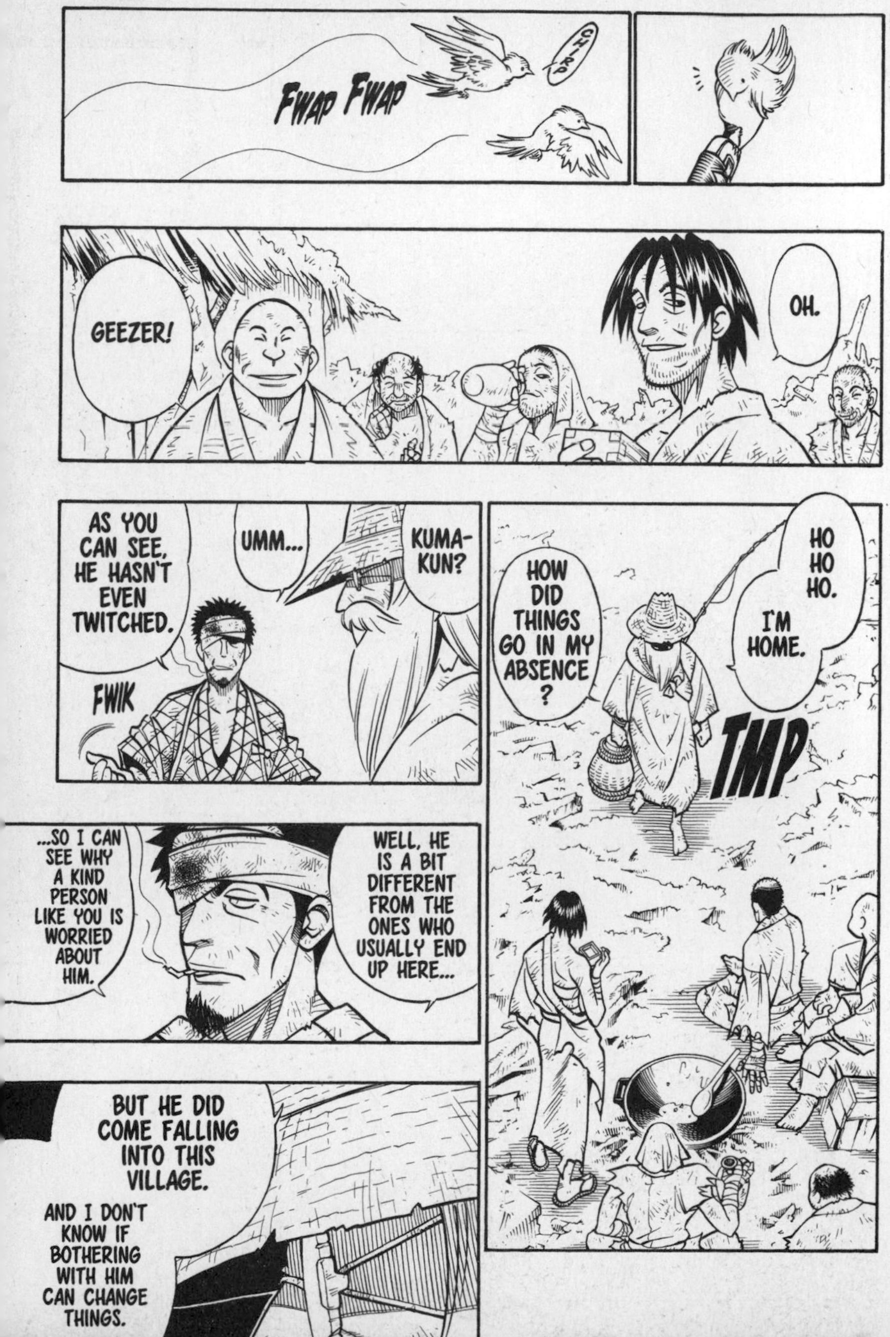
CHIRP
FWAP FWAP
OH.
GEEZER!
HO HO HO.
I'M HOME.
HOW DID THINGS GO IN MY ABSENCE?
TMP
KUMA-KUN?
UMM...
AS YOU CAN SEE, HE HASN'T EVEN TWITCHED.
FWIK
WELL, HE IS A BIT DIFFERENT FROM THE ONES WHO USUALLY END UP HERE...
...SO I CAN SEE WHY A KIND PERSON LIKE YOU IS WORRIED ABOUT HIM.
BUT HE DID COME FALLING INTO THIS VILLAGE.
AND I DON'T KNOW IF BOTHERING WITH HIM CAN CHANGE THINGS.

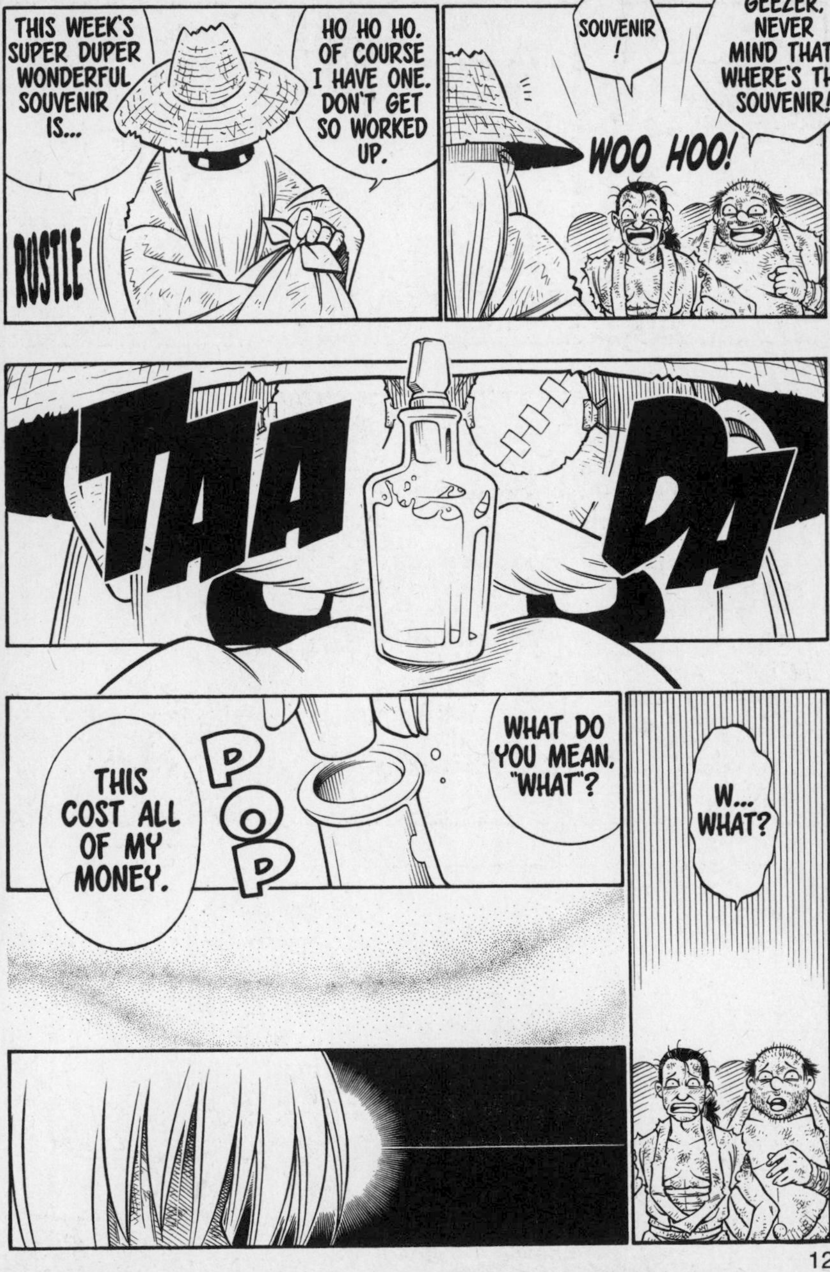
HEY GEEZER, NEVER MIND THAT. WHERE'S THE SOUVENIR!
SOUVENIR !
WOO HOO!
HO HO HO. OF COURSE I HAVE ONE. DON'T GET SO WORKED UP.
THIS WEEK'S SUPER DUPER WONDERFUL SOUVENIR IS...
RUSTLE
TAA DA
W... WHAT?
WHAT DO YOU MEAN, "WHAT"?
POP
THIS COST ALL OF MY MONEY.

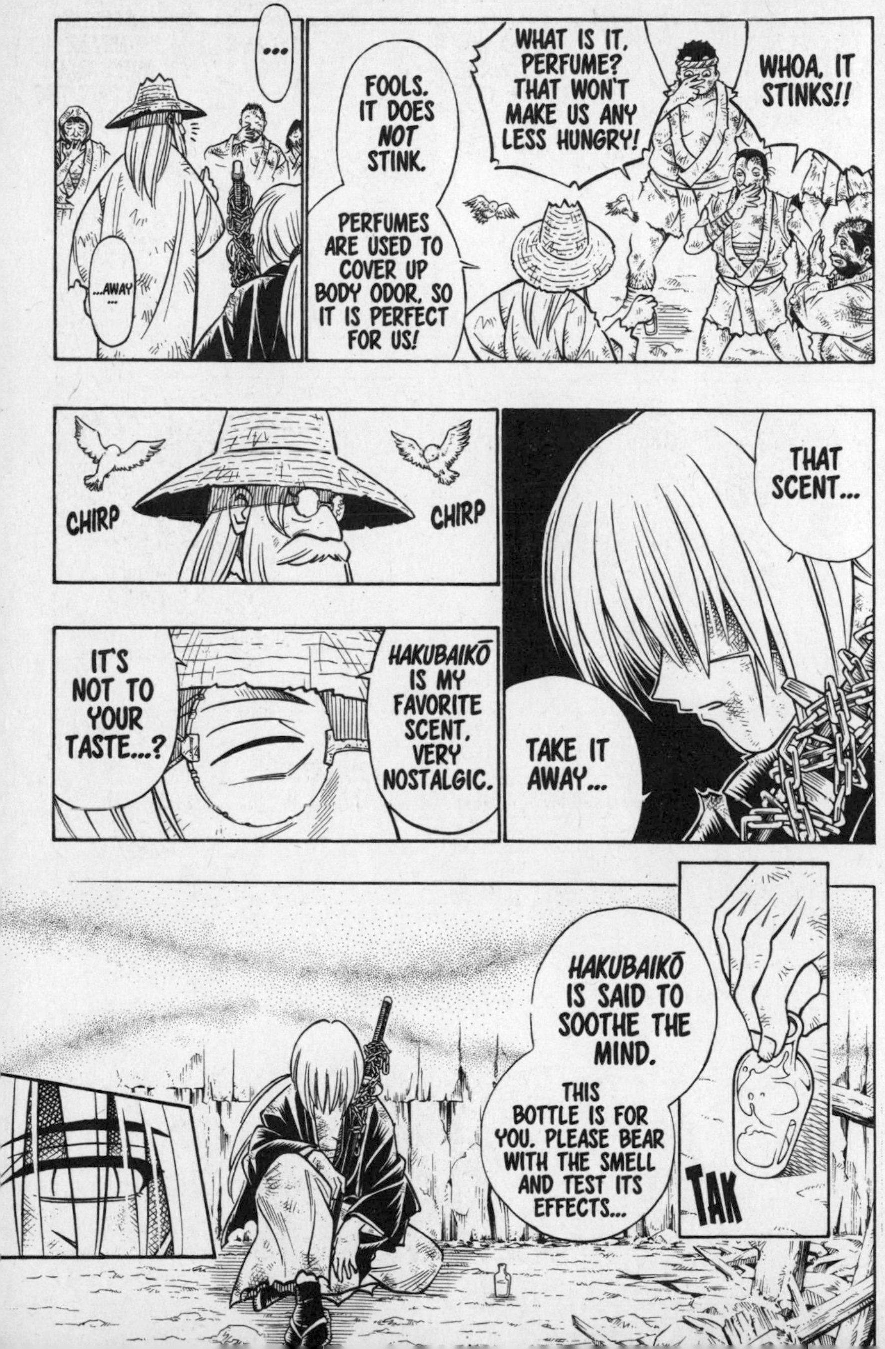
WHOA, IT STINKS!!
WHAT IS IT, PERFUME? THAT WON'T MAKE US ANY LESS HUNGRY!
FOOLS. IT DOES *NOT* STINK.
PERFUMES ARE USED TO COVER UP BODY ODOR, SO IT IS PERFECT FOR US!
...
...AWAY ...
THAT SCENT...
TAKE IT AWAY...
CHIRP
CHIRP
HAKUBAIKŌ IS MY FAVORITE SCENT, VERY NOSTALGIC.
IT'S NOT TO YOUR TASTE...?
TAK
HAKUBAIKŌ IS SAID TO SOOTHE THE MIND.
THIS BOTTLE IS FOR YOU. PLEASE BEAR WITH THE SMELL AND TEST ITS EFFECTS...

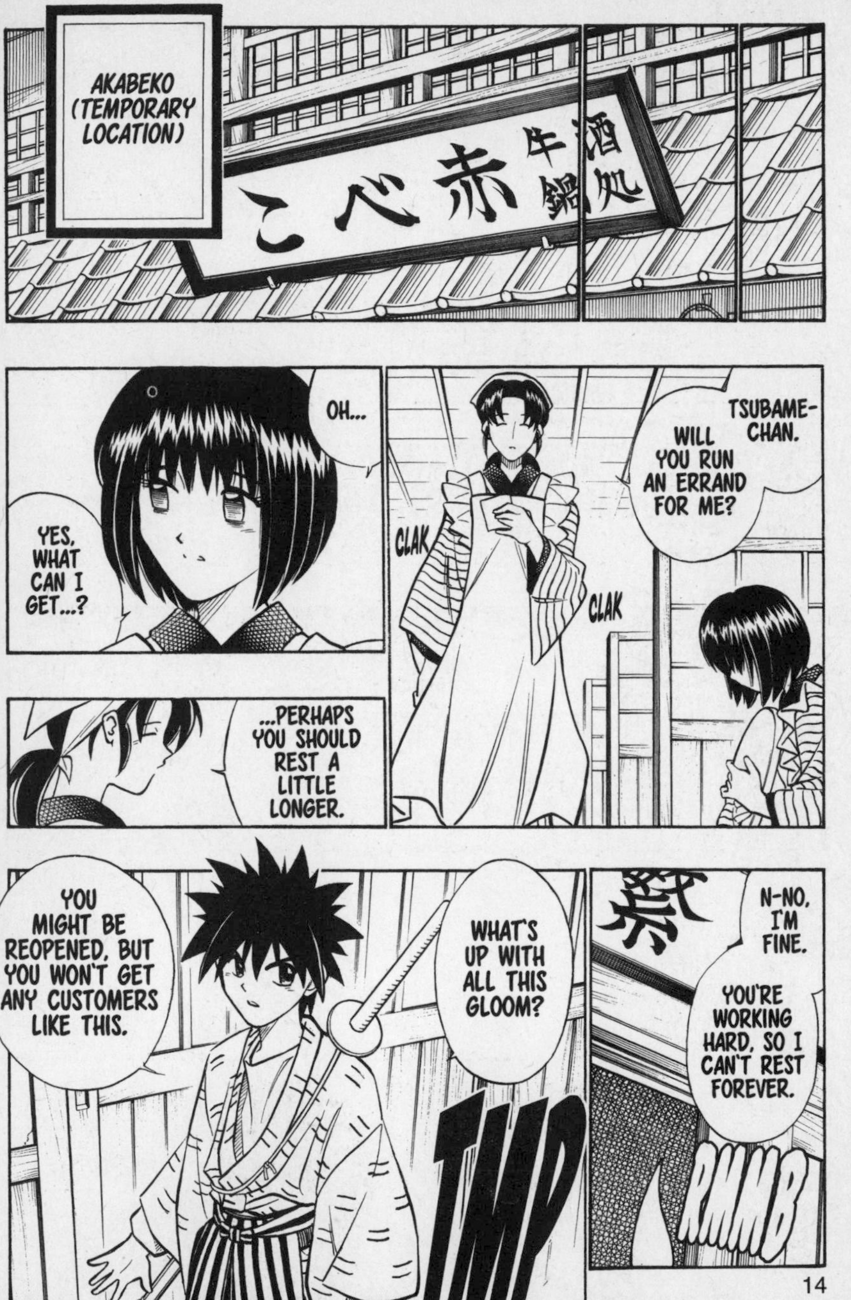
AKABEKO (TEMPORARY LOCATION)
酒処 牛鍋
赤べこ
TSUBAME-CHAN.
WILL YOU RUN AN ERRAND FOR ME?
CLAK
CLAK
OH...
YES, WHAT CAN I GET...?
...PERHAPS YOU SHOULD REST A LITTLE LONGER.
N-NO, I'M FINE.
YOU'RE WORKING HARD, SO I CAN'T REST FOREVER.
RMMB
TMP
WHAT'S UP WITH ALL THIS GLOOM?
YOU MIGHT BE REOPENED, BUT YOU WON'T GET ANY CUSTOMERS LIKE THIS.

READ THIS WAY

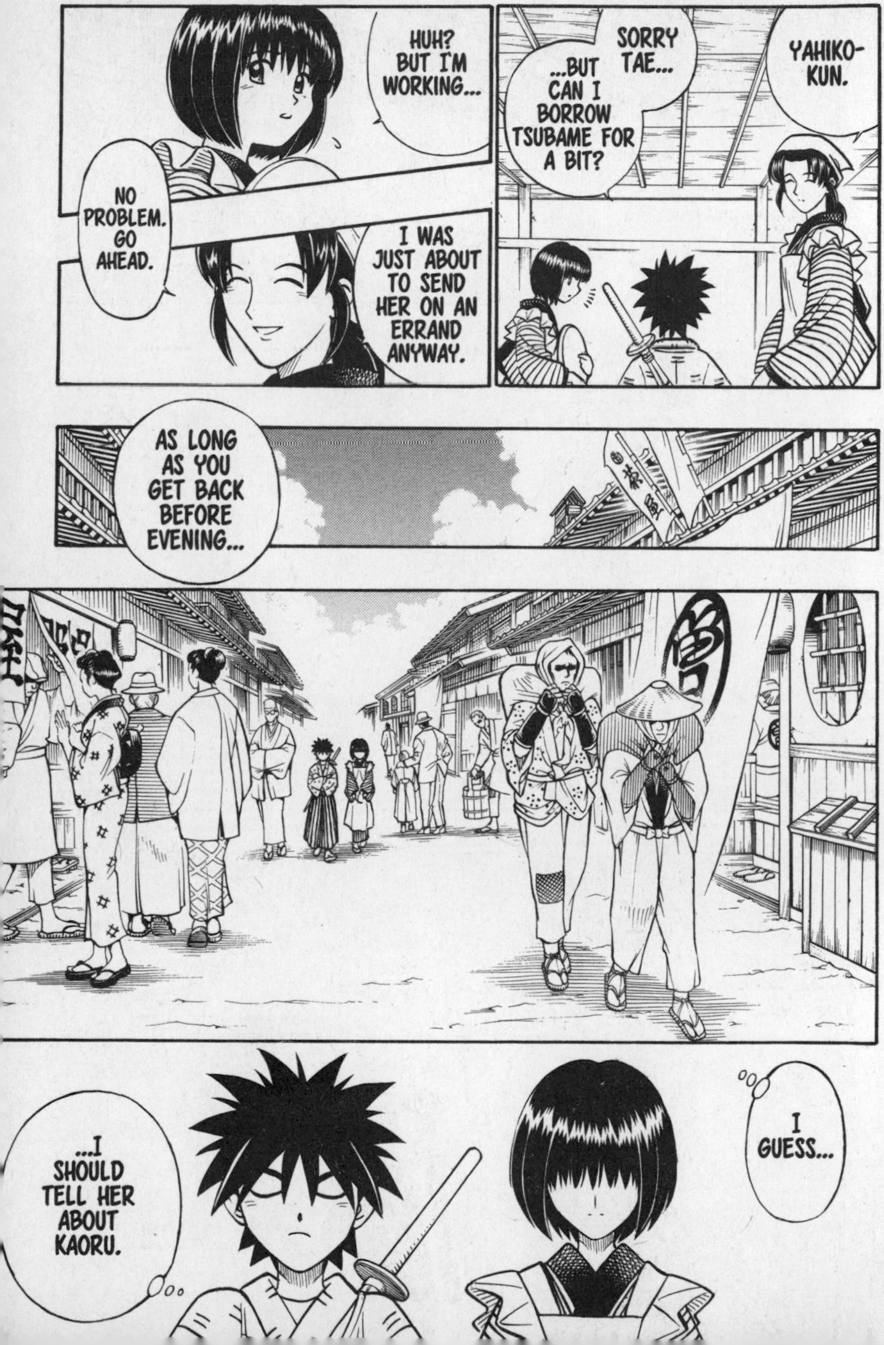
YAHIKO-KUN.
SORRY TAE...
...BUT CAN I BORROW TSUBAME FOR A BIT?
HUH? BUT I'M WORKING...
NO PROBLEM. GO AHEAD.
I WAS JUST ABOUT TO SEND HER ON AN ERRAND ANYWAY.
AS LONG AS YOU GET BACK BEFORE EVENING...
I GUESS...
...I SHOULD TELL HER ABOUT KAORU.

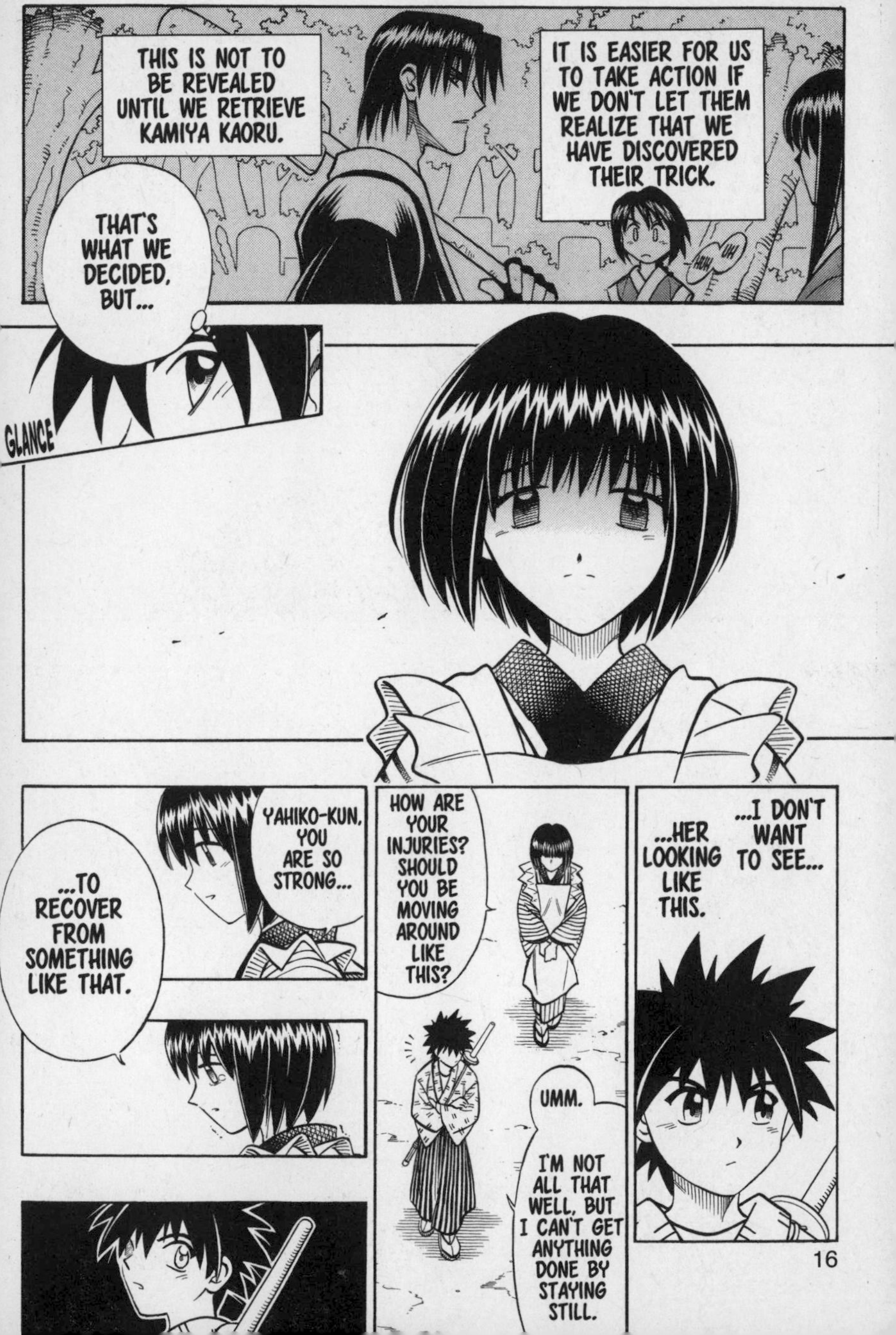
IT IS EASIER FOR US TO TAKE ACTION IF WE DON'T LET THEM REALIZE THAT WE HAVE DISCOVERED THEIR TRICK.
THIS IS NOT TO BE REVEALED UNTIL WE RETRIEVE KAMIYA KAORU.
UH HUH
THAT'S WHAT WE DECIDED, BUT...
GLANCE
...I DON'T WANT TO SEE...
...HER LOOKING LIKE THIS.
HOW ARE YOUR INJURIES? SHOULD YOU BE MOVING AROUND LIKE THIS?
UMM.
I'M NOT ALL THAT WELL, BUT I CAN'T GET ANYTHING DONE BY STAYING STILL.
YAHIKO-KUN, YOU ARE SO STRONG...
...TO RECOVER FROM SOMETHING LIKE THAT.

READ THIS WAY

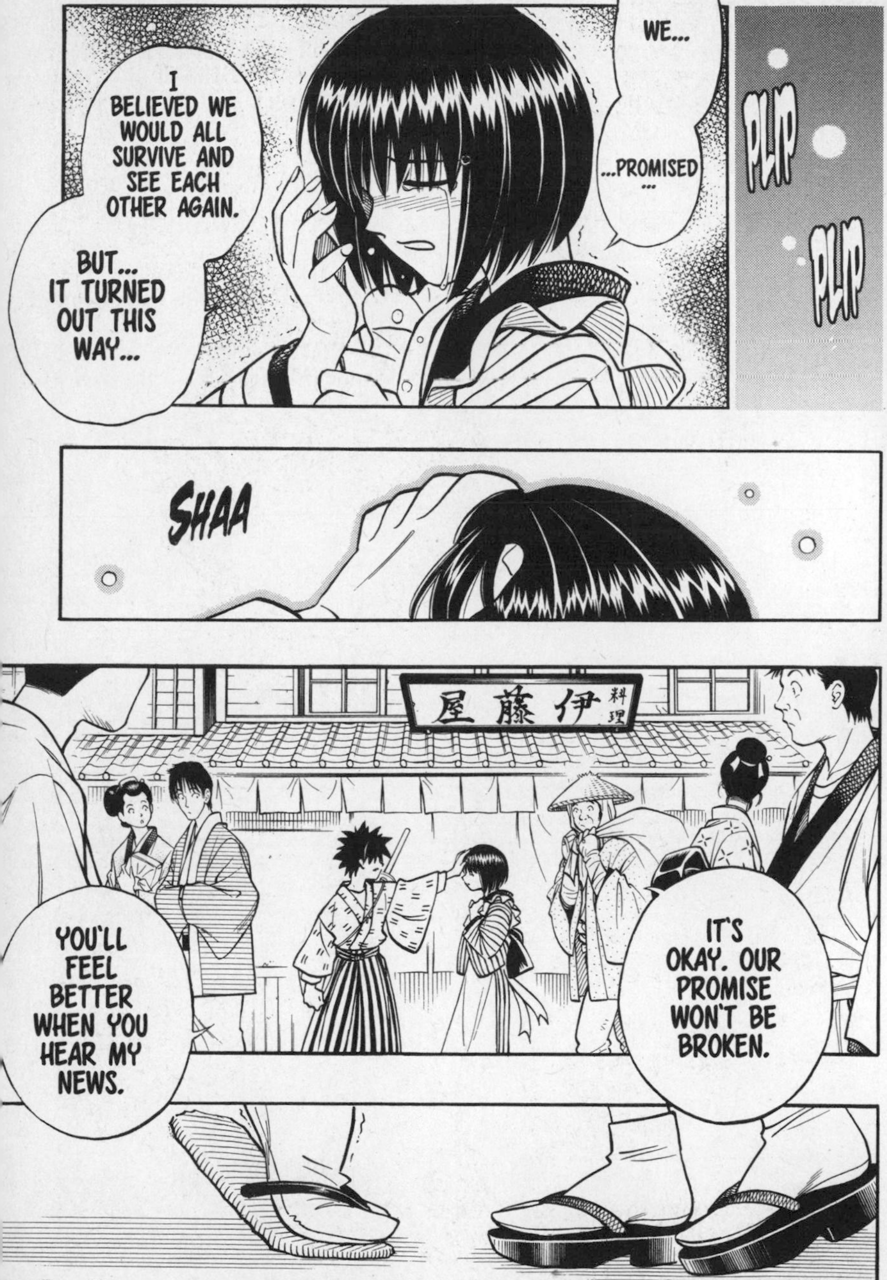
PLIP
PLIP
WE... ...PROMISED...
I BELIEVED WE WOULD ALL SURVIVE AND SEE EACH OTHER AGAIN.
BUT... IT TURNED OUT THIS WAY...
SHAA
料理 伊藤屋
IT'S OKAY. OUR PROMISE WON'T BE BROKEN.
YOU'LL FEEL BETTER WHEN YOU HEAR MY NEWS.

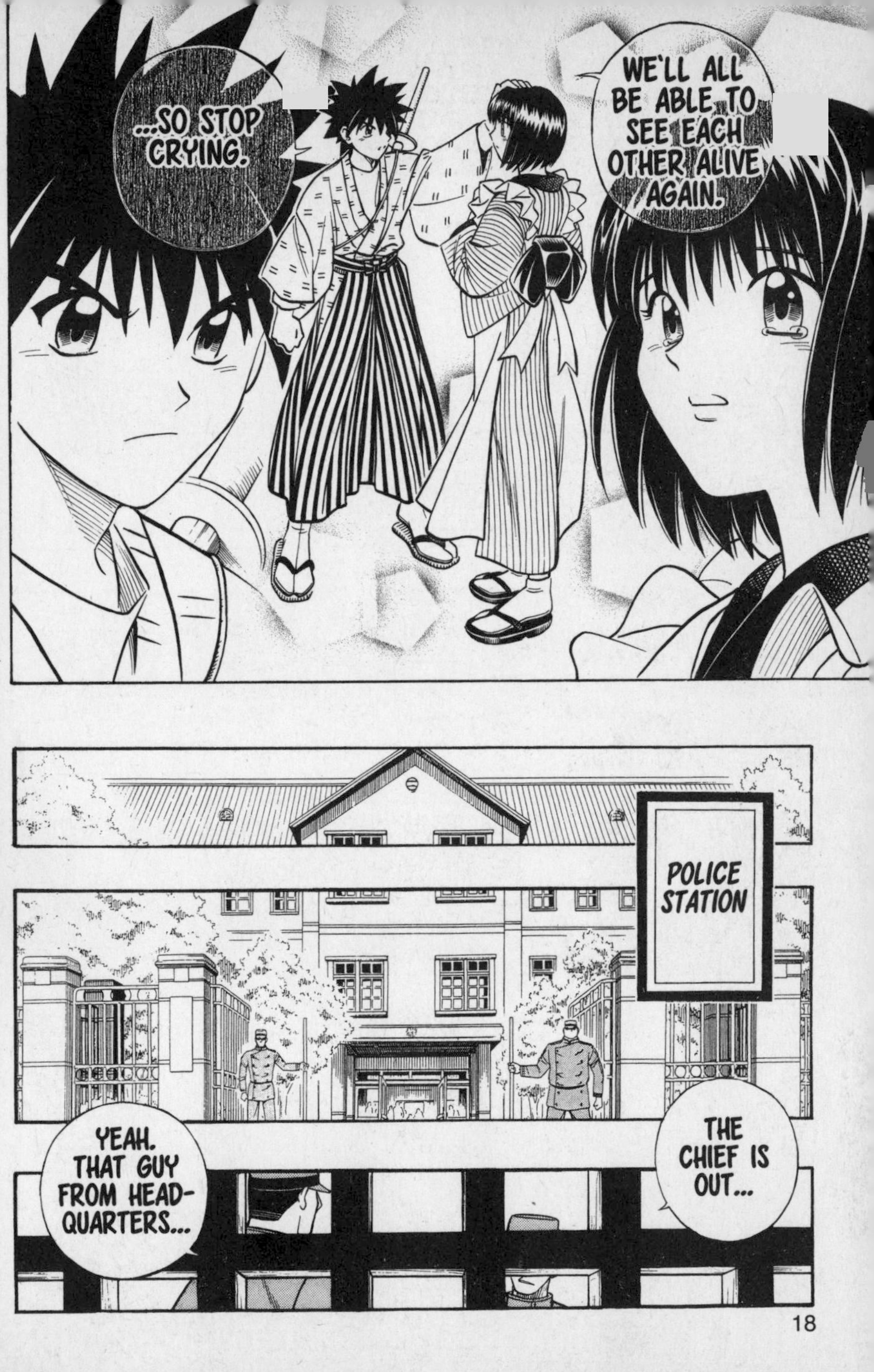
WE'LL ALL BE ABLE TO SEE EACH OTHER ALIVE AGAIN.
...SO STOP CRYING.
POLICE STATION
THE CHIEF IS OUT...
YEAH. THAT GUY FROM HEAD-QUARTERS...

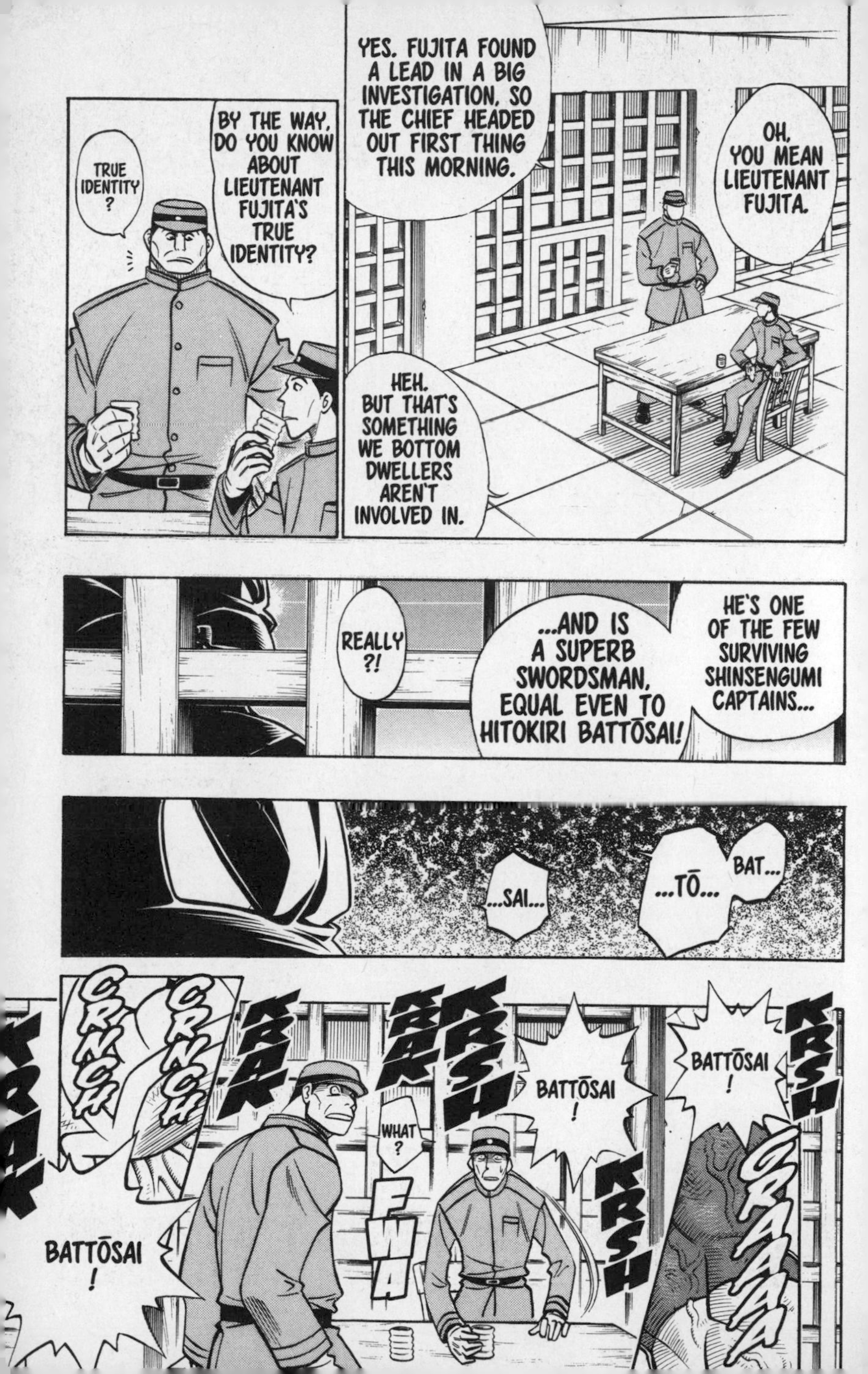
YES. FUJITA FOUND A LEAD IN A BIG INVESTIGATION, SO THE CHIEF HEADED OUT FIRST THING THIS MORNING.
OH, YOU MEAN LIEUTENANT FUJITA.
HEH. BUT THAT'S SOMETHING WE BOTTOM DWELLERS AREN'T INVOLVED IN.
BY THE WAY, DO YOU KNOW ABOUT LIEUTENANT FUJITA'S TRUE IDENTITY?
TRUE IDENTITY?
HE'S ONE OF THE FEW SURVIVING SHINSENGUMI CAPTAINS...
...AND IS A SUPERB SWORDSMAN, EQUAL EVEN TO HITOKIRI BATTŌSAI!
REALLY?!
BAT...
...TŌ...
...SAI...
KRSH
BATTŌSAI!
BATTŌSAI!
KRSH
KRSH
BAK
WHAT?
FWA
BAK
CRNCH
CRNCH
BATTŌSAI!
KRAK

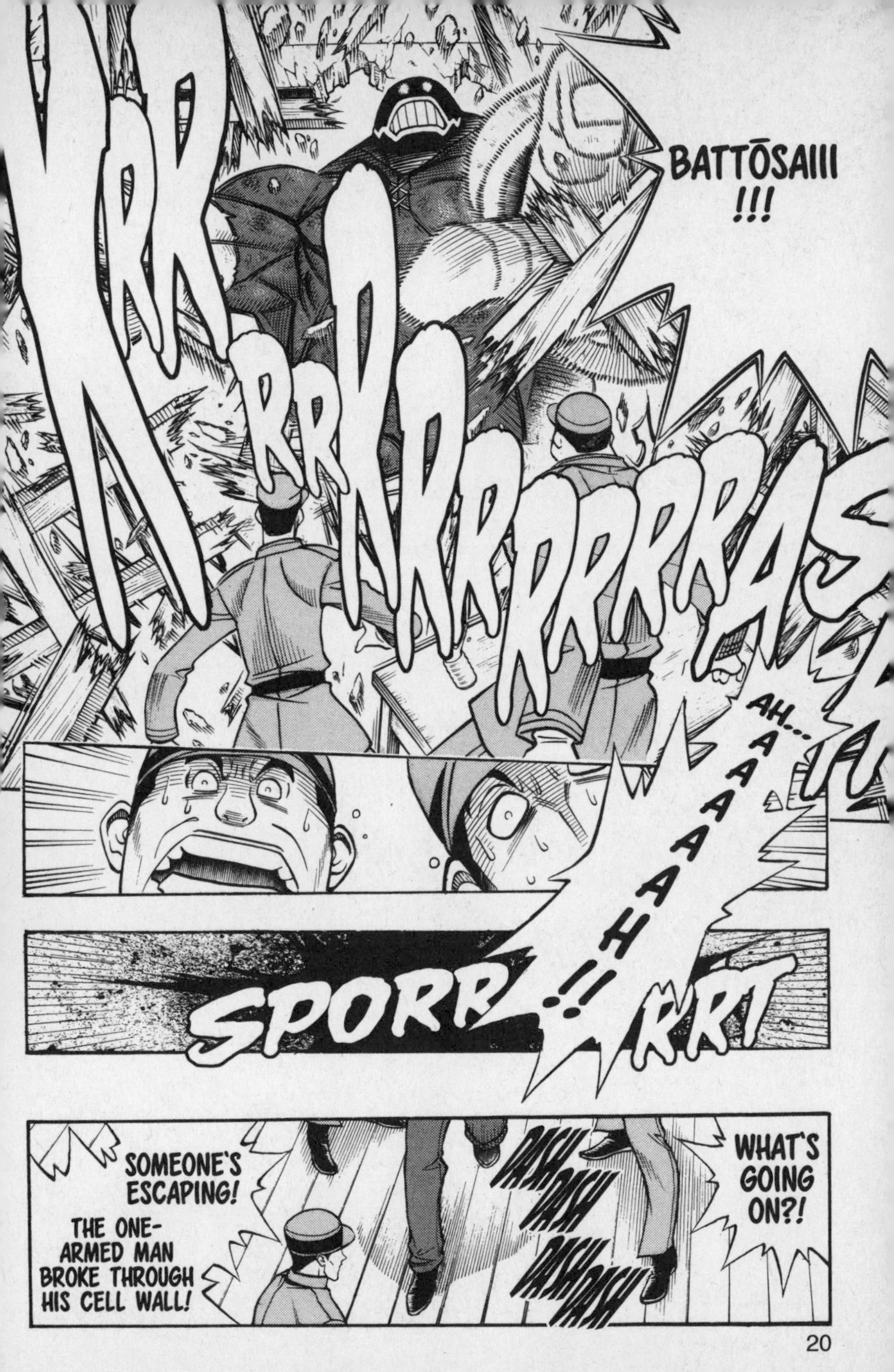
BATTŌSAIII !!!
AH... AAAAAAAH!!!
SPORR KRRT
WHAT'S GOING ON?!
SOMEONE'S ESCAPING!
THE ONE-ARMED MAN BROKE THROUGH HIS CELL WALL!

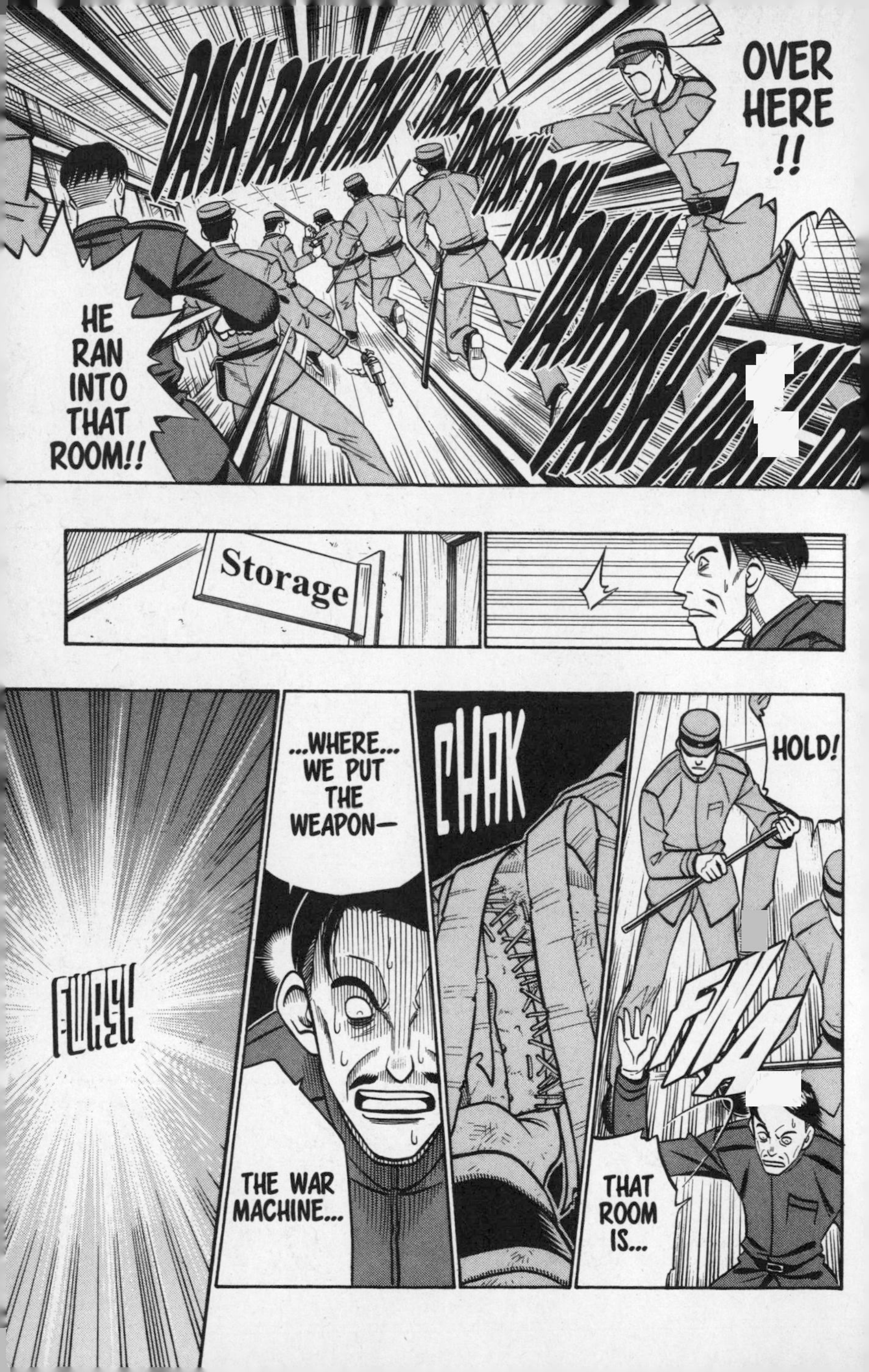
OVER HERE!!
DASH DASH DASH DASH DASH DASH DASH
HE RAN INTO THAT ROOM!!
Storage
HOLD!
FWA
THAT ROOM IS...
CHAK
...WHERE... WE PUT THE WEAPON—
THE WAR MACHINE...
FLASH

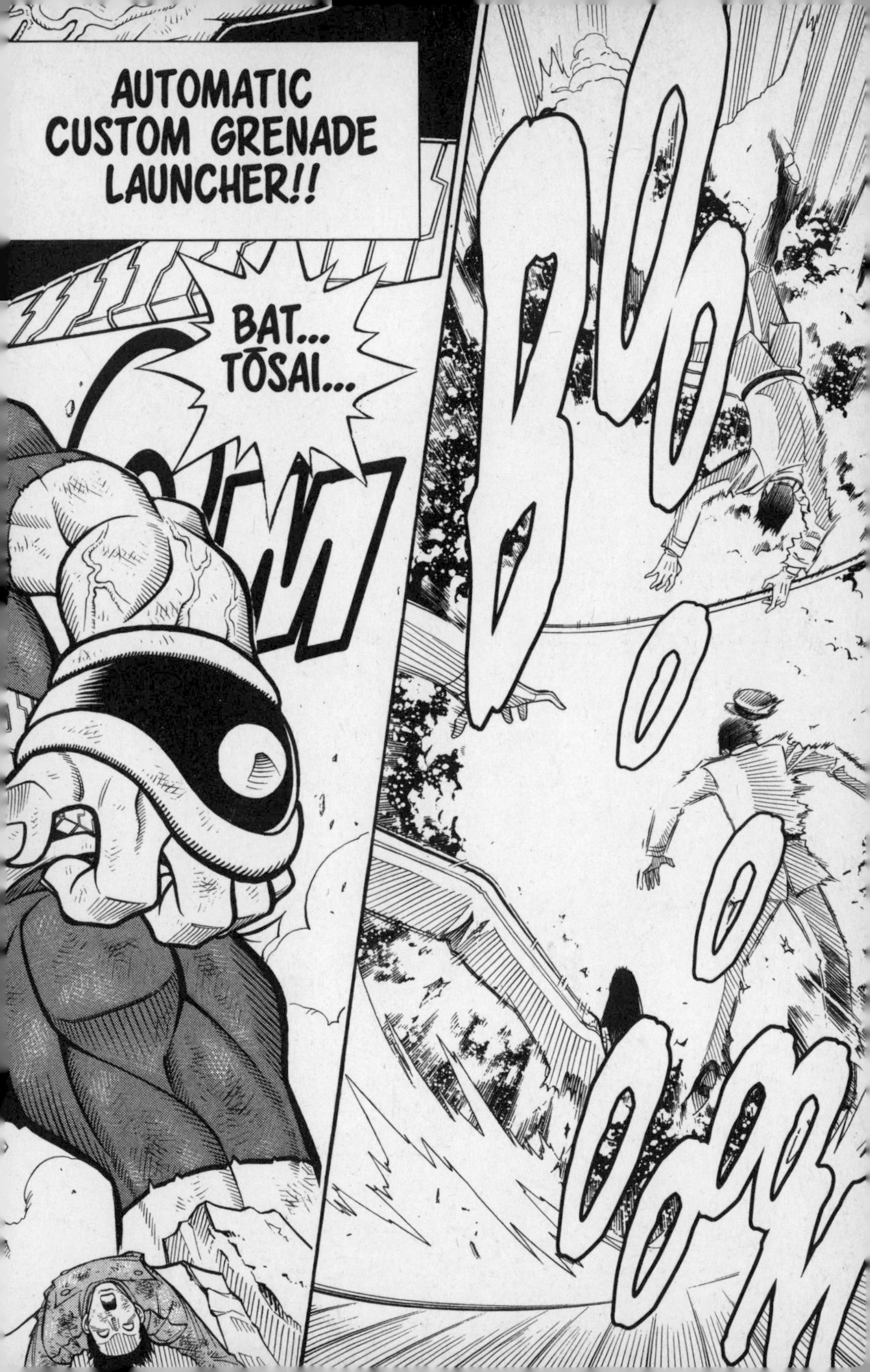
AUTOMATIC CUSTOM GRENADE LAUNCHER!!
BAT... TŌSAI...

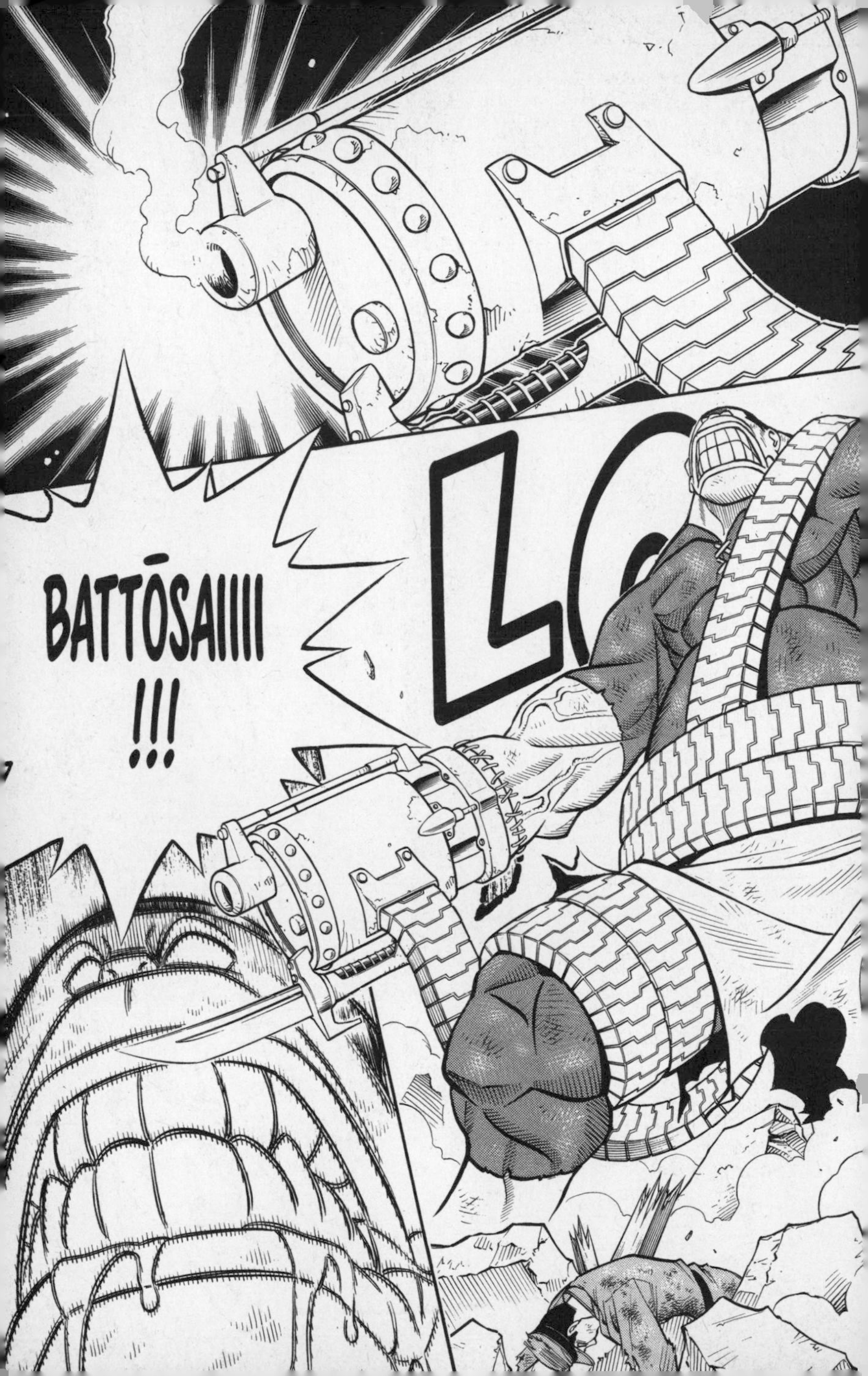
BATTŌSAIIIII
!!!

Rurouni Kenshin

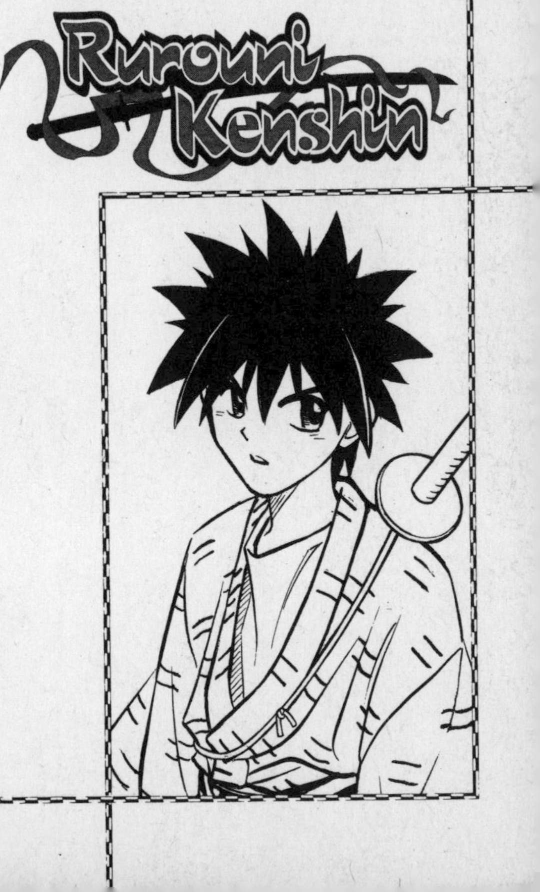

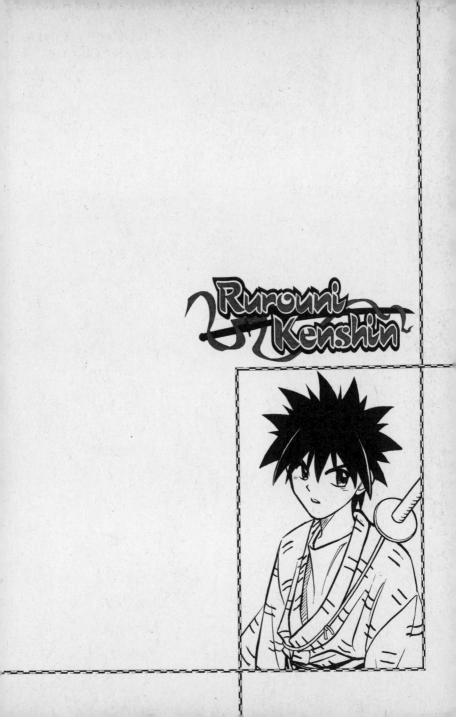

Act 219 Yahiko's True Battle (Part 1)

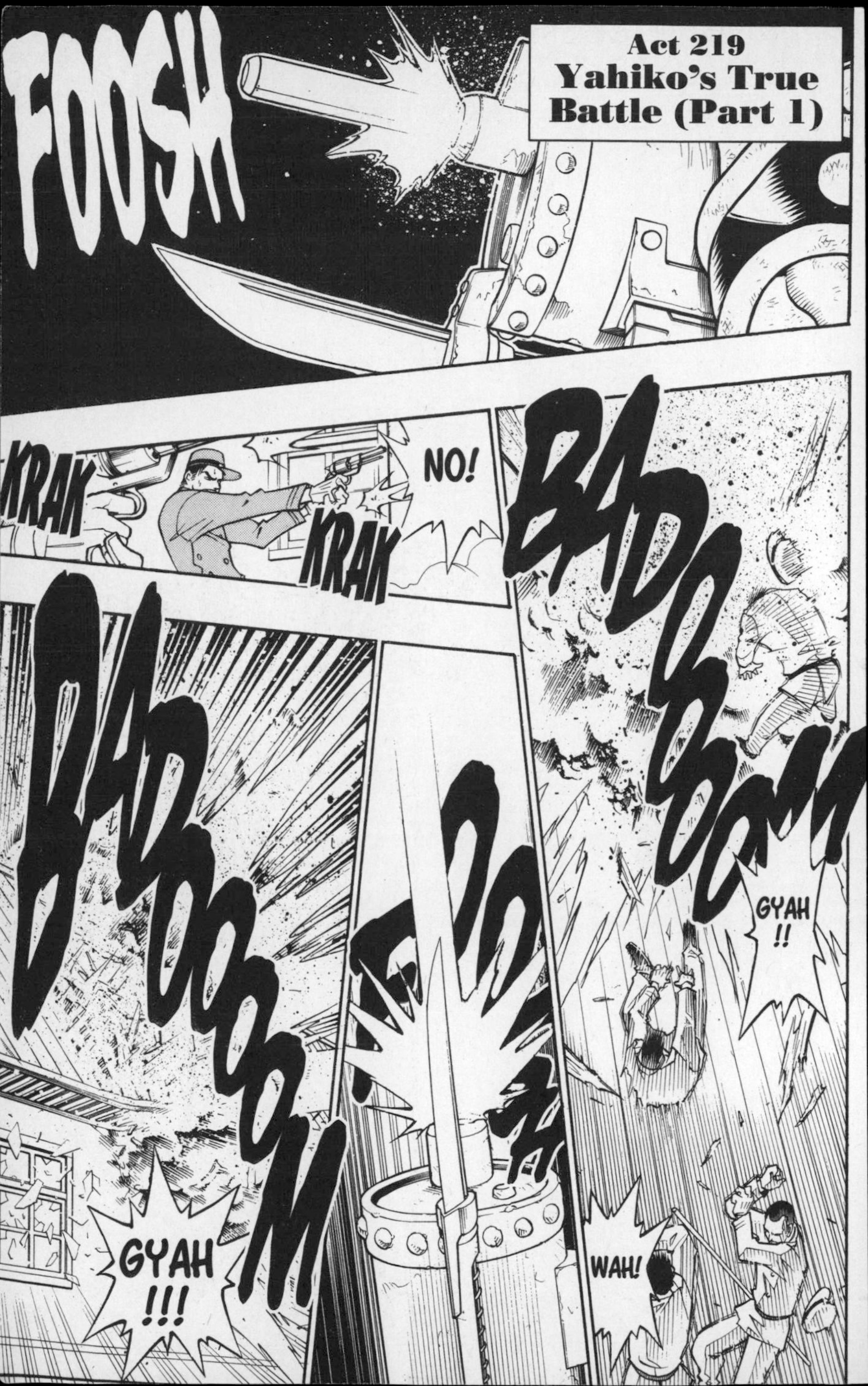
FOOSH
GYAH !!
WAH!
NO!
KRAK
KRAK
GYAH !!!

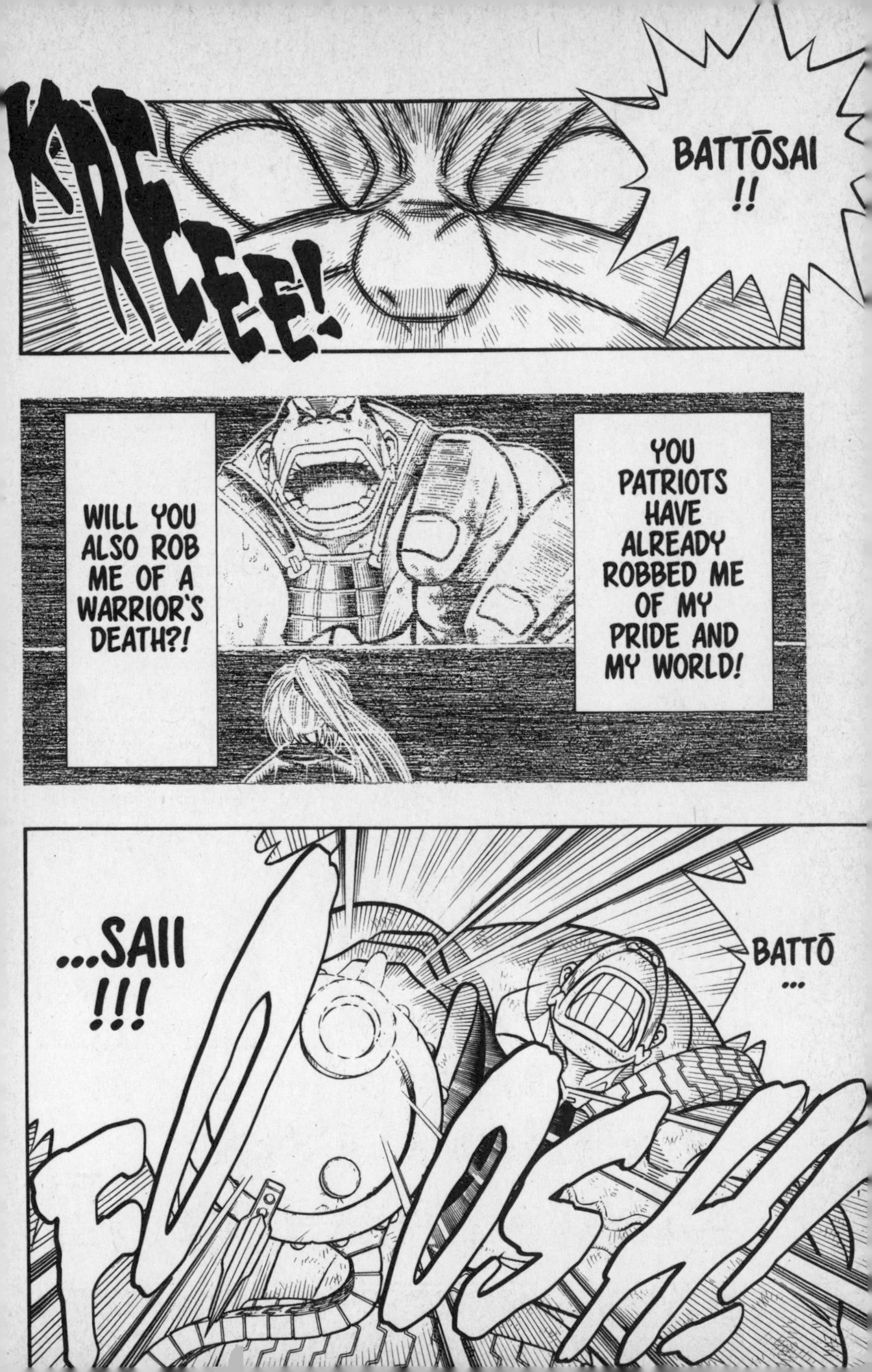
BATTŌSAI !!
YOU PATRIOTS HAVE ALREADY ROBBED ME OF MY PRIDE AND MY WORLD!
WILL YOU ALSO ROB ME OF A WARRIOR'S DEATH?!
BATTŌ ...
...SAII !!!

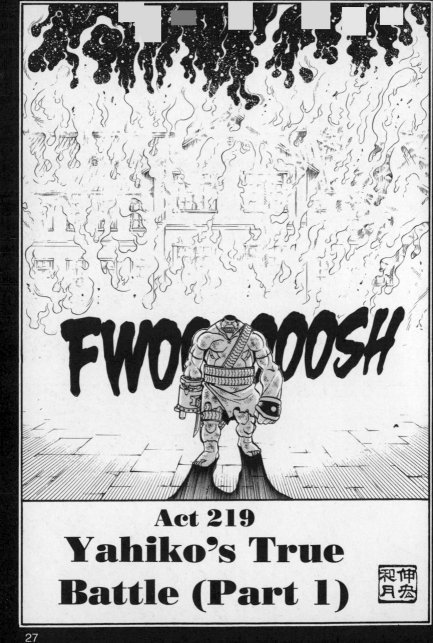

Act 219
Yahiko's True
Battle (Part 1)

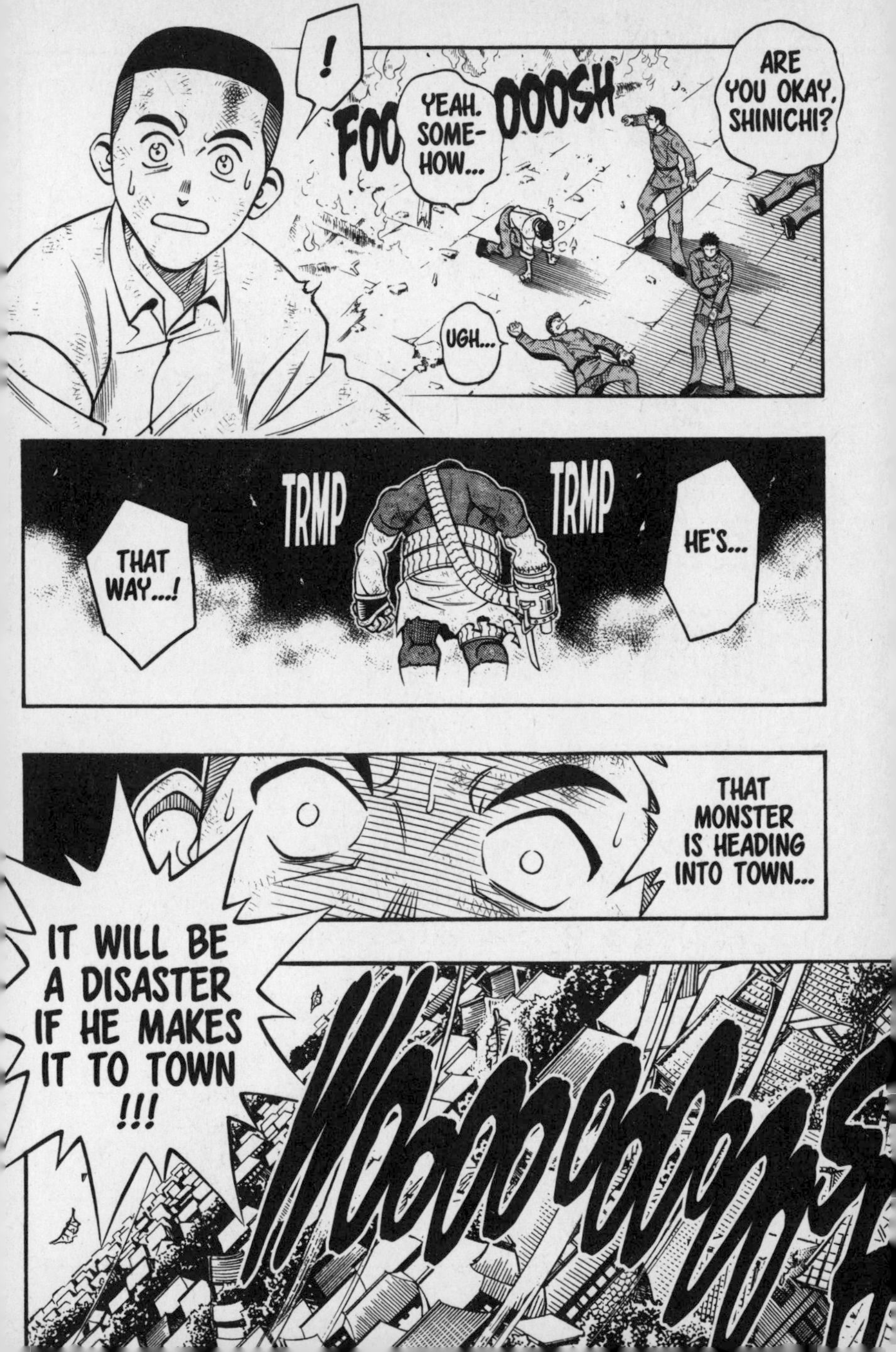
ARE YOU OKAY, SHINICHI?
FOOOOOSH
YEAH. SOMEHOW...
UGH...
!
HE'S...
TRMP
TRMP
THAT WAY...!
THAT MONSTER IS HEADING INTO TOWN...
IT WILL BE A DISASTER IF HE MAKES IT TO TOWN!!!

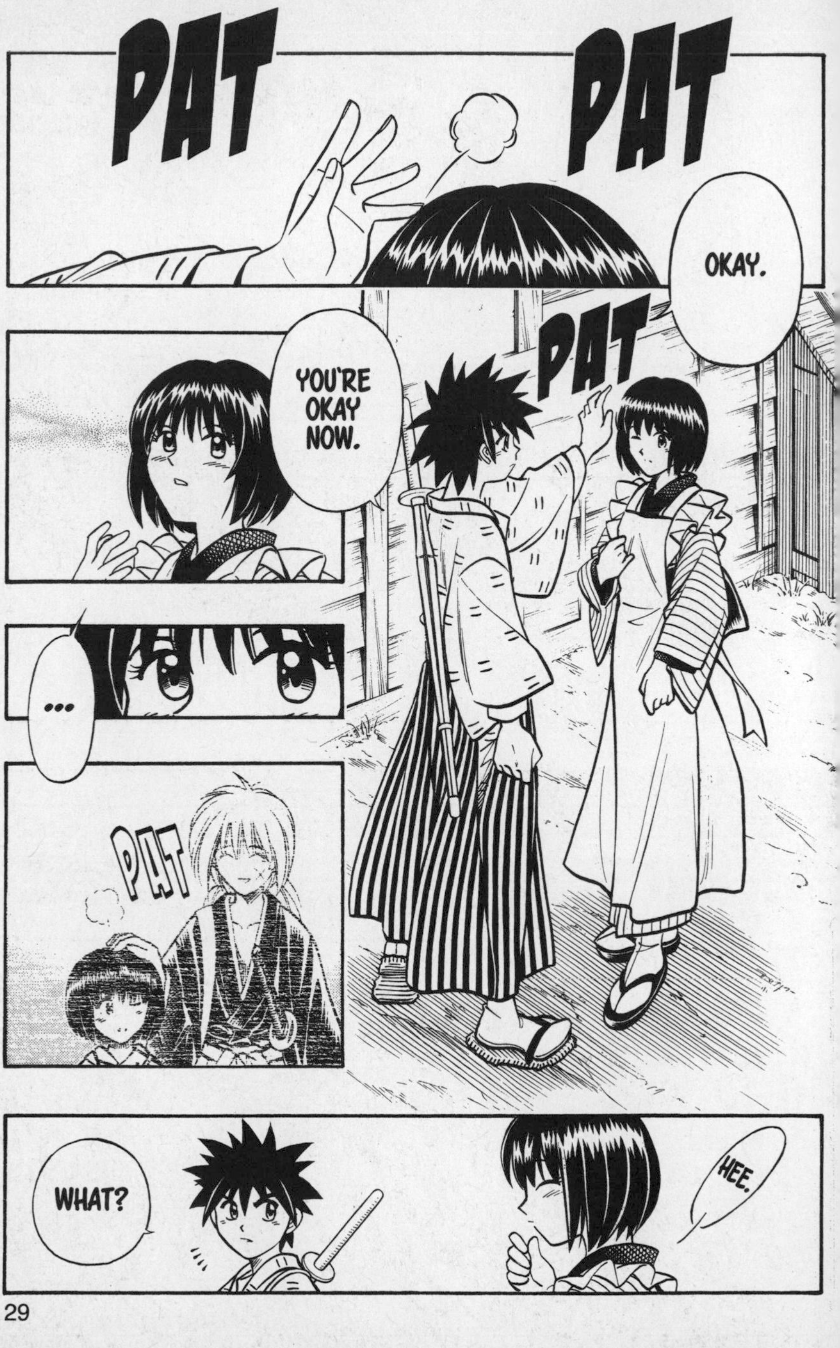
PAT
PAT
OKAY.
PAT
YOU'RE OKAY NOW.
...
PAT
HEE.
WHAT?

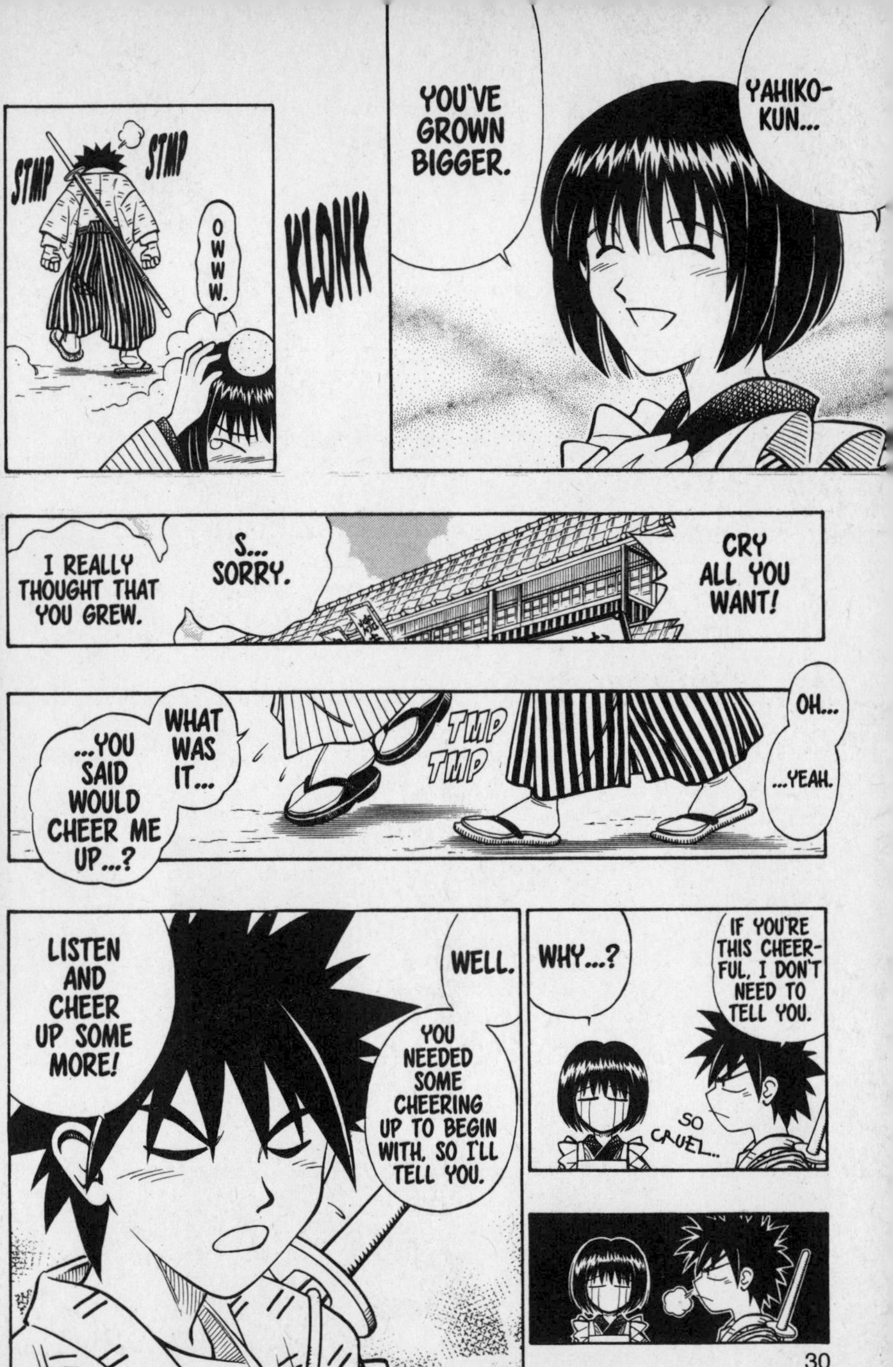
YAHIKO-KUN...
YOU'VE GROWN BIGGER.
KLONK
OWWW.
STMP
STMP
CRY ALL YOU WANT!
S... SORRY.
I REALLY THOUGHT THAT YOU GREW.
OH...
...YEAH.
TMP TMP
WHAT WAS IT...
...YOU SAID WOULD CHEER ME UP...?
IF YOU'RE THIS CHEERFUL, I DON'T NEED TO TELL YOU.
WHY...?
SO CRUEL...
WELL.
YOU NEEDED SOME CHEERING UP TO BEGIN WITH, SO I'LL TELL YOU.
LISTEN AND CHEER UP SOME MORE!

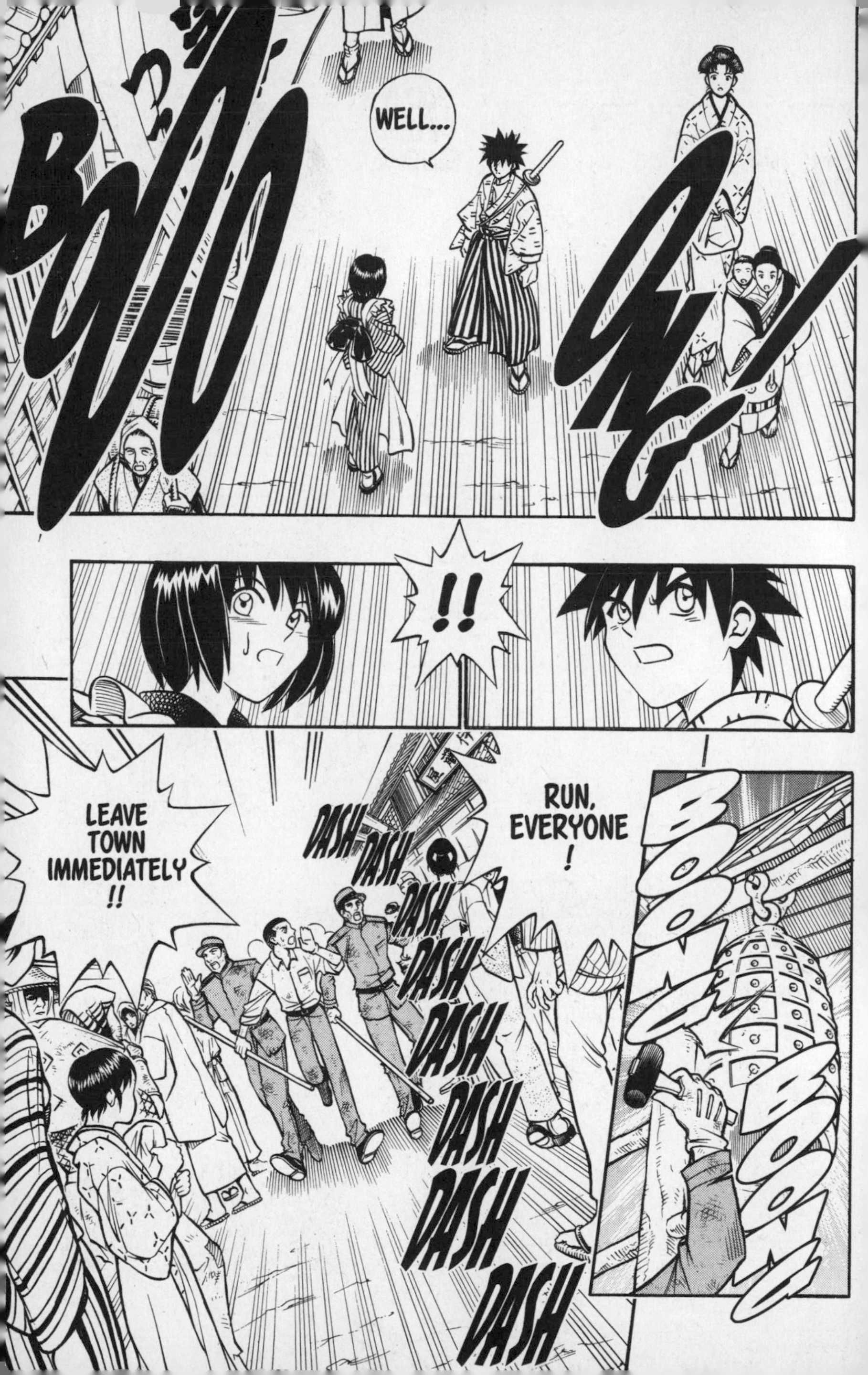
WELL...
!!
RUN, EVERYONE!
DASH DASH DASH DASH DASH DASH DASH DASH DASH DASH DASH
LEAVE TOWN IMMEDIATELY!!

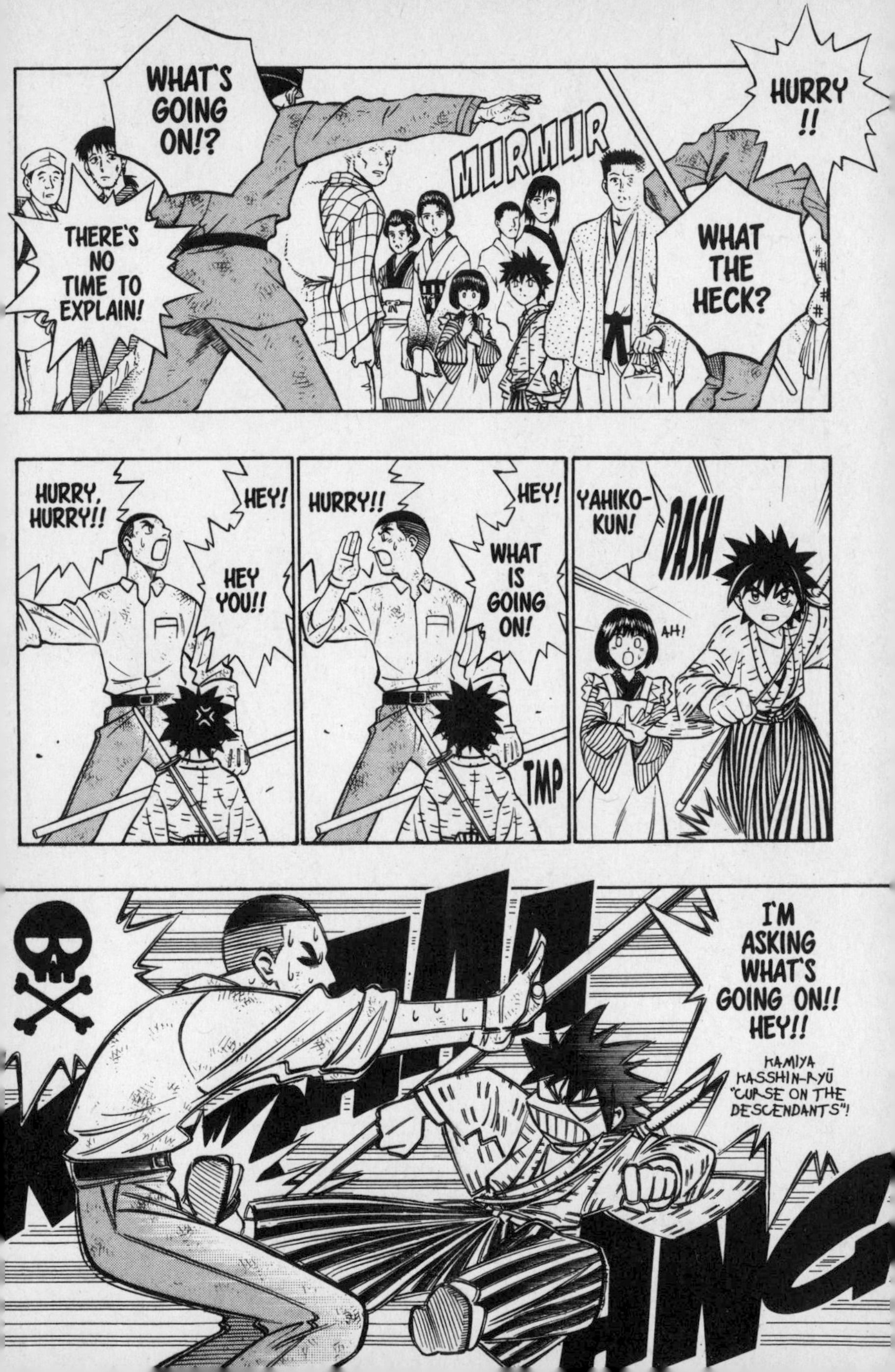
HURRY !!
WHAT THE HECK?
MURMUR
WHAT'S GOING ON!?
THERE'S NO TIME TO EXPLAIN!
YAHIKO-KUN!
DASH
AH!
HEY!
HURRY!!
WHAT IS GOING ON!
TMP
HEY!
HURRY, HURRY!!
HEY YOU!!
I'M ASKING WHAT'S GOING ON!! HEY!!
KAMIYA KASSHIN-RYŪ "CURSE ON THE DESCENDANTS"!

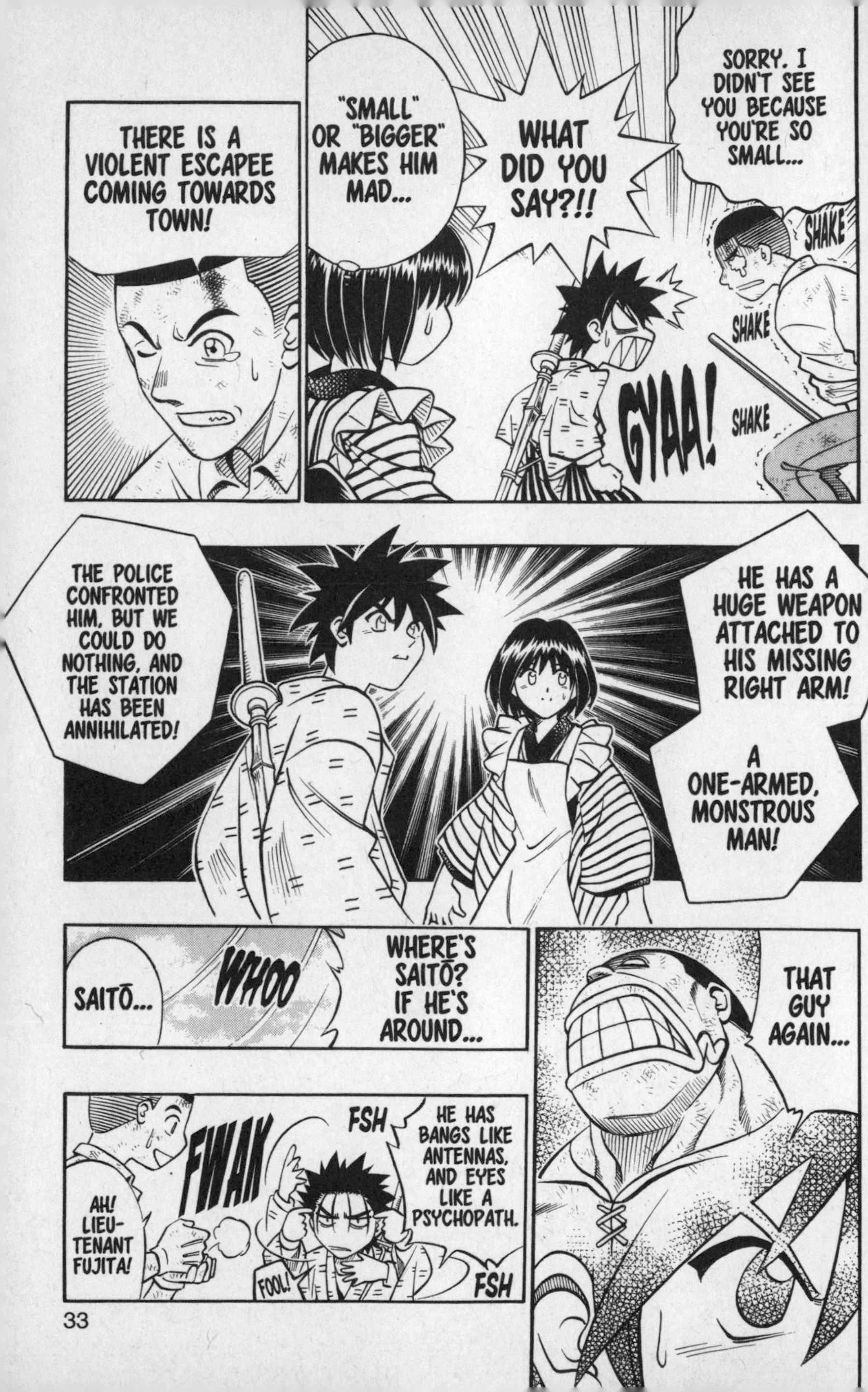
SORRY. I DIDN'T SEE YOU BECAUSE YOU'RE SO SMALL...
SHAKE
SHAKE
SHAKE
WHAT DID YOU SAY?!!
"SMALL" OR "BIGGER" MAKES HIM MAD...
GYAA!
THERE IS A VIOLENT ESCAPEE COMING TOWARDS TOWN!
HE HAS A HUGE WEAPON ATTACHED TO HIS MISSING RIGHT ARM!
A ONE-ARMED, MONSTROUS MAN!
THE POLICE CONFRONTED HIM, BUT WE COULD DO NOTHING, AND THE STATION HAS BEEN ANNIHILATED!
THAT GUY AGAIN...
WHERE'S SAITŌ? IF HE'S AROUND...
WHOO
SAITŌ...
FSH
HE HAS BANGS LIKE ANTENNAS, AND EYES LIKE A PSYCHOPATH.
FWAK
AH! LIEU-TENANT FUJITA!
FOOL!
FSH

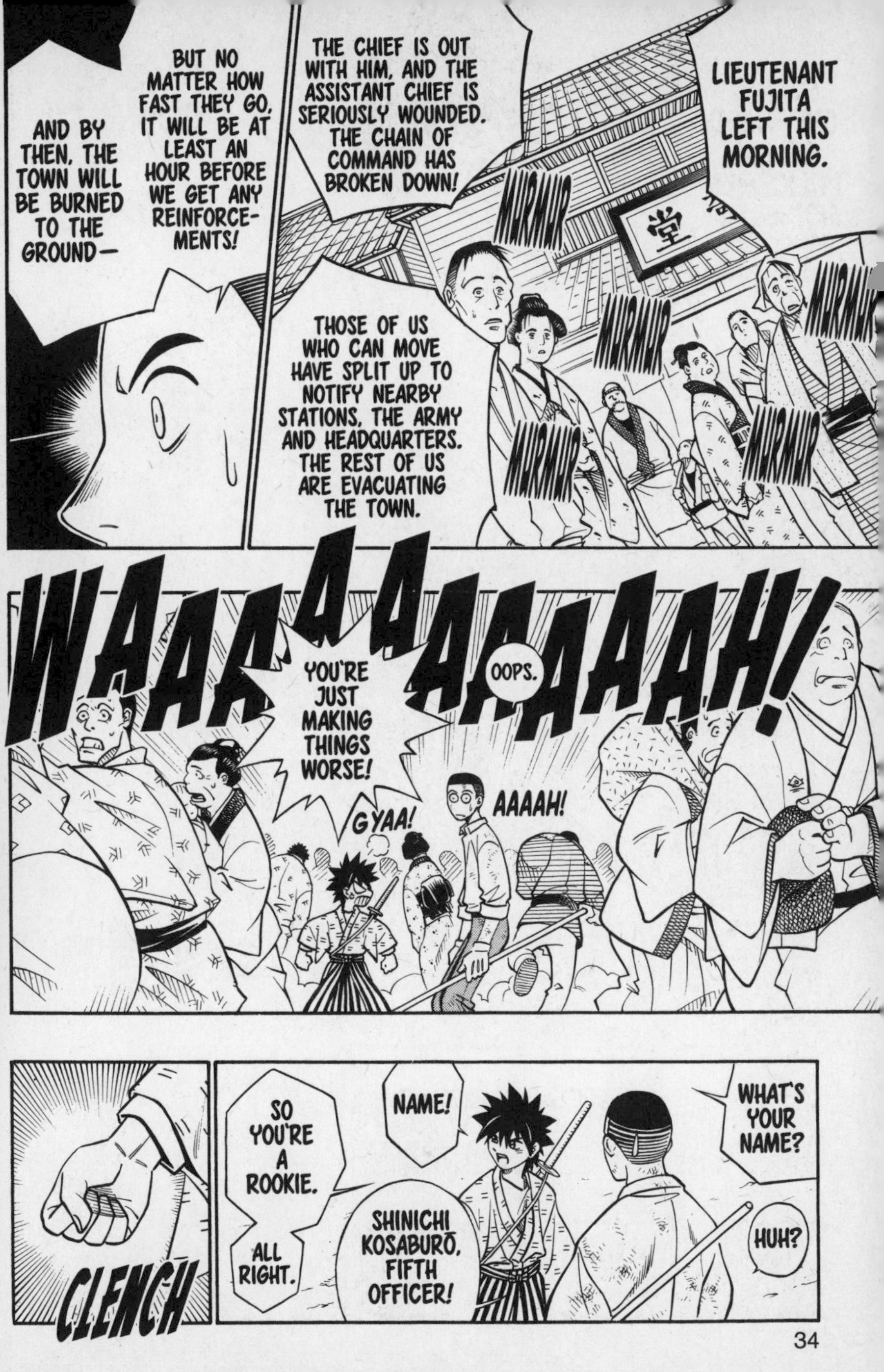
LIEUTENANT FUJITA LEFT THIS MORNING.
THE CHIEF IS OUT WITH HIM, AND THE ASSISTANT CHIEF IS SERIOUSLY WOUNDED. THE CHAIN OF COMMAND HAS BROKEN DOWN!
MURMUR
MURMUR
MURMUR
MURMUR
MURMUR
MURMUR
THOSE OF US WHO CAN MOVE HAVE SPLIT UP TO NOTIFY NEARBY STATIONS, THE ARMY AND HEADQUARTERS. THE REST OF US ARE EVACUATING THE TOWN.
BUT NO MATTER HOW FAST THEY GO, IT WILL BE AT LEAST AN HOUR BEFORE WE GET ANY REINFORCE-MENTS!
AND BY THEN, THE TOWN WILL BE BURNED TO THE GROUND—
WAAAAAAAAAAAH!
OOPS.
YOU'RE JUST MAKING THINGS WORSE!
AAAAH!
GYAA!
WHAT'S YOUR NAME?
HUH?
NAME!
SHINICHI KOSABURŌ, FIFTH OFFICER!
SO YOU'RE A ROOKIE.
ALL RIGHT.
CLENCH

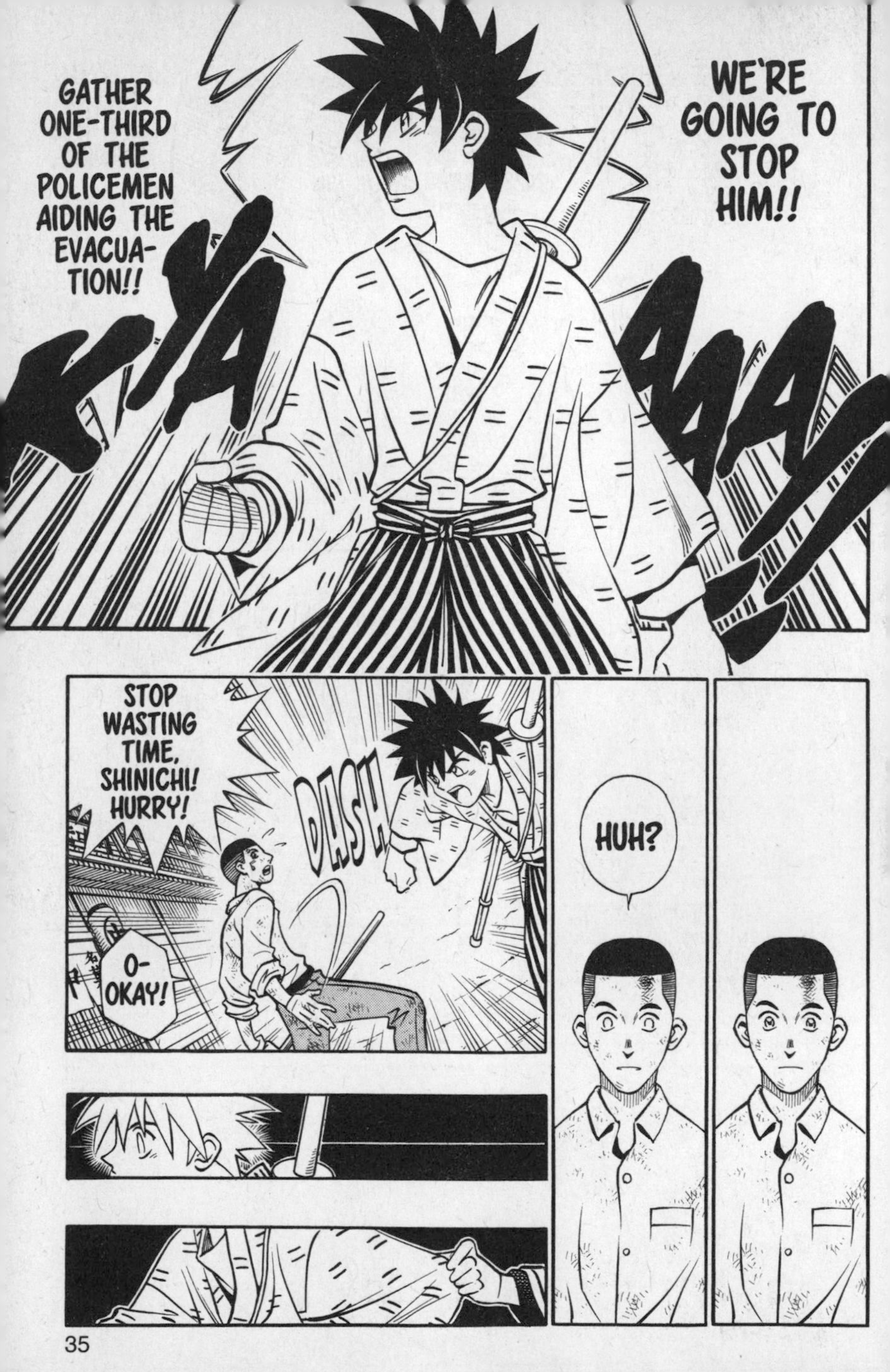
WE'RE GOING TO STOP HIM!!
GATHER ONE-THIRD OF THE POLICEMEN AIDING THE EVACUA-TION!!
HUH?
STOP WASTING TIME, SHINICHI! HURRY!
DASH
O-OKAY!

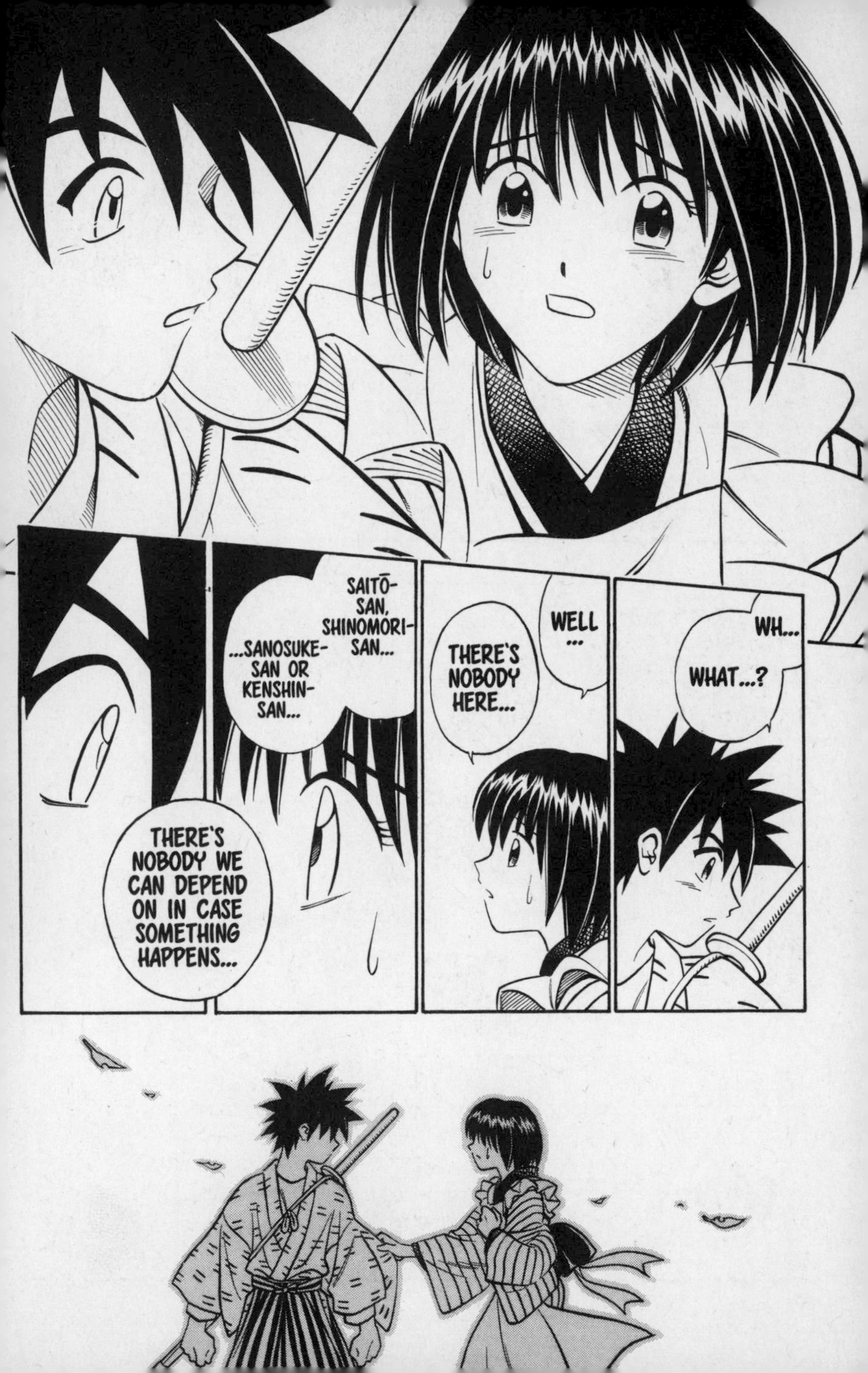
WH...
WHAT...?
WELL...
THERE'S NOBODY HERE...
SAITŌ-SAN, SHINOMORI-SAN...
...SANOSUKE-SAN OR KENSHIN-SAN...
THERE'S NOBODY WE CAN DEPEND ON IN CASE SOMETHING HAPPENS...

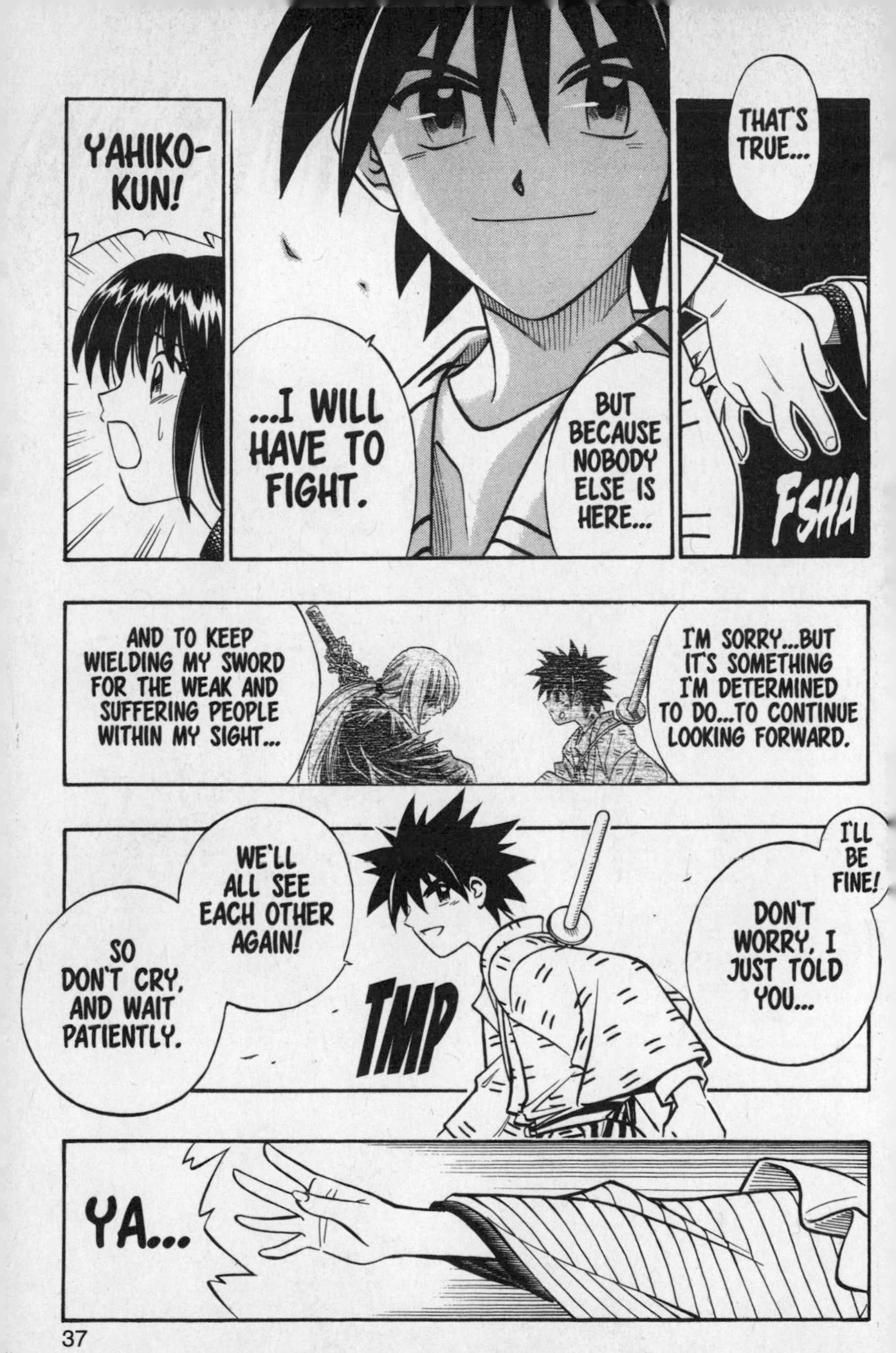

THAT'S TRUE...
FSHA
BUT BECAUSE NOBODY ELSE IS HERE...
...I WILL HAVE TO FIGHT.
YAHIKO-KUN!
I'M SORRY...BUT IT'S SOMETHING I'M DETERMINED TO DO...TO CONTINUE LOOKING FORWARD.
AND TO KEEP WIELDING MY SWORD FOR THE WEAK AND SUFFERING PEOPLE WITHIN MY SIGHT...
I'LL BE FINE!
DON'T WORRY, I JUST TOLD YOU...
WE'LL ALL SEE EACH OTHER AGAIN!
TMP
SO DON'T CRY, AND WAIT PATIENTLY.
YA...

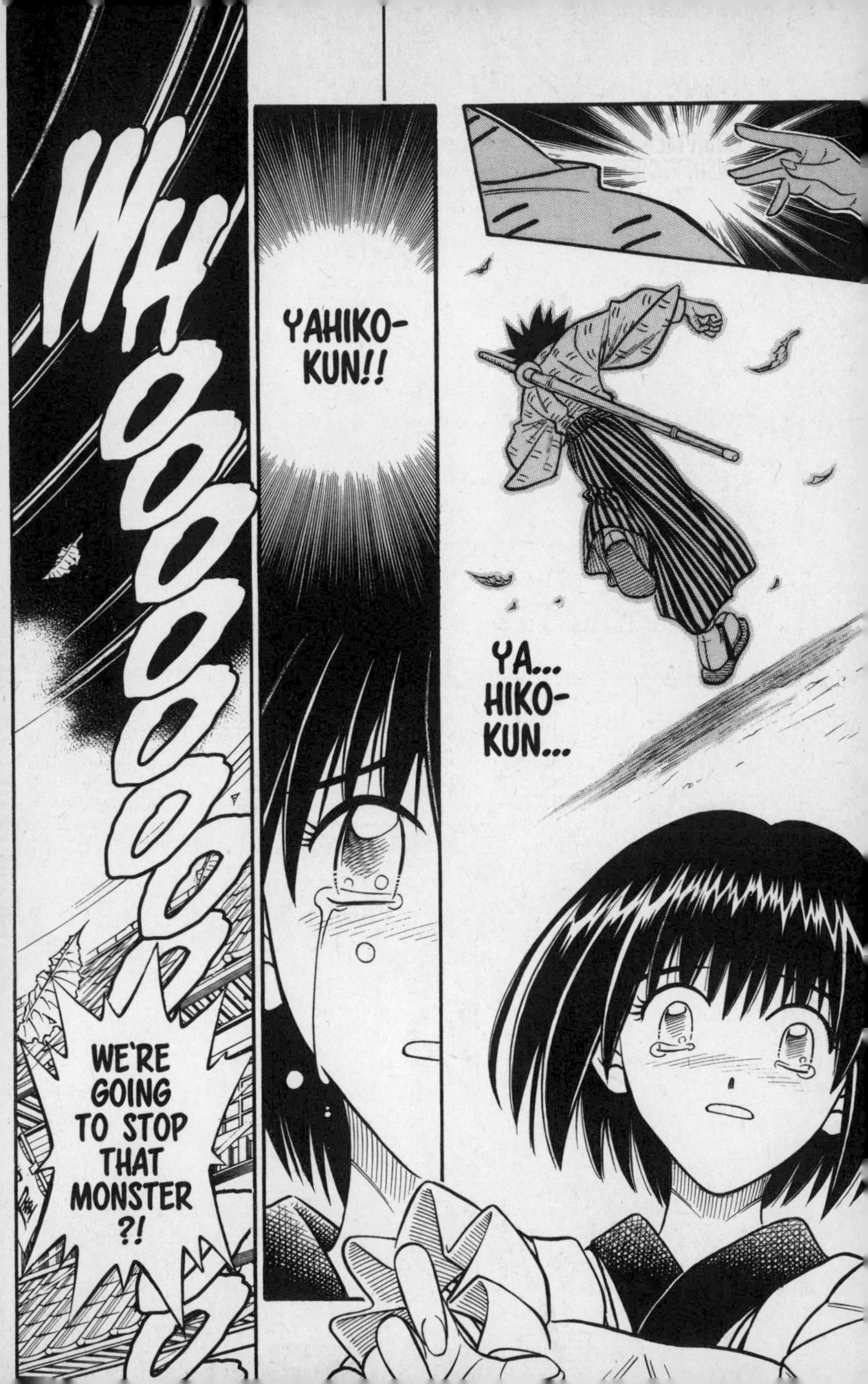
YA... HIKO-KUN...
YAHIKO-KUN!!
WHOOOOOOOA
WE'RE GOING TO STOP THAT MONSTER?!

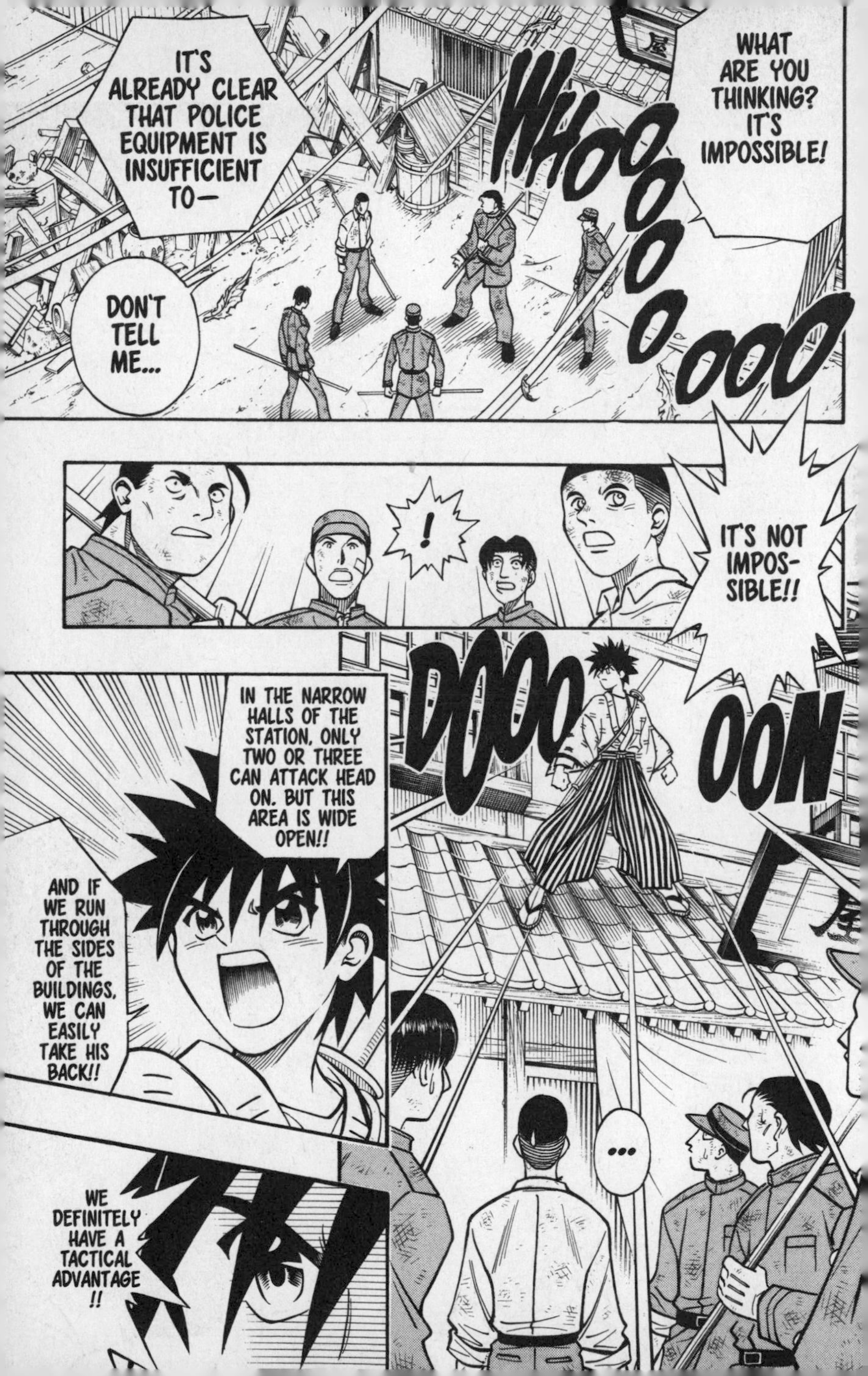
WHAT ARE YOU THINKING? IT'S IMPOSSIBLE!
WHOOOOOOOOO
IT'S ALREADY CLEAR THAT POLICE EQUIPMENT IS INSUFFICIENT TO—
DON'T TELL ME...
IT'S NOT IMPOSSIBLE!!
!
DOOOOOON
...
IN THE NARROW HALLS OF THE STATION, ONLY TWO OR THREE CAN ATTACK HEAD ON. BUT THIS AREA IS WIDE OPEN!!
AND IF WE RUN THROUGH THE SIDES OF THE BUILDINGS, WE CAN EASILY TAKE HIS BACK!!
WE DEFINITELY HAVE A TACTICAL ADVANTAGE!!

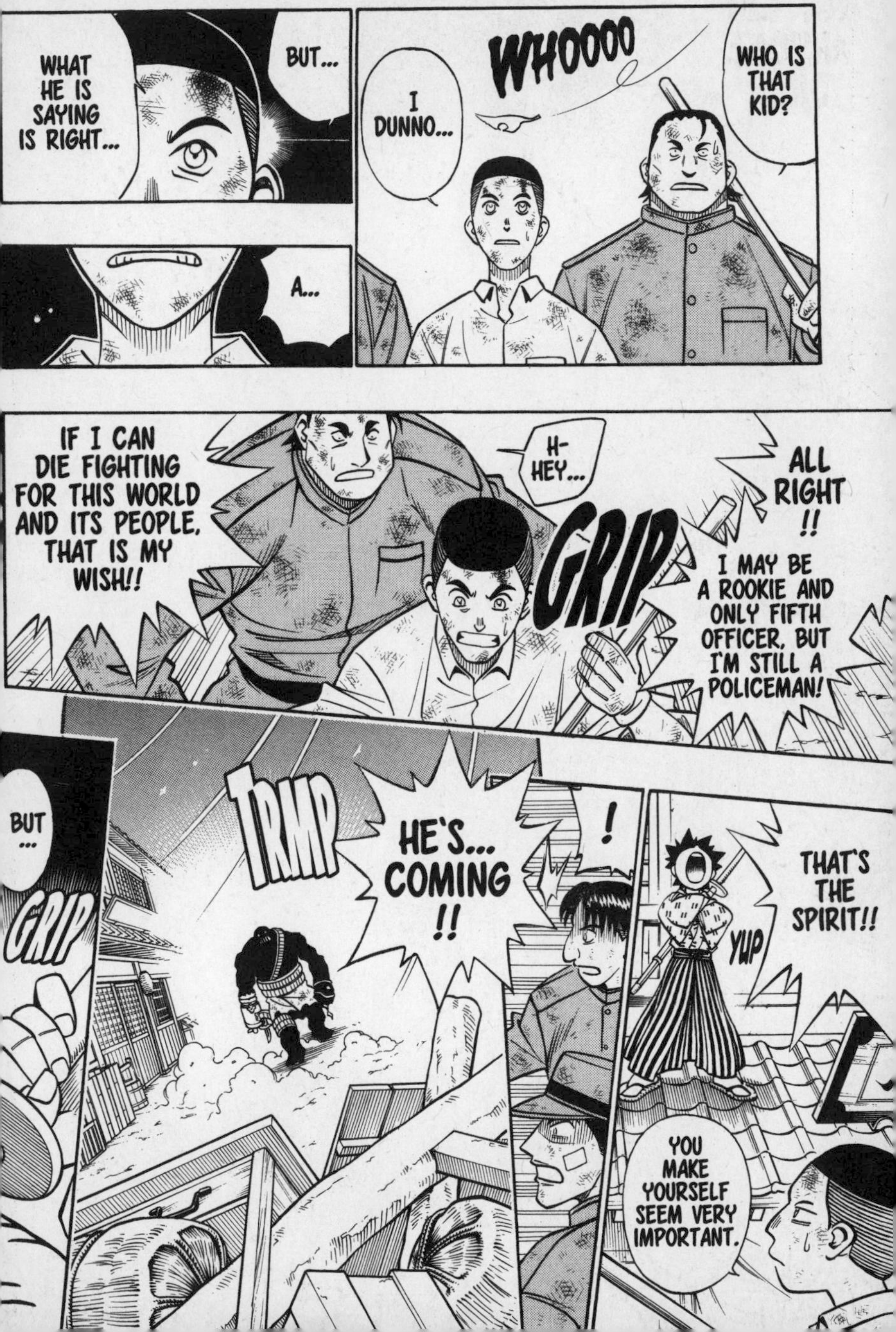
WHO IS THAT KID?
WHOOOO
I DUNNO...
BUT...
WHAT HE IS SAYING IS RIGHT...
A...
ALL RIGHT!!
I MAY BE A ROOKIE AND ONLY FIFTH OFFICER, BUT I'M STILL A POLICEMAN!
GRIP
H-HEY...
IF I CAN DIE FIGHTING FOR THIS WORLD AND ITS PEOPLE, THAT IS MY WISH!!
THAT'S THE SPIRIT!!
YUP
YOU MAKE YOURSELF SEEM VERY IMPORTANT.
!
HE'S... COMING!!
TRMP
BUT...
GRIP

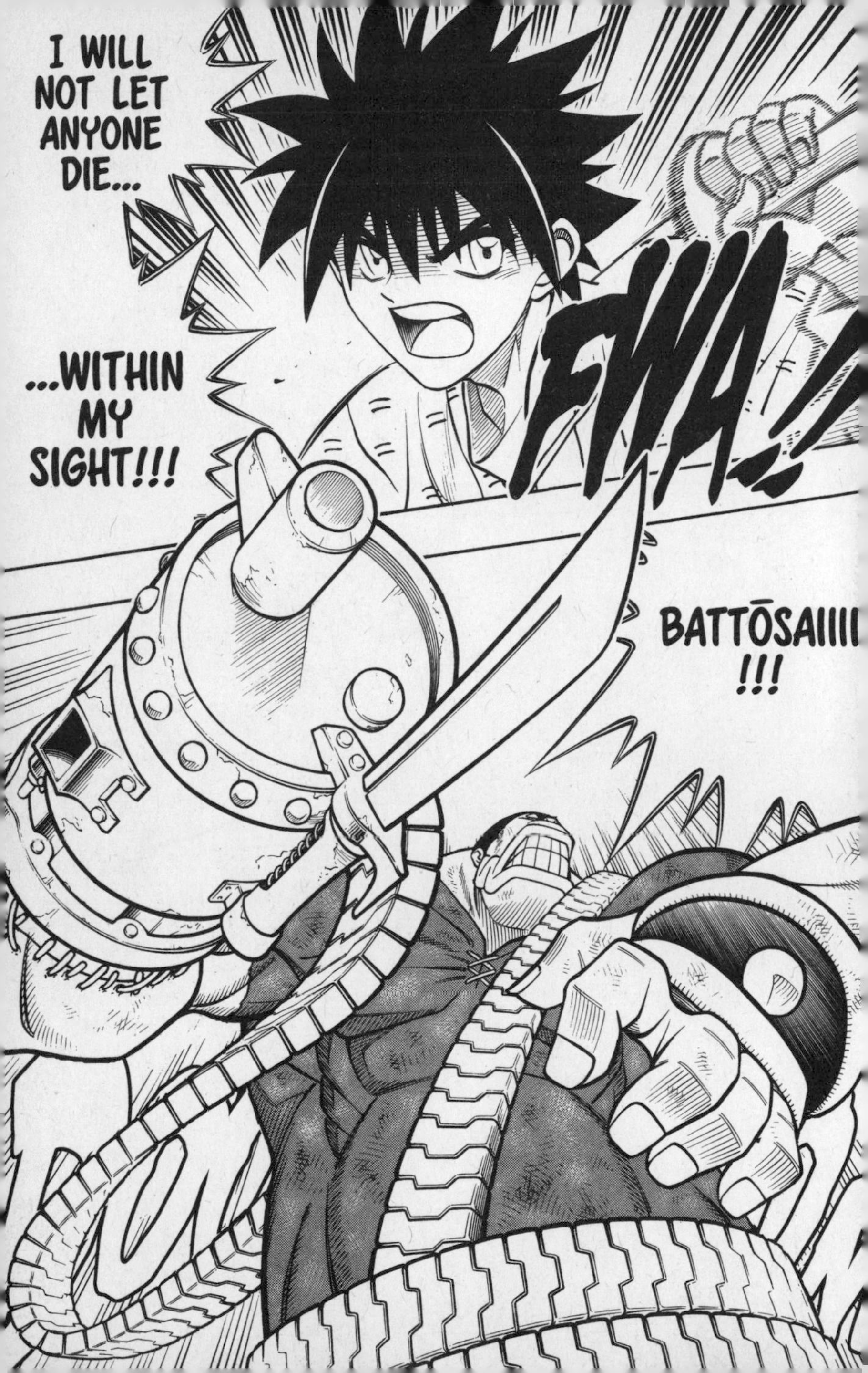

FWA!!
I WILL NOT LET ANYONE DIE...
...WITHIN MY SIGHT!!!
BATTŌSAIIIII!!!

Rurouni Kenshin

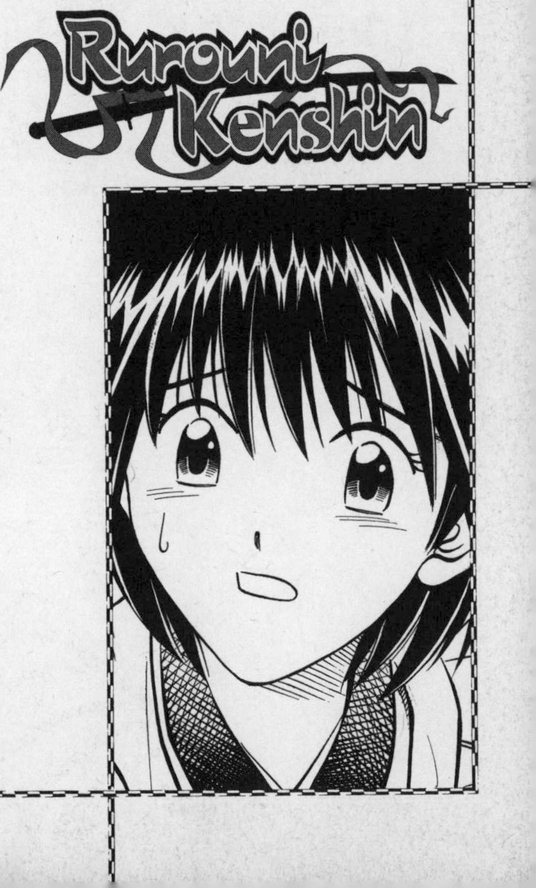

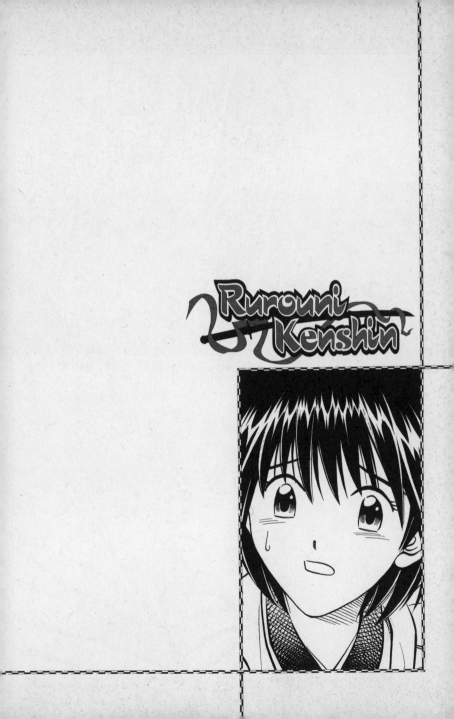

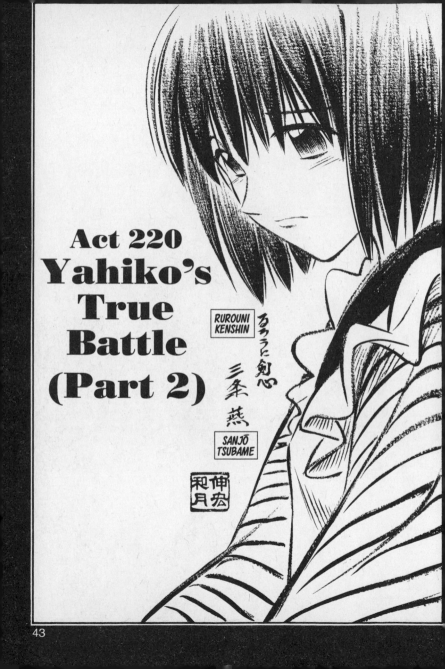

Act 220
Yahiko's True Battle (Part 2)

RUROUNI KENSHIN
るろうに剣心

三条 燕

SANJŌ TSUBAME

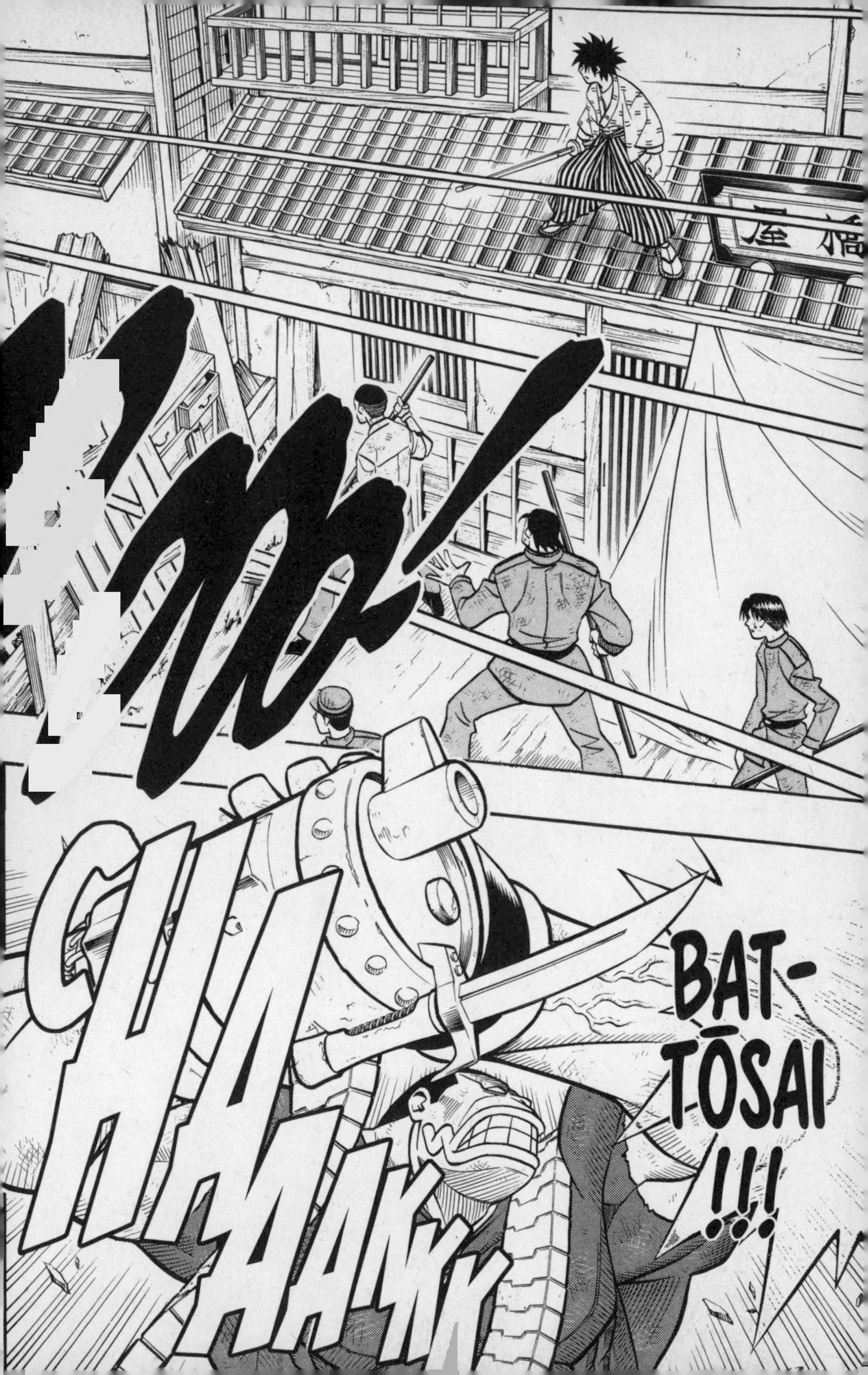
屋 橋
CHAANK
BAT-
TŌSAI
!!!

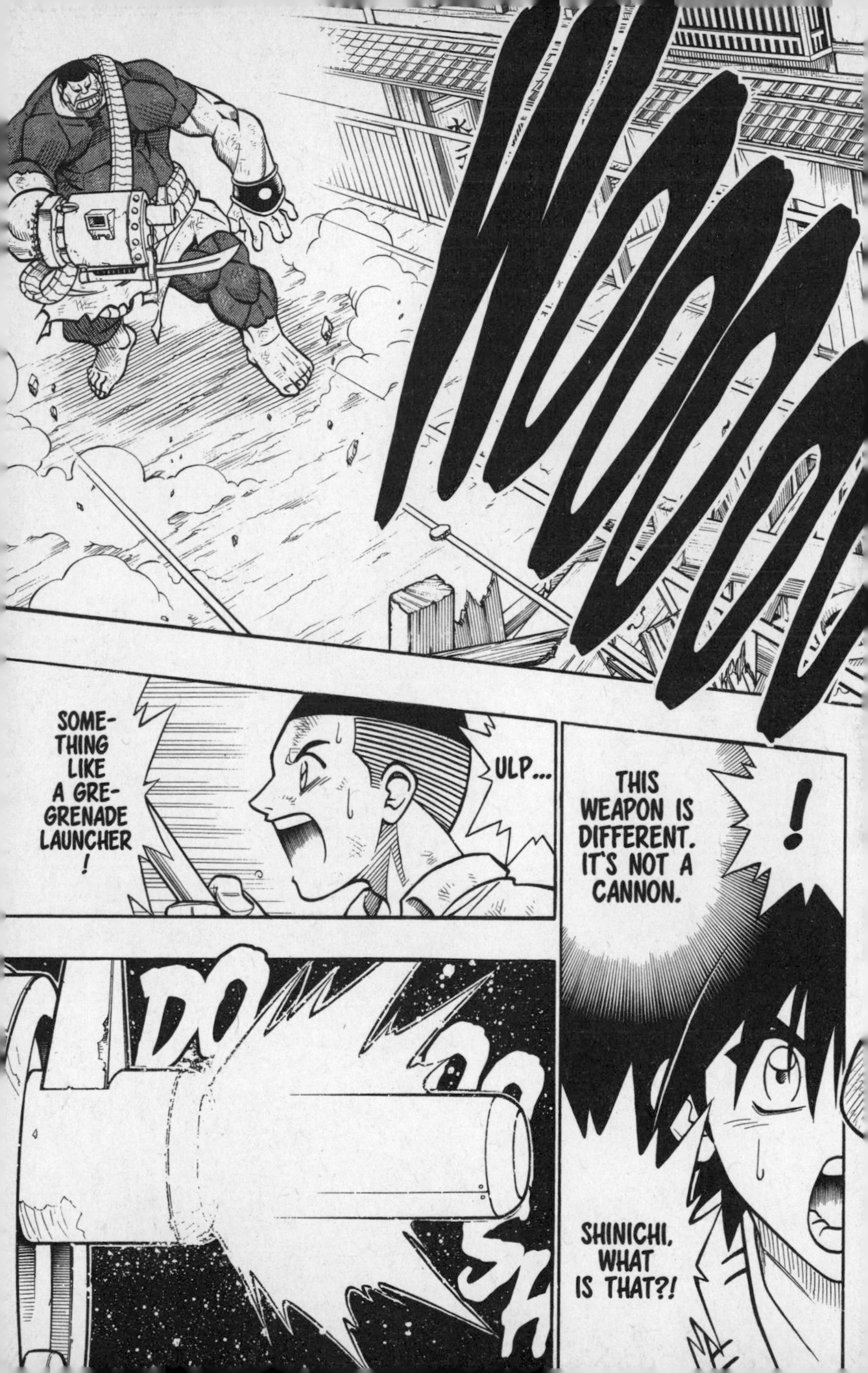
!
THIS WEAPON IS DIFFERENT. IT'S NOT A CANNON.
SHINICHI, WHAT IS THAT?!
ULP...
SOME-THING LIKE A GRE-GRENADE LAUNCHER!

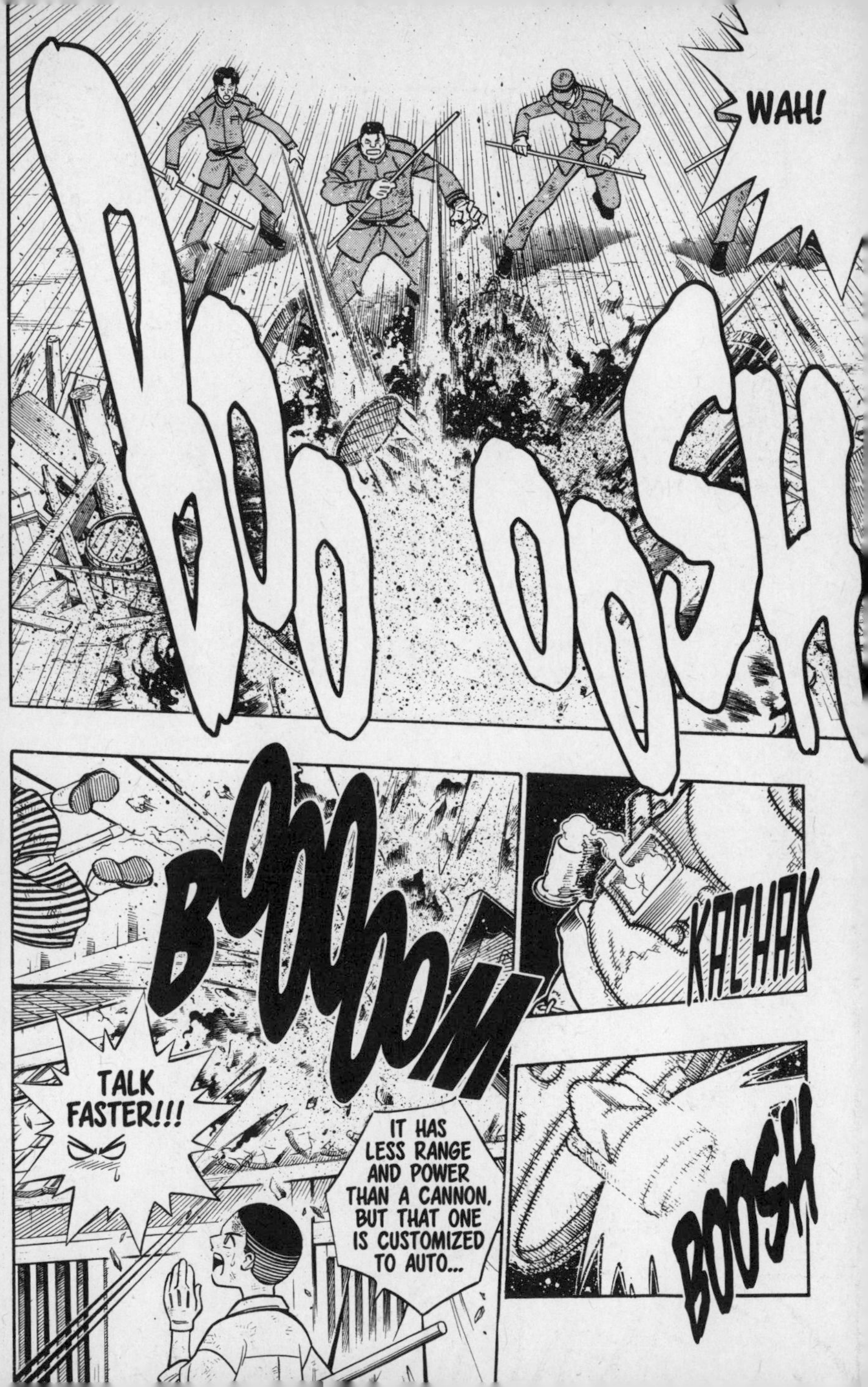
WAH!
BOOOOSH
KACHAK
BOOSH
BOOOOM
TALK FASTER!!!
IT HAS LESS RANGE AND POWER THAN A CANNON, BUT THAT ONE IS CUSTOMIZED TO AUTO...

READ THIS WAY

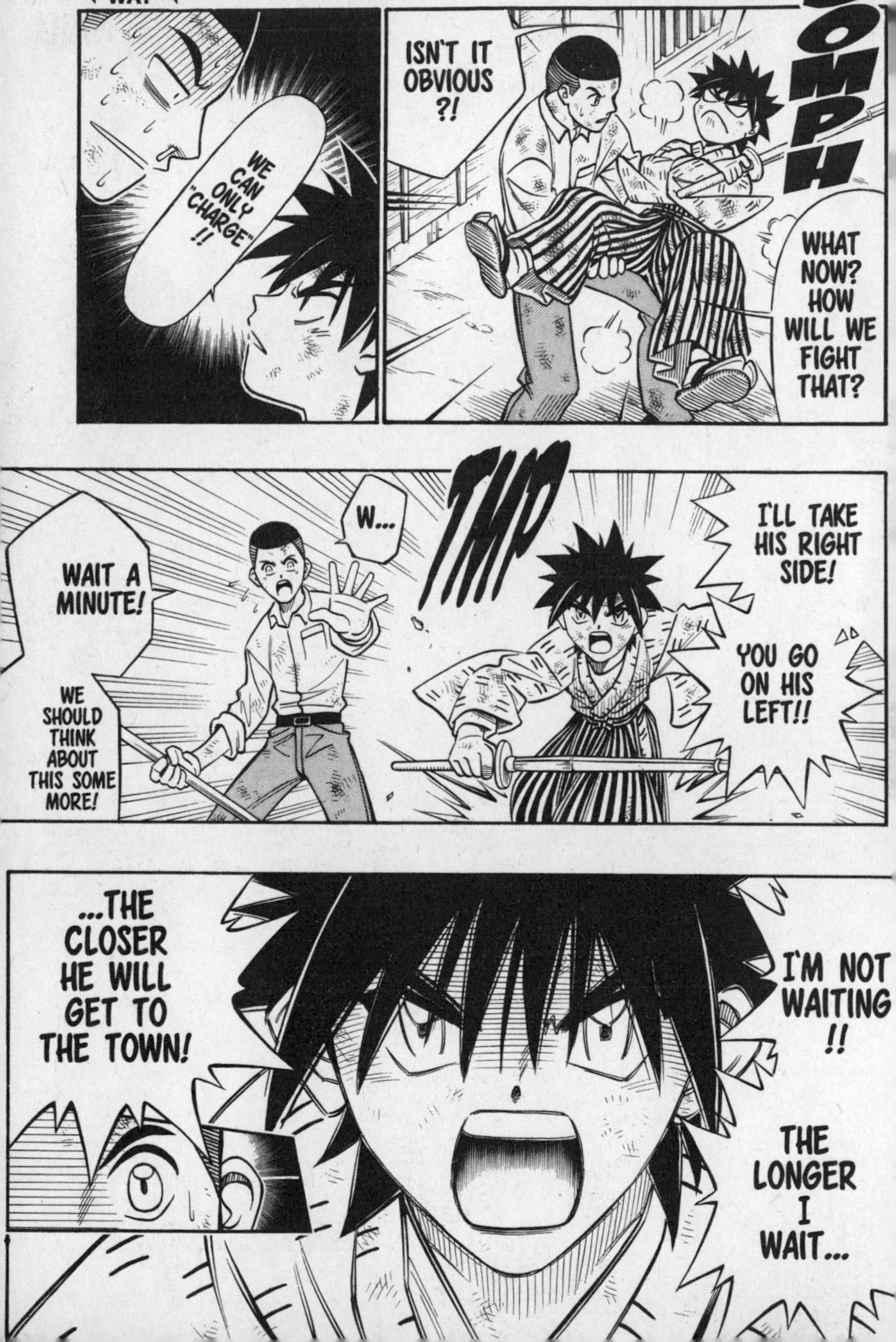
BOMPH
WHAT NOW? HOW WILL WE FIGHT THAT?
ISN'T IT OBVIOUS?!
WE CAN ONLY "CHARGE"!!
I'LL TAKE HIS RIGHT SIDE!
YOU GO ON HIS LEFT!!
TMP
W...
WAIT A MINUTE!
WE SHOULD THINK ABOUT THIS SOME MORE!
I'M NOT WAITING!!
THE LONGER I WAIT...
...THE CLOSER HE WILL GET TO THE TOWN!

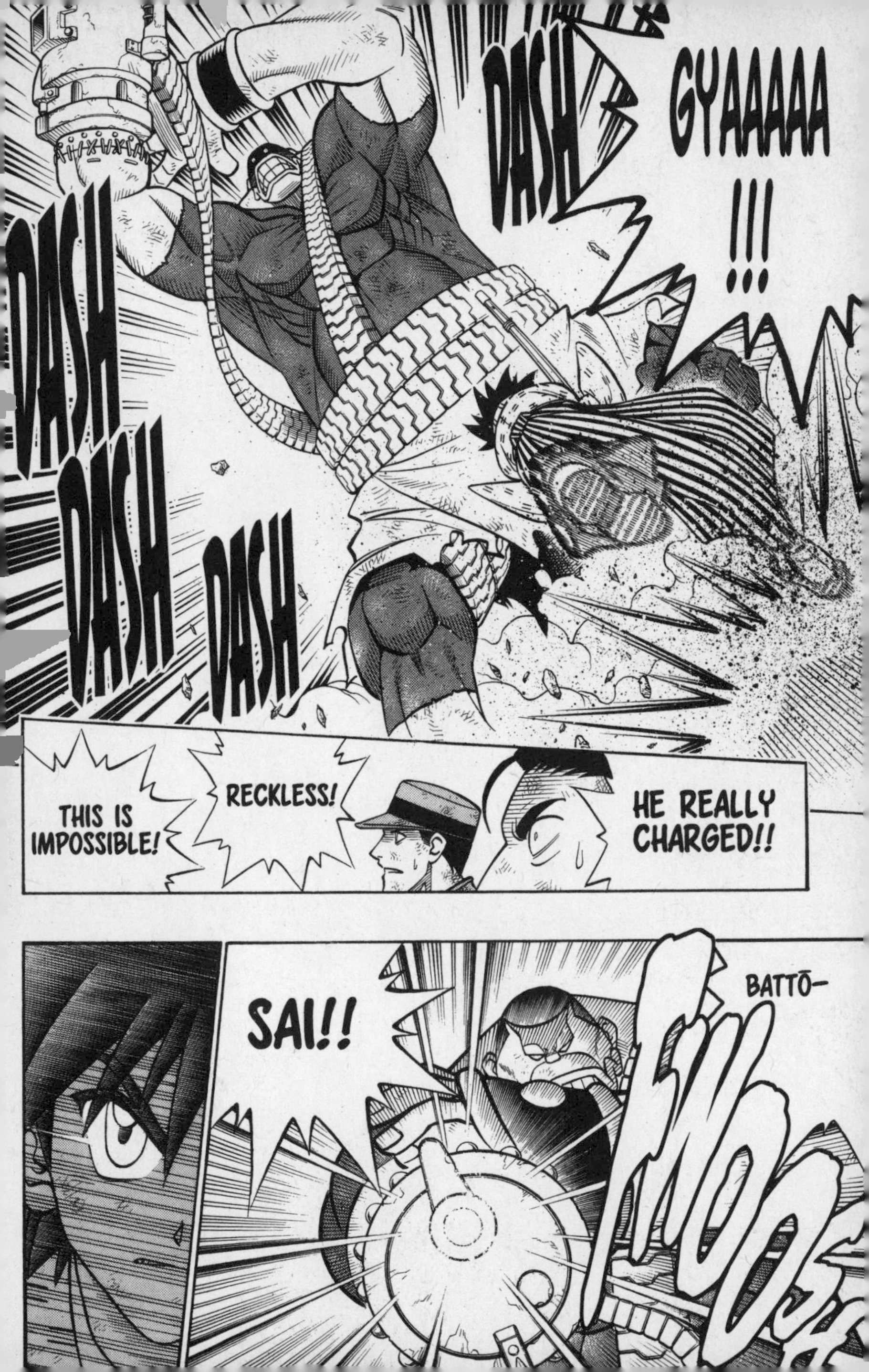
GYAAAAA!!!
DASH
DASH
DASH
DASH
HE REALLY CHARGED!!
RECKLESS!
THIS IS IMPOSSIBLE!
BATTŌ-
SAI!!

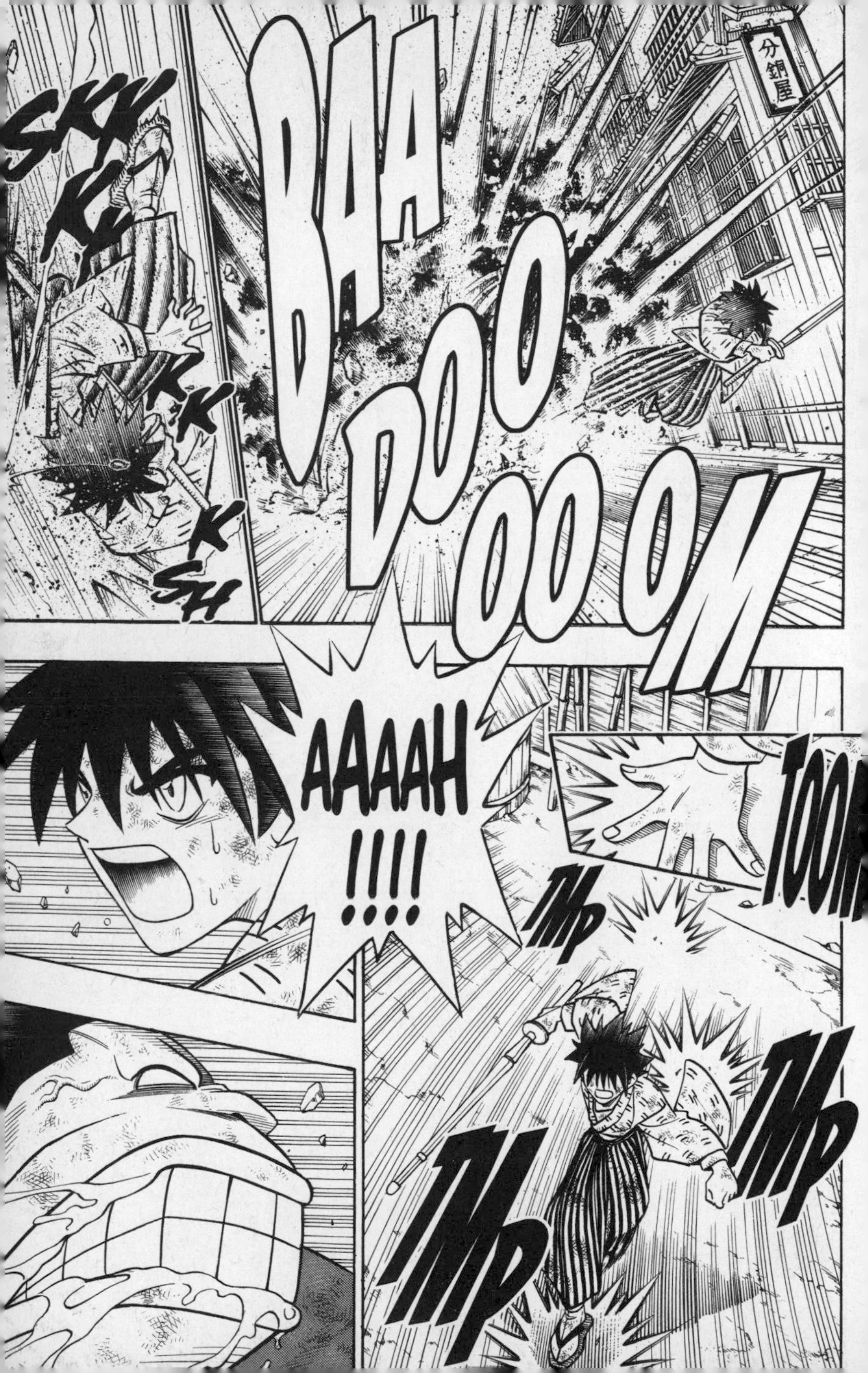
BAA
DOOOOOOM
SH
TOOM
AAAAH
!!!!
TMP
TMP
TMP

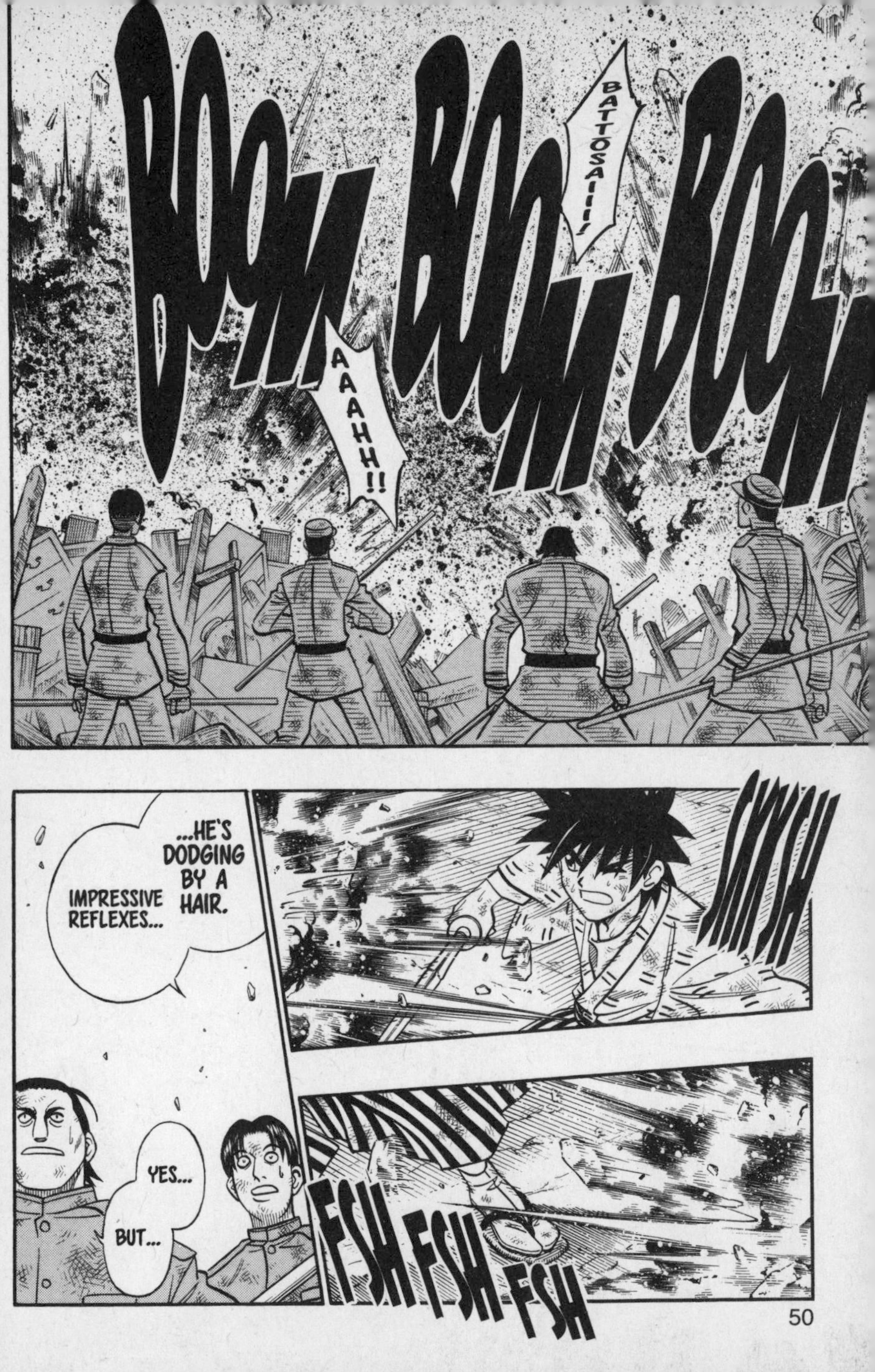
BOOM BOOM BOOM
BATTOSAIII!
AAAAHH!!
...HE'S DODGING BY A HAIR. IMPRESSIVE REFLEXES...
FSH FSH FSH
YES...
BUT...

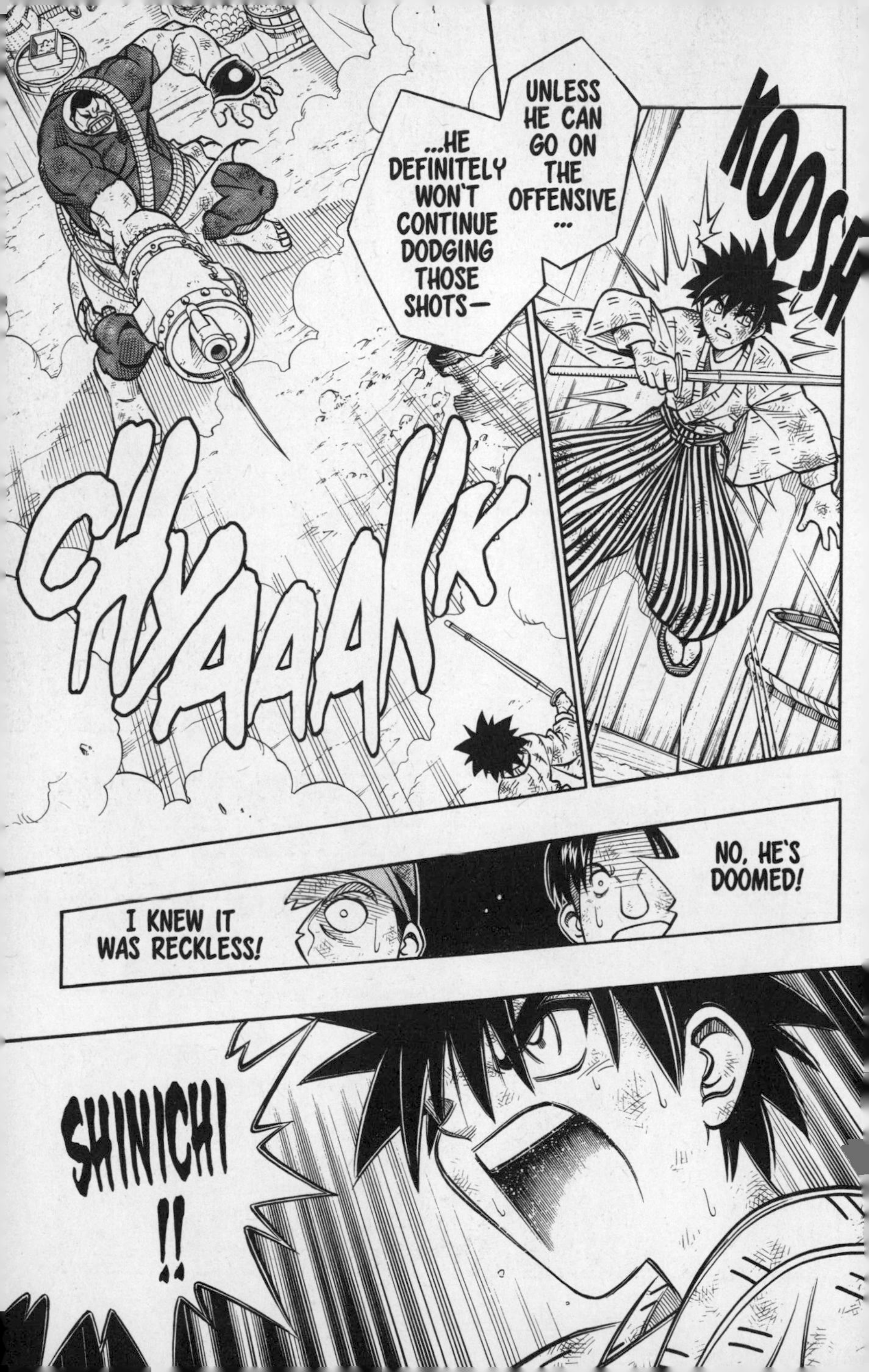
KOOSH
UNLESS HE CAN GO ON THE OFFENSIVE...
...HE DEFINITELY WON'T CONTINUE DODGING THOSE SHOTS—
CHAAAKK
NO, HE'S DOOMED!
I KNEW IT WAS RECKLESS!
SHINICHI !!

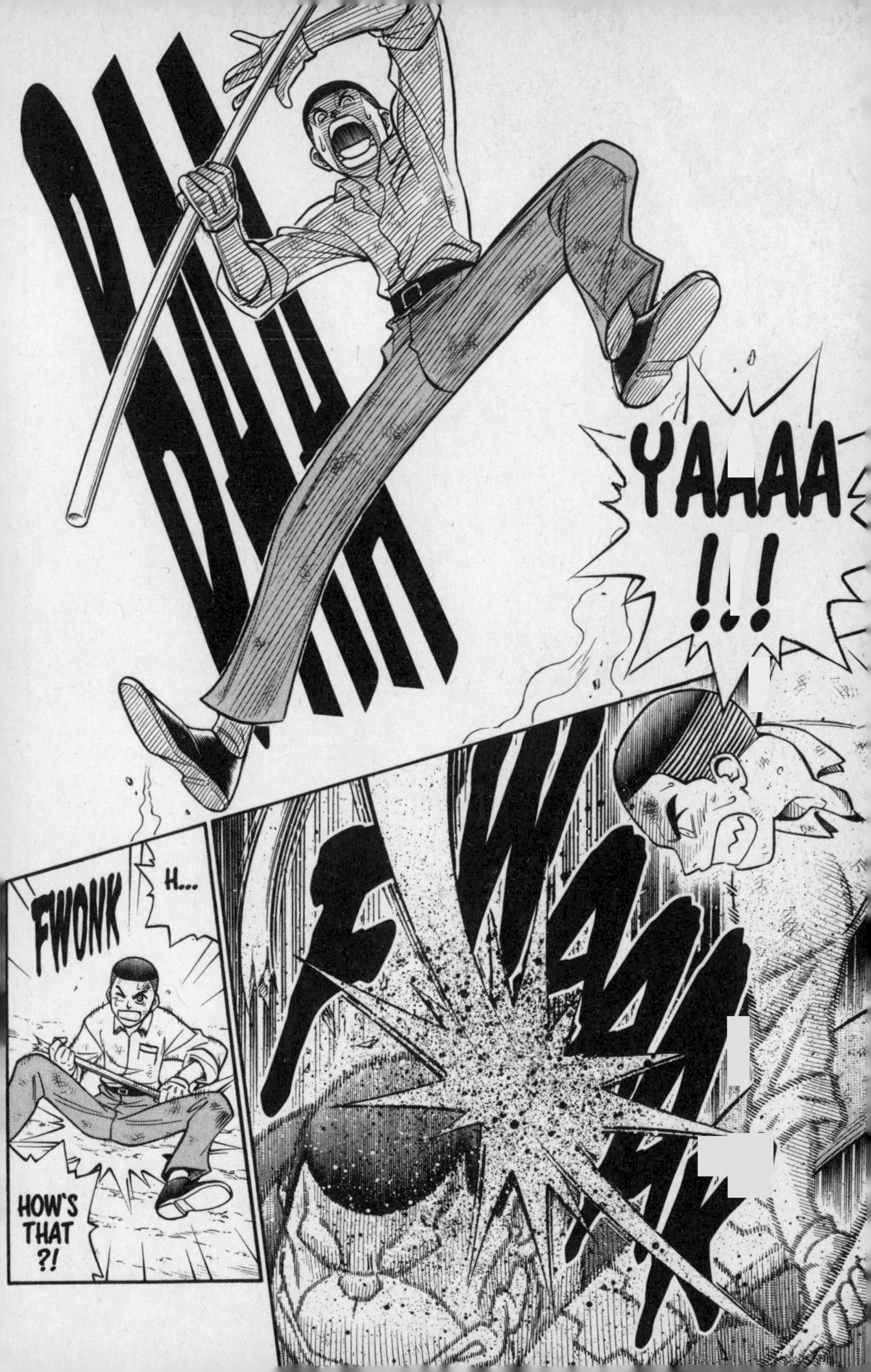
YAAAA !!!
H...
FWONK
HOW'S THAT ?!

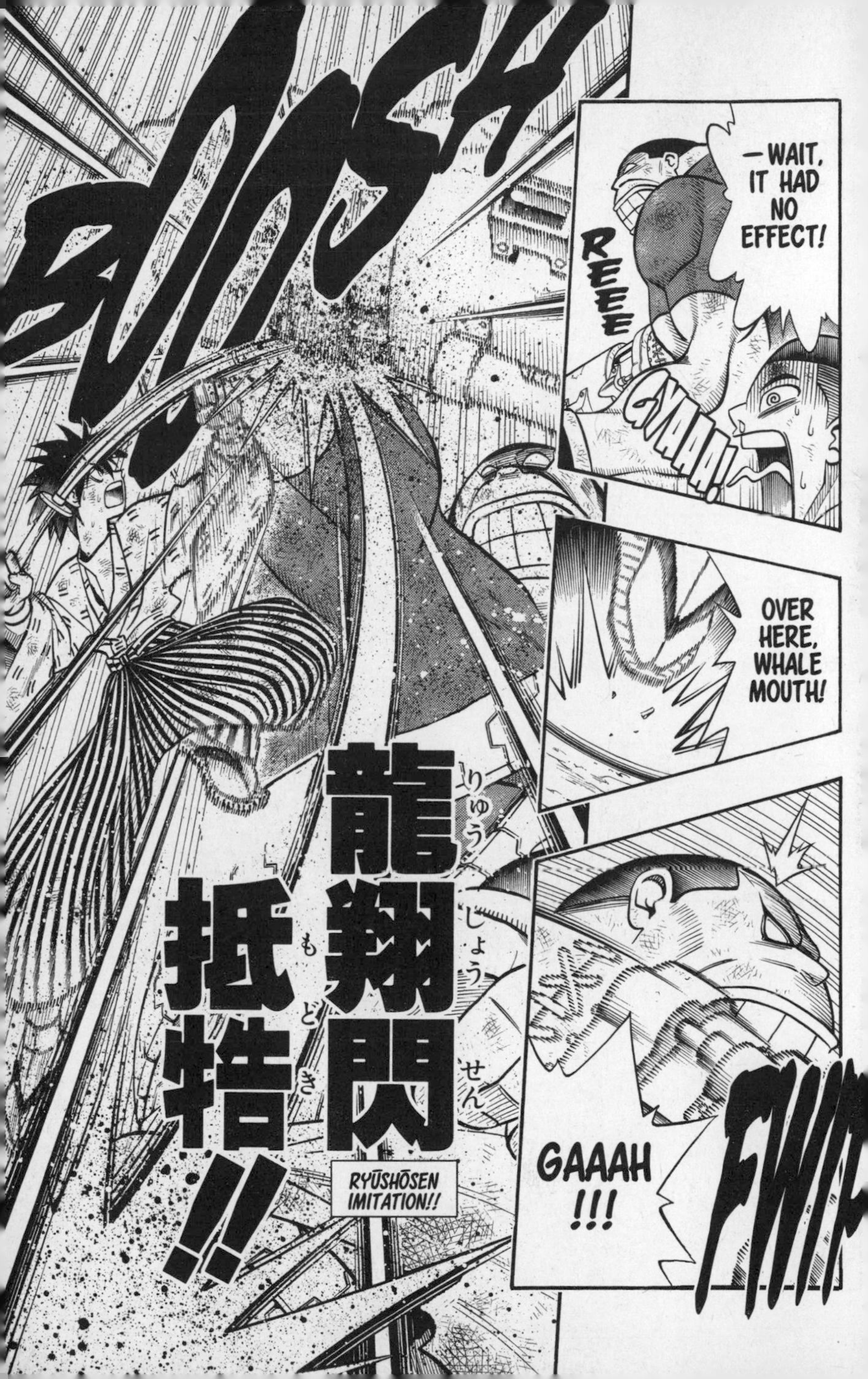
—WAIT, IT HAD NO EFFECT!
REEEE
GYAAAH!
OVER HERE, WHALE MOUTH!
GAAAH !!!
FWIP
龍翔閃抵牾!!
りゅうしょうせんもどき
RYŪSHŌSEN IMITATION!!

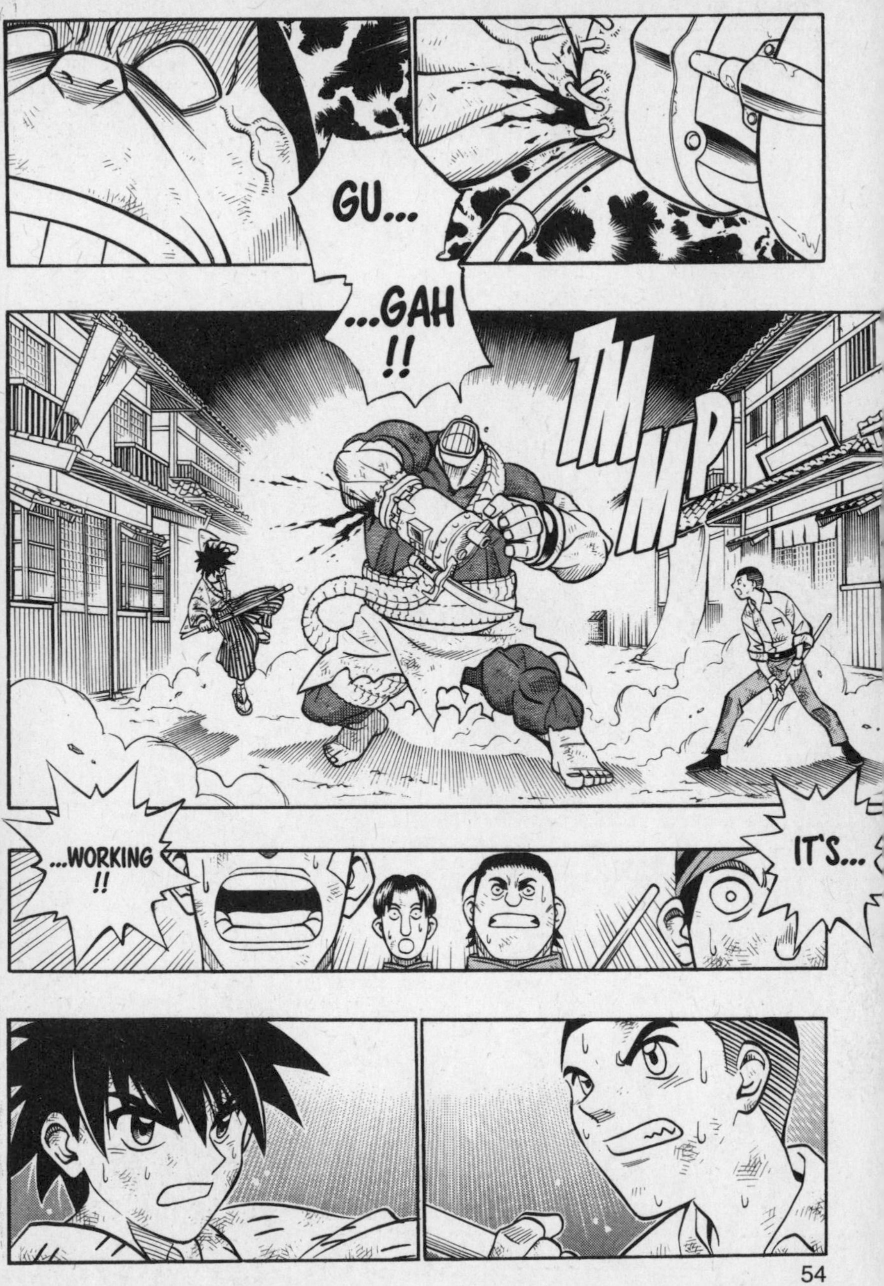
GU...
...GAH !!
TMMP
IT'S...
...WORKING !!

READ THIS WAY

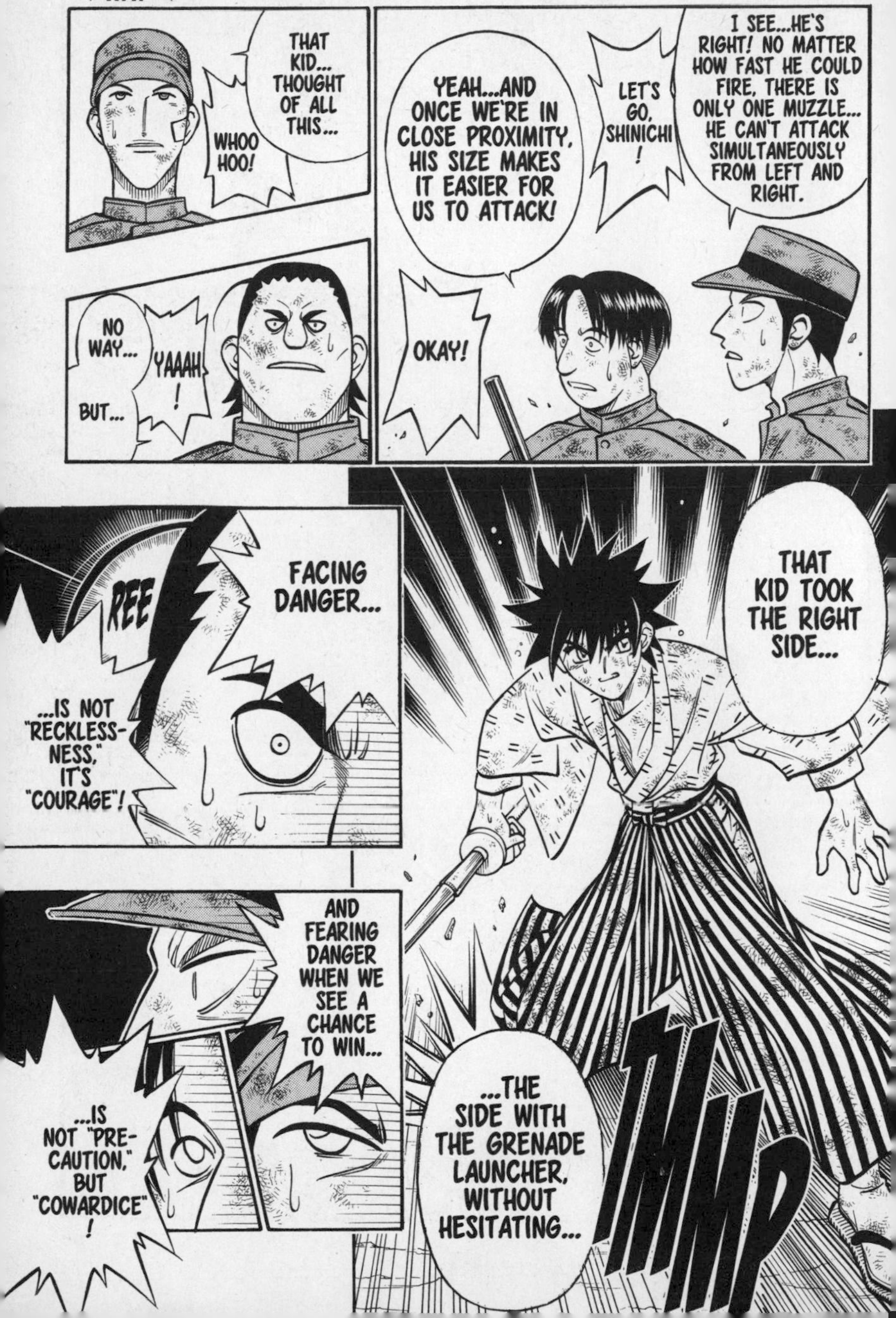
I SEE...HE'S RIGHT! NO MATTER HOW FAST HE COULD FIRE, THERE IS ONLY ONE MUZZLE... HE CAN'T ATTACK SIMULTANEOUSLY FROM LEFT AND RIGHT.
LET'S GO, SHINICHI!
YEAH...AND ONCE WE'RE IN CLOSE PROXIMITY, HIS SIZE MAKES IT EASIER FOR US TO ATTACK!
OKAY!
THAT KID... THOUGHT OF ALL THIS...
WHOO HOO!
YAAAH!
NO WAY...
BUT...
THAT KID TOOK THE RIGHT SIDE...
...THE SIDE WITH THE GRENADE LAUNCHER, WITHOUT HESITATING...
TMMP
REE
FACING DANGER...
...IS NOT "RECKLESS-NESS," IT'S "COURAGE"!
AND FEARING DANGER WHEN WE SEE A CHANCE TO WIN...
...IS NOT "PRE-CAUTION," BUT "COWARDICE"!

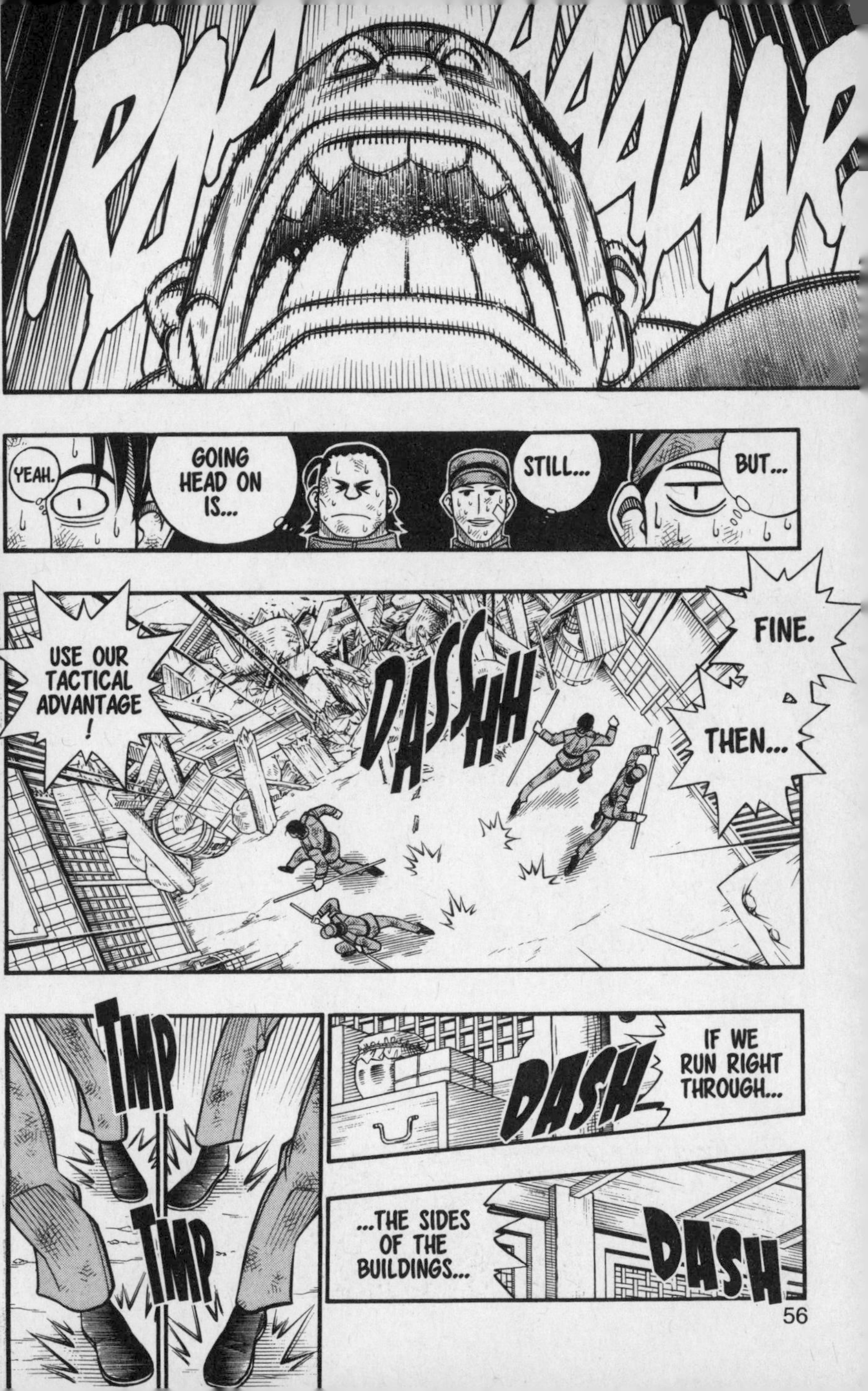
BUT...
STILL...
GOING HEAD ON IS...
YEAH.
FINE.
THEN...
DASHHH
USE OUR TACTICAL ADVANTAGE!
IF WE RUN RIGHT THROUGH...
DASH
...THE SIDES OF THE BUILDINGS...
DASH
TMP
TMP

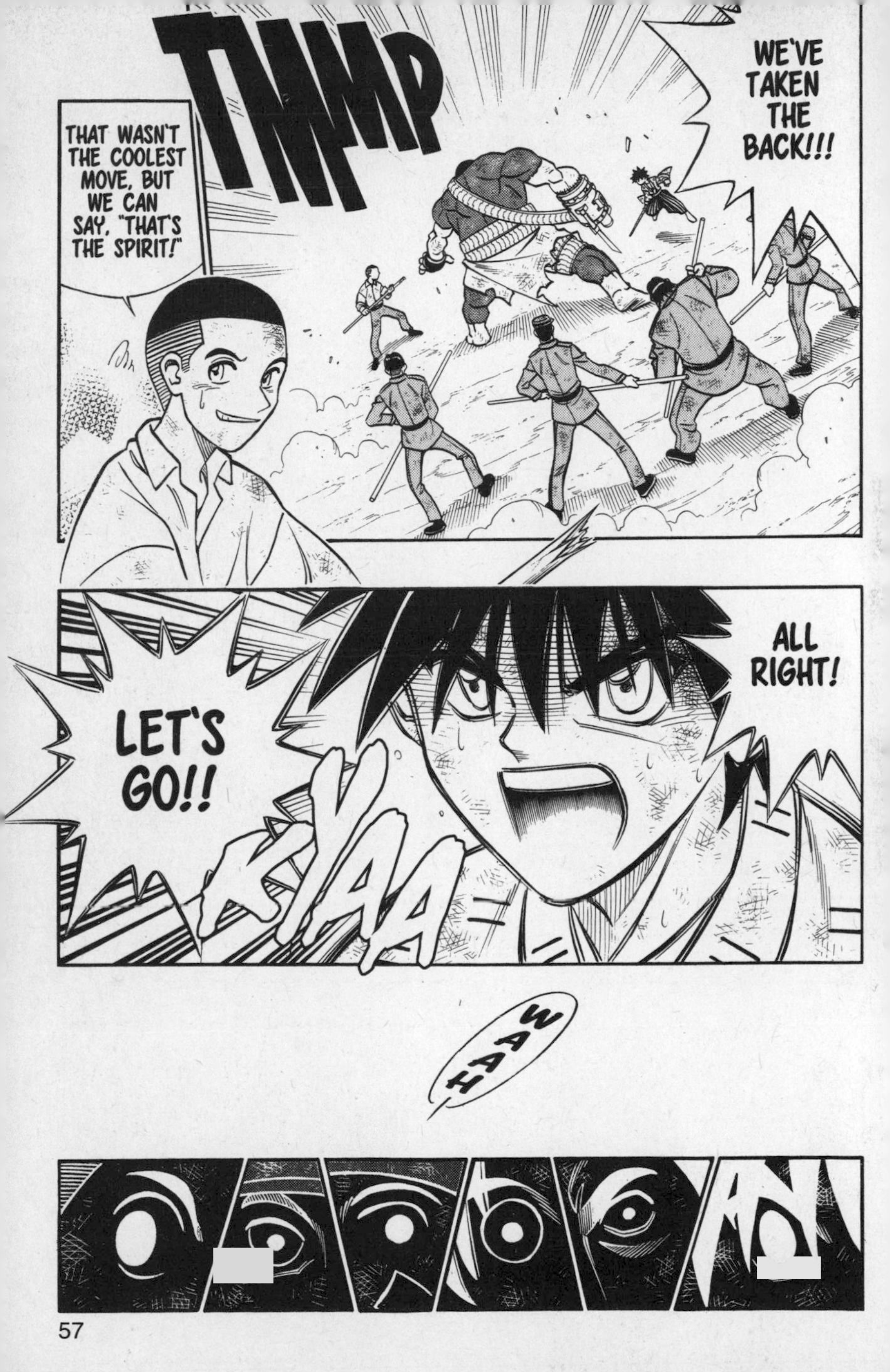
WE'VE TAKEN THE BACK!!!
TMMP
THAT WASN'T THE COOLEST MOVE, BUT WE CAN SAY, "THAT'S THE SPIRIT!"
ALL RIGHT!
LET'S GO!!
KIAA
WAAH

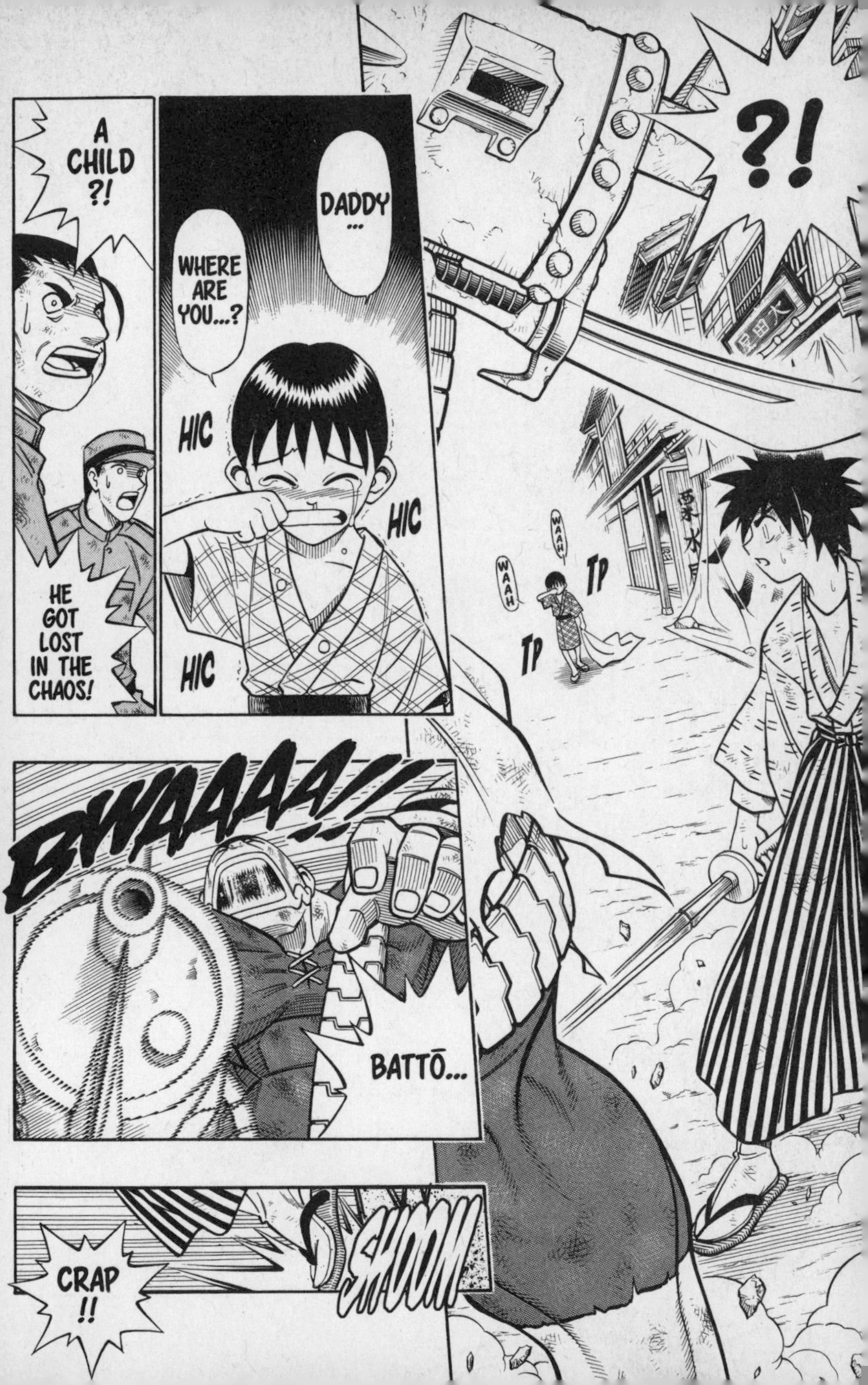
?!
WAAH
WAAH
TP
TP
DADDY ...
WHERE ARE YOU...?
HIC
HIC
HIC
A CHILD ?!
HE GOT LOST IN THE CHAOS!
BWAAAAA!!
BATTŌ...
SHOOM
CRAP !!

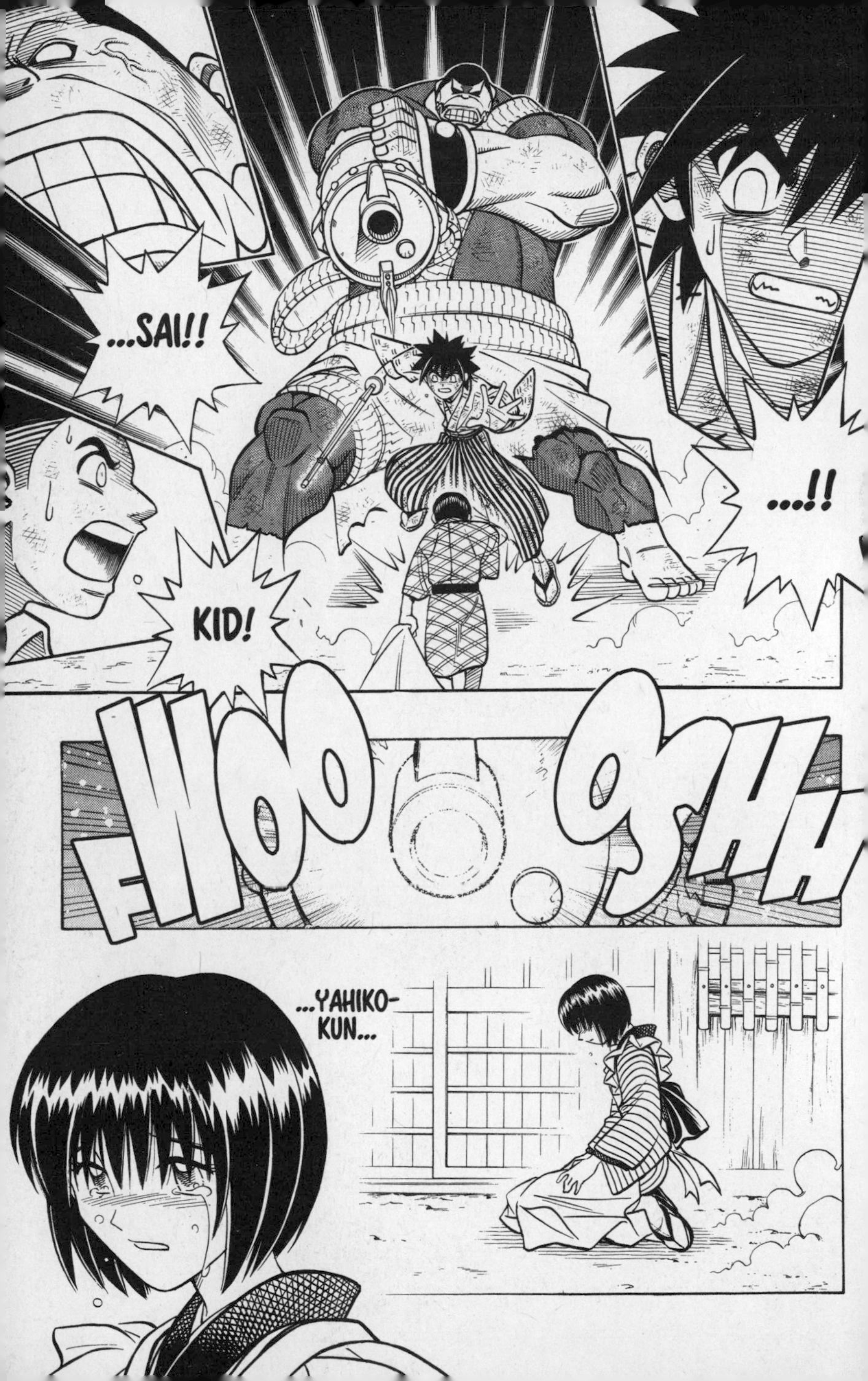
...!!
...SAI!!
KID!
WHOOOSH
...YAHIKO-KUN...

Rurouni Kenshin

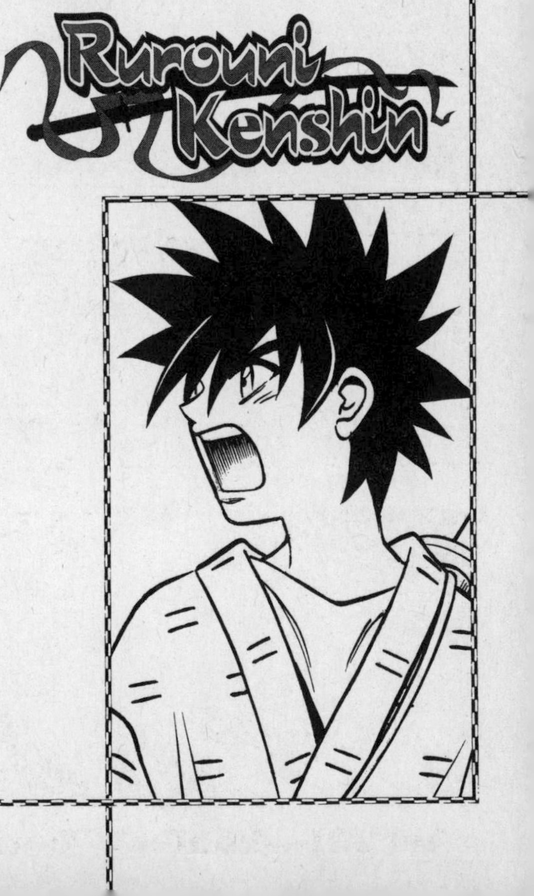

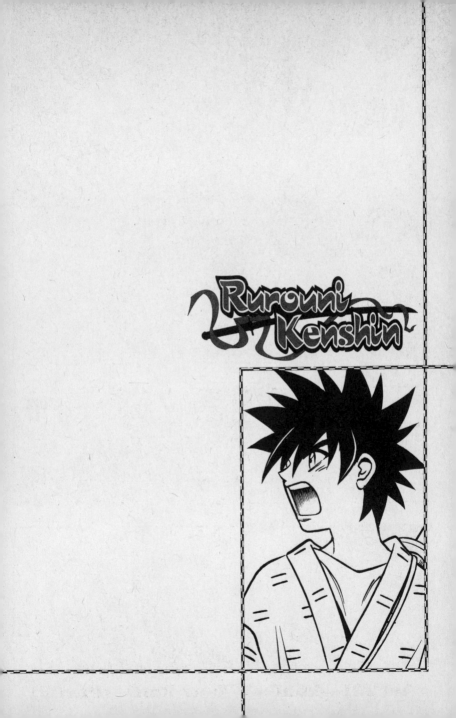

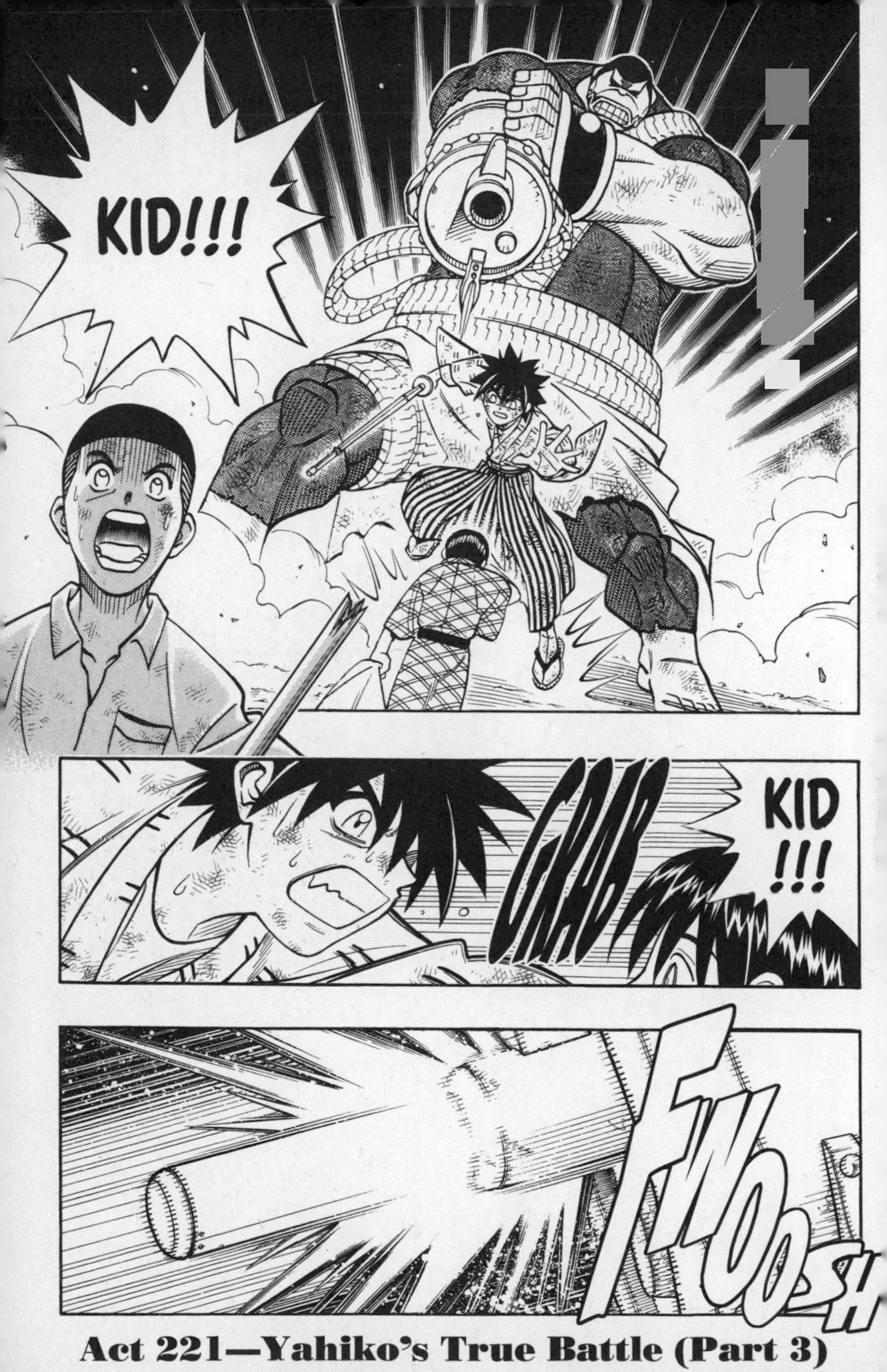
KID!!!
KID
!!!
GRAB
FWOOSH

Act 221—Yahiko's True Battle (Part 3)

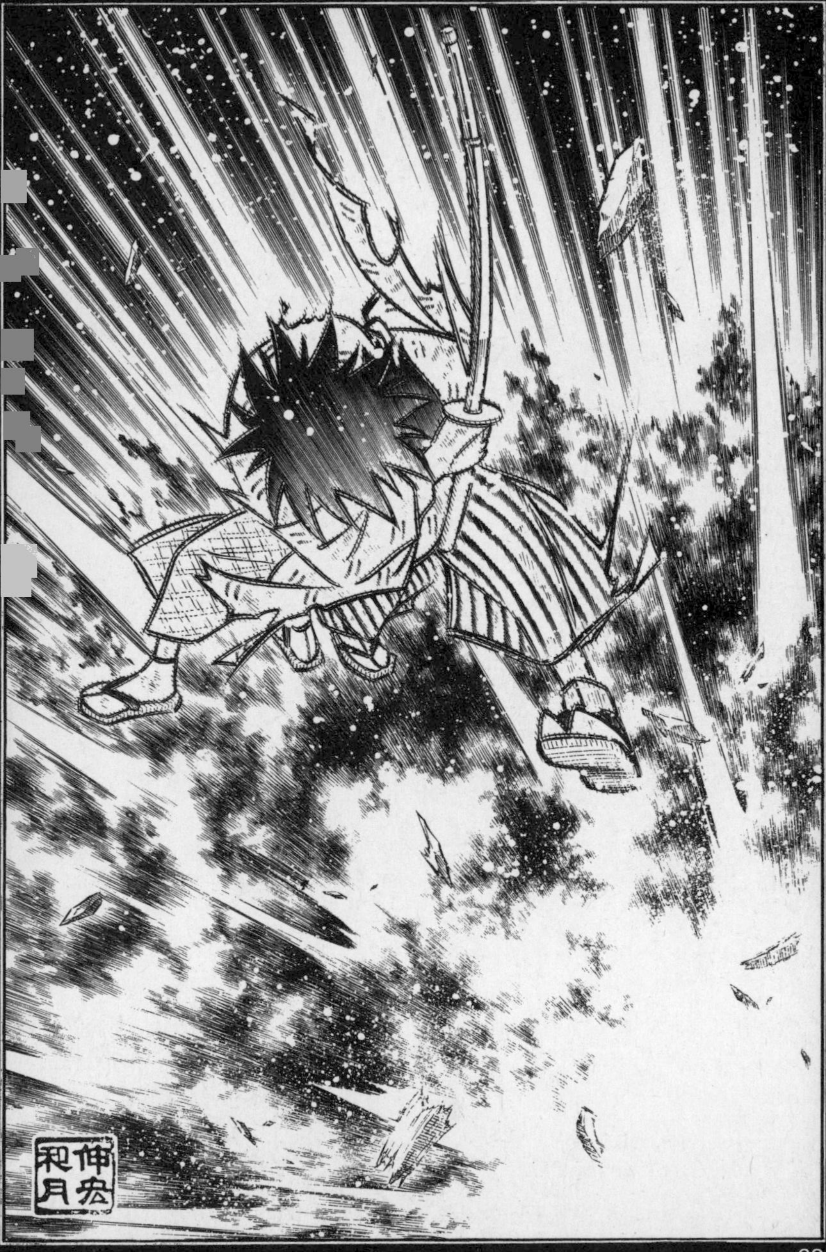

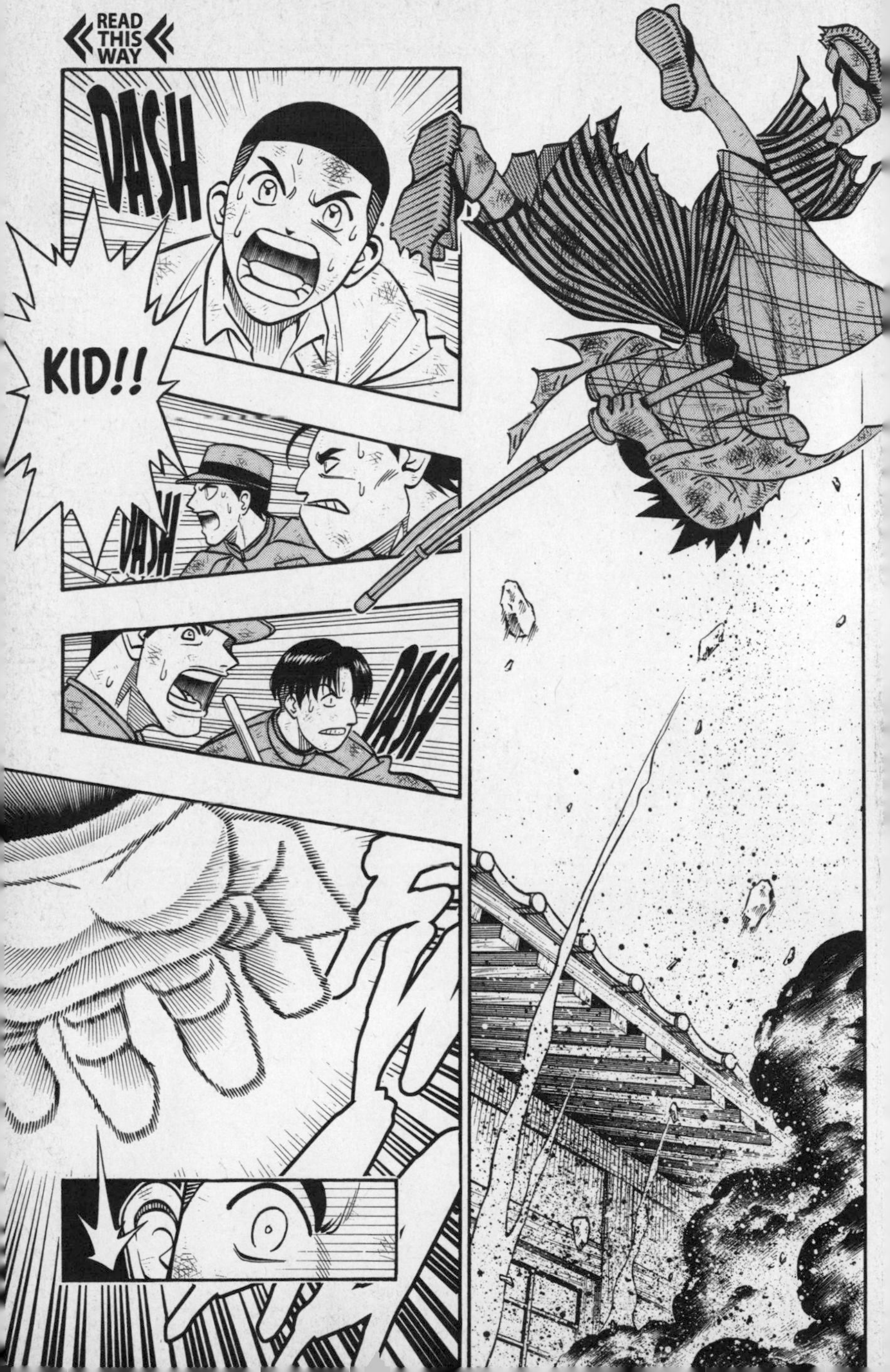
READ THIS WAY
DASH
KID!!
DASH
DASH

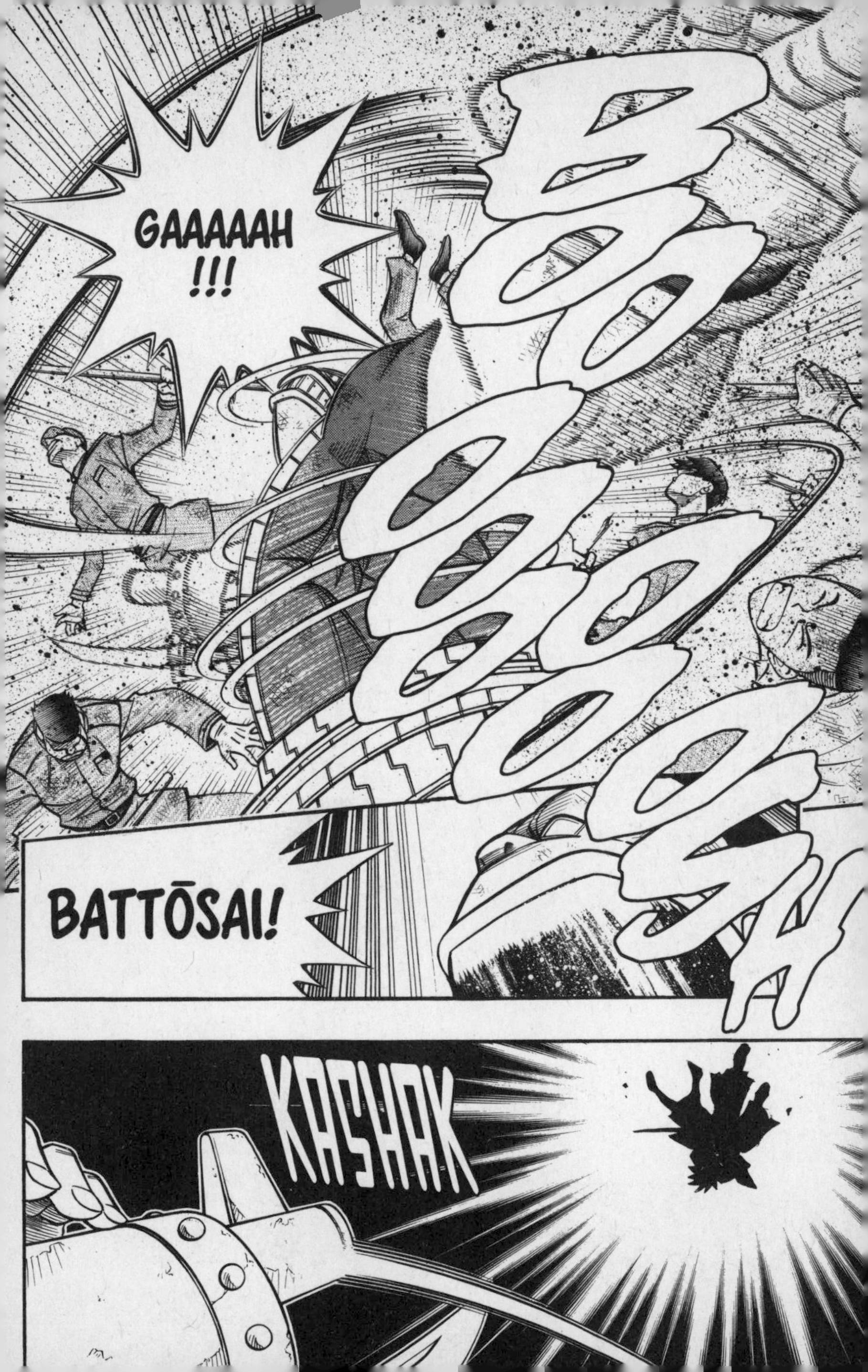
BOOOOOOOOSH
GAAAAAH !!!
BATTŌSAI!
KASHAK

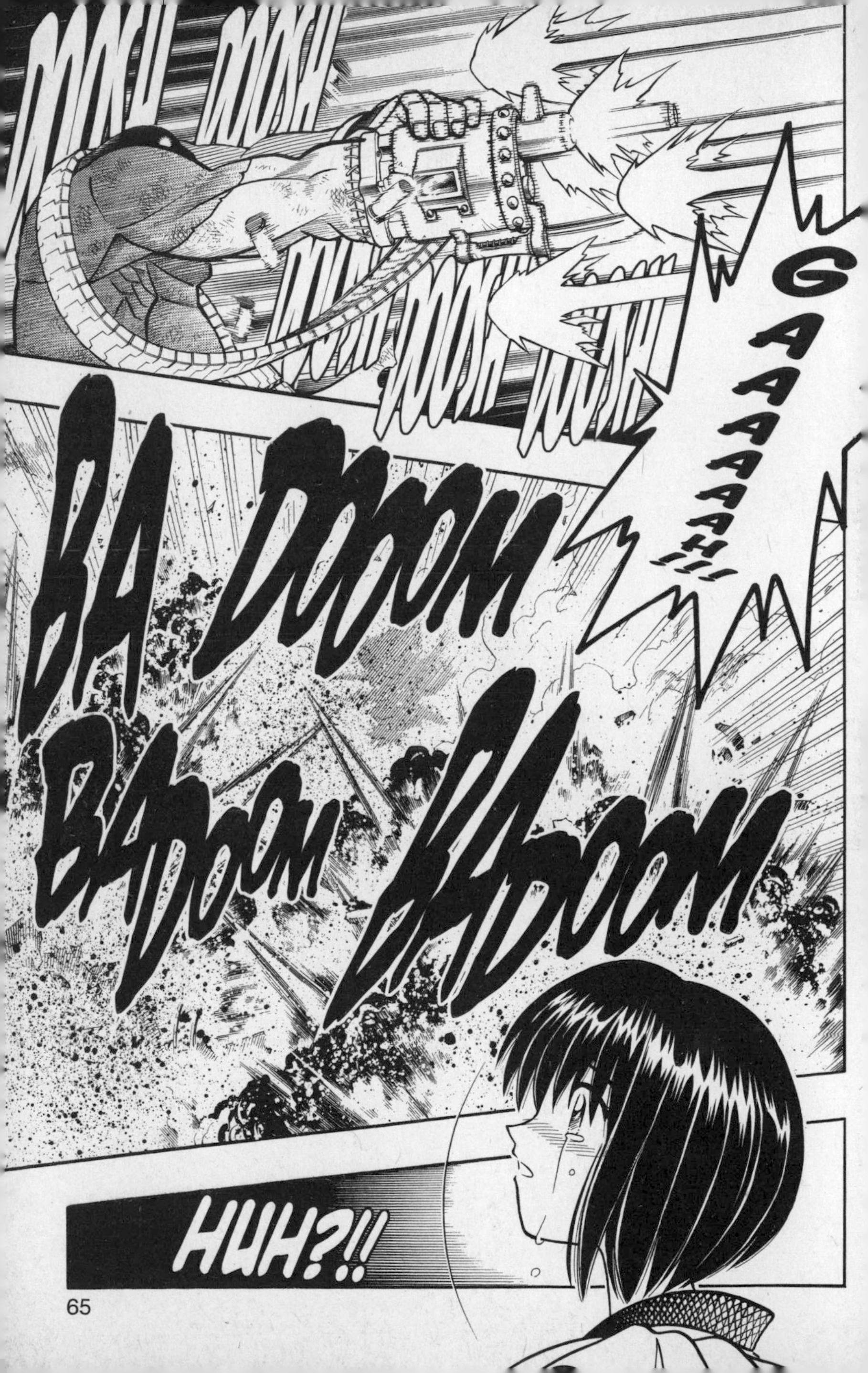
GAAAAAAAH!!!
DOOSH DOOSH
BA DOOM
BADOOM
HUH?!!

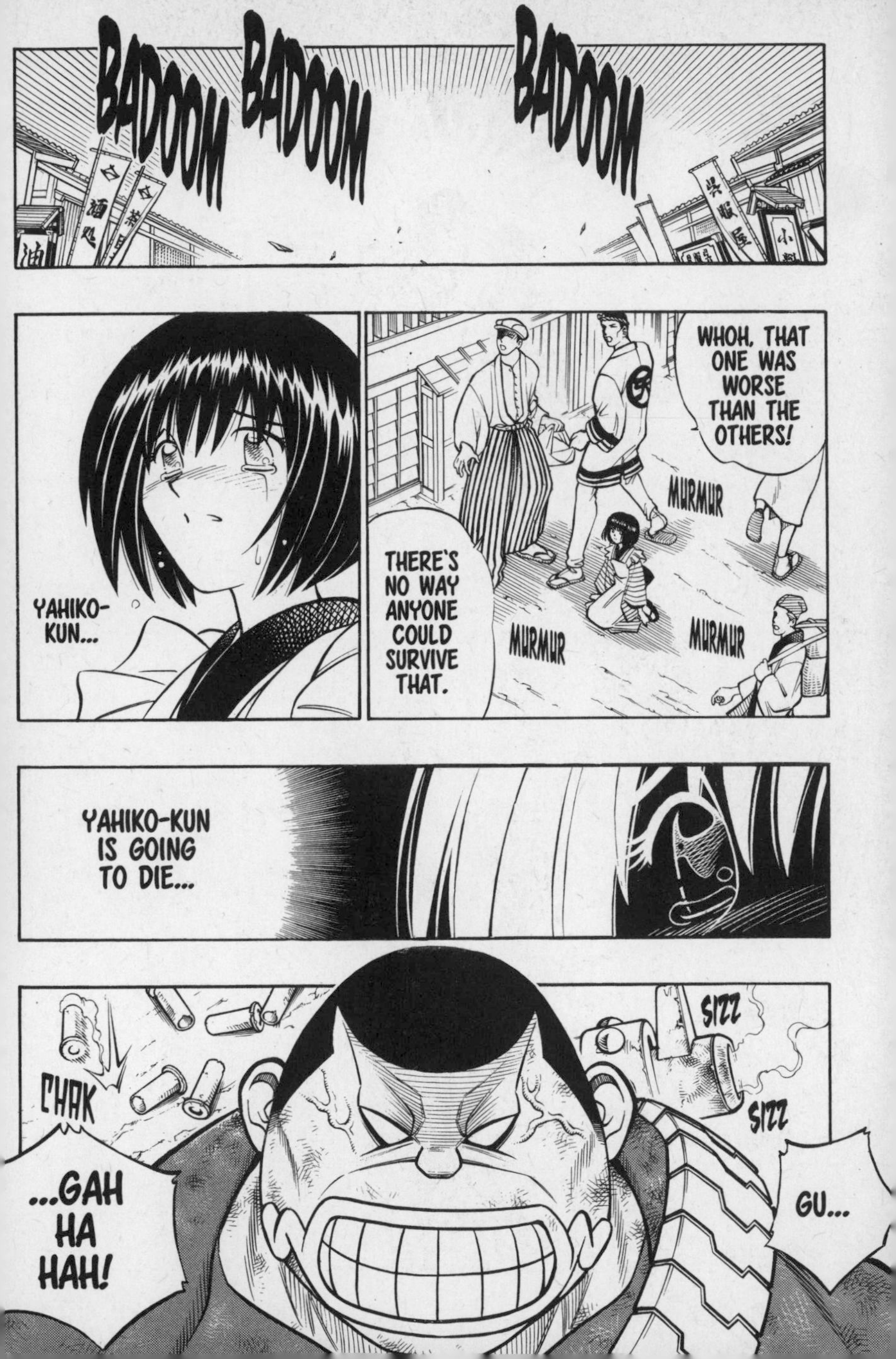
BADOOM
BADOOM
BADOOM
WHOH, THAT ONE WAS WORSE THAN THE OTHERS!
MURMUR
MURMUR
THERE'S NO WAY ANYONE COULD SURVIVE THAT.
MURMUR
YAHIKO-KUN...
YAHIKO-KUN IS GOING TO DIE...
SIZZ
SIZZ
GU...
C'HAK
...GAH HA HAH!

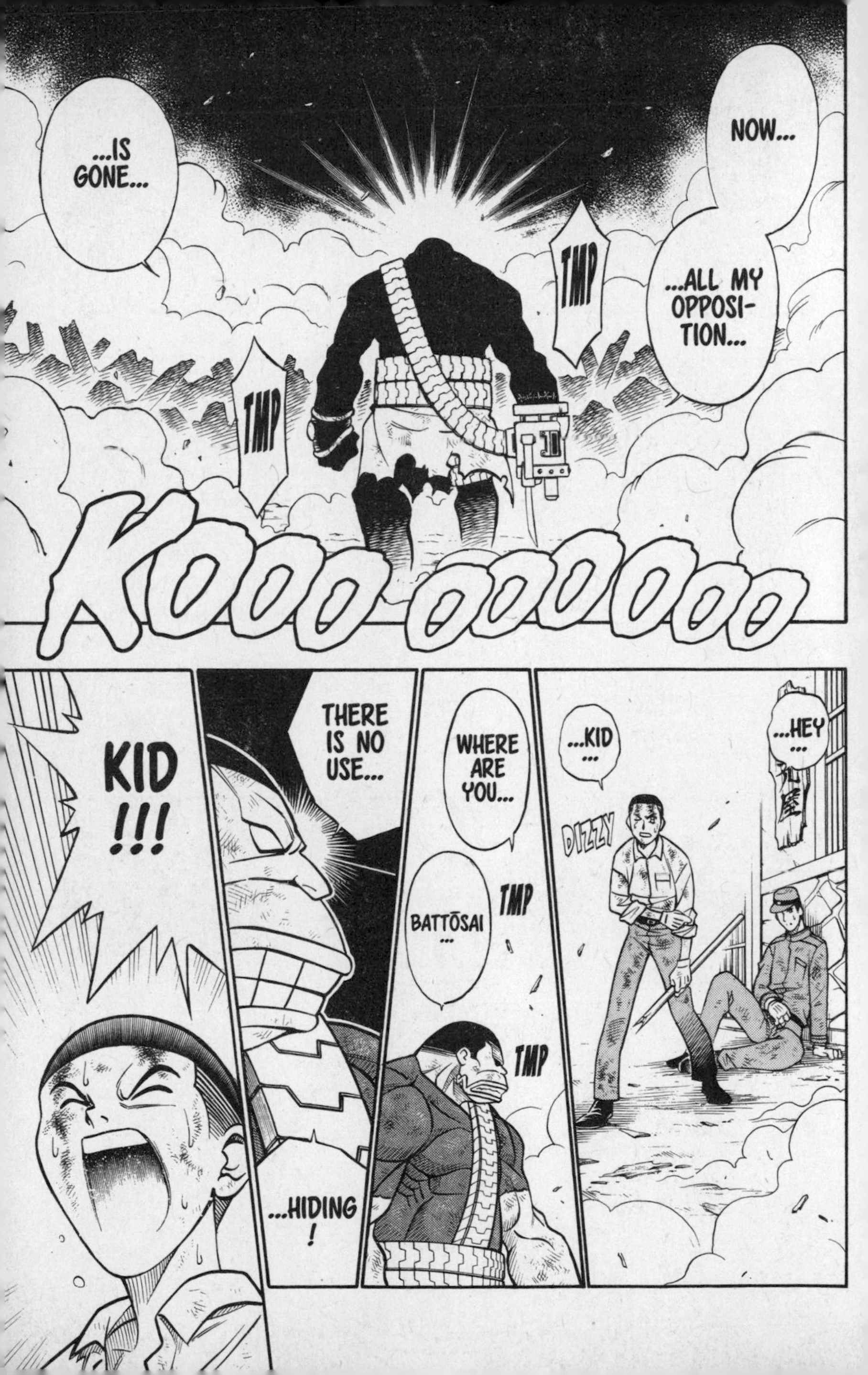
NOW...
...ALL MY OPPOSITION...
TMP
TMP
...IS GONE...
KOOO OOOOOO
...HEY ...
...KID ...
DIZZY
WHERE ARE YOU...
TMP
BATTŌSAI ...
TMP
THERE IS NO USE...
...HIDING !
KID !!!

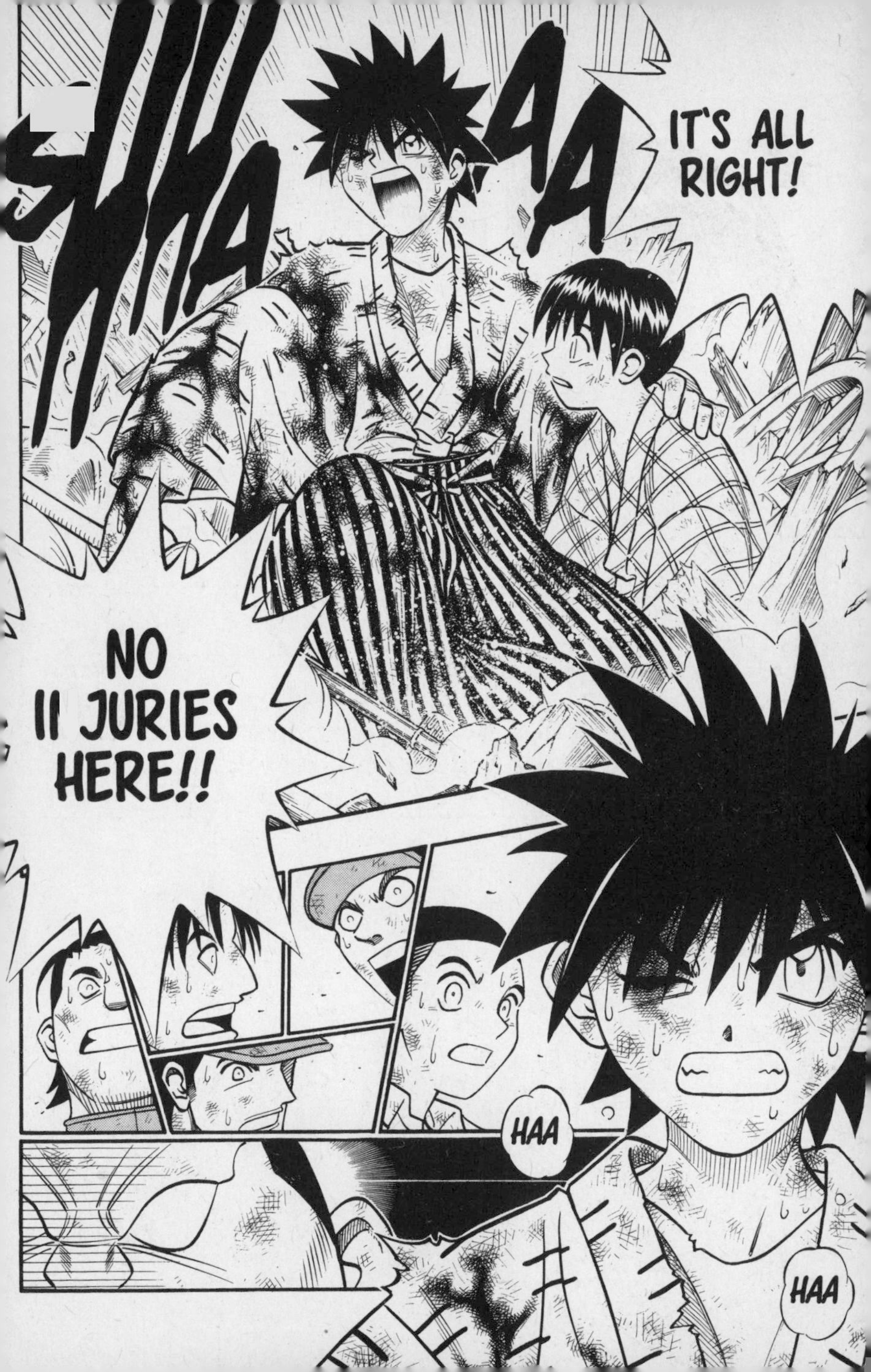
SHHAAA
IT'S ALL RIGHT!
NO II JURIES HERE!!
HAA
HAA

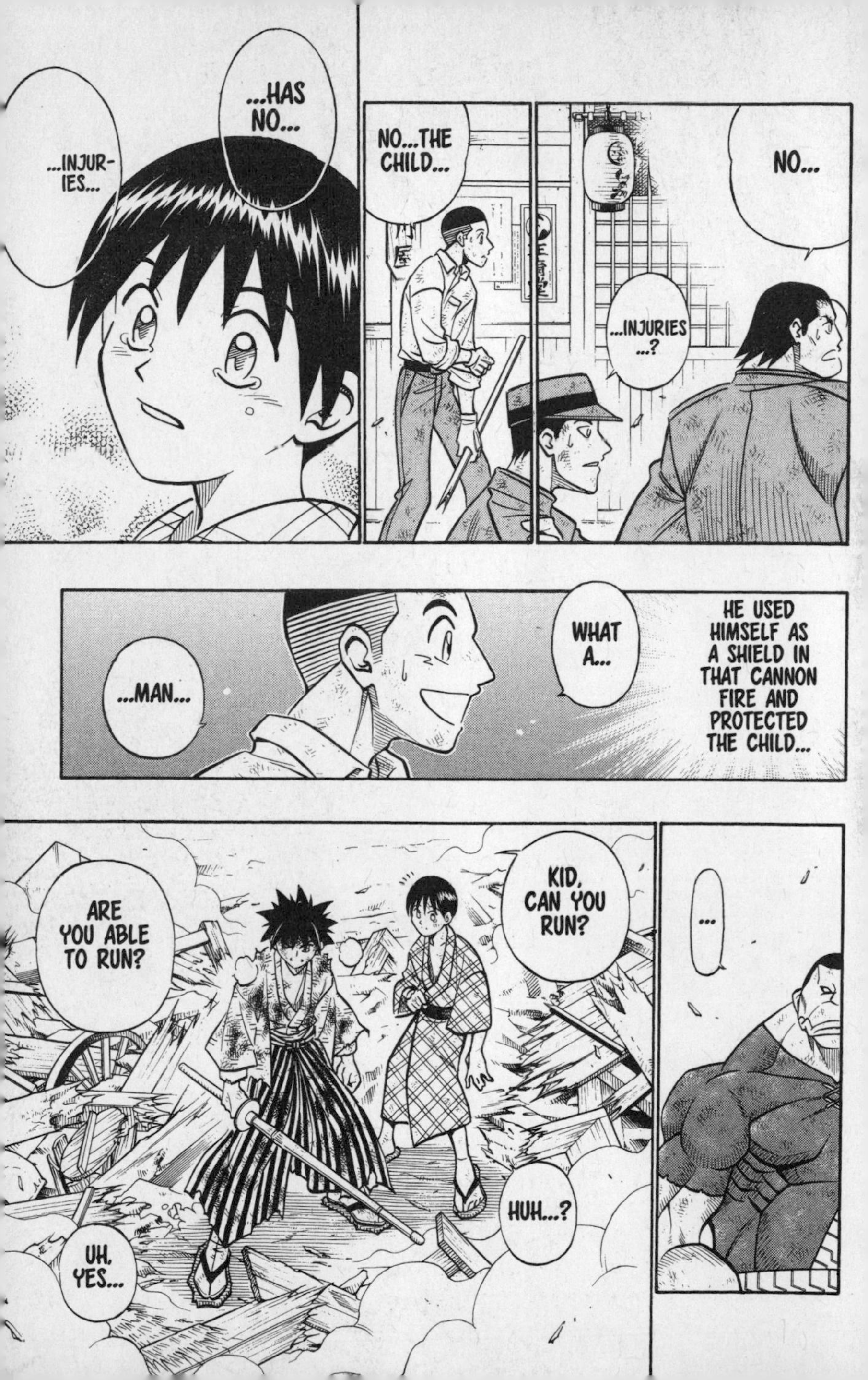
NO...
...INJURIES ...?
NO...THE CHILD...
...HAS NO...
...INJURIES...
HE USED HIMSELF AS A SHIELD IN THAT CANNON FIRE AND PROTECTED THE CHILD...
WHAT A...
...MAN...
...
KID, CAN YOU RUN?
HUH...?
ARE YOU ABLE TO RUN?
UH, YES...

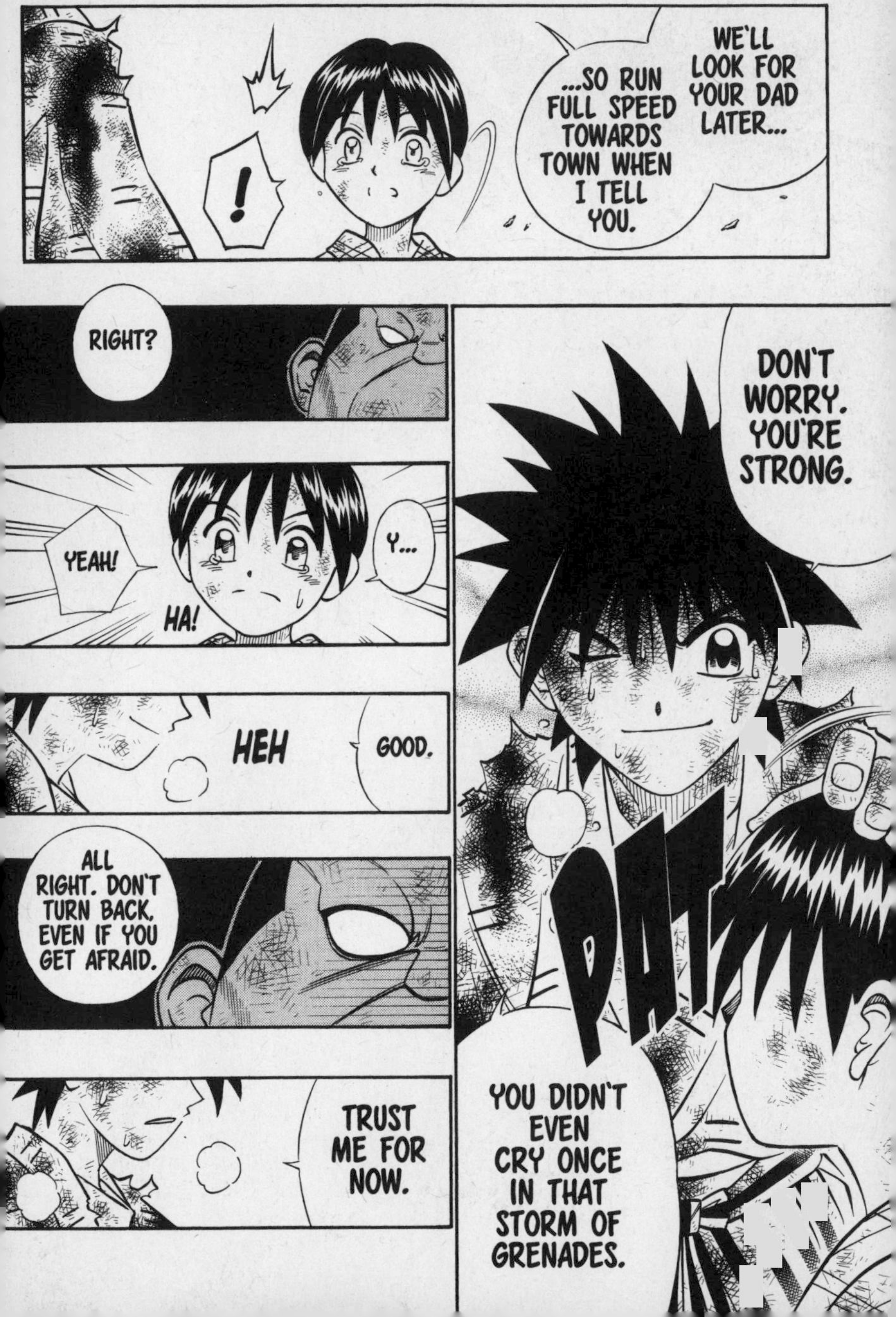
WE'LL LOOK FOR YOUR DAD LATER...
...SO RUN FULL SPEED TOWARDS TOWN WHEN I TELL YOU.
!
DON'T WORRY. YOU'RE STRONG.
PAT
YOU DIDN'T EVEN CRY ONCE IN THAT STORM OF GRENADES.
RIGHT?
Y...
YEAH!
HA!
GOOD.
HEH
ALL RIGHT. DON'T TURN BACK, EVEN IF YOU GET AFRAID.
TRUST ME FOR NOW.

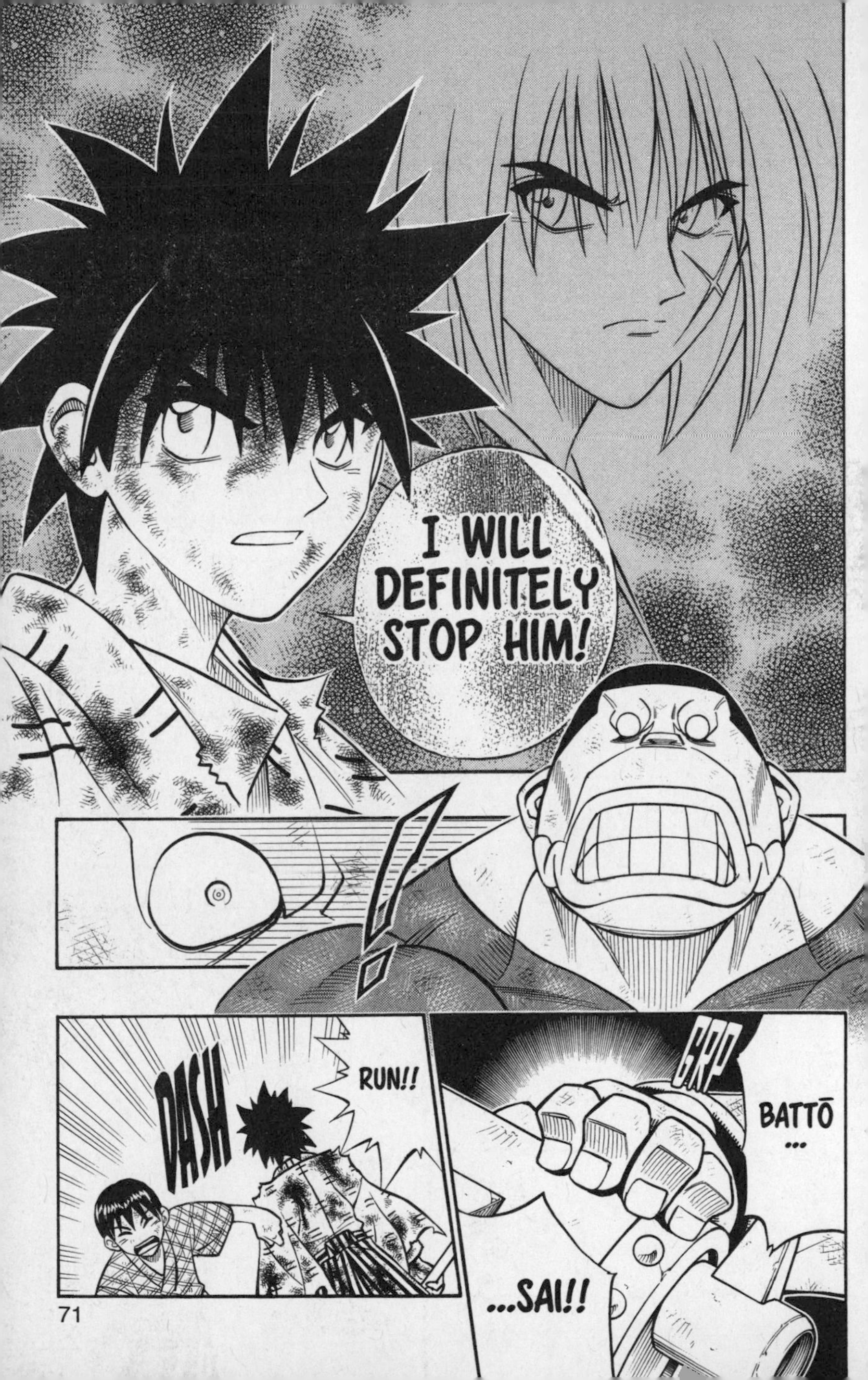
I WILL DEFINITELY STOP HIM!
GRP
BATTŌ ...
...SAI!!
RUN!!
DASH

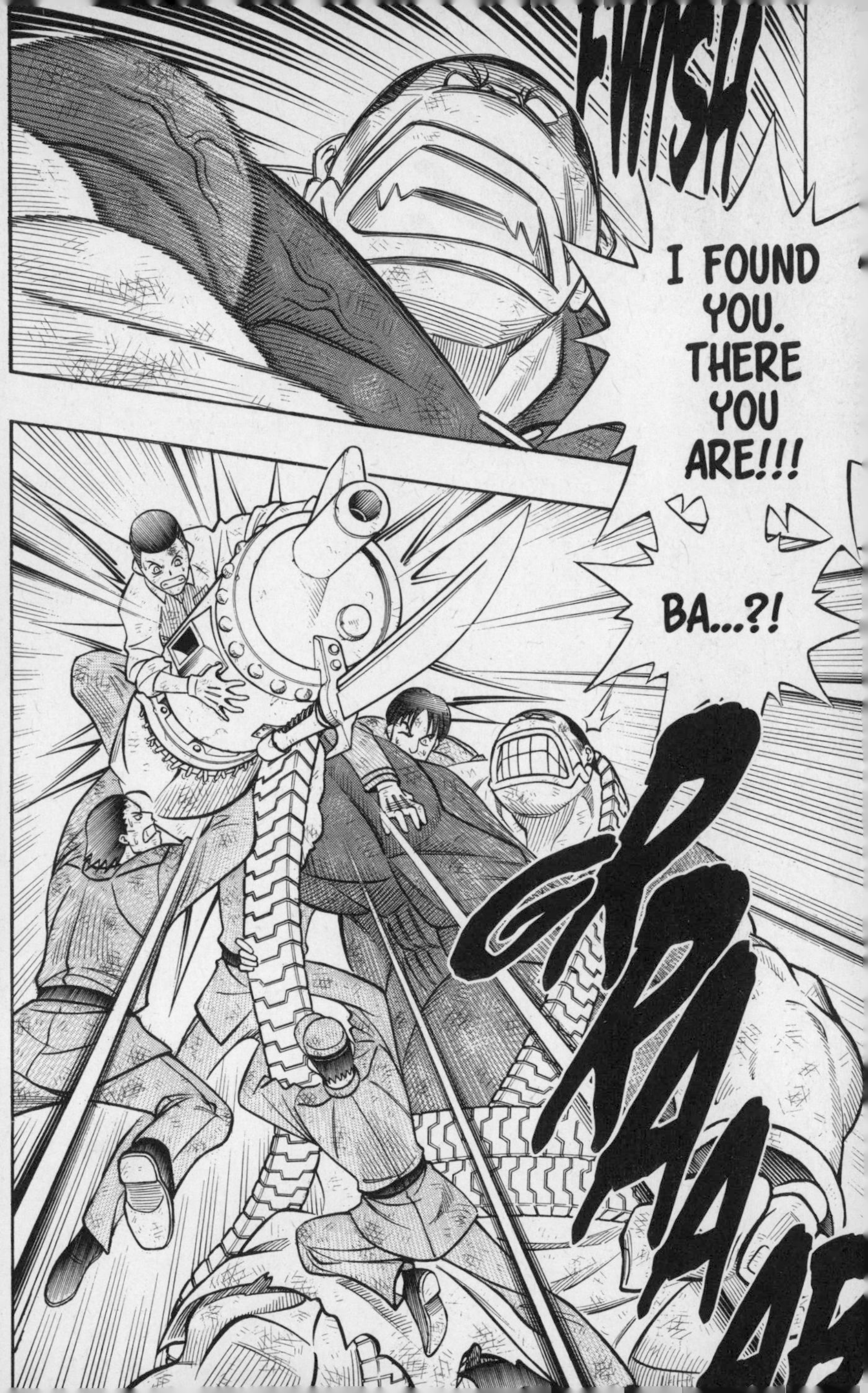
FWISH
I FOUND YOU. THERE YOU ARE!!!
BA...?!

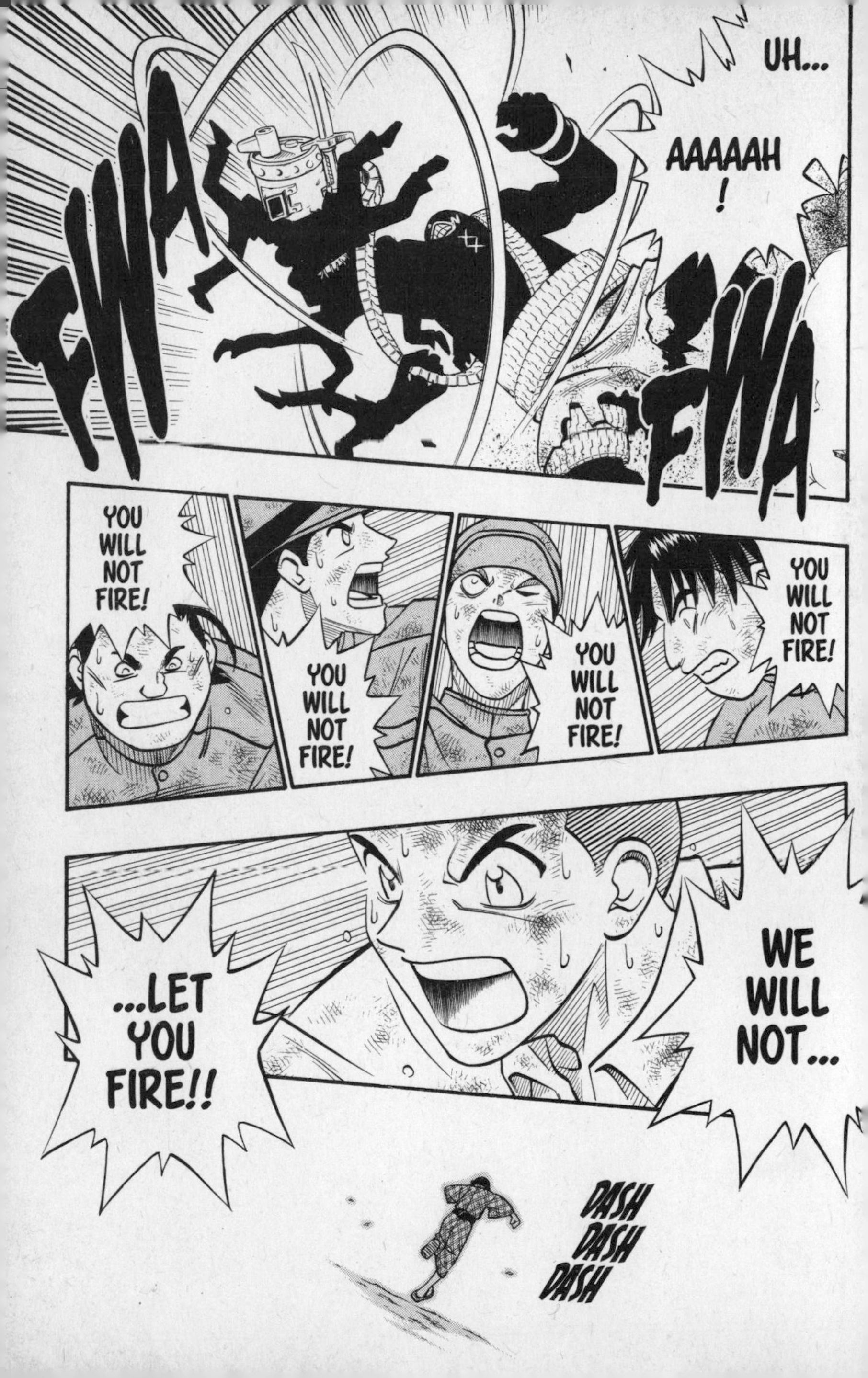

UH...
AAAAAH!
FWA
FWA
YOU WILL NOT FIRE!
YOU WILL NOT FIRE!
YOU WILL NOT FIRE!
YOU WILL NOT FIRE!
WE WILL NOT...
...LET YOU FIRE!!
DASH DASH DASH

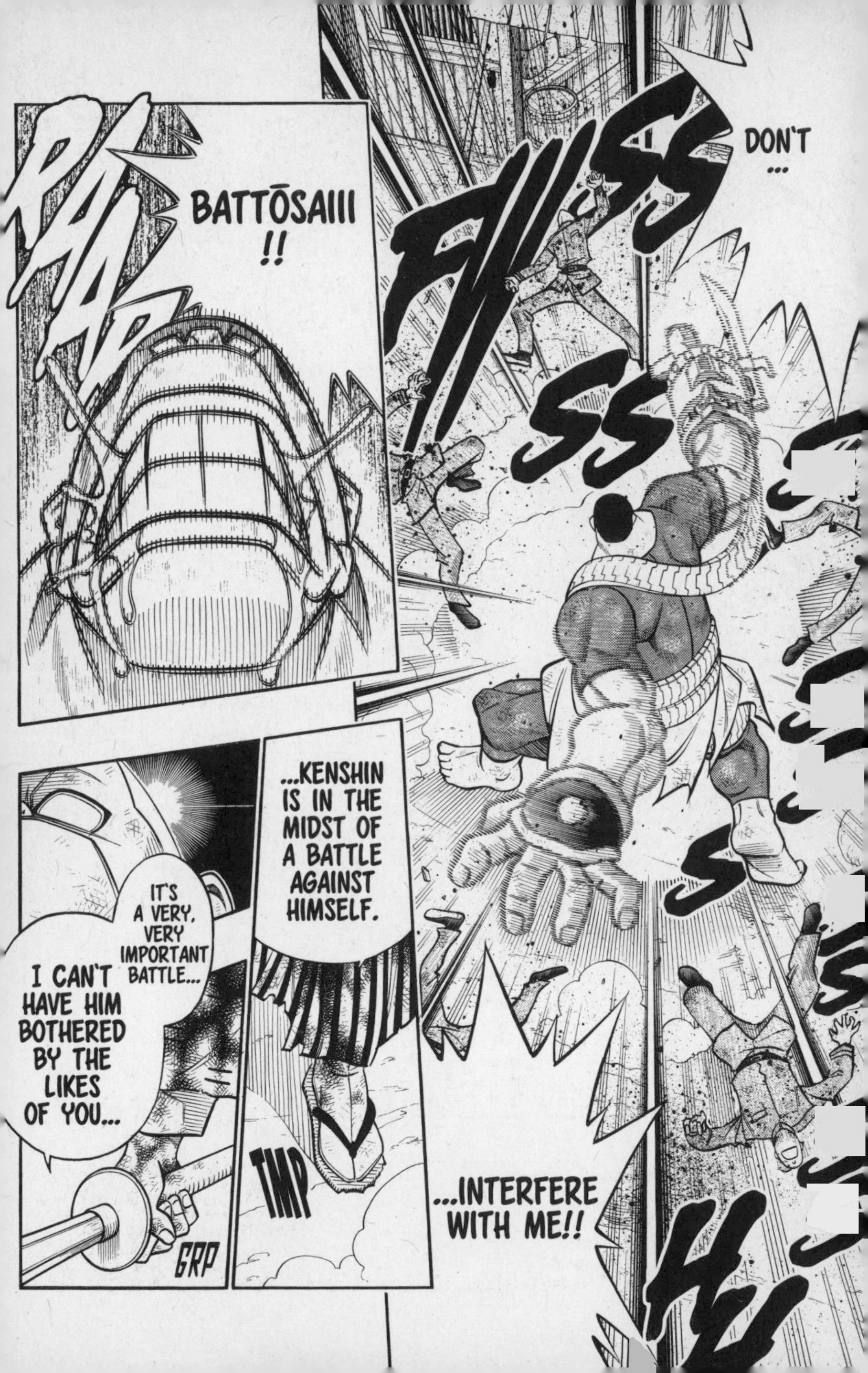
DON'T ...
...INTERFERE WITH ME!!
BATTŌSAIII !!
...KENSHIN IS IN THE MIDST OF A BATTLE AGAINST HIMSELF.
TMP
IT'S A VERY, VERY IMPORTANT BATTLE...
I CAN'T HAVE HIM BOTHERED BY THE LIKES OF YOU...
GRP

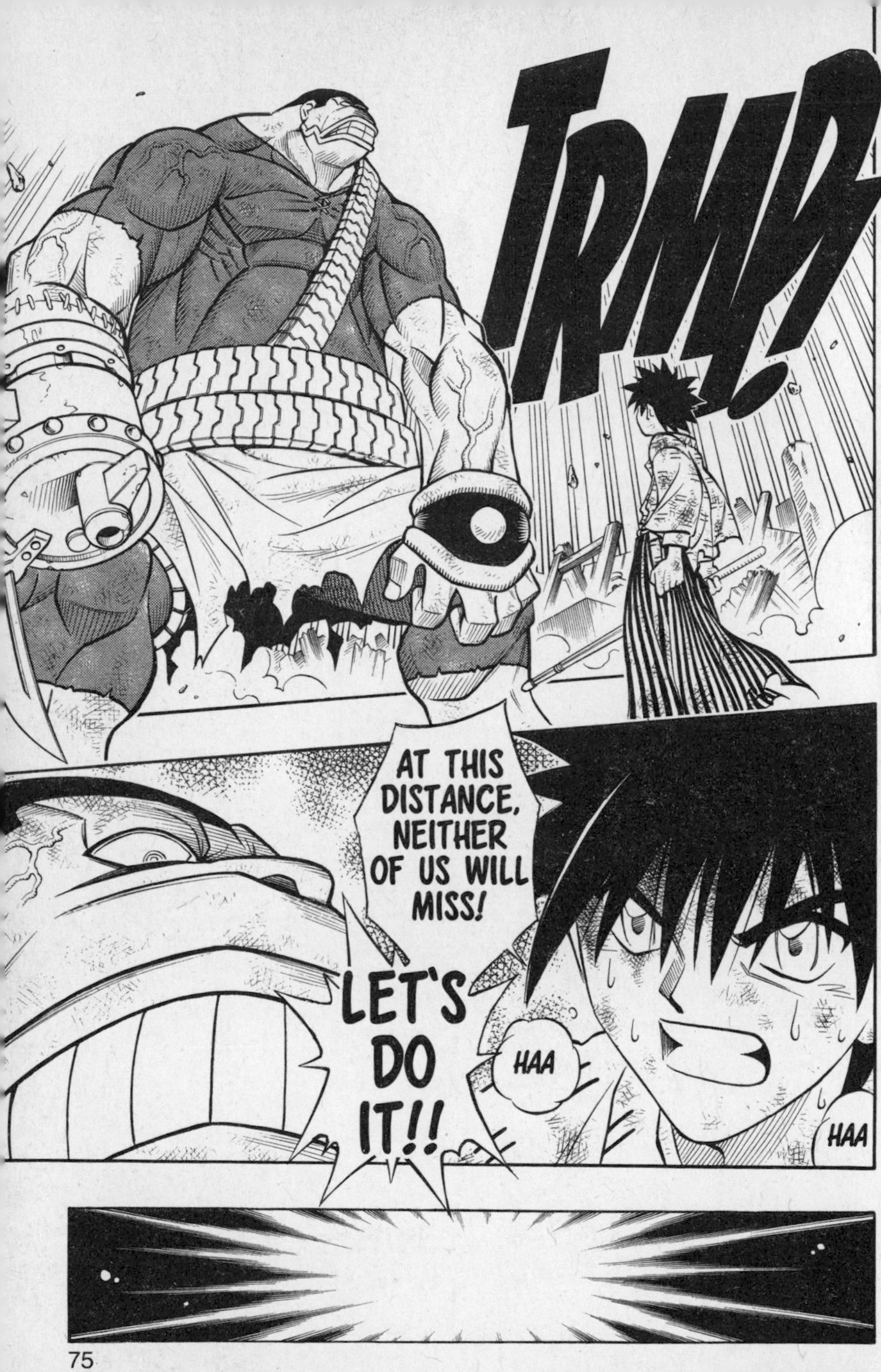
TPMB!
AT THIS DISTANCE, NEITHER OF US WILL MISS!
LET'S DO IT!!
HAA
HAA

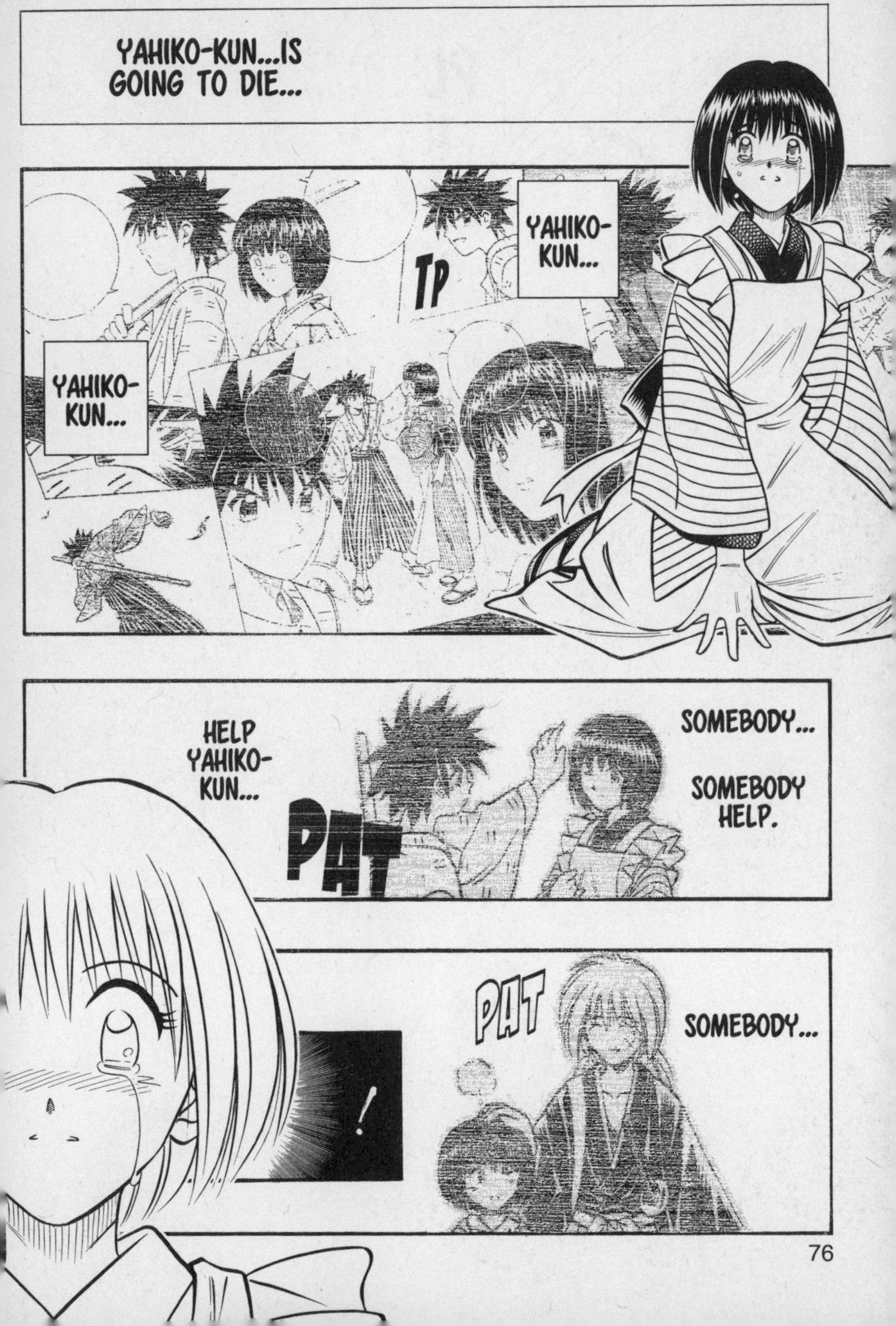
YAHIKO-KUN...IS GOING TO DIE...
YAHIKO-KUN...
TP
YAHIKO-KUN...
SOMEBODY...
SOMEBODY HELP.
HELP YAHIKO-KUN...
PAT
SOMEBODY...
PAT
!

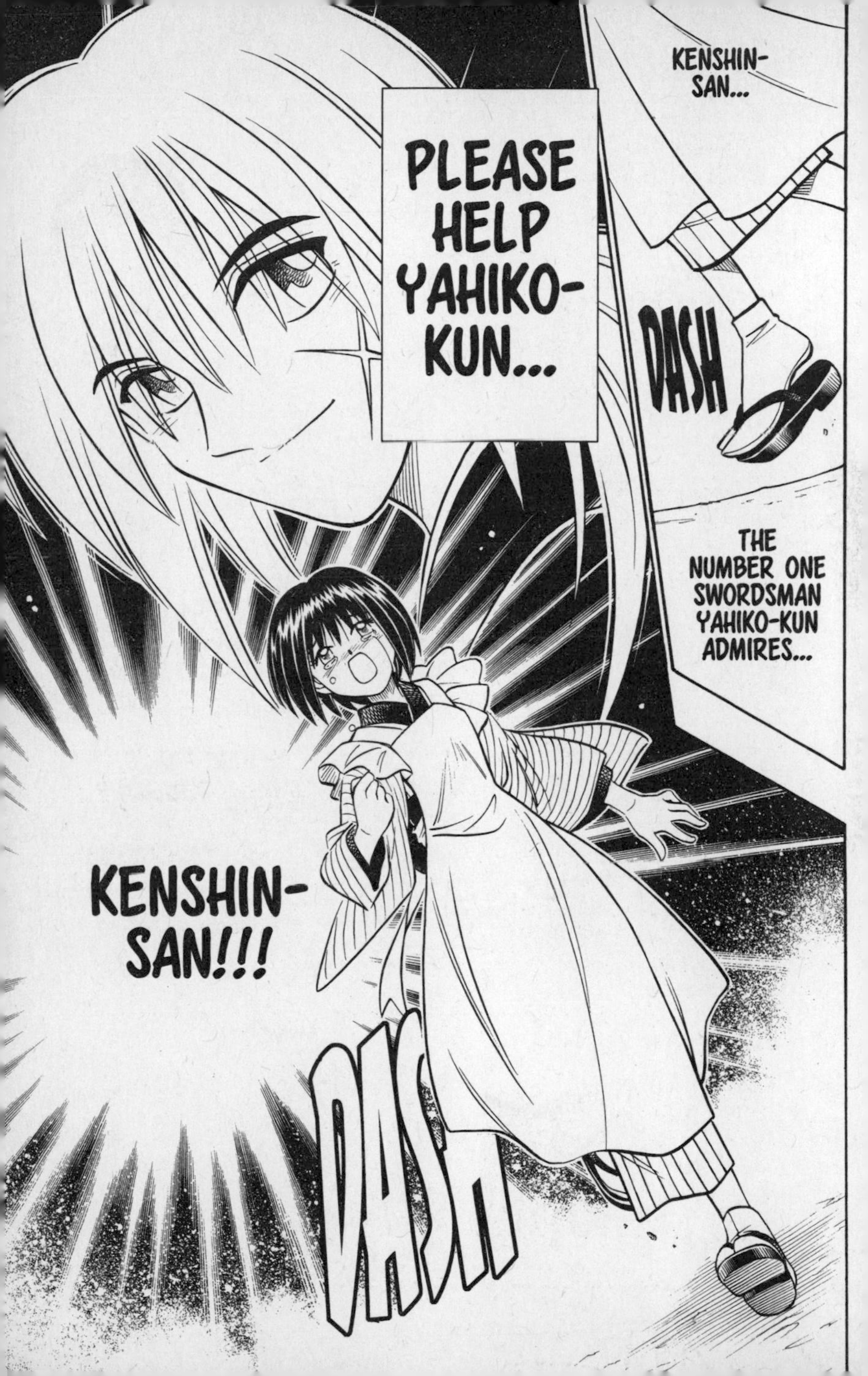
KENSHIN-SAN...
DASH
PLEASE HELP YAHIKO-KUN...
THE NUMBER ONE SWORDSMAN YAHIKO-KUN ADMIRES...
KENSHIN-SAN!!!
DASH

Rurouni Kenshin

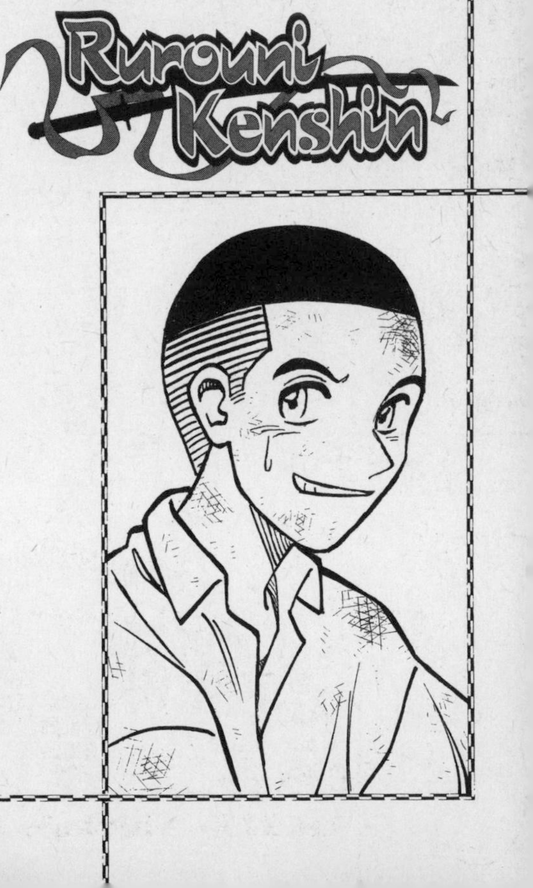

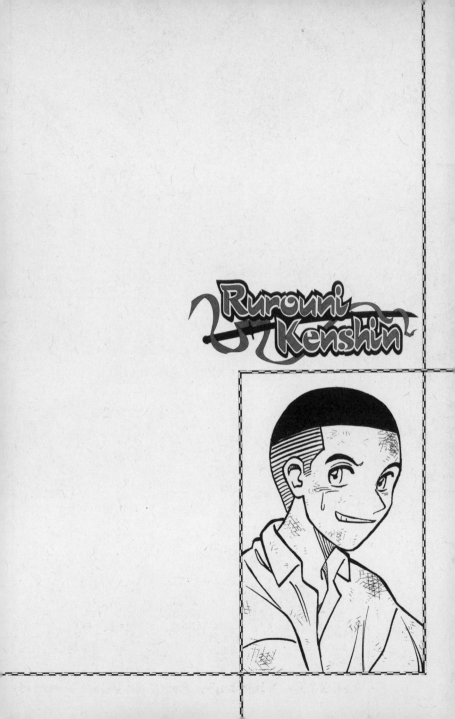

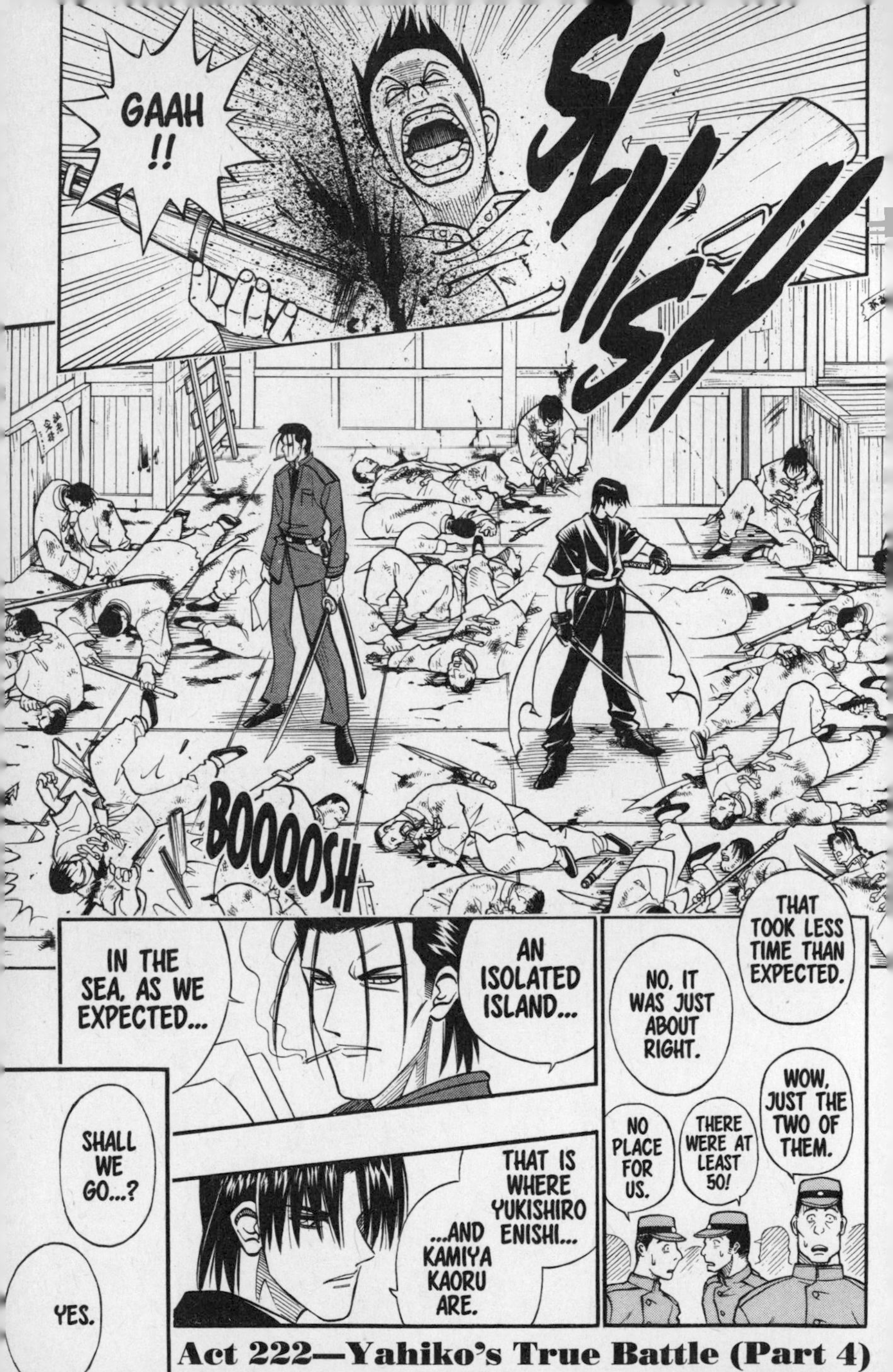
SWISH
GAAH!!
BOOOOSH
THAT TOOK LESS TIME THAN EXPECTED.
NO, IT WAS JUST ABOUT RIGHT.
WOW, JUST THE TWO OF THEM.
THERE WERE AT LEAST 50!
NO PLACE FOR US.
AN ISOLATED ISLAND...
IN THE SEA, AS WE EXPECTED...
THAT IS WHERE YUKISHIRO ENISHI...
...AND KAMIYA KAORU ARE.
SHALL WE GO...?
YES.

Act 222—Yahiko's True Battle (Part 4)

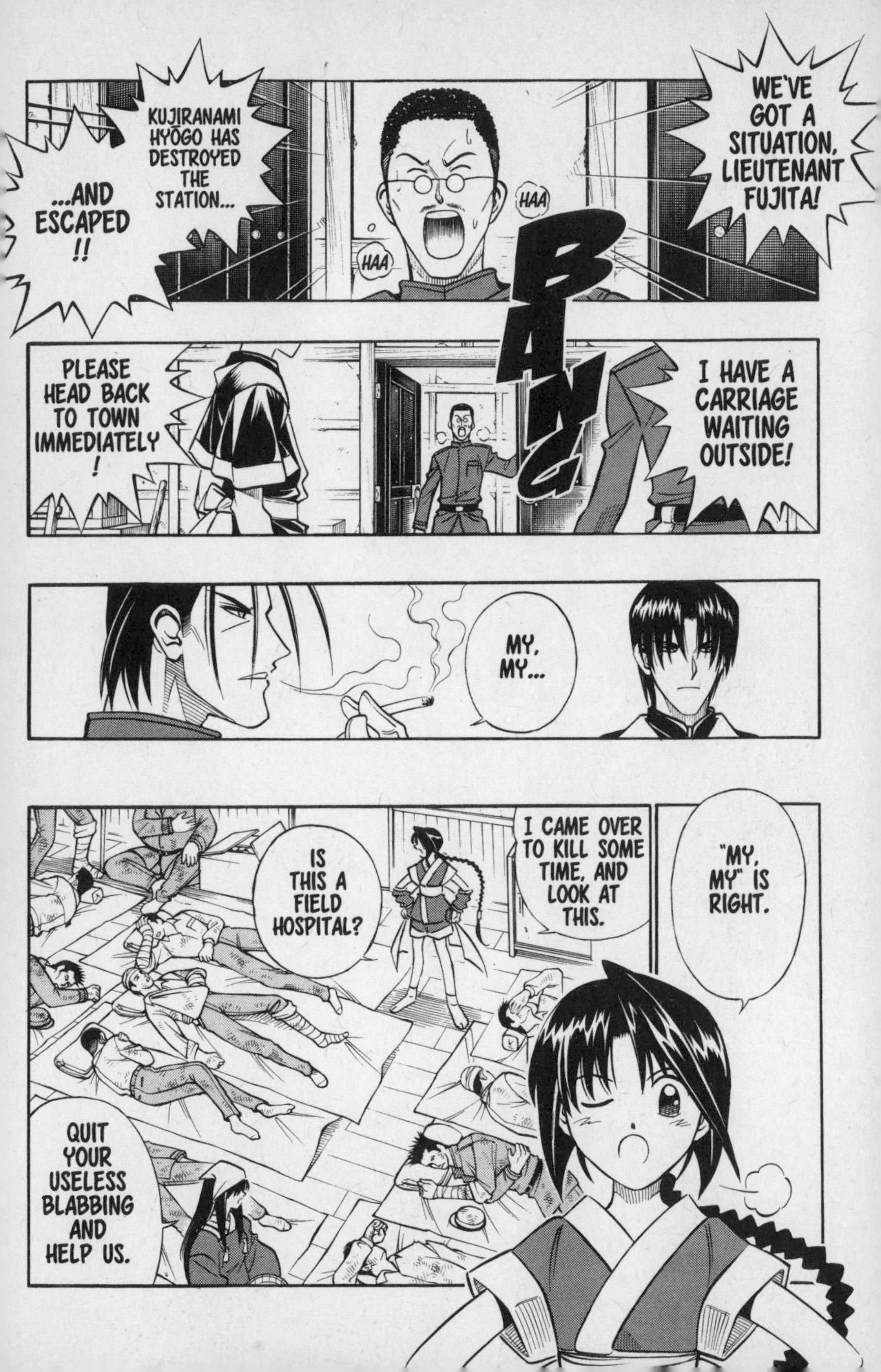
WE'VE GOT A SITUATION, LIEUTENANT FUJITA!
HAA
HAA
KUJIRANAMI HYŌGO HAS DESTROYED THE STATION...
...AND ESCAPED !!
BANG
I HAVE A CARRIAGE WAITING OUTSIDE!
PLEASE HEAD BACK TO TOWN IMMEDIATELY !
MY, MY...
"MY, MY" IS RIGHT.
I CAME OVER TO KILL SOME TIME, AND LOOK AT THIS.
IS THIS A FIELD HOSPITAL?
QUIT YOUR USELESS BLABBING AND HELP US.

READ THIS WAY

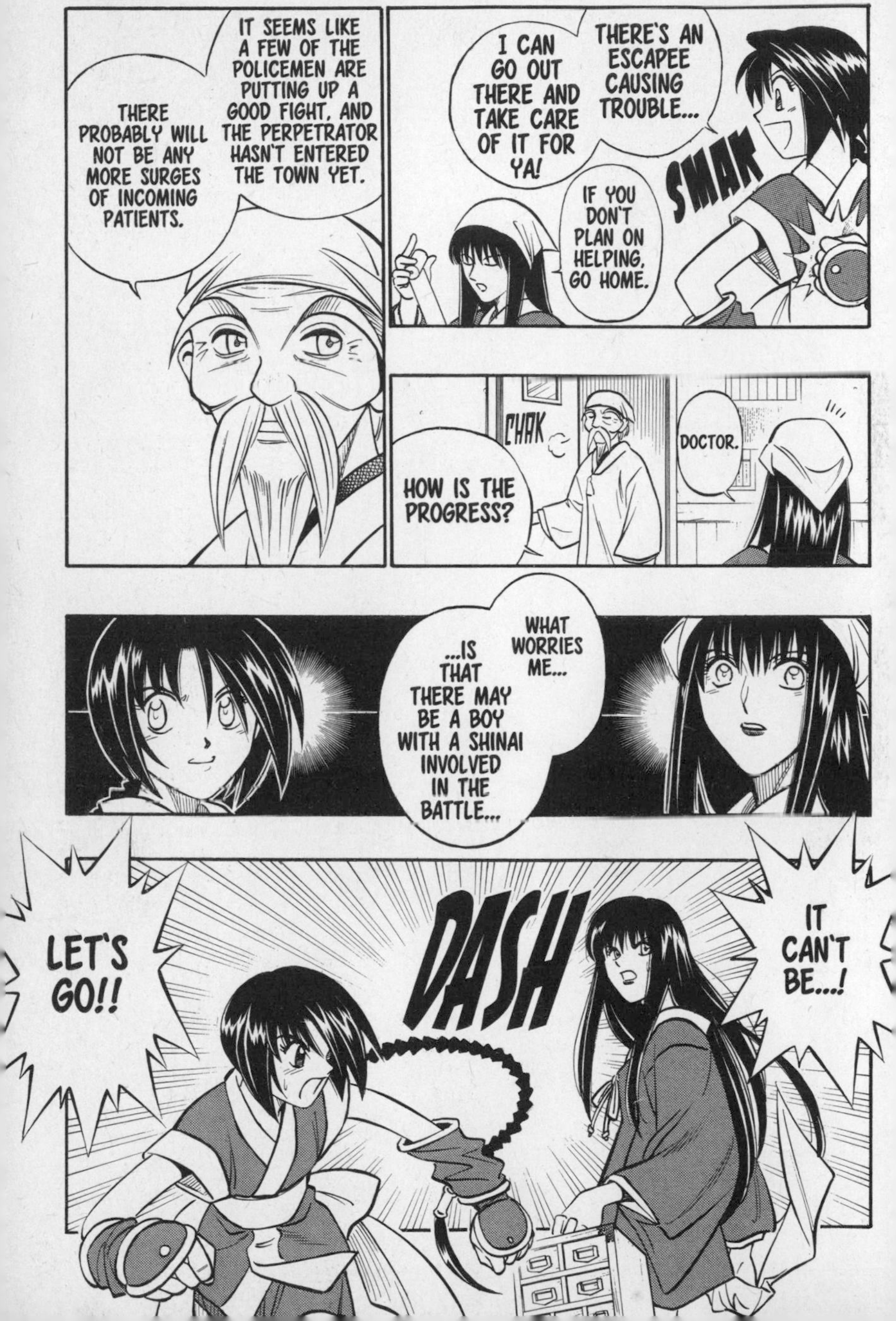
THERE'S AN ESCAPEE CAUSING TROUBLE...
I CAN GO OUT THERE AND TAKE CARE OF IT FOR YA!
SMAK
IF YOU DON'T PLAN ON HELPING, GO HOME.
DOCTOR.
CHAK
HOW IS THE PROGRESS?
IT SEEMS LIKE A FEW OF THE POLICEMEN ARE PUTTING UP A GOOD FIGHT, AND THE PERPETRATOR HASN'T ENTERED THE TOWN YET.
THERE PROBABLY WILL NOT BE ANY MORE SURGES OF INCOMING PATIENTS.
WHAT WORRIES ME...
...IS THAT THERE MAY BE A BOY WITH A SHINAI INVOLVED IN THE BATTLE...
IT CAN'T BE...!
DASH
LET'S GO!!

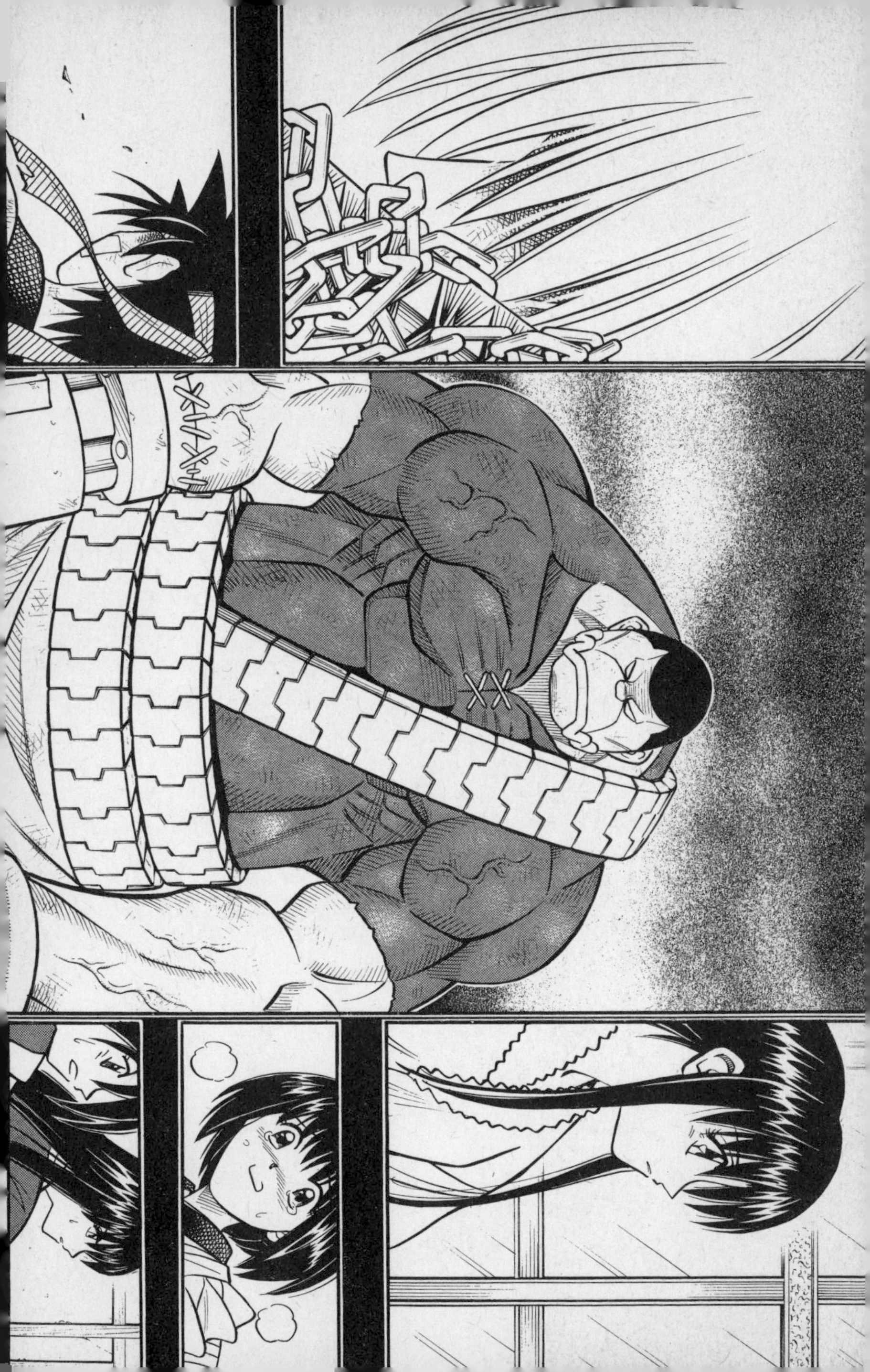

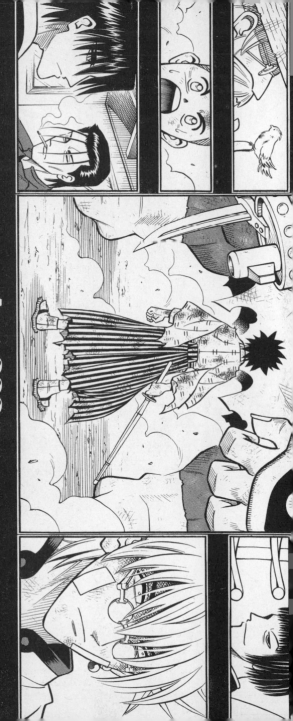

Act 222
Yahiko's True Battle (Part 4)

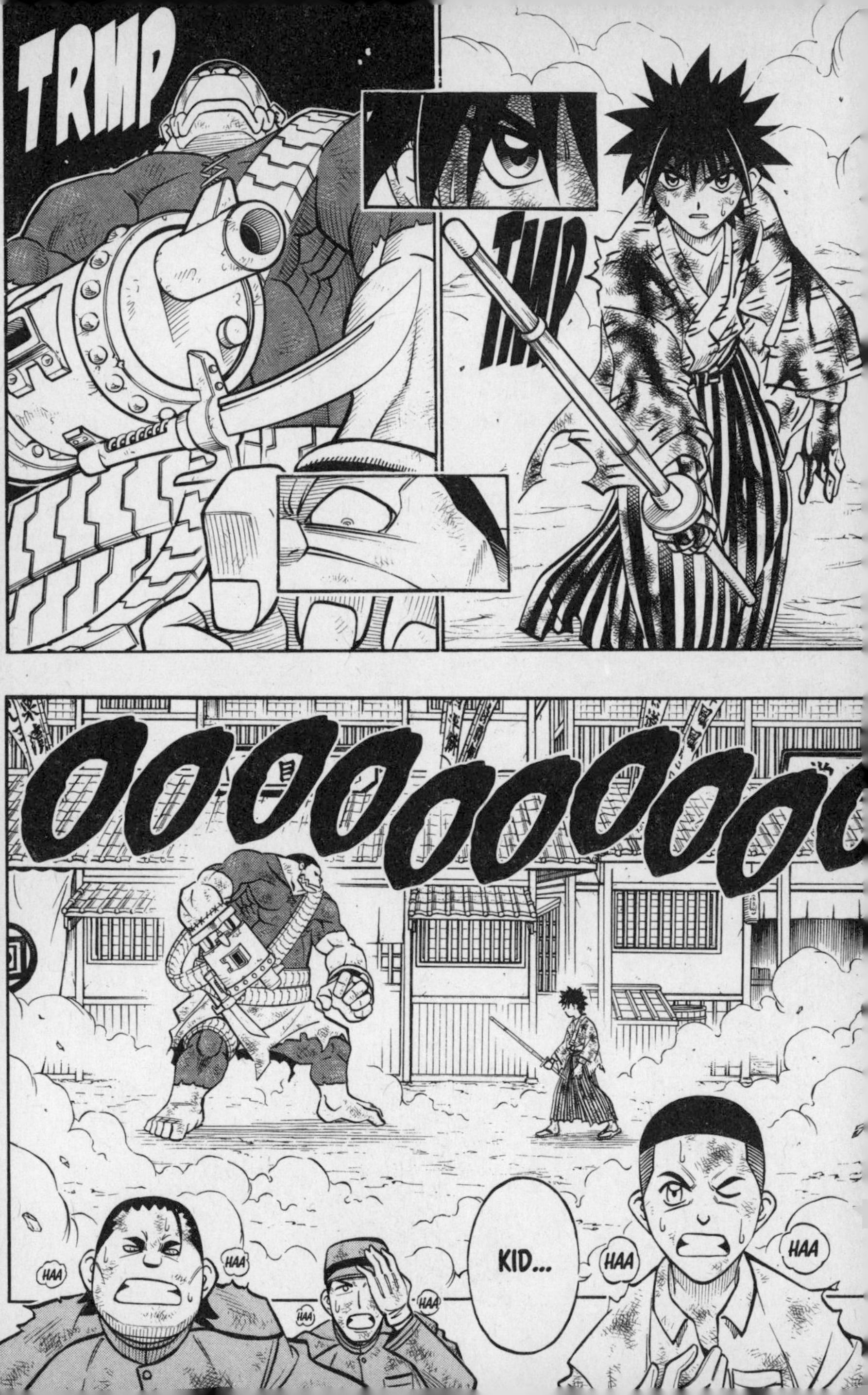

TMP
TRMP
OOOOOOOOOO
HAA
HAA
KID...
HAA
HAA
HAA
HAA

READ THIS WAY

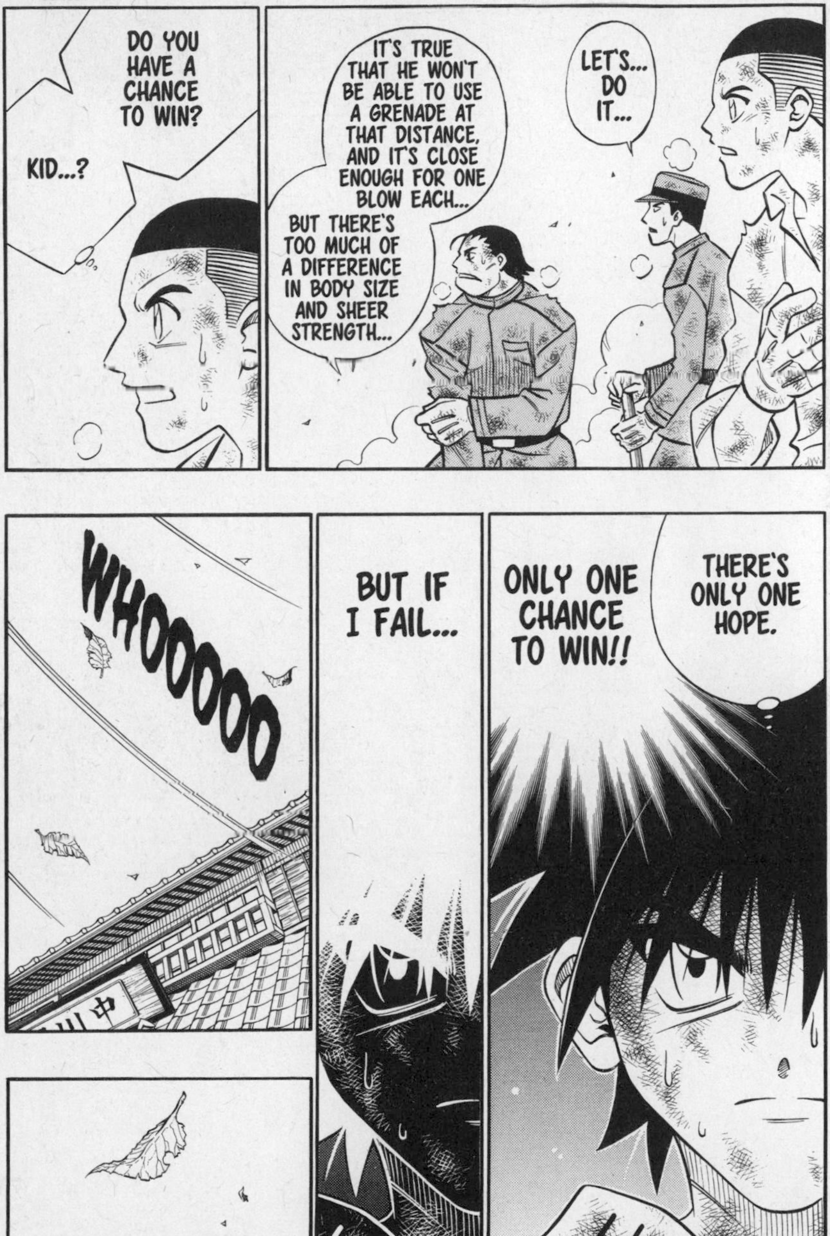
LET'S... DO IT...
IT'S TRUE THAT HE WON'T BE ABLE TO USE A GRENADE AT THAT DISTANCE, AND IT'S CLOSE ENOUGH FOR ONE BLOW EACH...
BUT THERE'S TOO MUCH OF A DIFFERENCE IN BODY SIZE AND SHEER STRENGTH...
DO YOU HAVE A CHANCE TO WIN?
KID...?
THERE'S ONLY ONE HOPE.
ONLY ONE CHANCE TO WIN!!
BUT IF I FAIL...
WHOOOOOO

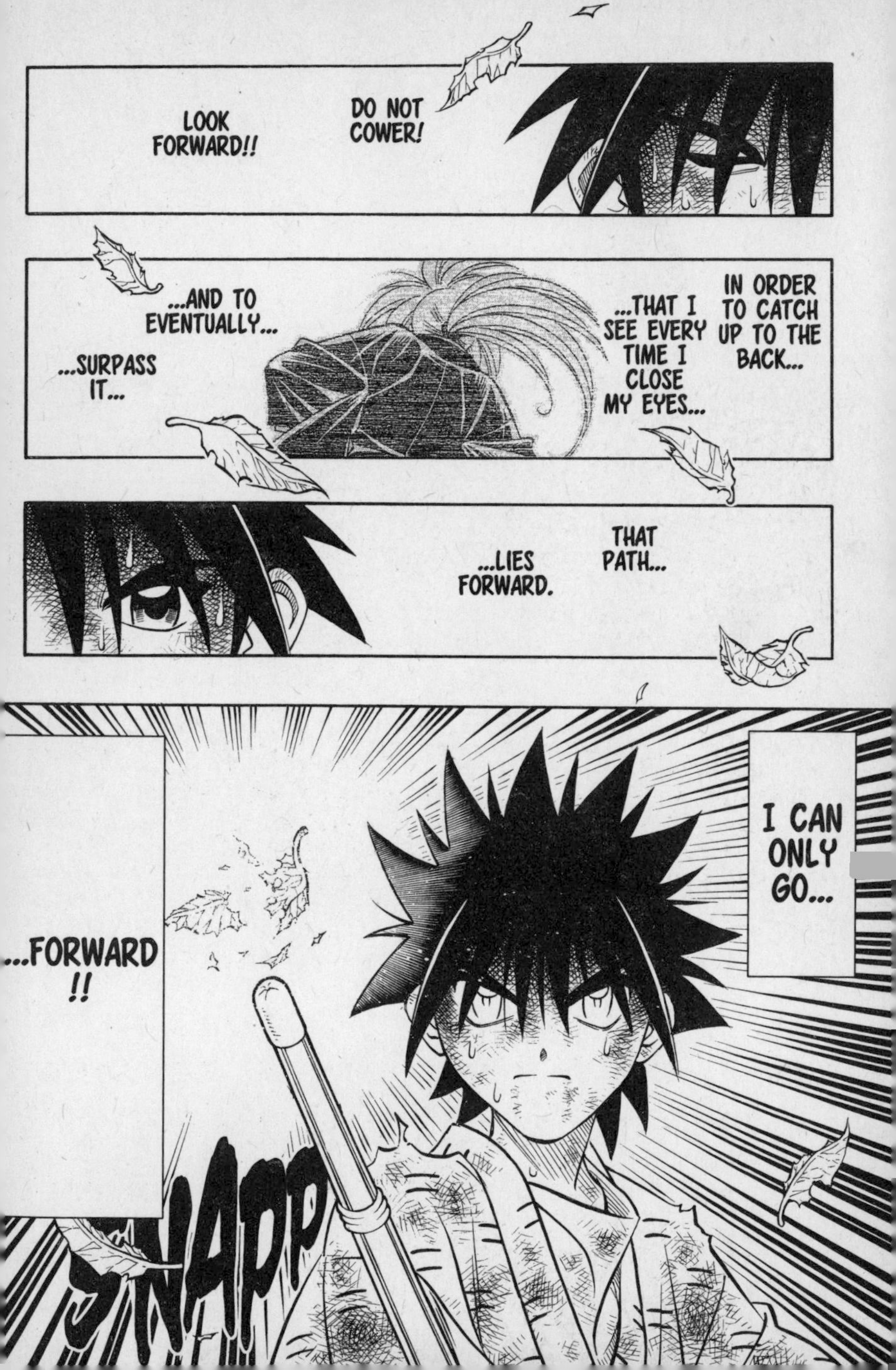
DO NOT COWER!
LOOK FORWARD!!
IN ORDER TO CATCH UP TO THE BACK...
...THAT I SEE EVERY TIME I CLOSE MY EYES...
...AND TO EVENTUALLY...
...SURPASS IT...
THAT PATH...
...LIES FORWARD.
I CAN ONLY GO...
...FORWARD!!
SNAPP

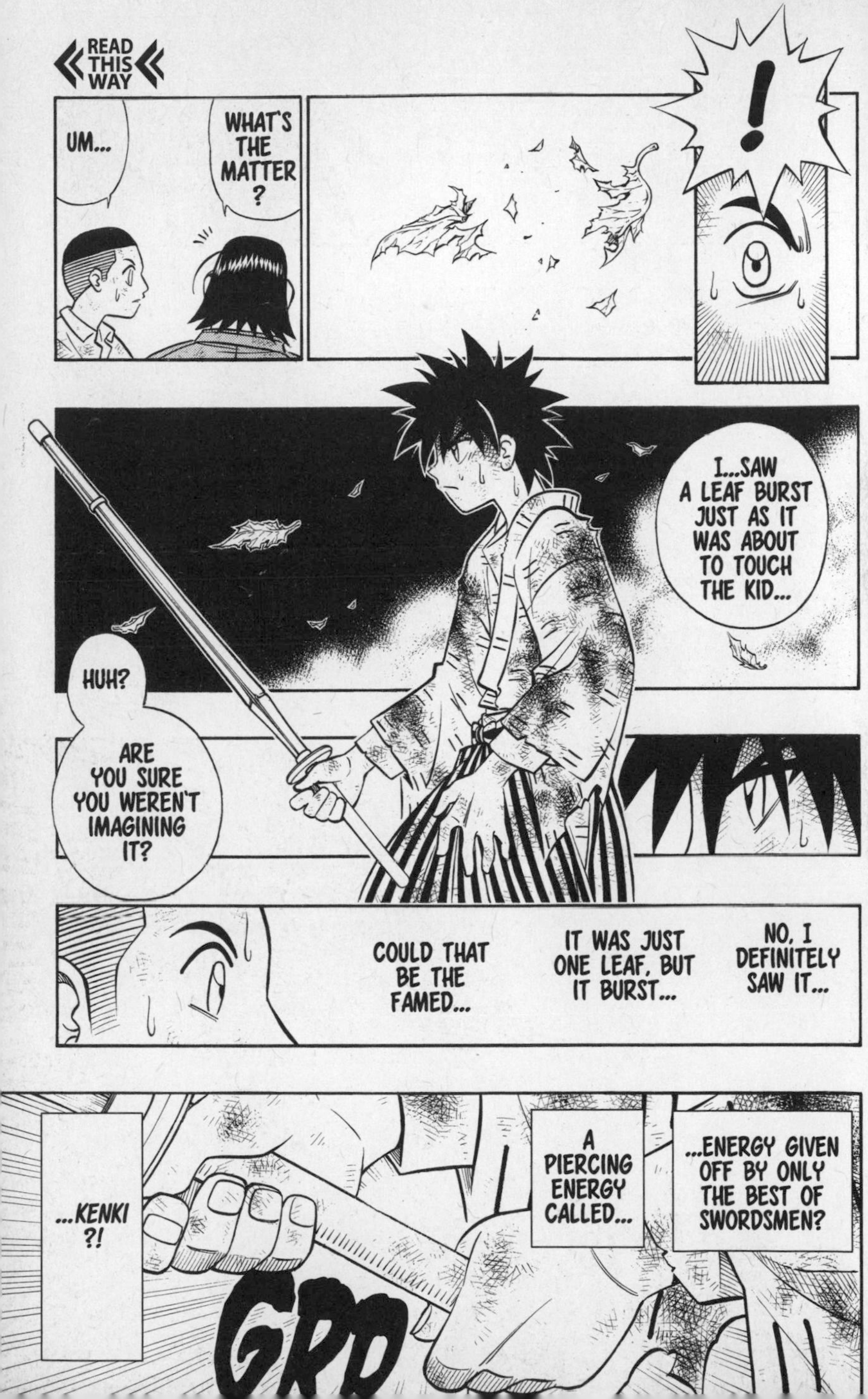
READ THIS WAY
!
WHAT'S THE MATTER ?
UM...
I...SAW A LEAF BURST JUST AS IT WAS ABOUT TO TOUCH THE KID...
HUH?
ARE YOU SURE YOU WEREN'T IMAGINING IT?
NO, I DEFINITELY SAW IT...
IT WAS JUST ONE LEAF, BUT IT BURST...
COULD THAT BE THE FAMED...
...ENERGY GIVEN OFF BY ONLY THE BEST OF SWORDSMEN?
A PIERCING ENERGY CALLED...
...KENKI ?!
GRD

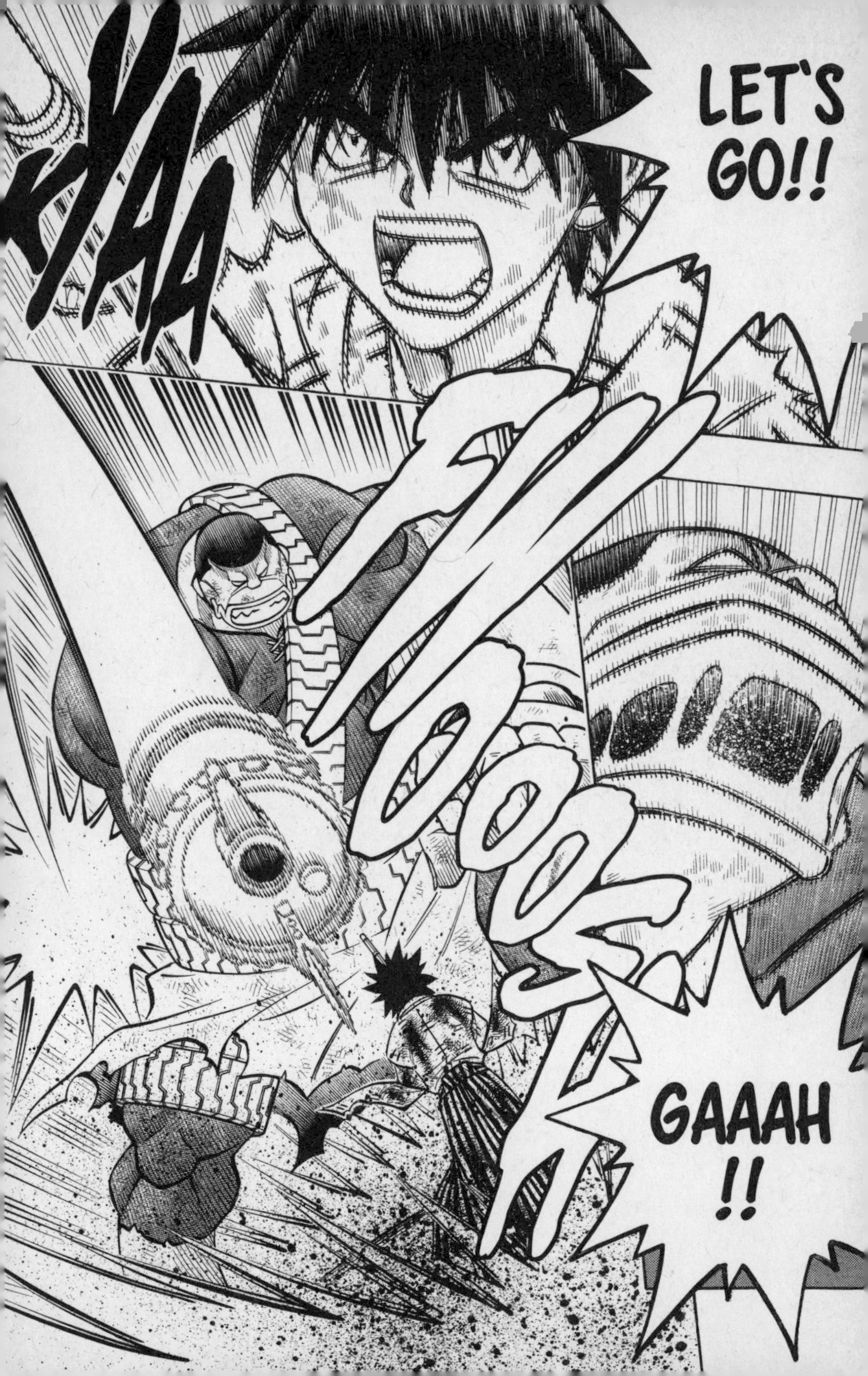
LET'S GO!!
KYAA
GAAAH!!

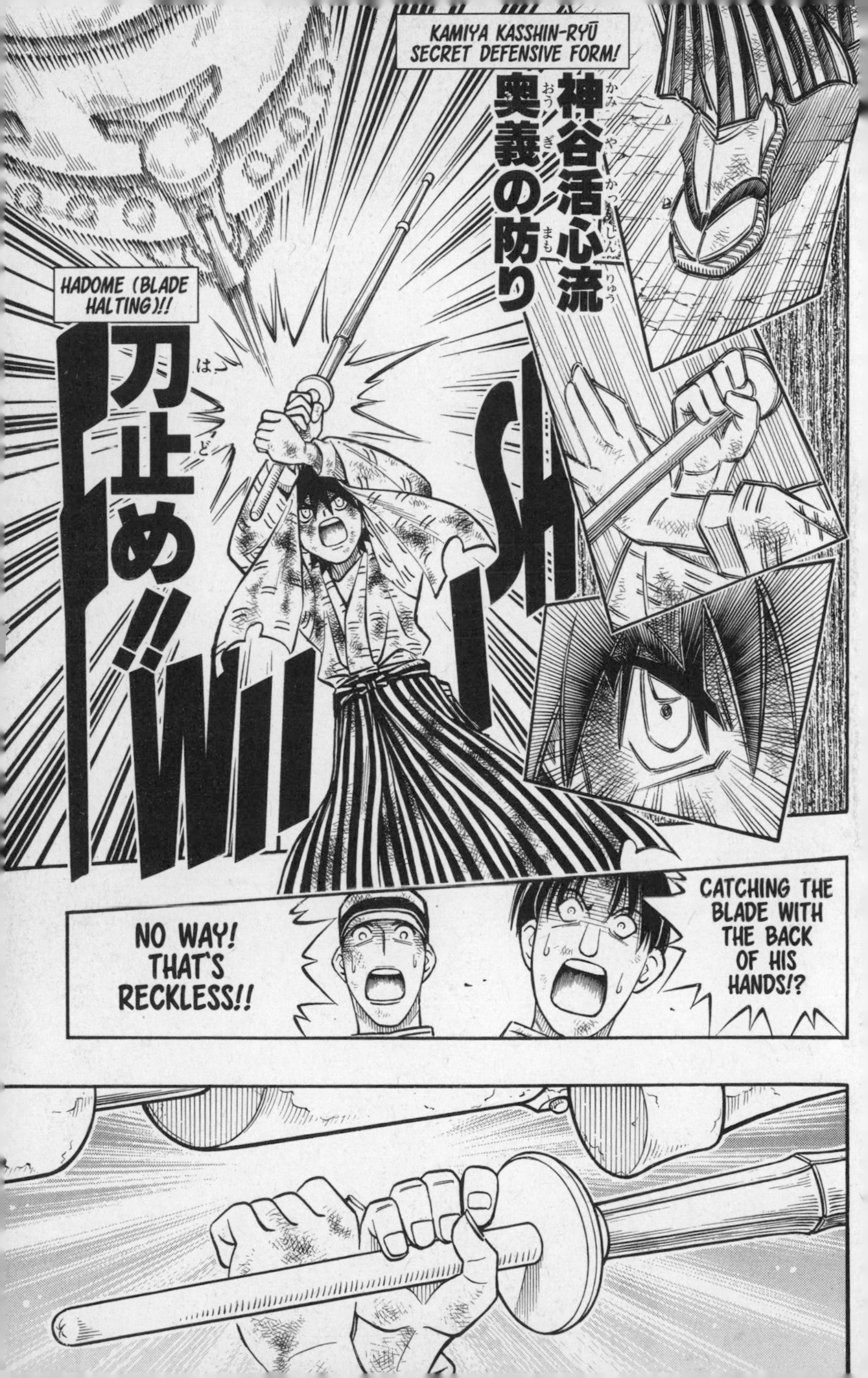
KAMIYA KASSHIN-RYŪ SECRET DEFENSIVE FORM!
神谷活心流奥義の防り
HADOME (BLADE HALTING)!!
刃止め!!
SHWII
CATCHING THE BLADE WITH THE BACK OF HIS HANDS!?
NO WAY! THAT'S RECKLESS!!

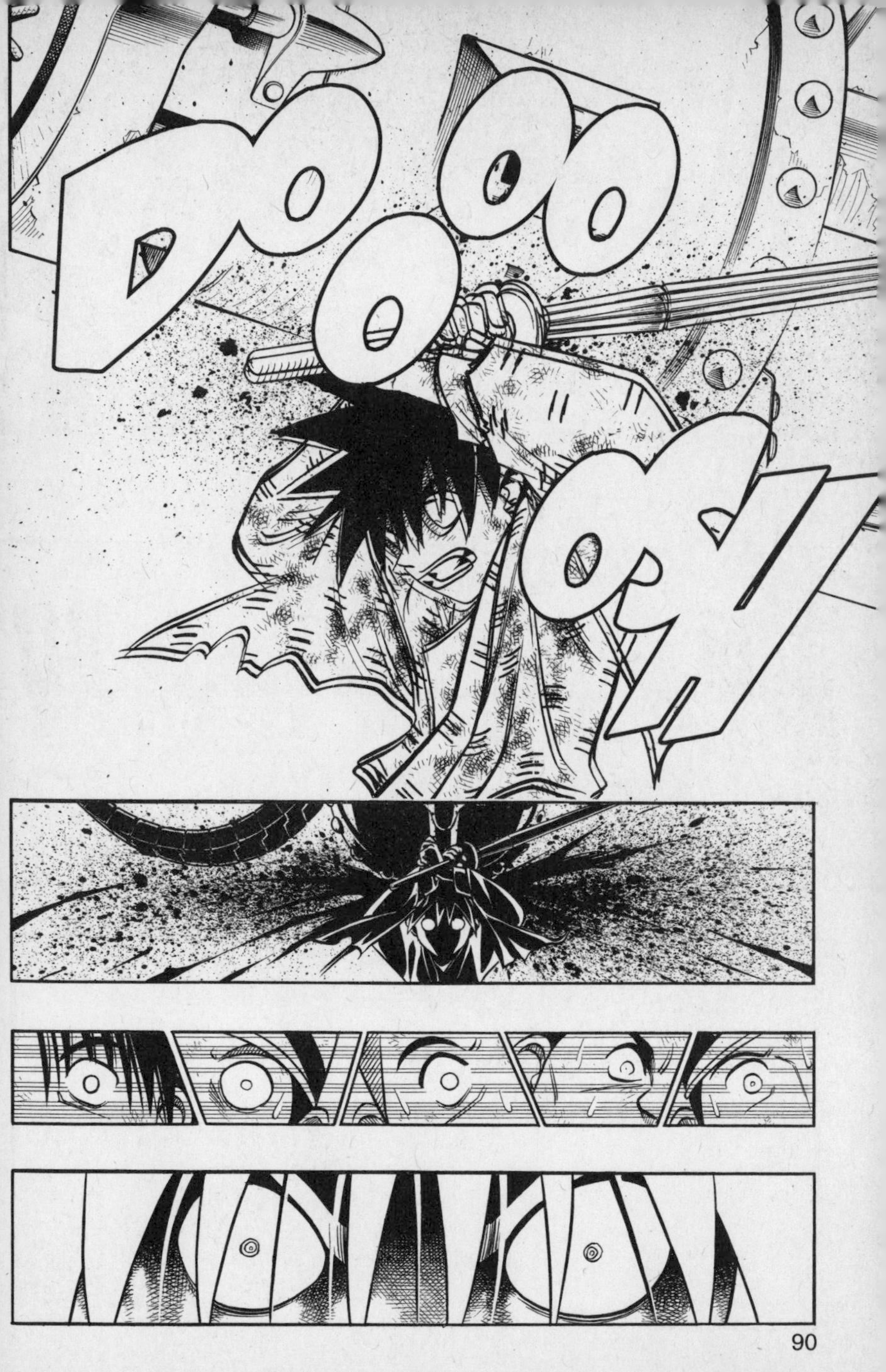
DOOOOOM

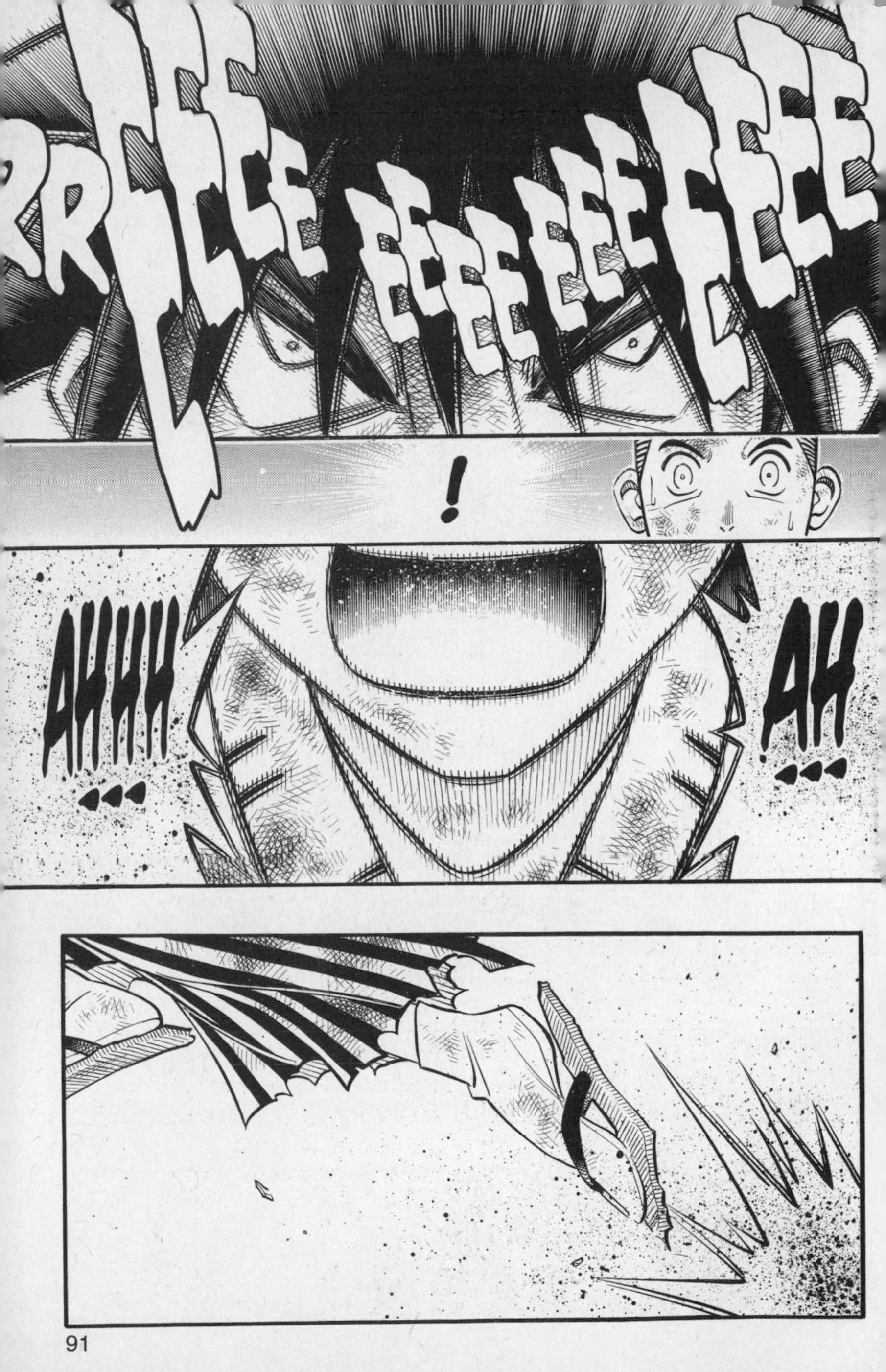

RREEE EEEEEEEEEEEEE
!
AHHH...
AH!...

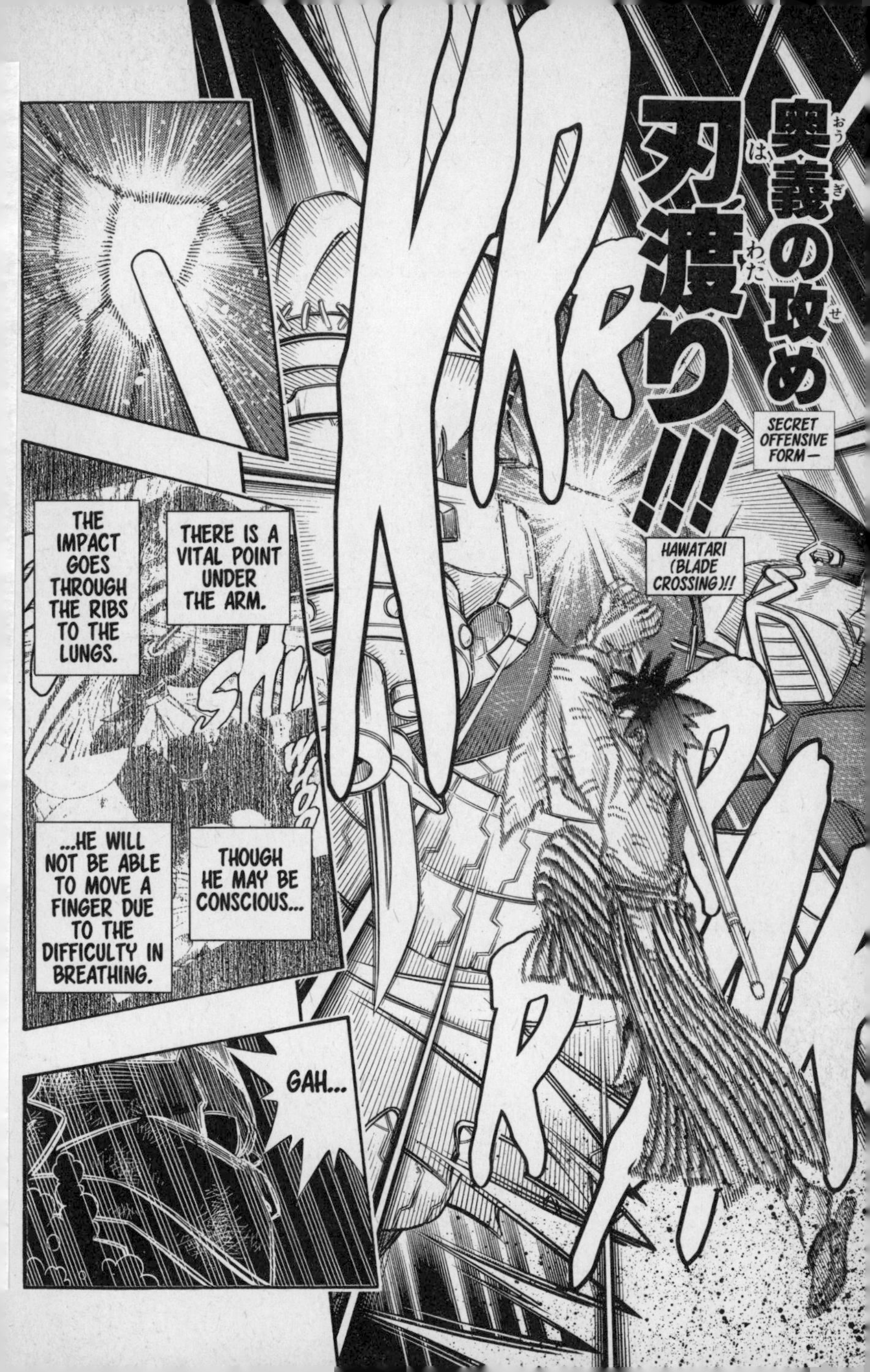
奥義の攻め
刃渡り!!!
SECRET OFFENSIVE FORM—
HAWATARI (BLADE CROSSING)!!
THERE IS A VITAL POINT UNDER THE ARM.
THE IMPACT GOES THROUGH THE RIBS TO THE LUNGS.
THOUGH HE MAY BE CONSCIOUS...
...HE WILL NOT BE ABLE TO MOVE A FINGER DUE TO THE DIFFICULTY IN BREATHING.
GAH...

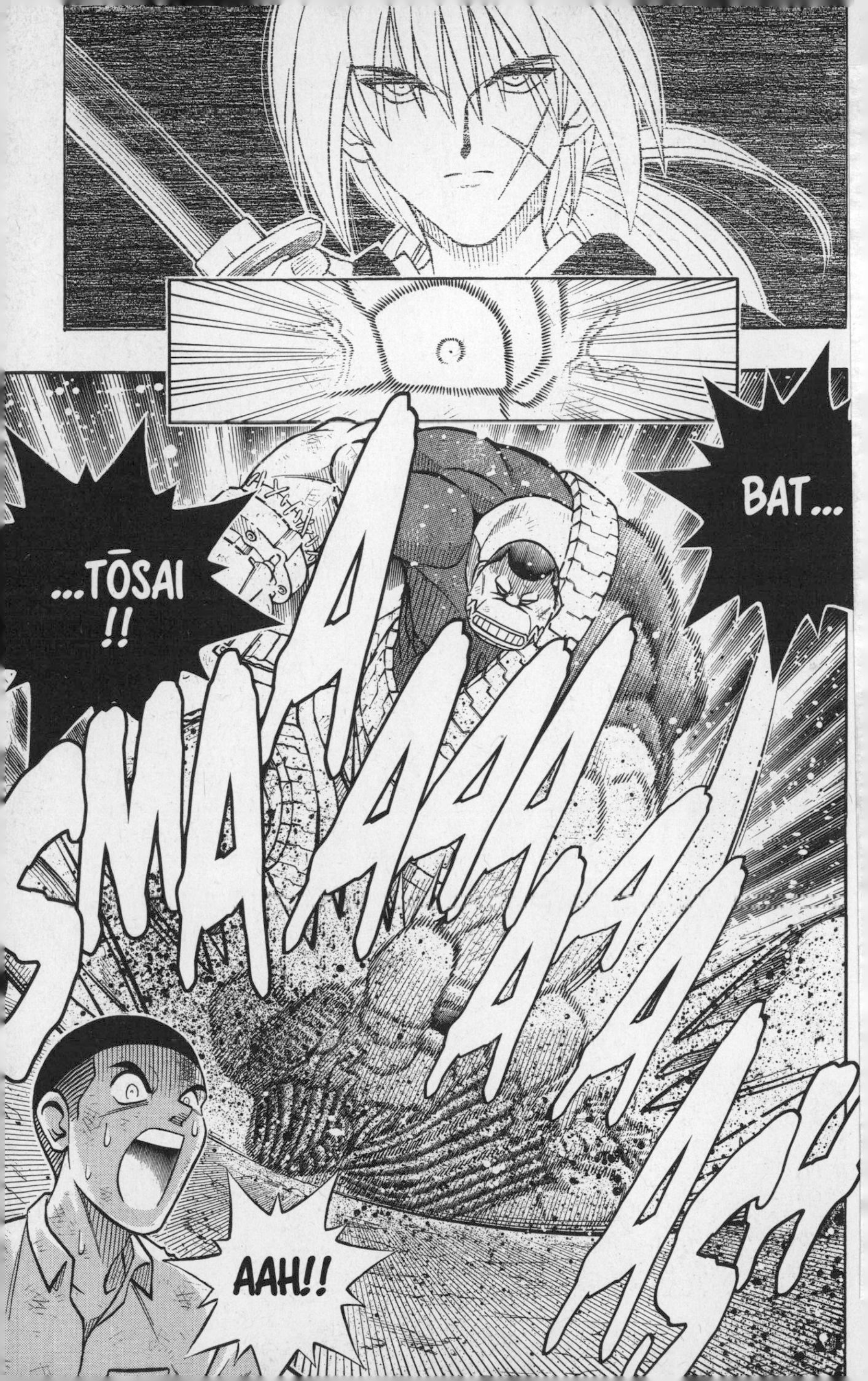
BAT...
...TŌSAI !!
AAH!!

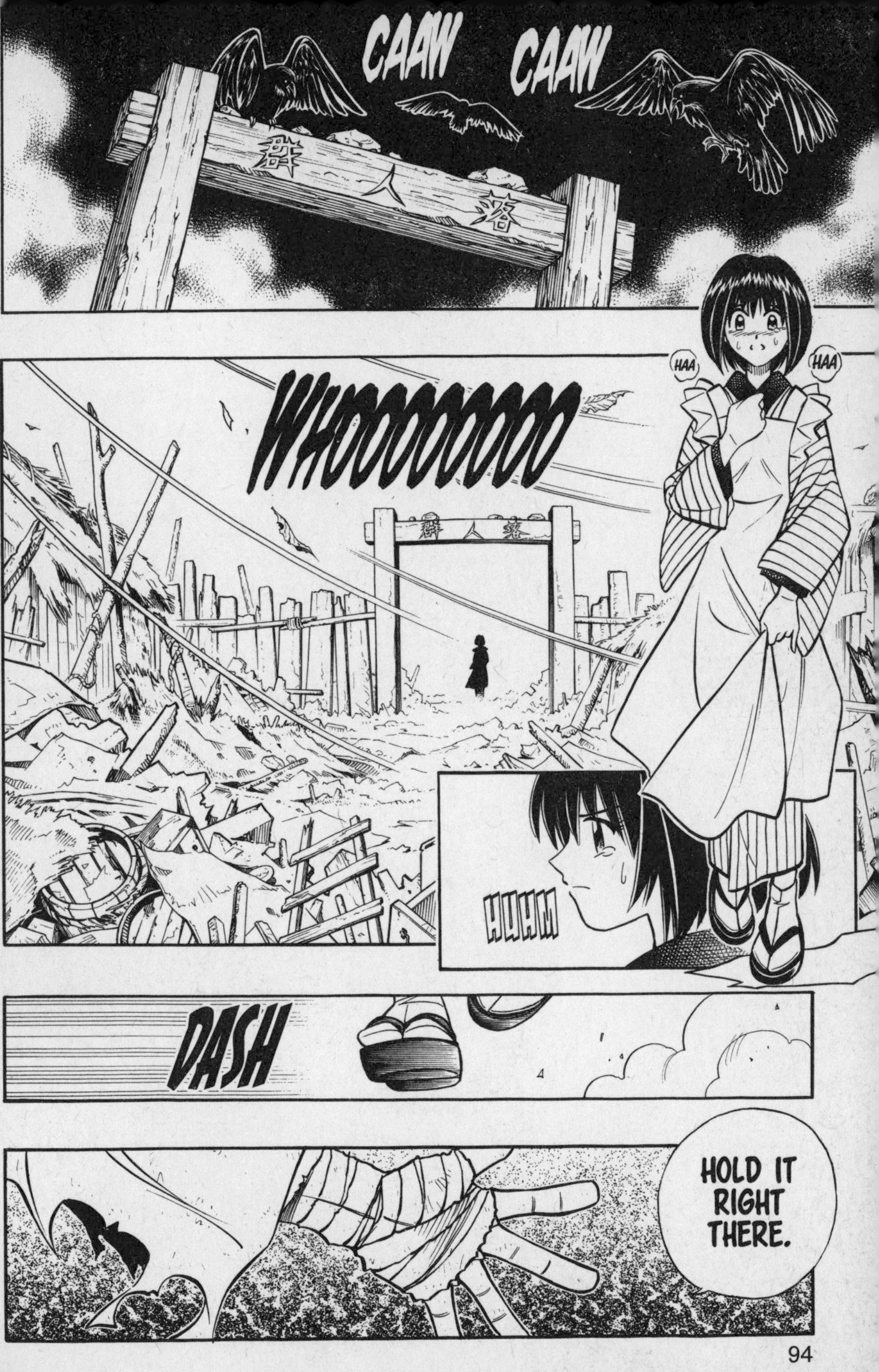

CAAW CAAW
落人群
HAA HAA
WHOOOOOOOOO
落人群
HUHM
DASH
HOLD IT RIGHT THERE.

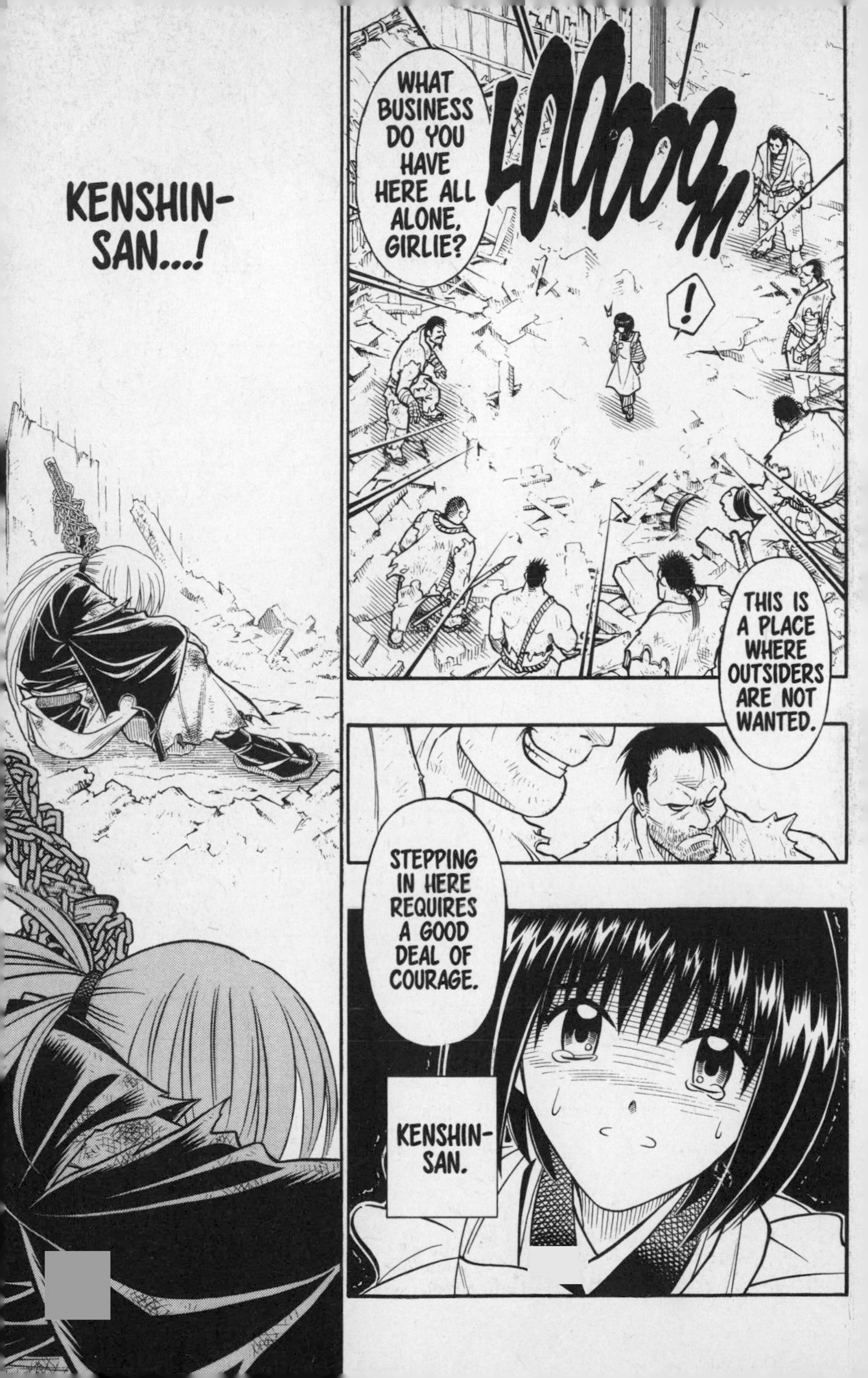
LOOOOM
WHAT BUSINESS DO YOU HAVE HERE ALL ALONE, GIRLIE?
!
THIS IS A PLACE WHERE OUTSIDERS ARE NOT WANTED.
STEPPING IN HERE REQUIRES A GOOD DEAL OF COURAGE.
KENSHIN-SAN.
KENSHIN-SAN...!

Rurouni Kenshin

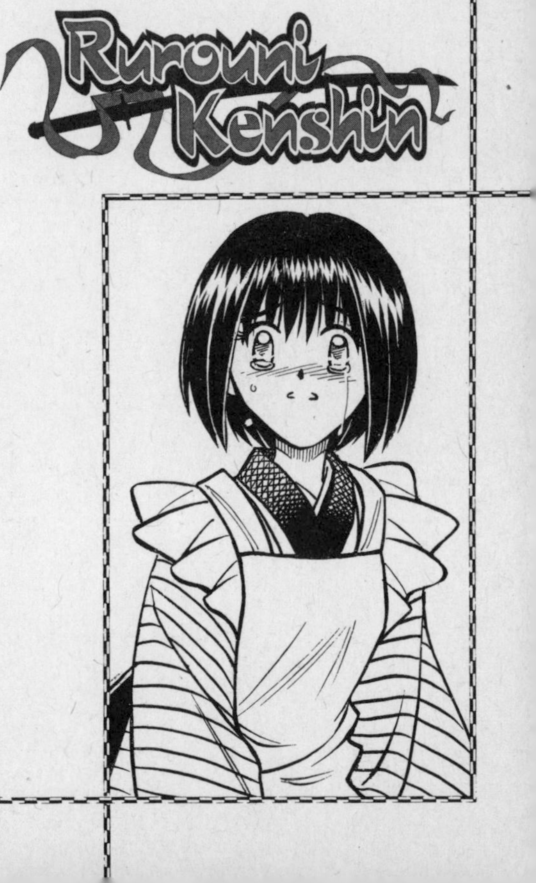

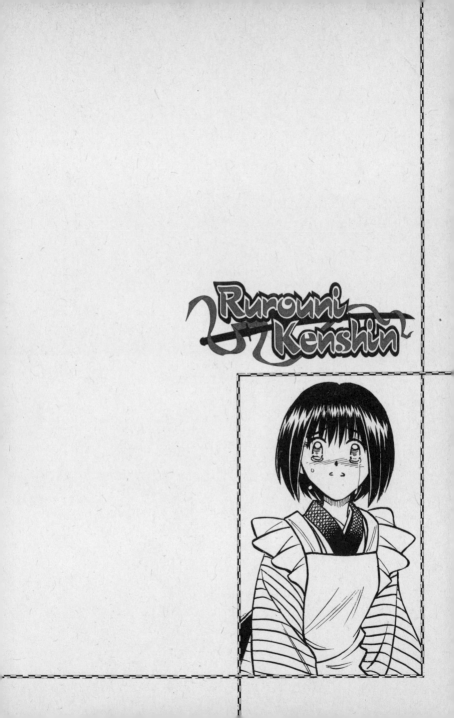

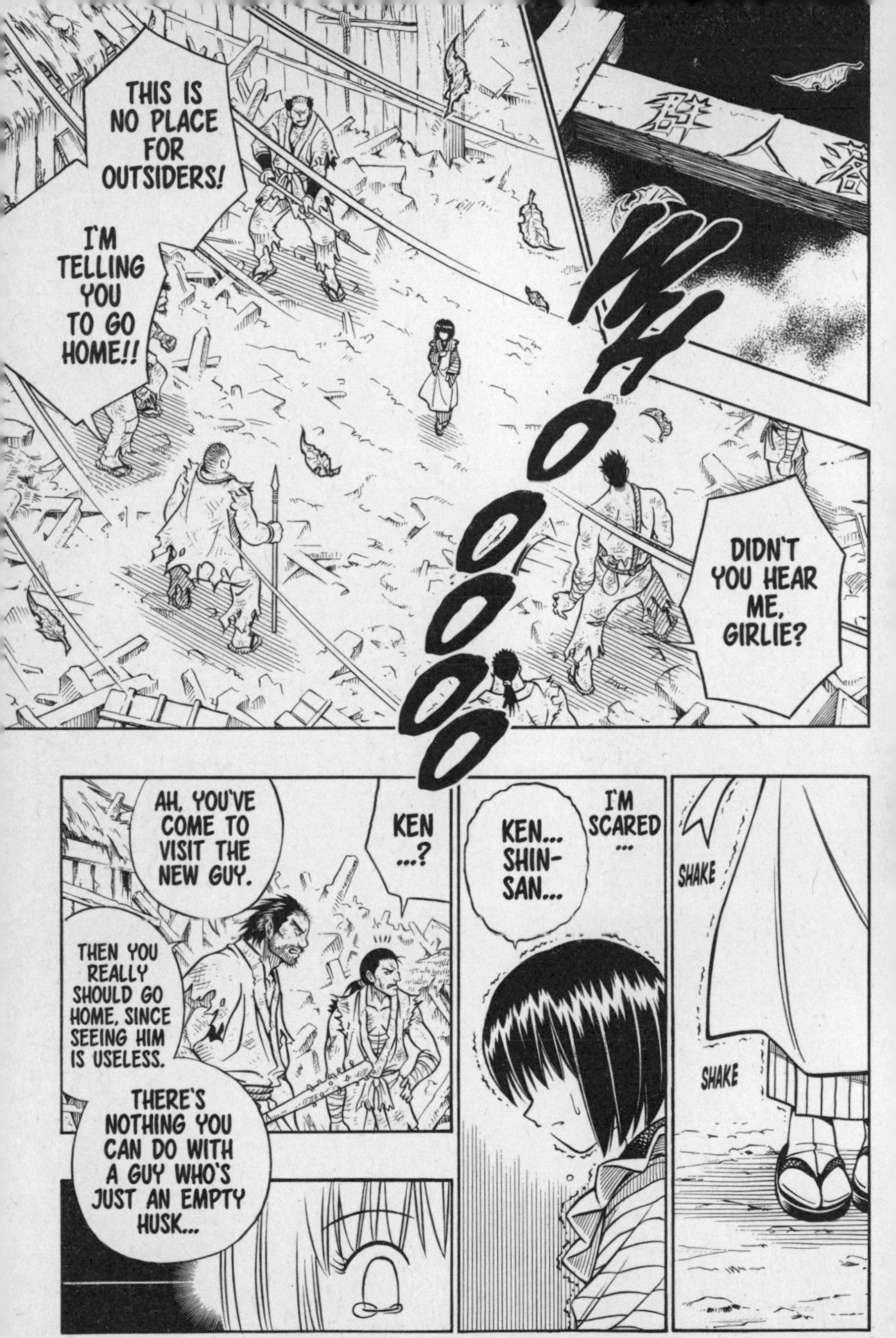
WHOOOOOO
THIS IS NO PLACE FOR OUTSIDERS!
I'M TELLING YOU TO GO HOME!!
DIDN'T YOU HEAR ME, GIRLIE?
SHAKE
SHAKE
I'M SCARED...
KEN... SHIN-SAN...
KEN...?
AH, YOU'VE COME TO VISIT THE NEW GUY.
THEN YOU REALLY SHOULD GO HOME, SINCE SEEING HIM IS USELESS.
THERE'S NOTHING YOU CAN DO WITH A GUY WHO'S JUST AN EMPTY HUSK...

Act 223—Dream, Reality and Illusions

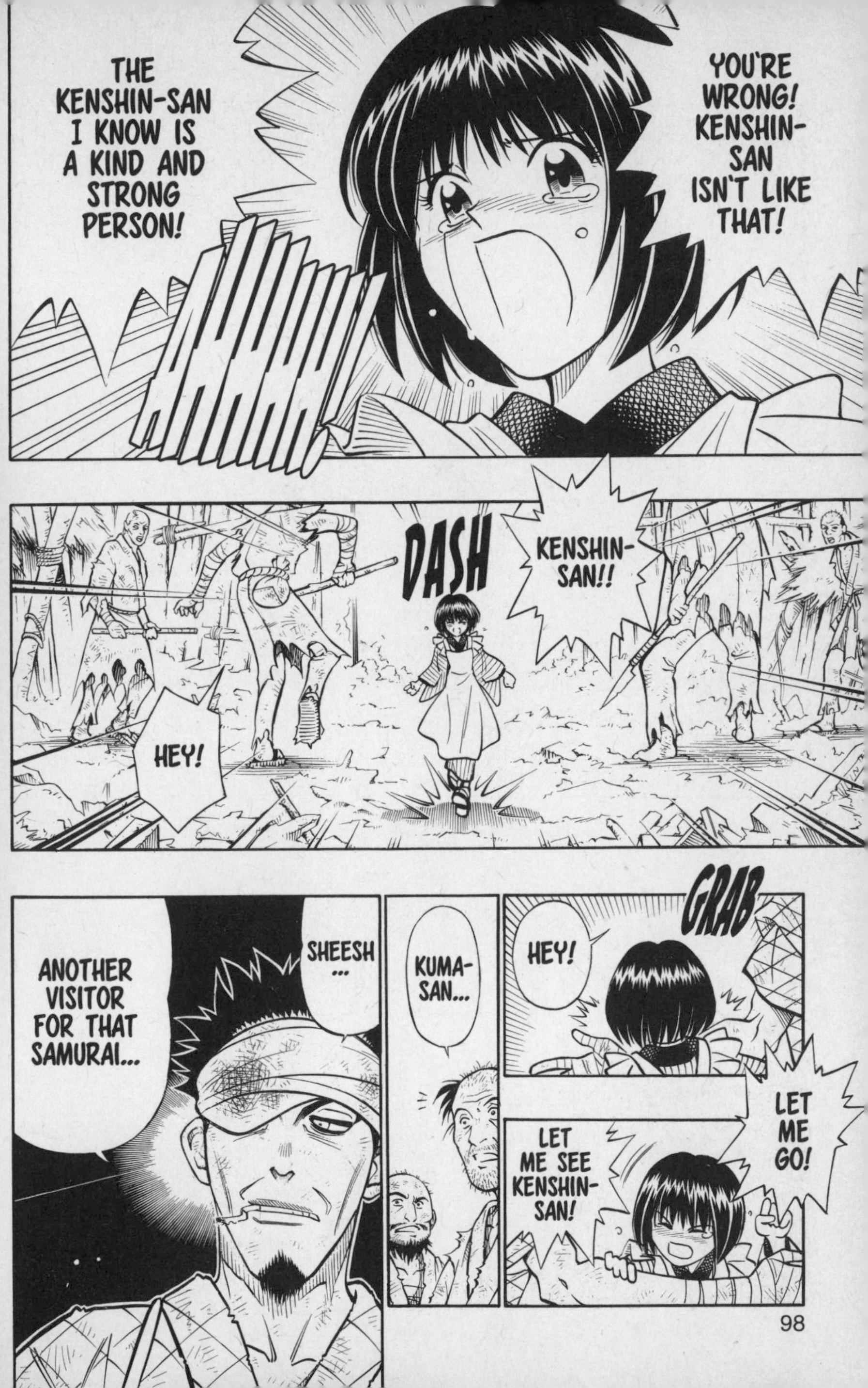
YOU'RE WRONG! KENSHIN-SAN ISN'T LIKE THAT!
THE KENSHIN-SAN I KNOW IS A KIND AND STRONG PERSON!
KENSHIN-SAN!!
DASH
HEY!
GRAB
HEY!
LET ME GO!
LET ME SEE KENSHIN-SAN!
KUMA-SAN...
SHEESH...
ANOTHER VISITOR FOR THAT SAMURAI...

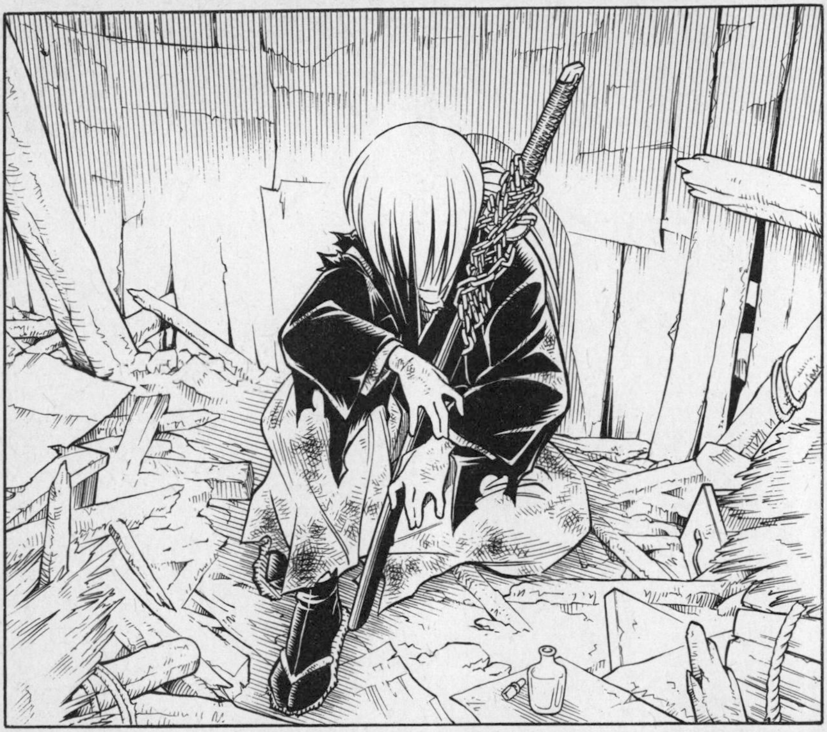

Act 223
Dream, Reality and Illusions

伸宏和月

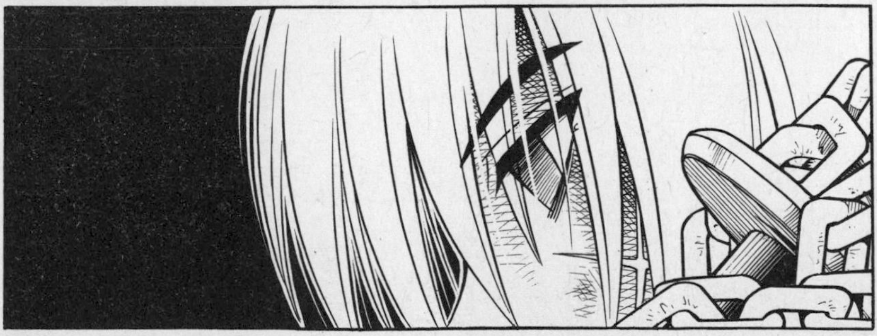

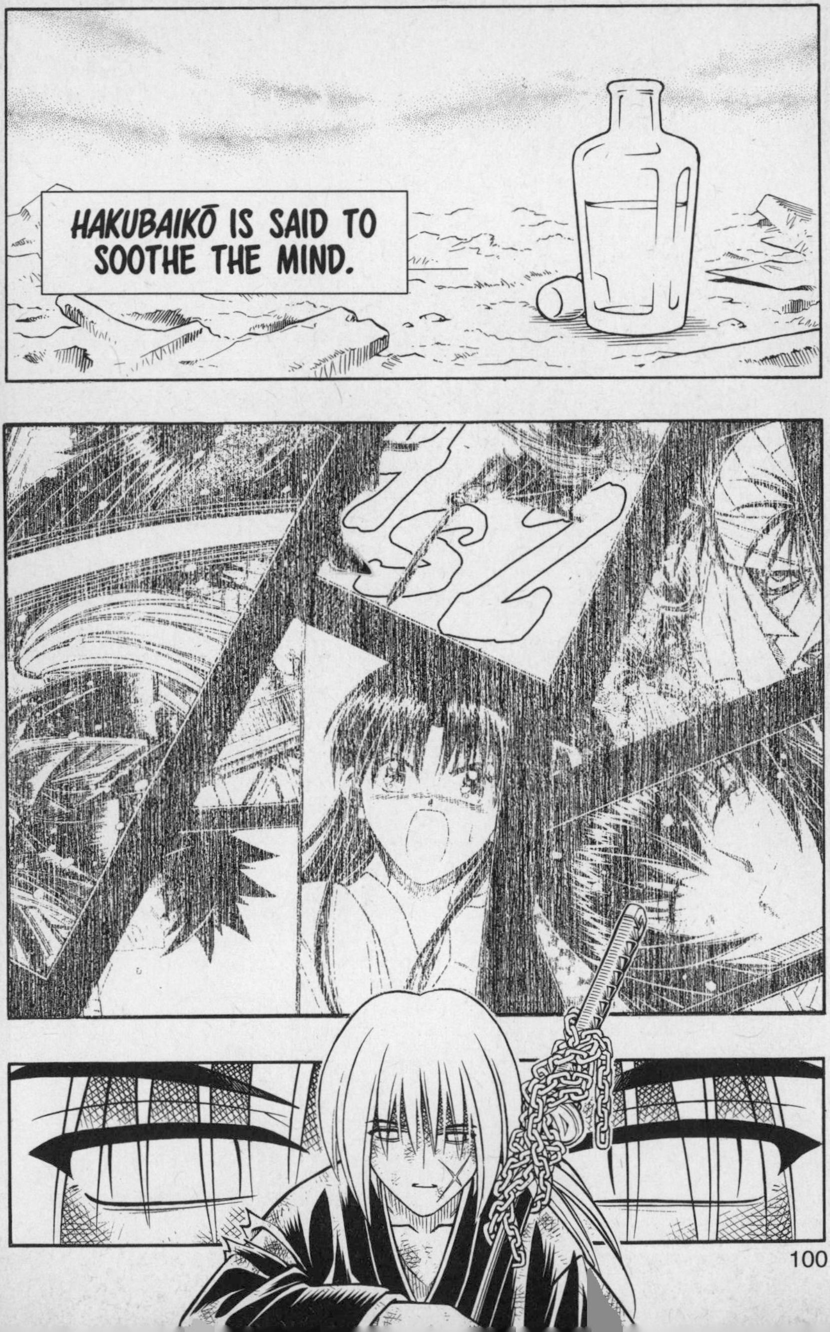
HAKUBAIKŌ IS SAID TO SOOTHE THE MIND.

READ THIS WAY

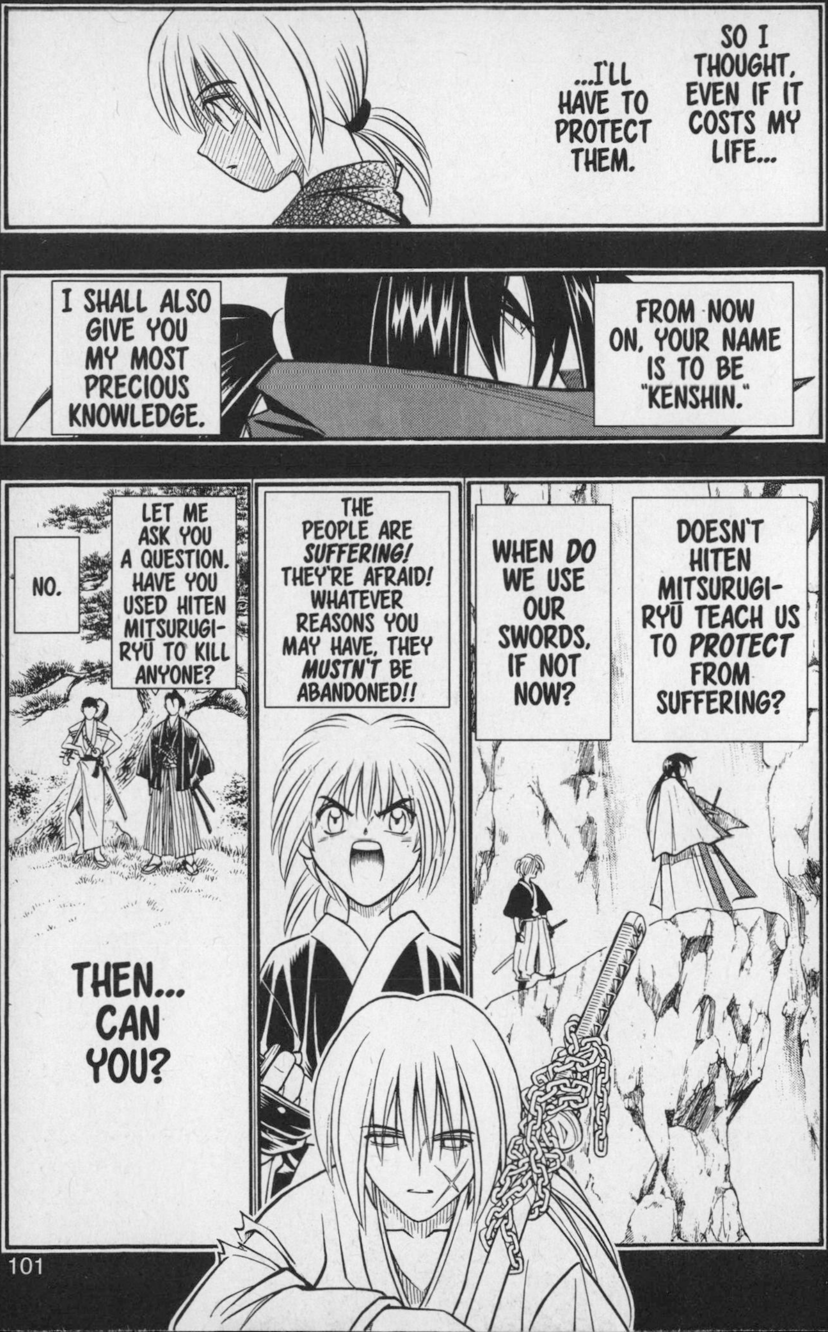

SO I THOUGHT, EVEN IF IT COSTS MY LIFE...
...I'LL HAVE TO PROTECT THEM.
FROM NOW ON, YOUR NAME IS TO BE "KENSHIN."
I SHALL ALSO GIVE YOU MY MOST PRECIOUS KNOWLEDGE.
DOESN'T HITEN MITSURUGI-RYŪ TEACH US TO *PROTECT* FROM SUFFERING?
WHEN *DO* WE USE OUR SWORDS, IF NOT NOW?
THE PEOPLE ARE *SUFFERING!* THEY'RE AFRAID! WHATEVER REASONS YOU MAY HAVE, THEY *MUSTN'T* BE ABANDONED!!
LET ME ASK YOU A QUESTION. HAVE YOU USED HITEN MITSURUGI-RYŪ TO KILL ANYONE?
NO.
THEN... CAN YOU?

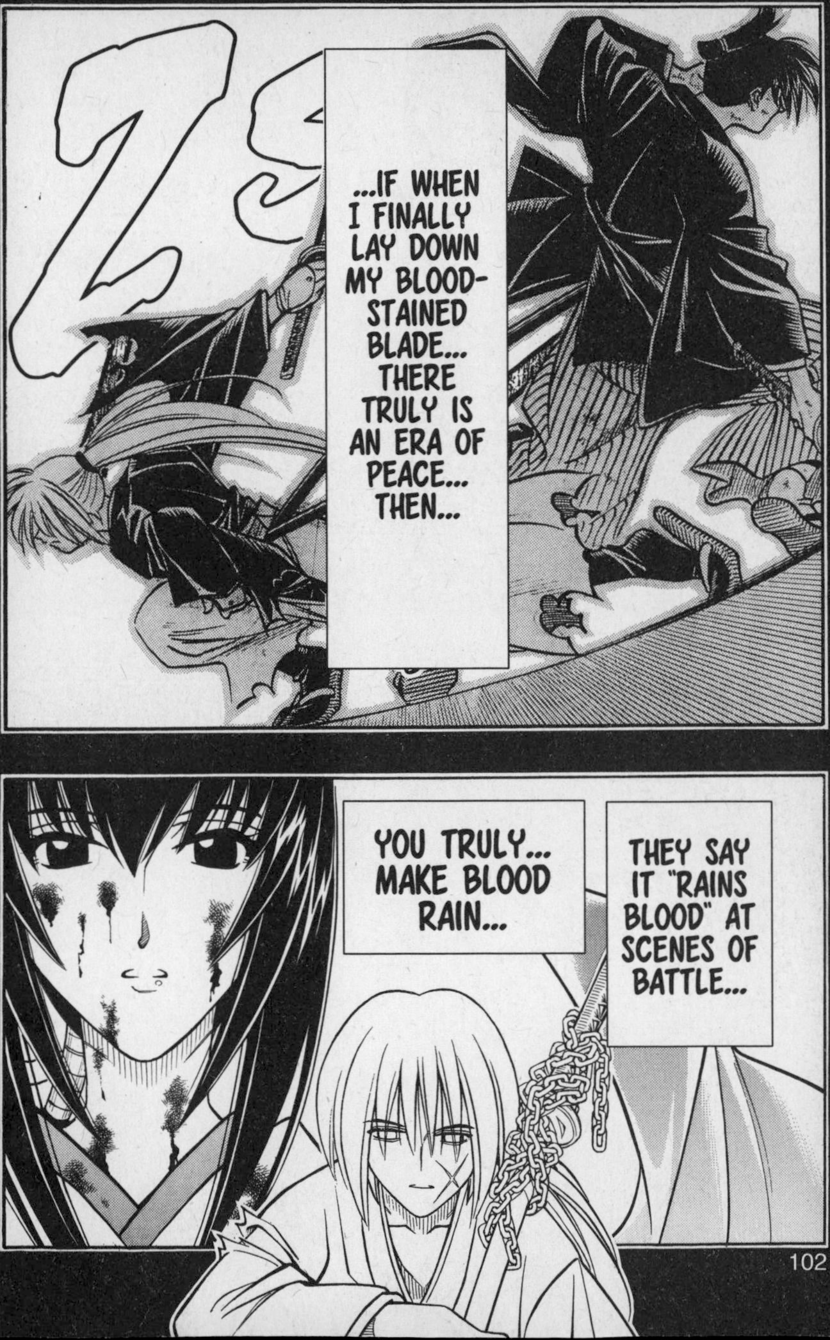
...IF WHEN I FINALLY LAY DOWN MY BLOOD-STAINED BLADE... THERE TRULY IS AN ERA OF PEACE... THEN...
THEY SAY IT "RAINS BLOOD" AT SCENES OF BATTLE...
YOU TRULY... MAKE BLOOD RAIN...

READ THIS WAY

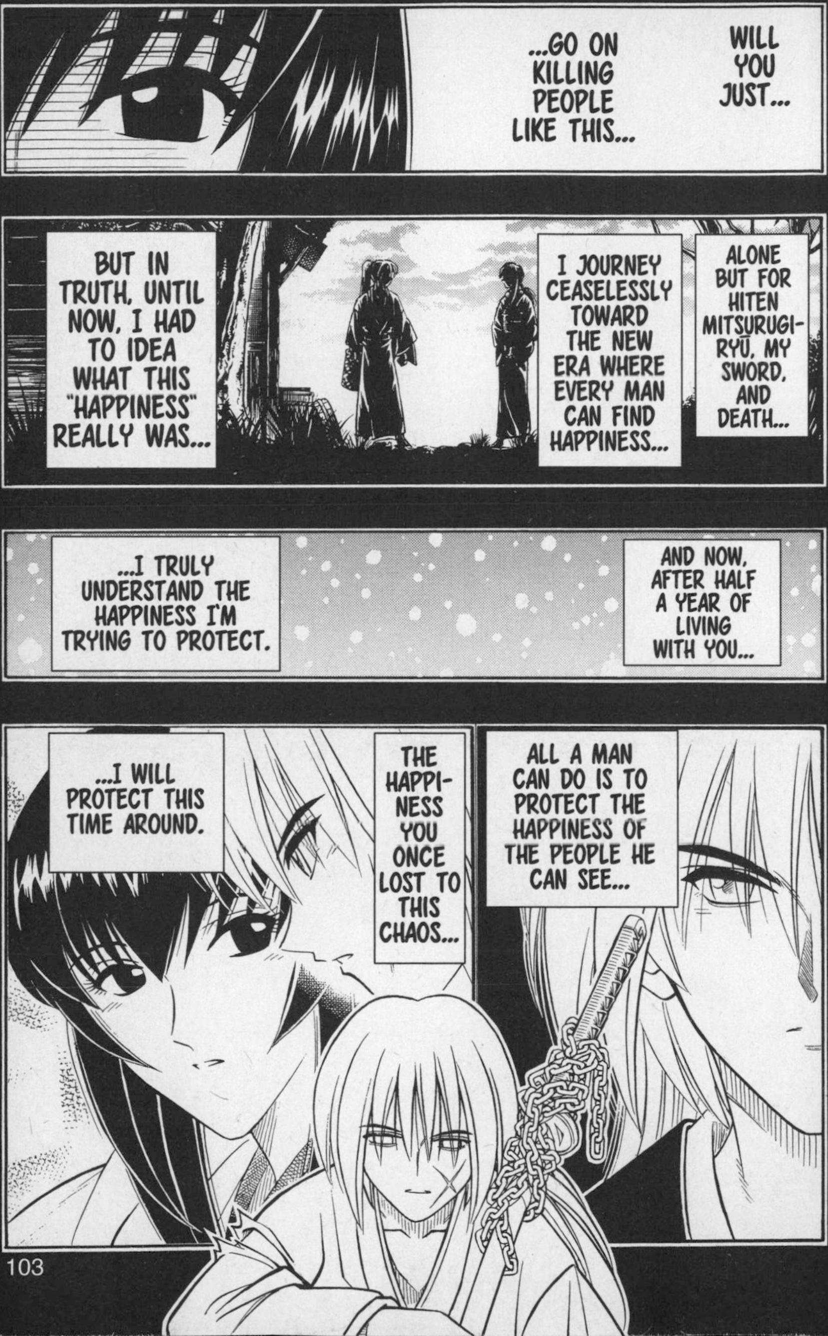
WILL YOU JUST...
...GO ON KILLING PEOPLE LIKE THIS...
ALONE BUT FOR HITEN MITSURUGI-RYŪ, MY SWORD, AND DEATH...
I JOURNEY CEASELESSLY TOWARD THE NEW ERA WHERE EVERY MAN CAN FIND HAPPINESS...
BUT IN TRUTH, UNTIL NOW, I HAD TO IDEA WHAT THIS "HAPPINESS" REALLY WAS...
AND NOW, AFTER HALF A YEAR OF LIVING WITH YOU...
...I TRULY UNDERSTAND THE HAPPINESS I'M TRYING TO PROTECT.
ALL A MAN CAN DO IS TO PROTECT THE HAPPINESS OF THE PEOPLE HE CAN SEE...
THE HAPPI-NESS YOU ONCE LOST TO THIS CHAOS...
...I WILL PROTECT THIS TIME AROUND.

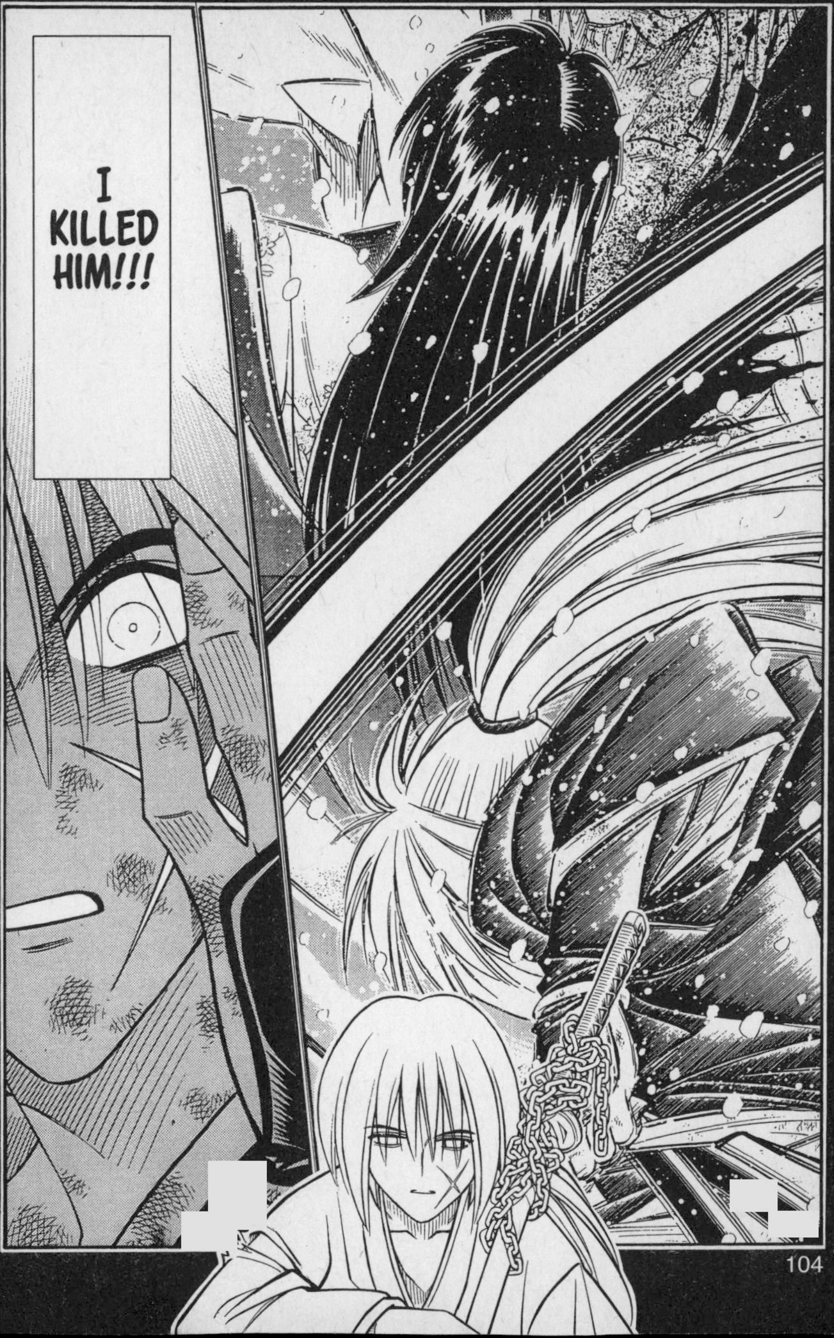
I KILLED HIM!!!

READ THIS WAY

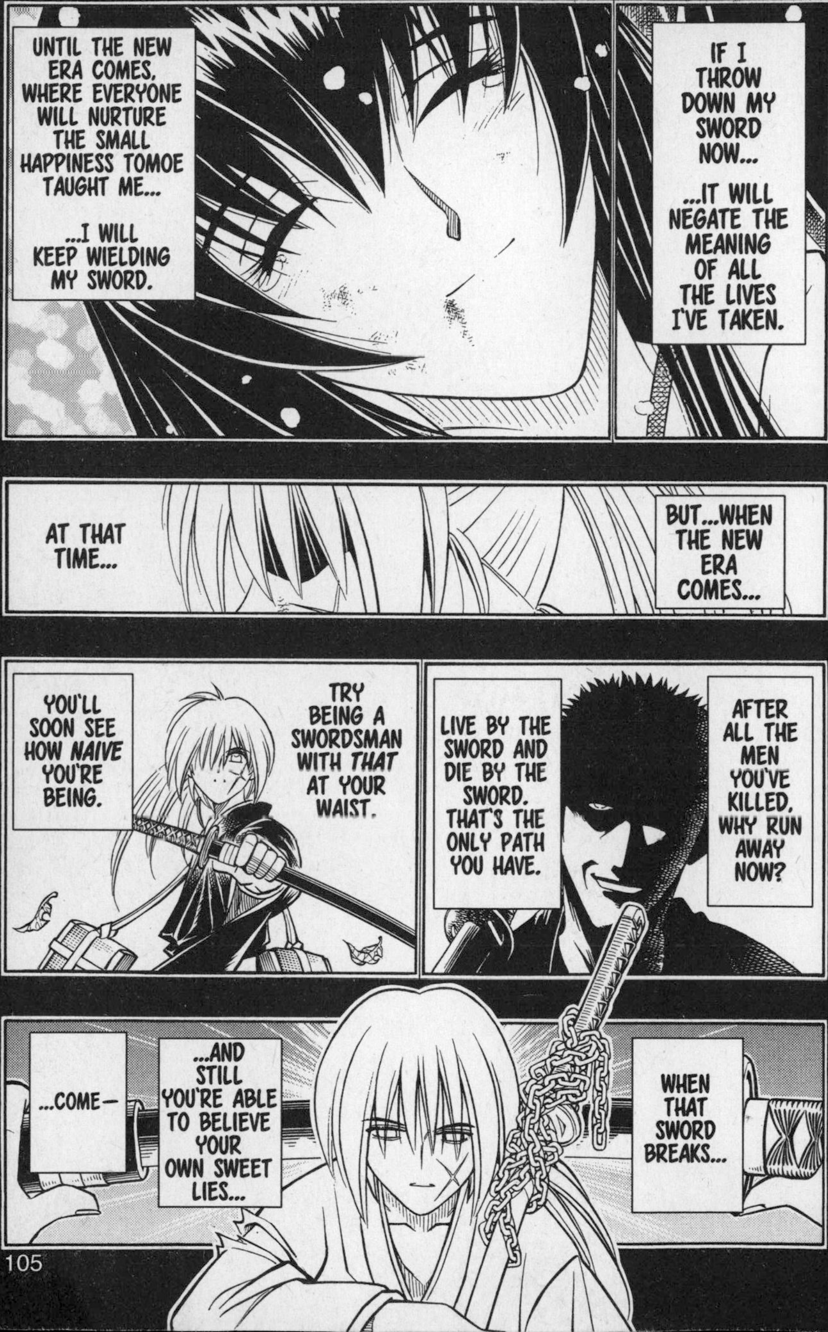

IF I THROW DOWN MY SWORD NOW...
...IT WILL NEGATE THE MEANING OF ALL THE LIVES I'VE TAKEN.
UNTIL THE NEW ERA COMES, WHERE EVERYONE WILL NURTURE THE SMALL HAPPINESS TOMOE TAUGHT ME...
...I WILL KEEP WIELDING MY SWORD.
BUT...WHEN THE NEW ERA COMES...
AT THAT TIME...
AFTER ALL THE MEN YOU'VE KILLED, WHY RUN AWAY NOW?
LIVE BY THE SWORD AND DIE BY THE SWORD. THAT'S THE ONLY PATH YOU HAVE.
TRY BEING A SWORDSMAN WITH *THAT* AT YOUR WAIST.
YOU'LL SOON SEE HOW *NAIVE* YOU'RE BEING.
WHEN THAT SWORD BREAKS...
...AND STILL YOU'RE ABLE TO BELIEVE YOUR OWN SWEET LIES...
...COME—

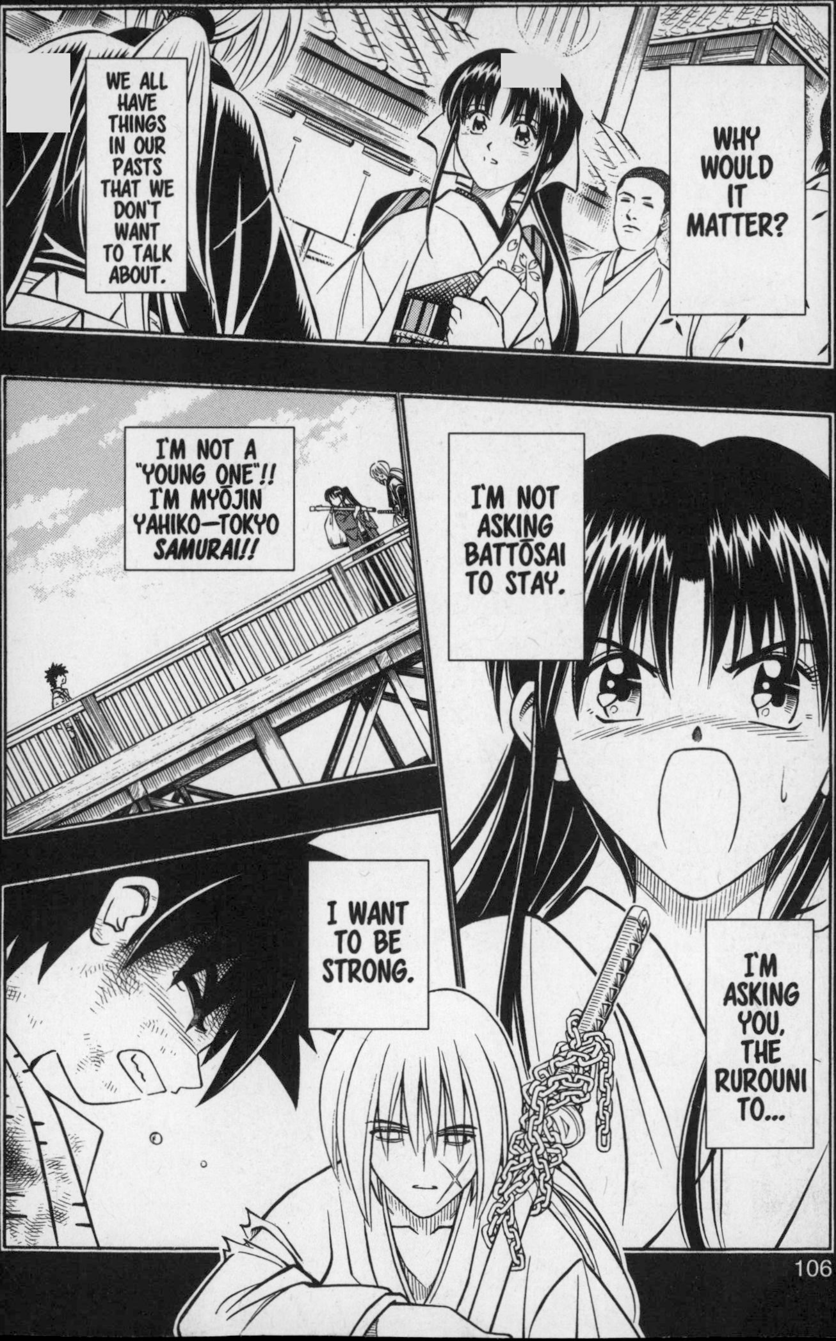
WHY WOULD IT MATTER?
WE ALL HAVE THINGS IN OUR PASTS THAT WE DON'T WANT TO TALK ABOUT.
I'M NOT ASKING BATTŌSAI TO STAY.
I'M ASKING YOU, THE RUROUNI TO...
I'M NOT A "YOUNG ONE"!! I'M MYŌJIN YAHIKO—TOKYO *SAMURAI!!*
I WANT TO BE STRONG.

READ THIS WAY

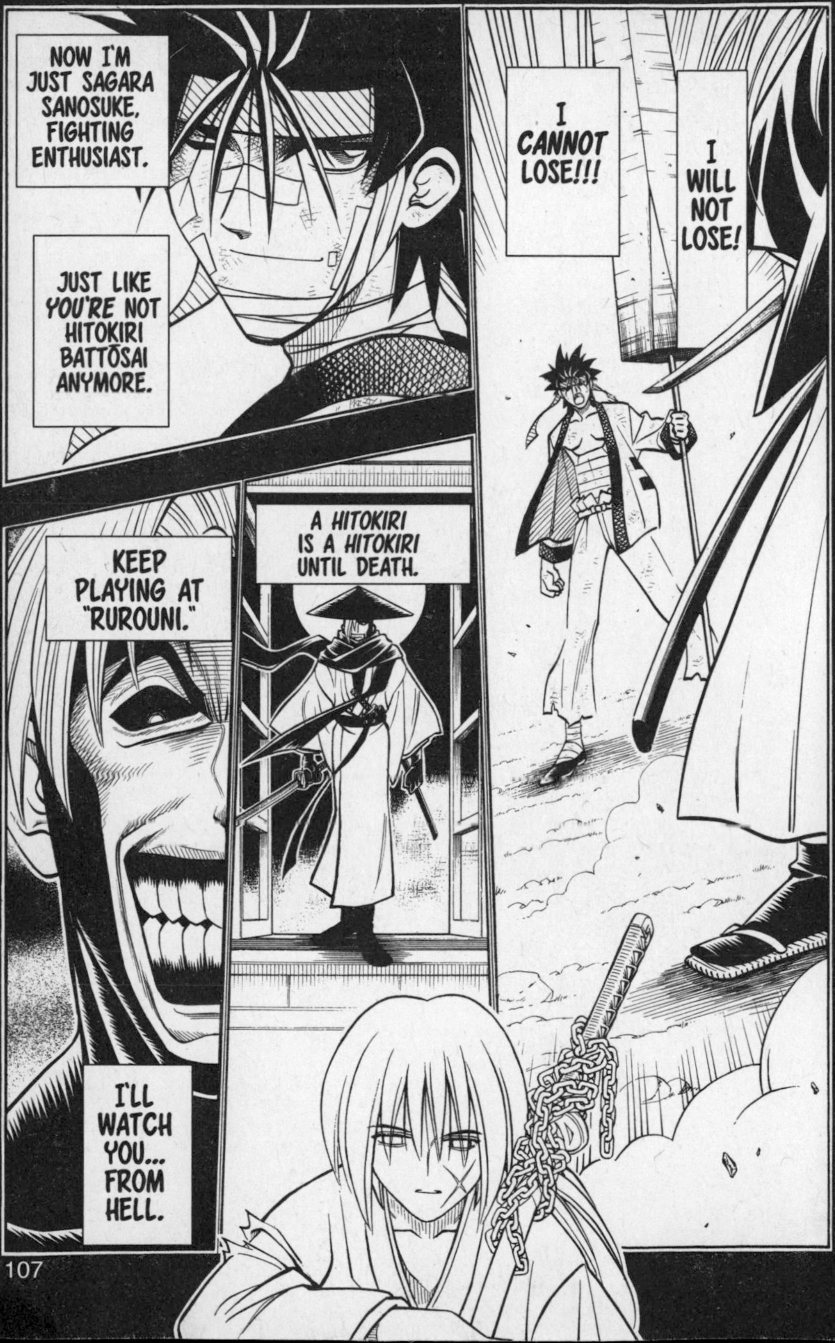

I WILL NOT LOSE!
I CANNOT LOSE!!!
NOW I'M JUST SAGARA SANOSUKE, FIGHTING ENTHUSIAST.
JUST LIKE YOU'RE NOT HITOKIRI BATTŌSAI ANYMORE.
A HITOKIRI IS A HITOKIRI UNTIL DEATH.
KEEP PLAYING AT "RUROUNI."
I'LL WATCH YOU... FROM HELL.

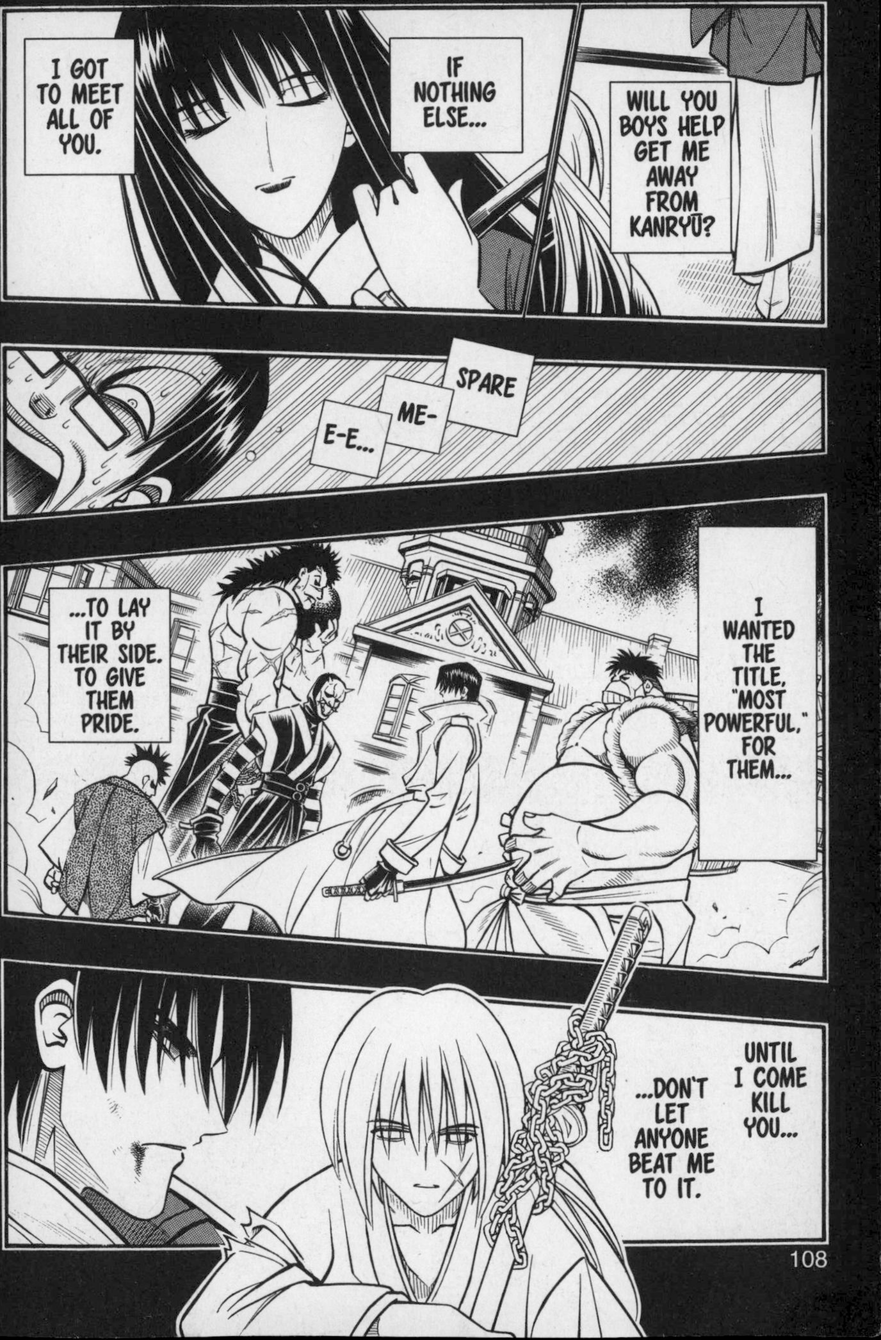
WILL YOU BOYS HELP GET ME AWAY FROM KANRYŪ?
IF NOTHING ELSE...
I GOT TO MEET ALL OF YOU.
SPARE
ME-
E-E...
I WANTED THE TITLE, "MOST POWERFUL," FOR THEM...
...TO LAY IT BY THEIR SIDE. TO GIVE THEM PRIDE.
UNTIL I COME KILL YOU...
...DON'T LET ANYONE BEAT ME TO IT.

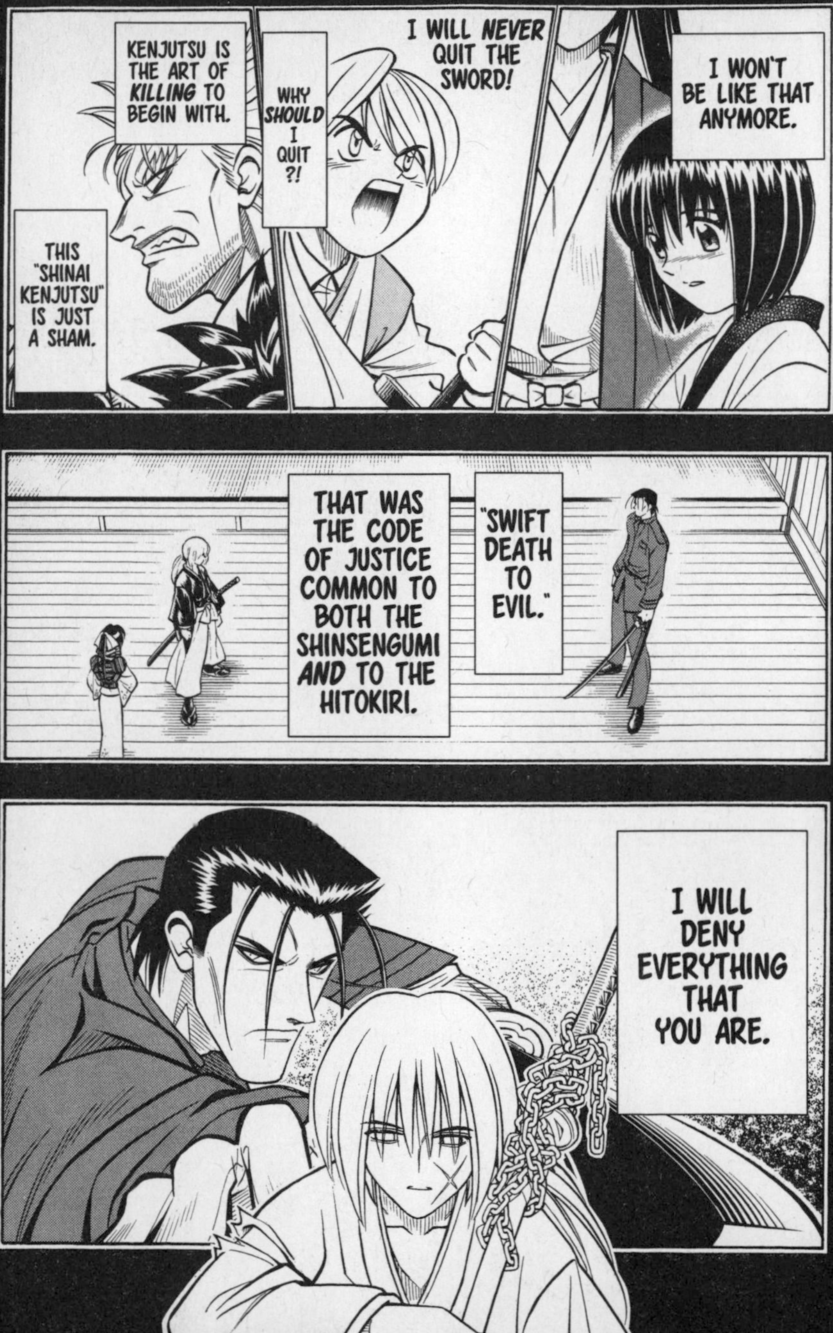
I WON'T BE LIKE THAT ANYMORE.
I WILL NEVER QUIT THE SWORD!
WHY SHOULD I QUIT ?!
KENJUTSU IS THE ART OF KILLING TO BEGIN WITH.
THIS "SHINAI KENJUTSU" IS JUST A SHAM.
"SWIFT DEATH TO EVIL."
THAT WAS THE CODE OF JUSTICE COMMON TO BOTH THE SHINSENGUMI AND TO THE HITOKIRI.
I WILL DENY EVERYTHING THAT YOU ARE.

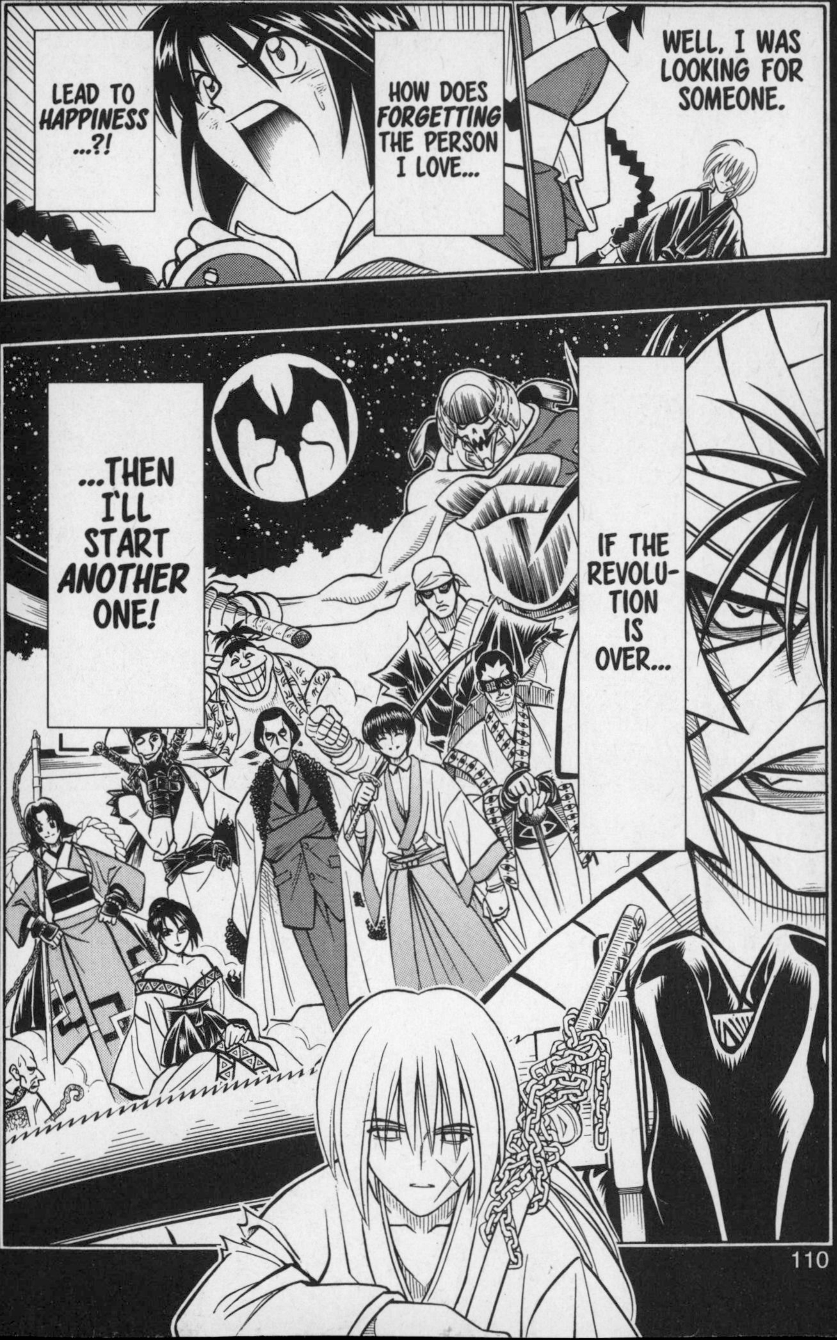
WELL, I WAS LOOKING FOR SOMEONE.
HOW DOES FORGETTING THE PERSON I LOVE...
LEAD TO HAPPINESS...?!
IF THE REVOLUTION IS OVER...
...THEN I'LL START ANOTHER ONE!

READ THIS WAY

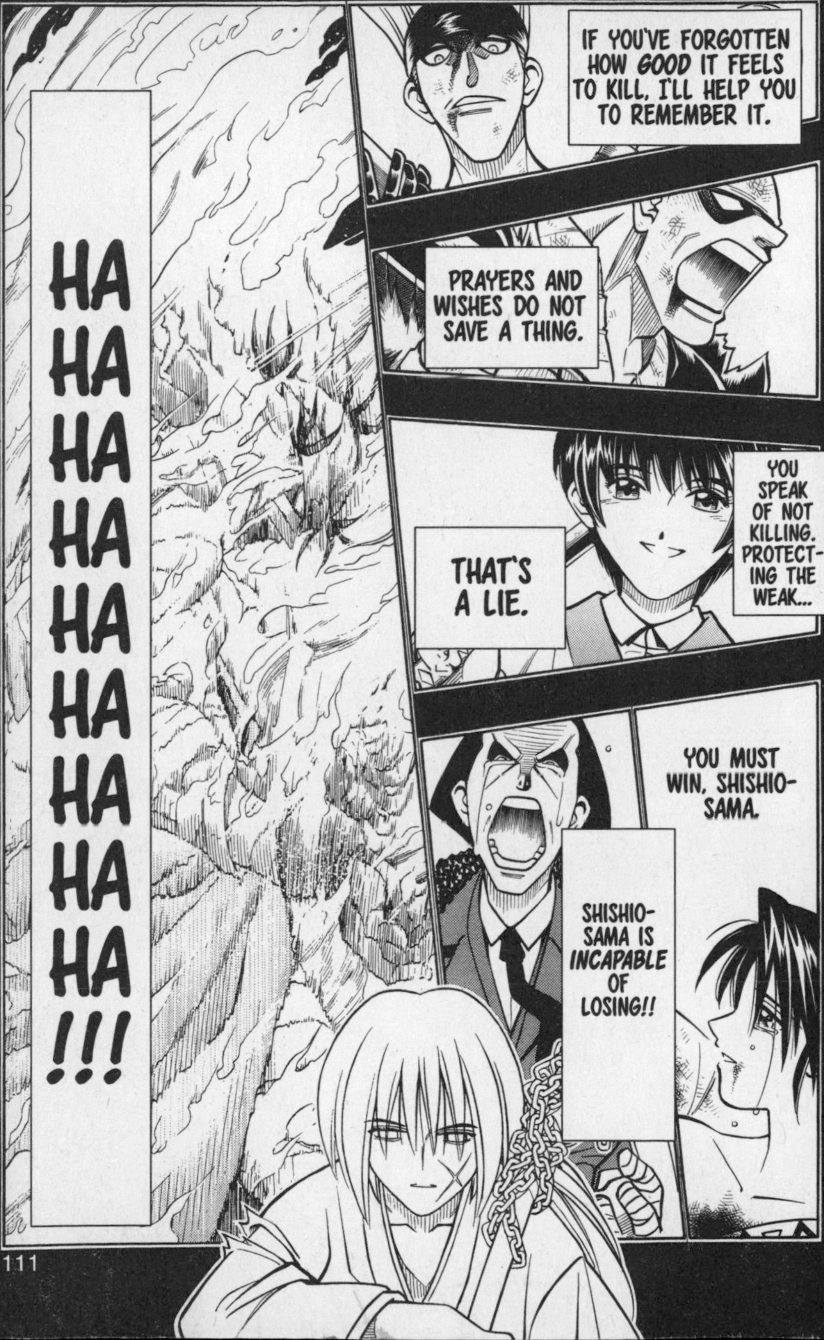

IF YOU'VE FORGOTTEN HOW GOOD IT FEELS TO KILL, I'LL HELP YOU TO REMEMBER IT.
PRAYERS AND WISHES DO NOT SAVE A THING.
YOU SPEAK OF NOT KILLING. PROTECTING THE WEAK...
THAT'S A LIE.
YOU MUST WIN, SHISHIO-SAMA.
SHISHIO-SAMA IS INCAPABLE OF LOSING!!
HA HA HA HA HA HA HA HA HA HA!!!

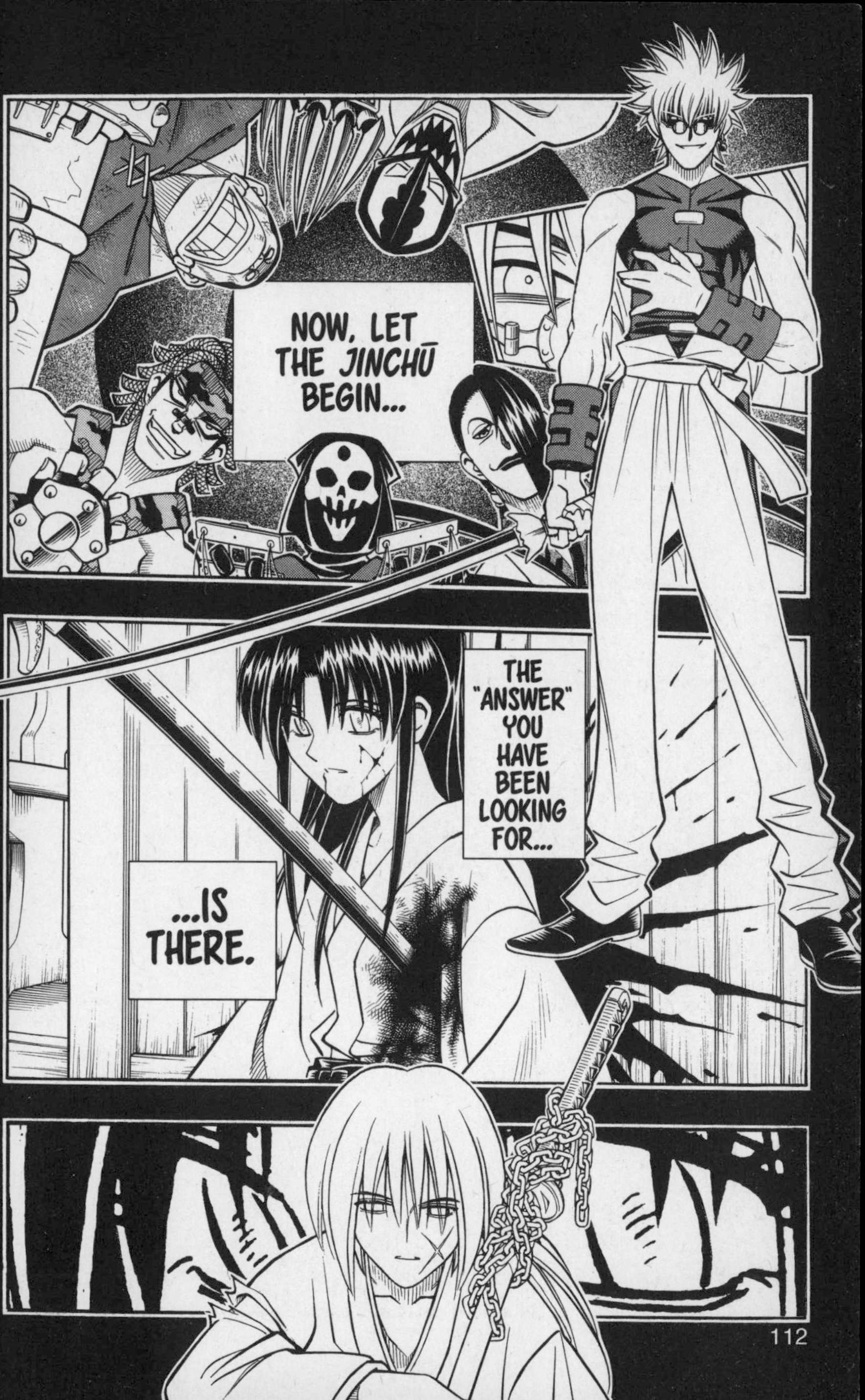
NOW, LET THE JINCHŪ BEGIN...
THE "ANSWER" YOU HAVE BEEN LOOKING FOR...
...IS THERE.

READ THIS WAY

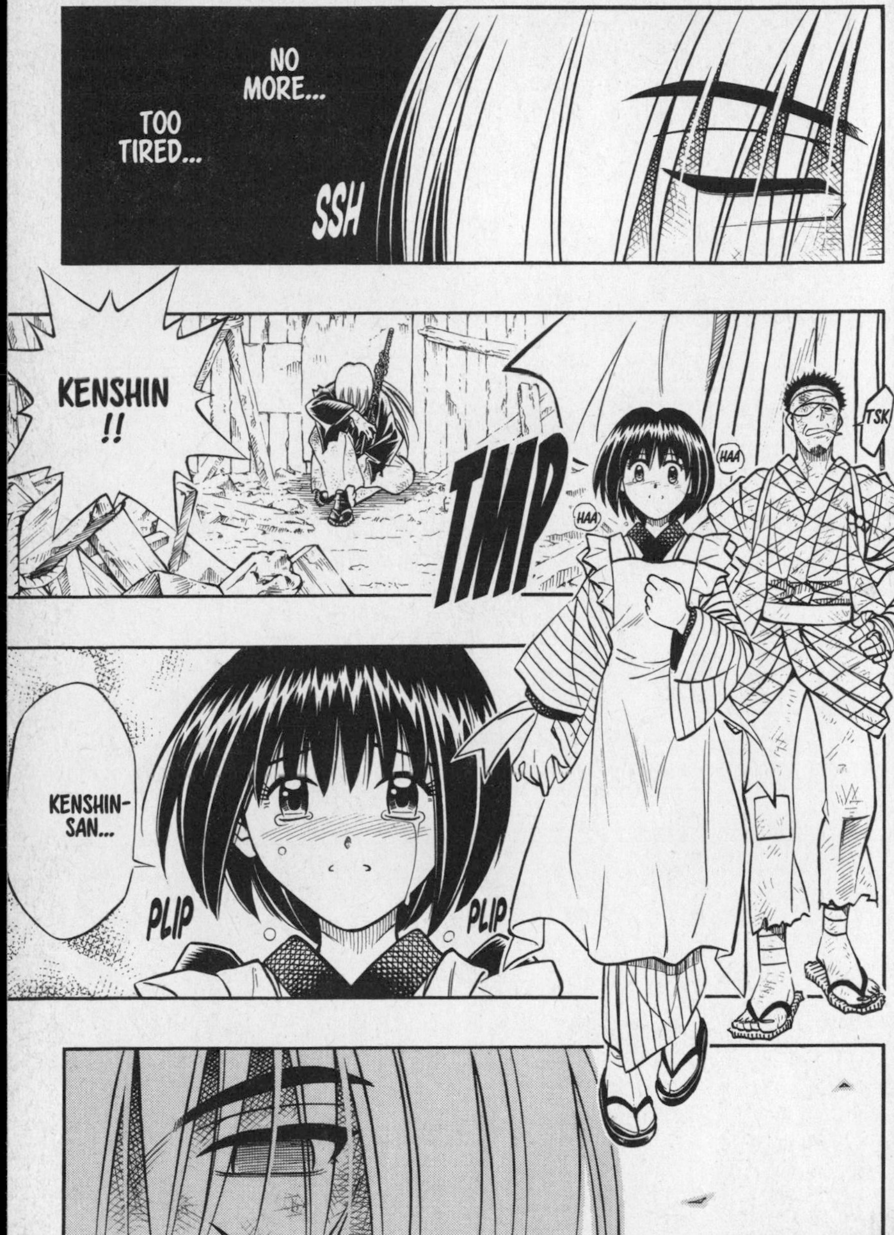

NO MORE...
TOO TIRED...
SSH
TSK
HAA
TMP
HAA
KENSHIN!!
PLIP
KENSHIN-SAN...
PLIP

Rurouni Kenshin

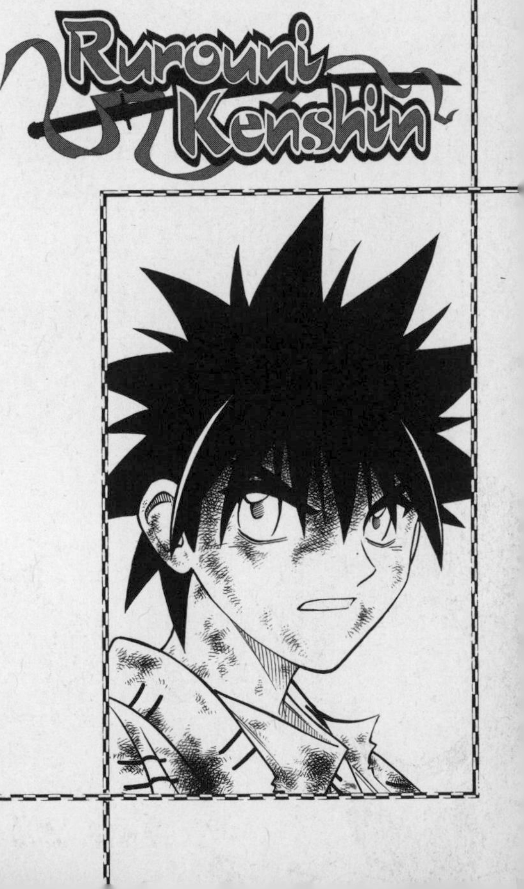

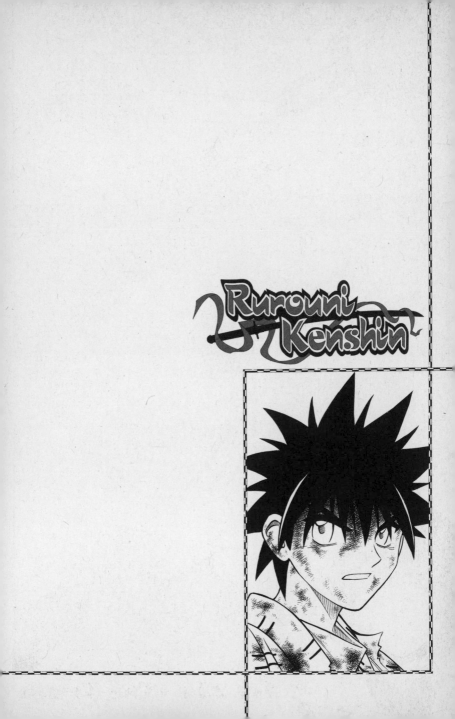

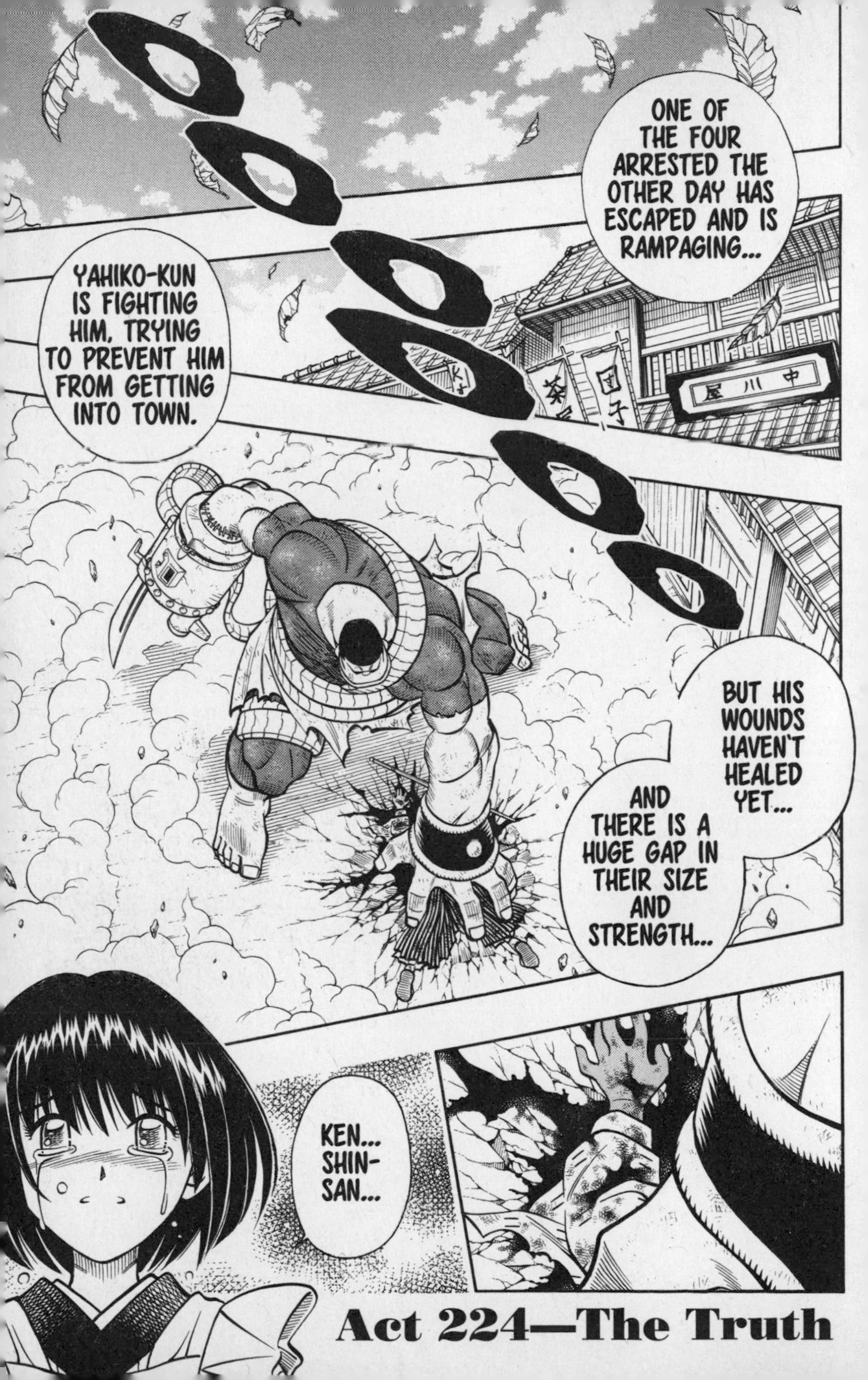
ONE OF THE FOUR ARRESTED THE OTHER DAY HAS ESCAPED AND IS RAMPAGING...
YAHIKO-KUN IS FIGHTING HIM, TRYING TO PREVENT HIM FROM GETTING INTO TOWN.
中川屋
団子
BUT HIS WOUNDS HAVEN'T HEALED YET...
AND THERE IS A HUGE GAP IN THEIR SIZE AND STRENGTH...
KEN... SHIN-SAN...

Act 224—The Truth

Act 224—The Truth

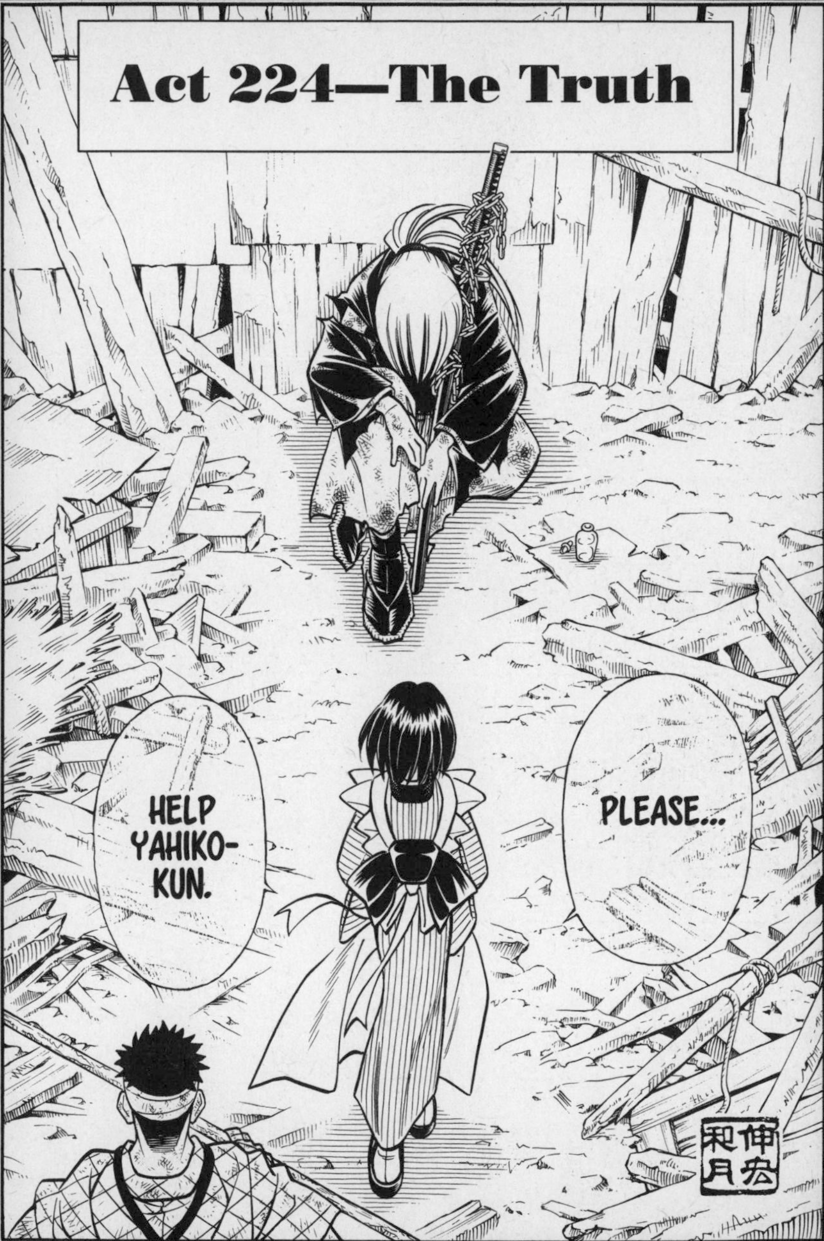
PLEASE...
HELP YAHIKO-KUN.

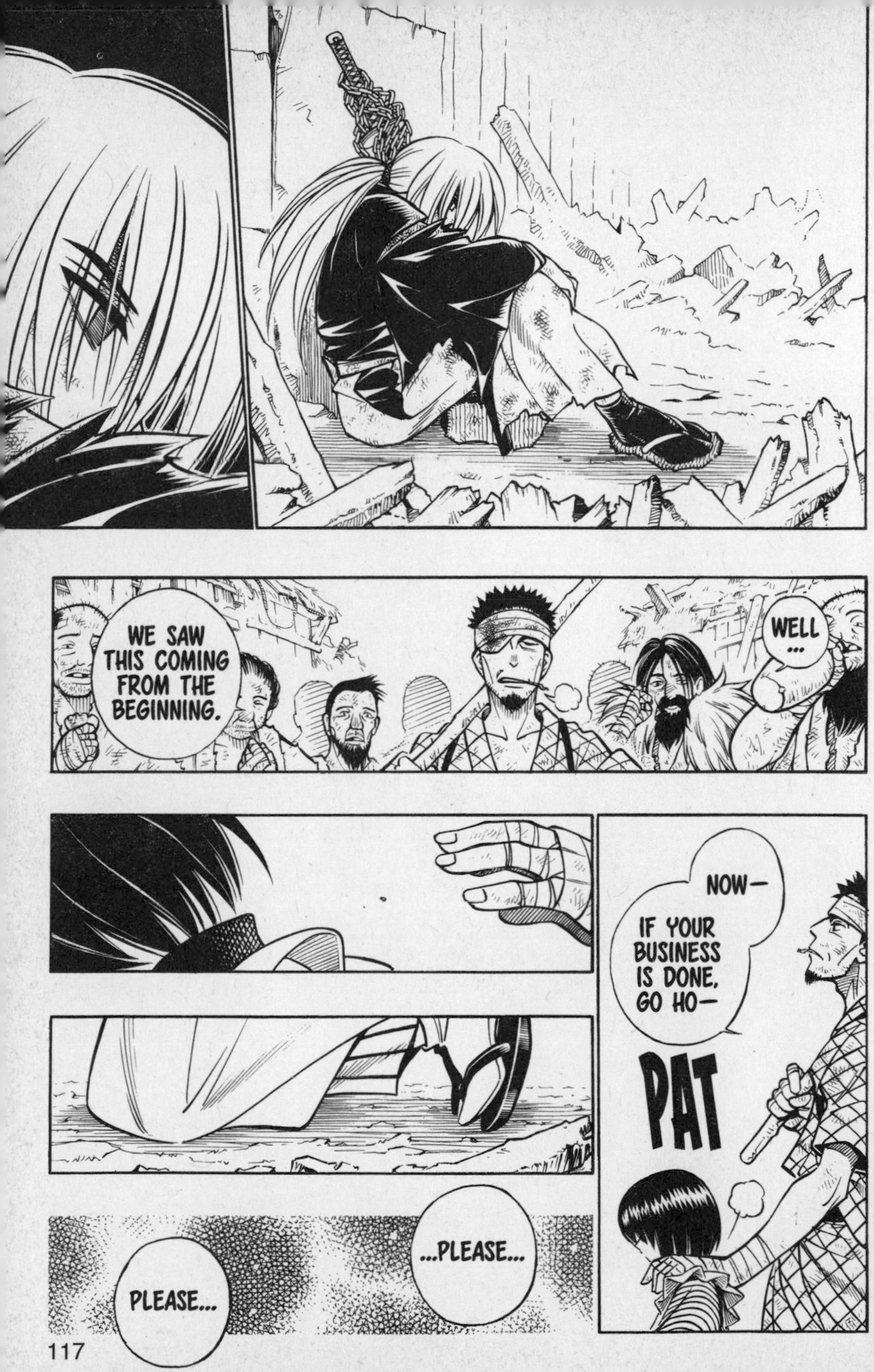

WELL ...
WE SAW THIS COMING FROM THE BEGINNING.
NOW—
IF YOUR BUSINESS IS DONE, GO HO—
PAT
...PLEASE...
PLEASE...

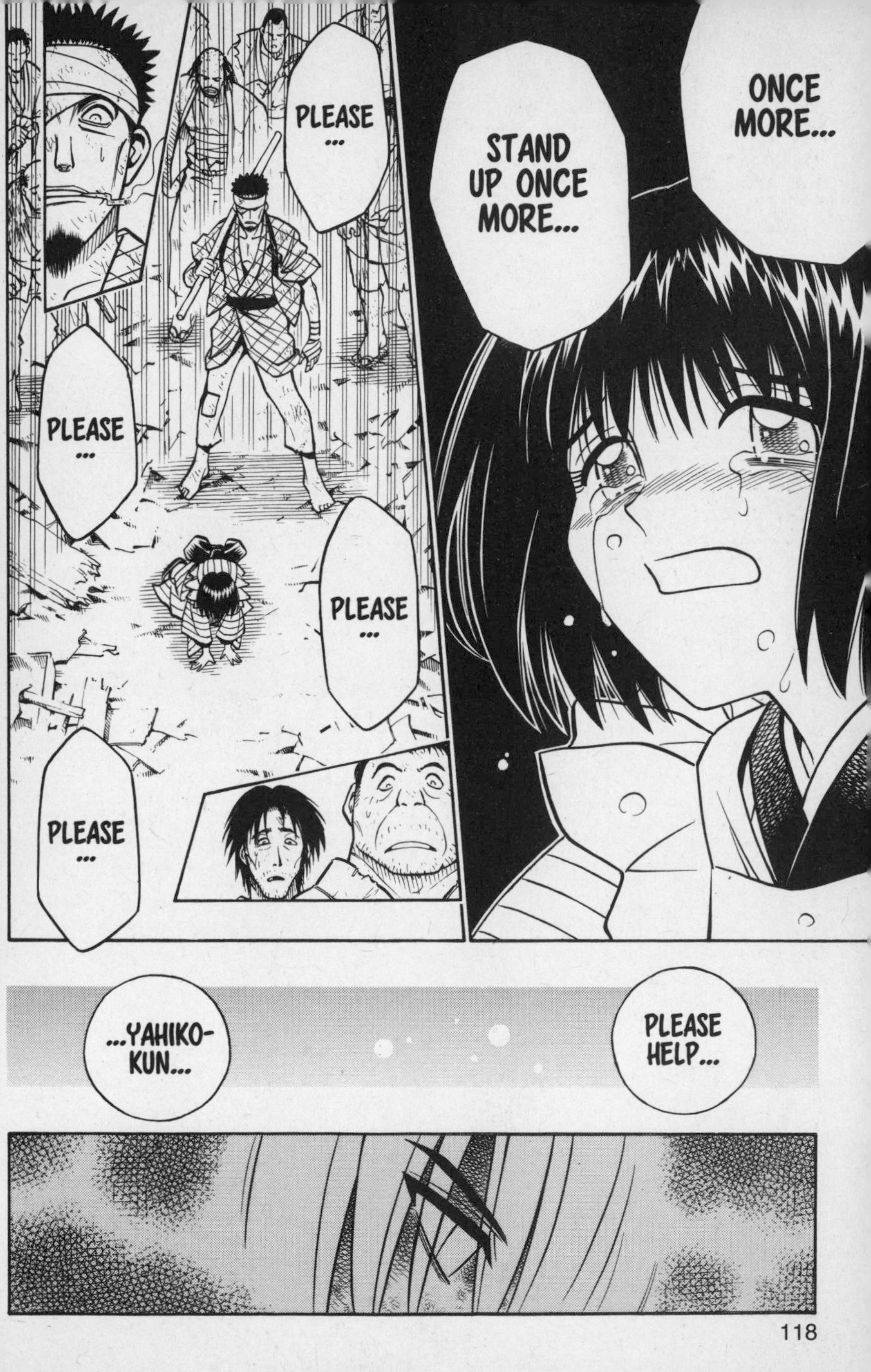
ONCE MORE...
STAND UP ONCE MORE...
PLEASE ...
PLEASE ...
PLEASE ...
PLEASE ...
PLEASE HELP...
...YAHIKO-KUN...

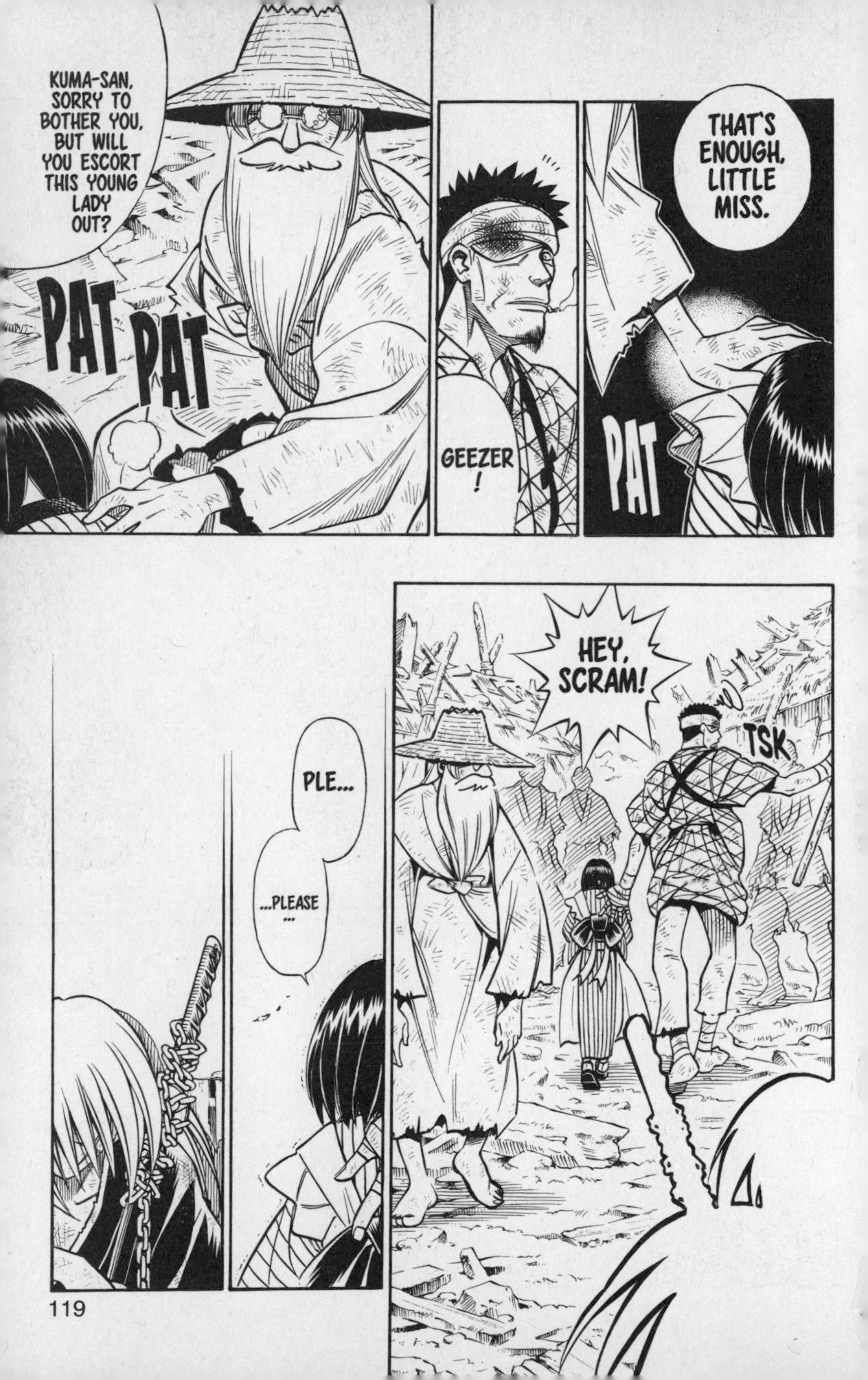
THAT'S ENOUGH, LITTLE MISS.
PAT
GEEZER!
KUMA-SAN, SORRY TO BOTHER YOU, BUT WILL YOU ESCORT THIS YOUNG LADY OUT?
PAT PAT
HEY, SCRAM!
TSK
PLE...
...PLEASE...

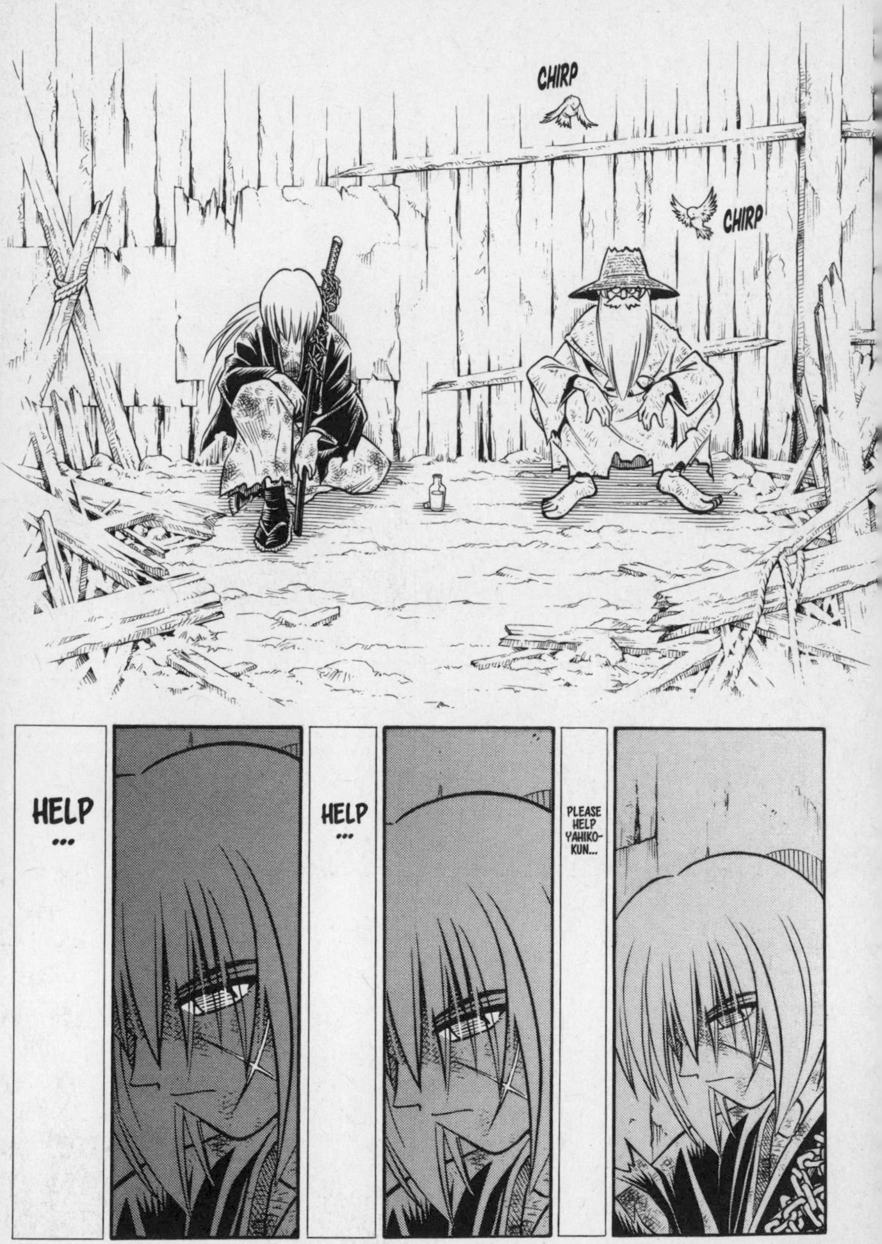
CHIRP
CHIRP
PLEASE HELP YAHIKO-KUN...
HELP ...
HELP ...

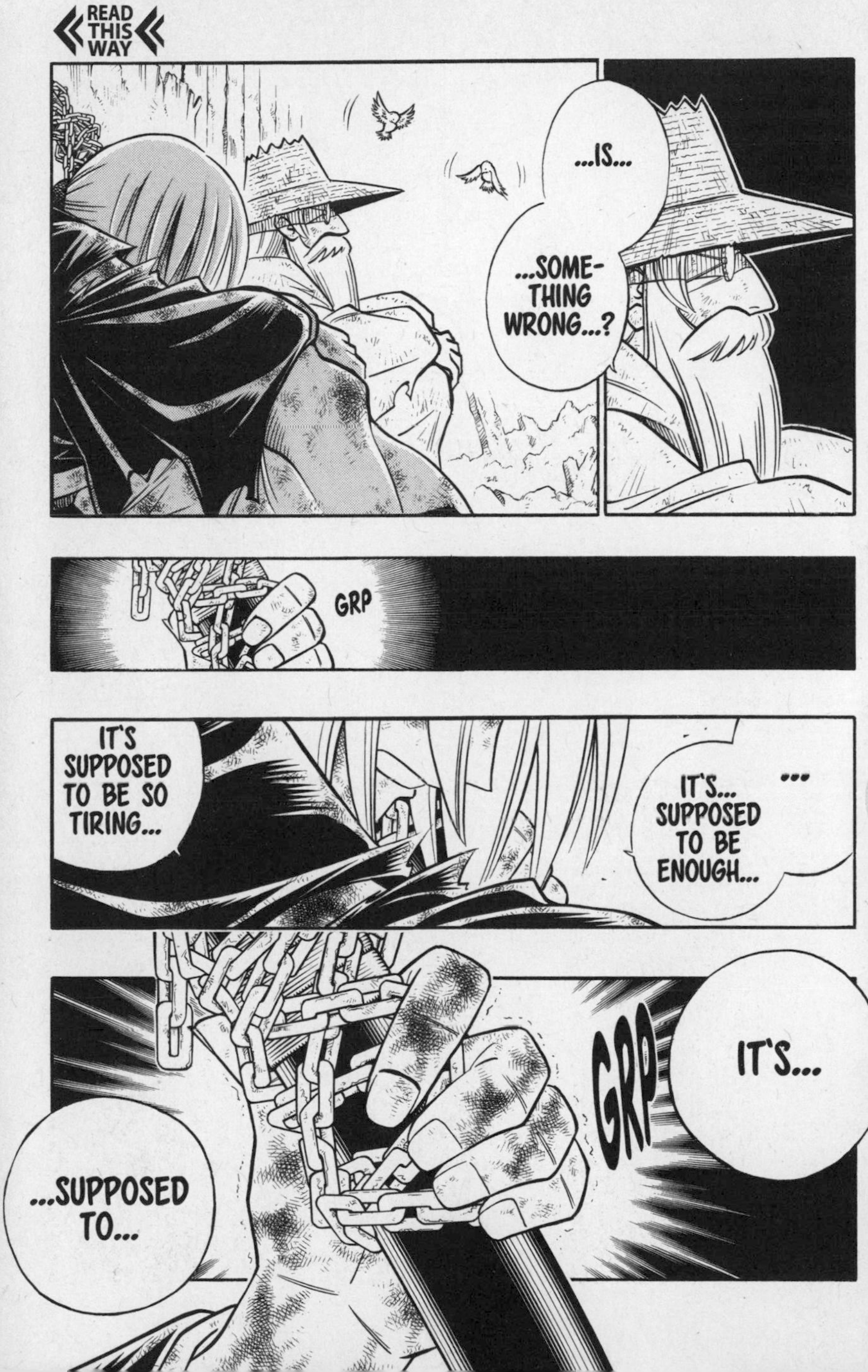
READ THIS WAY
...IS...
...SOME-THING WRONG...?
GRP
...
IT'S... SUPPOSED TO BE ENOUGH...
IT'S SUPPOSED TO BE SO TIRING...
IT'S...
GRP
...SUPPOSED TO...

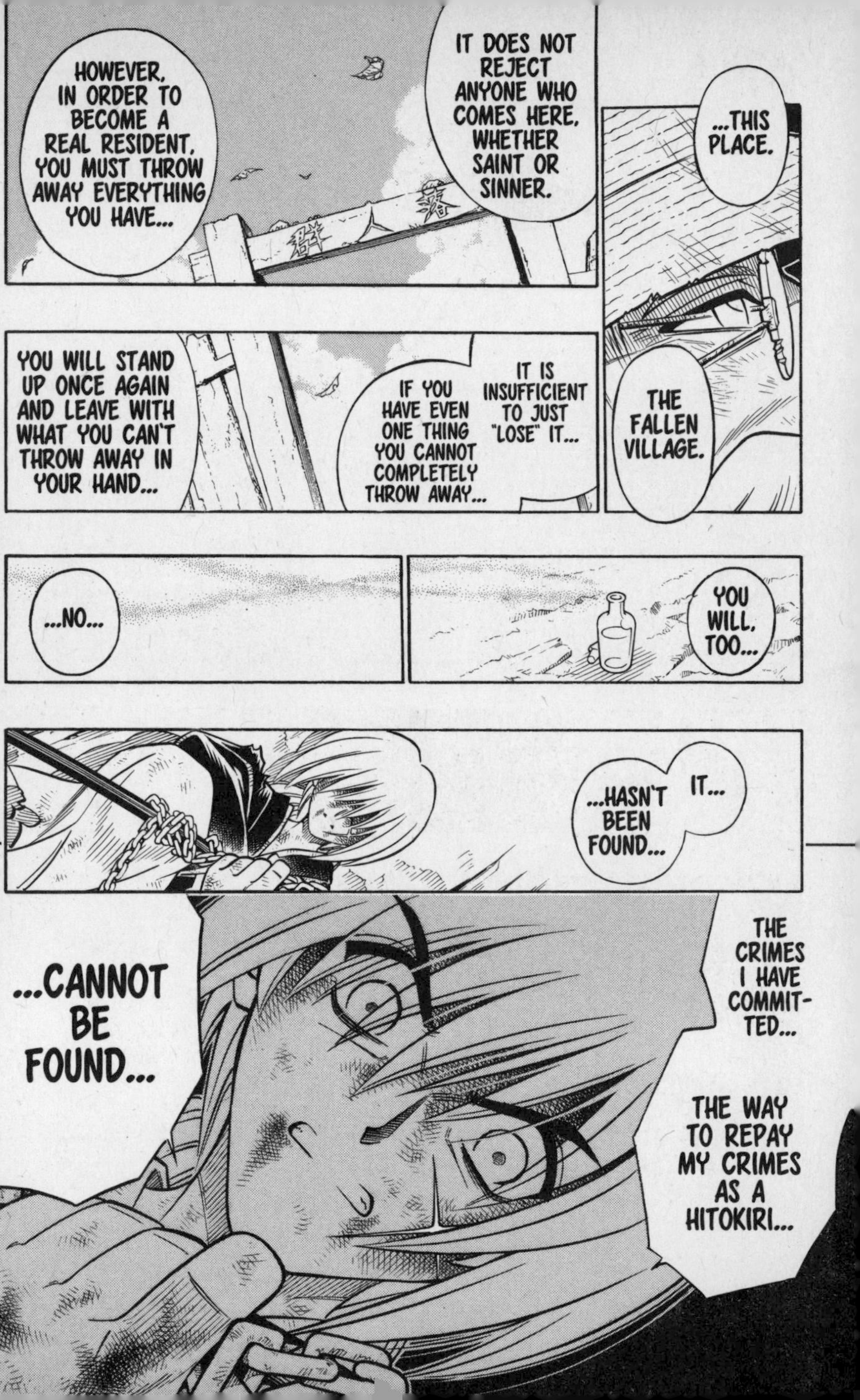
...THIS PLACE.
THE FALLEN VILLAGE.
IT DOES NOT REJECT ANYONE WHO COMES HERE, WHETHER SAINT OR SINNER.
HOWEVER, IN ORDER TO BECOME A REAL RESIDENT, YOU MUST THROW AWAY EVERYTHING YOU HAVE...
IT IS INSUFFICIENT TO JUST "LOSE" IT...
IF YOU HAVE EVEN ONE THING YOU CANNOT COMPLETELY THROW AWAY...
YOU WILL STAND UP ONCE AGAIN AND LEAVE WITH WHAT YOU CAN'T THROW AWAY IN YOUR HAND...
YOU WILL, TOO...
...NO...
IT...
...HASN'T BEEN FOUND...
THE CRIMES I HAVE COMMITTED...
THE WAY TO REPAY MY CRIMES AS A HITOKIRI...
...CANNOT BE FOUND...

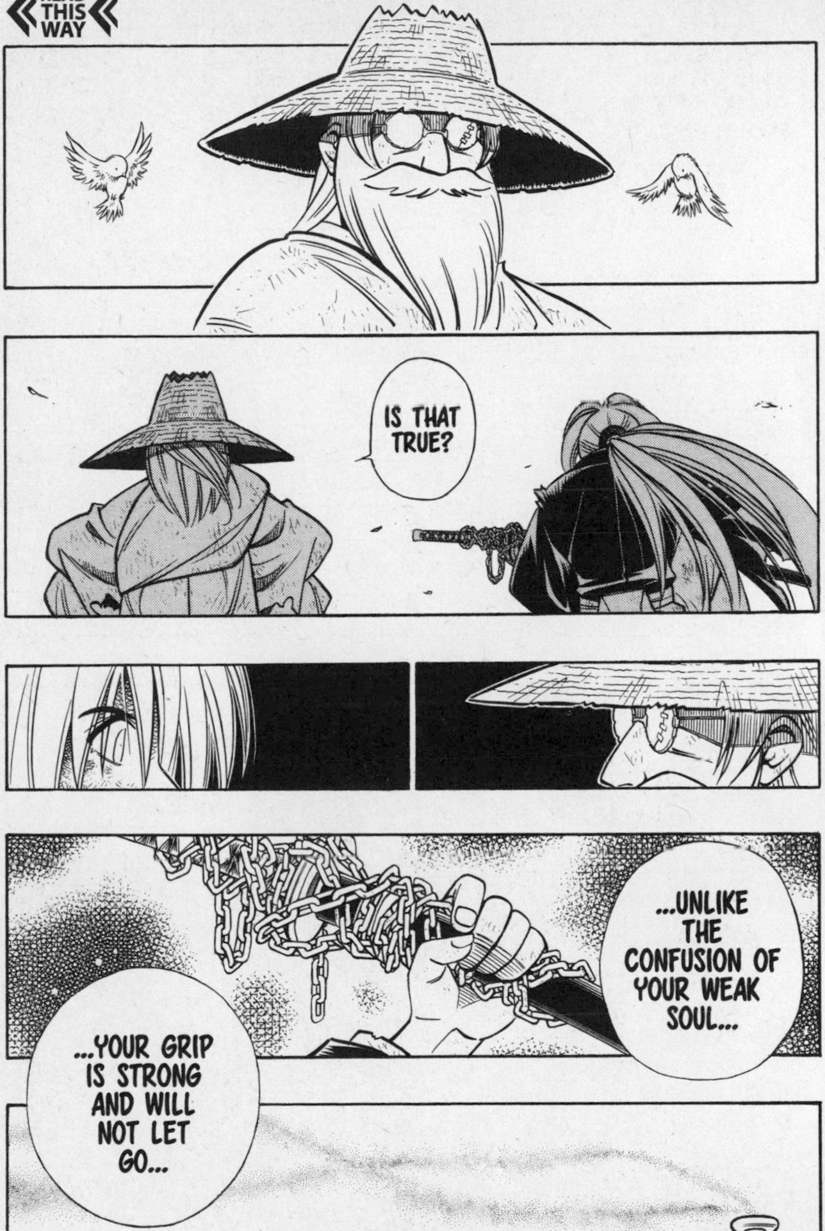
IS THAT TRUE?
...UNLIKE THE CONFUSION OF YOUR WEAK SOUL...
...YOUR GRIP IS STRONG AND WILL NOT LET GO...

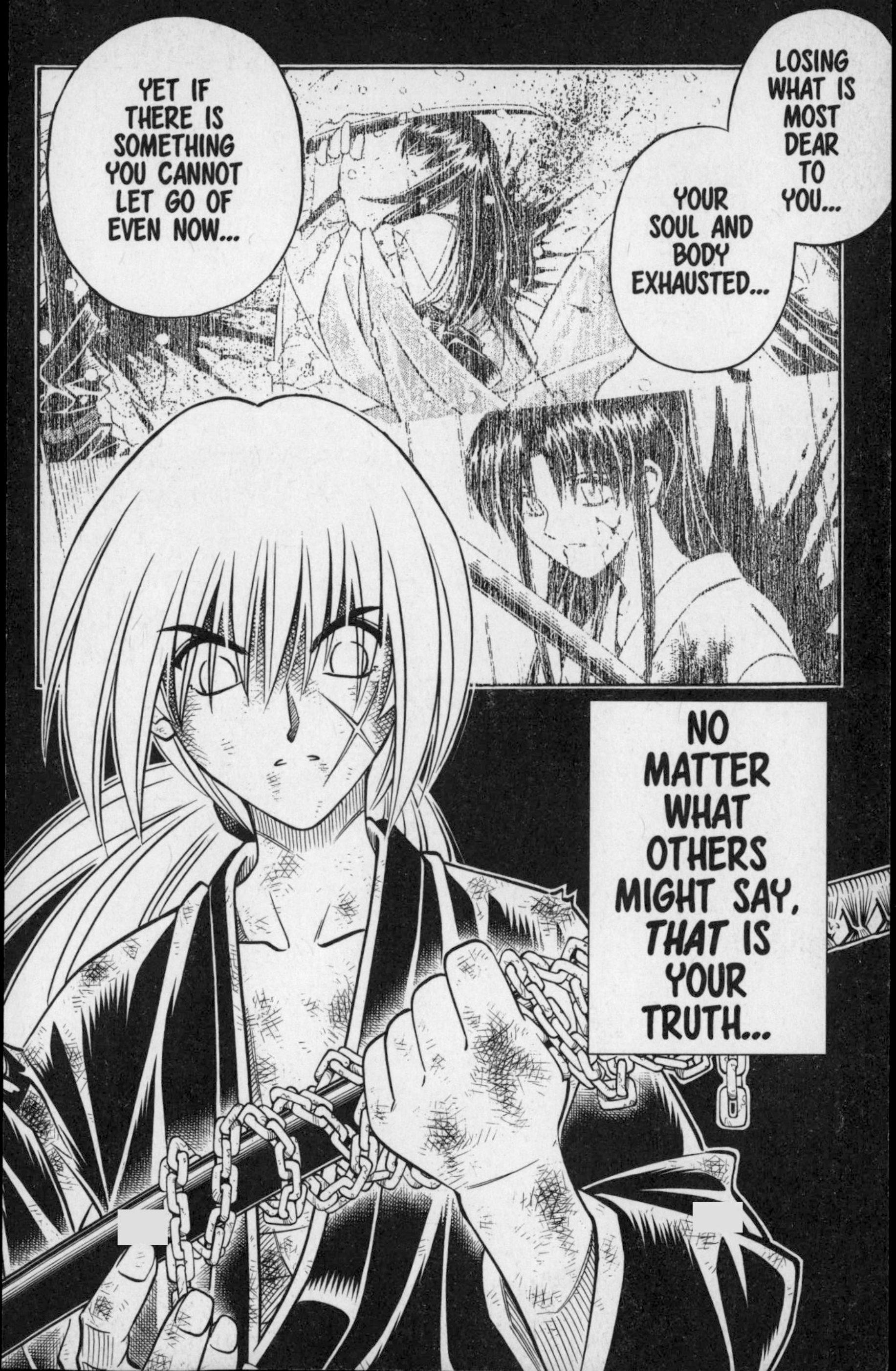
LOSING WHAT IS MOST DEAR TO YOU...
YOUR SOUL AND BODY EXHAUSTED...
YET IF THERE IS SOMETHING YOU CANNOT LET GO OF EVEN NOW...
NO MATTER WHAT OTHERS MIGHT SAY, *THAT* IS YOUR TRUTH...

READ THIS WAY

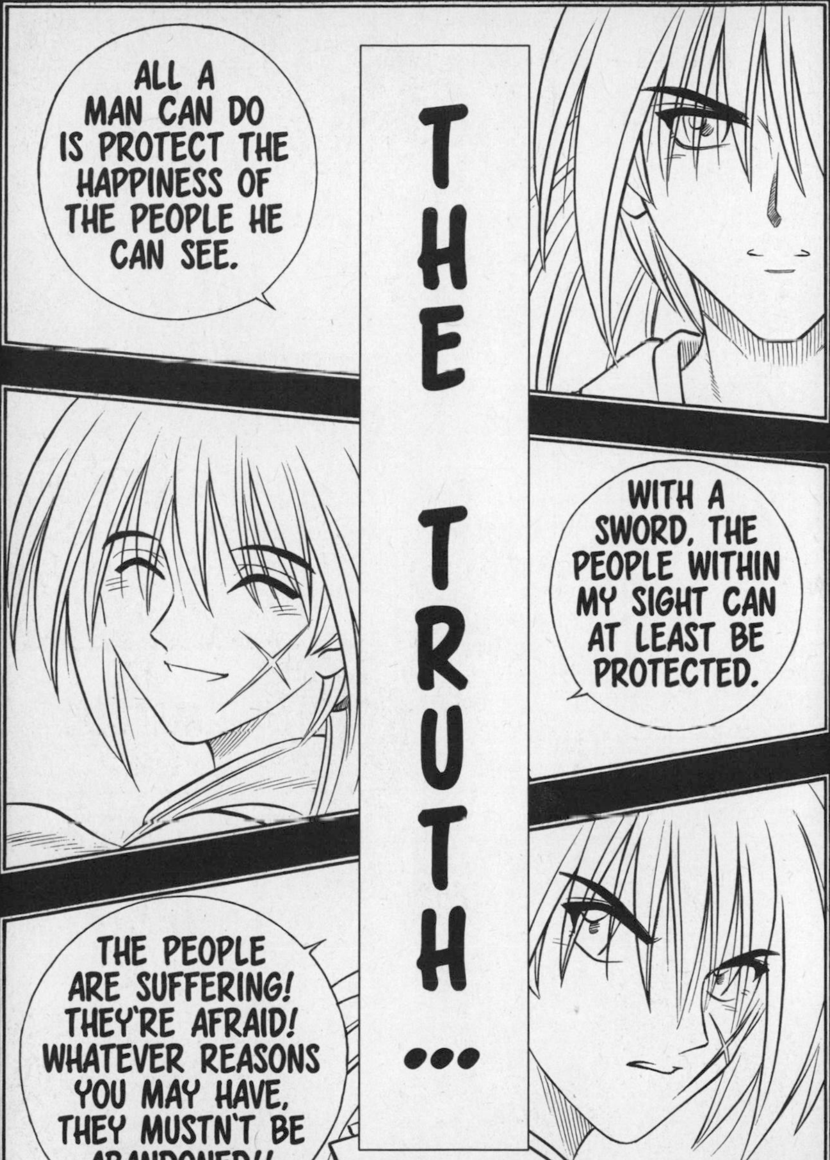
ALL A MAN CAN DO IS PROTECT THE HAPPINESS OF THE PEOPLE HE CAN SEE.
THE TRUTH...
WITH A SWORD, THE PEOPLE WITHIN MY SIGHT CAN AT LEAST BE PROTECTED.
THE PEOPLE ARE SUFFERING! THEY'RE AFRAID! WHATEVER REASONS YOU MAY HAVE, THEY MUSTN'T BE ABANDONED!!

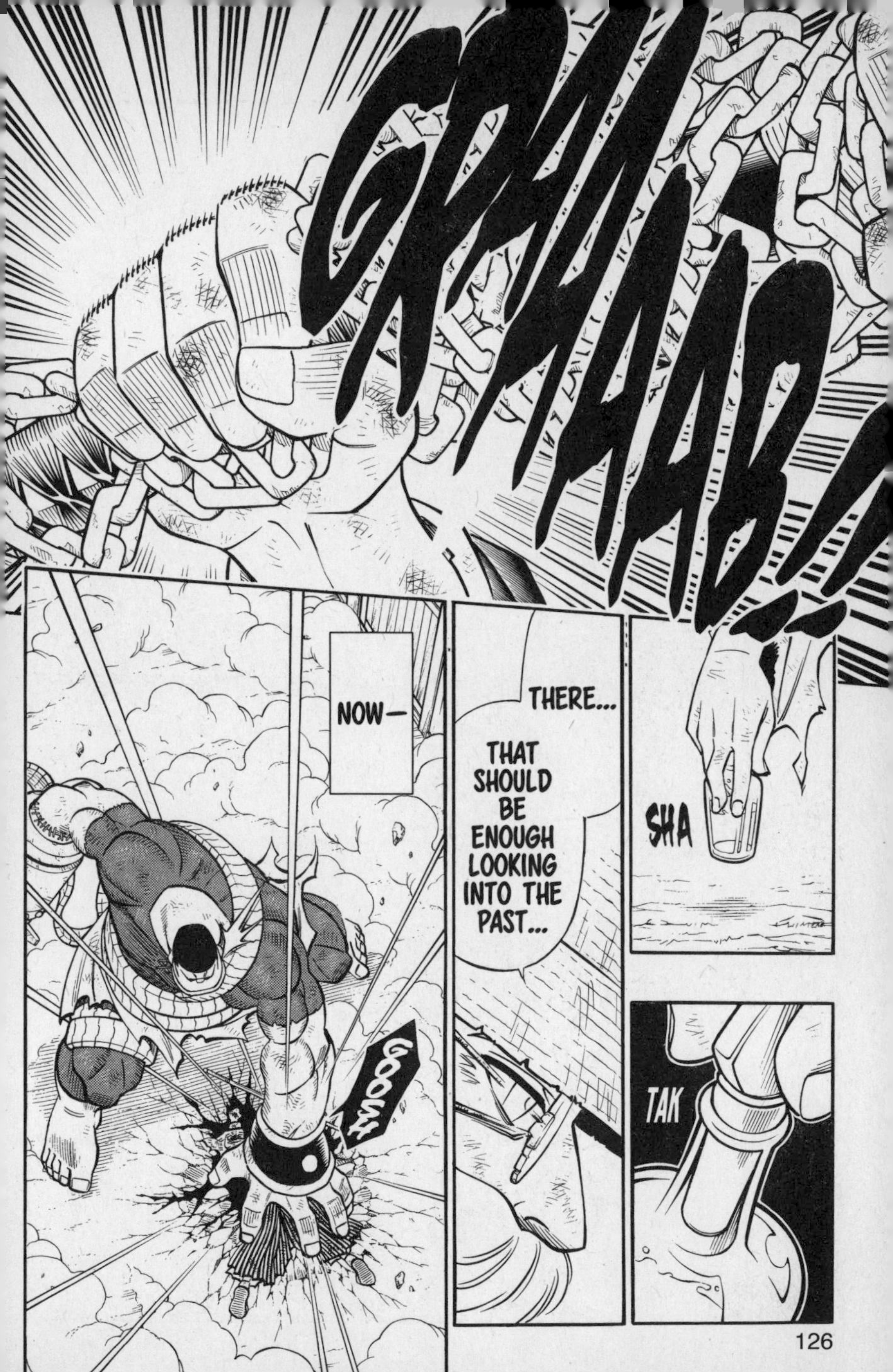
SHA
TAK
THERE...
THAT SHOULD BE ENOUGH LOOKING INTO THE PAST...
NOW—
GOOOSH

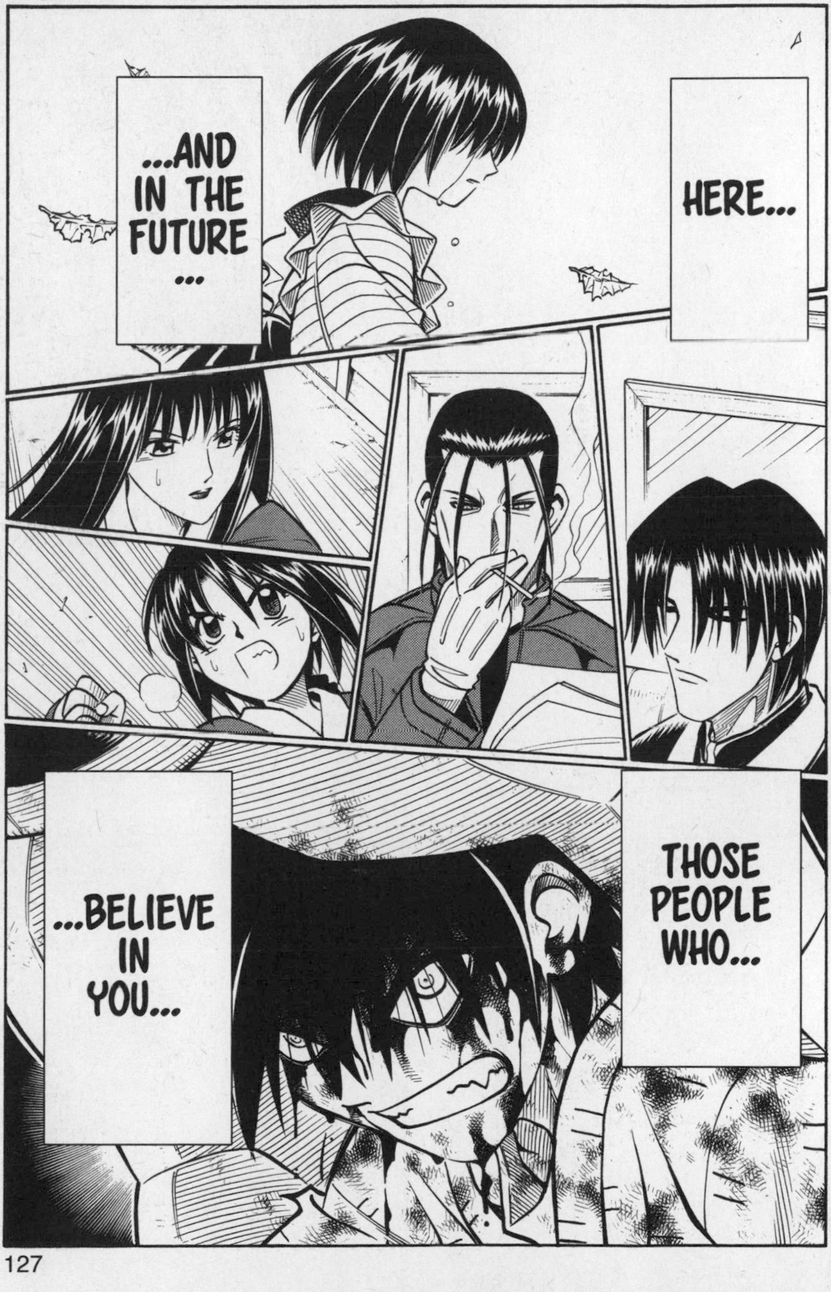
HERE...
...AND IN THE FUTURE ...
THOSE PEOPLE WHO...
...BELIEVE IN YOU...

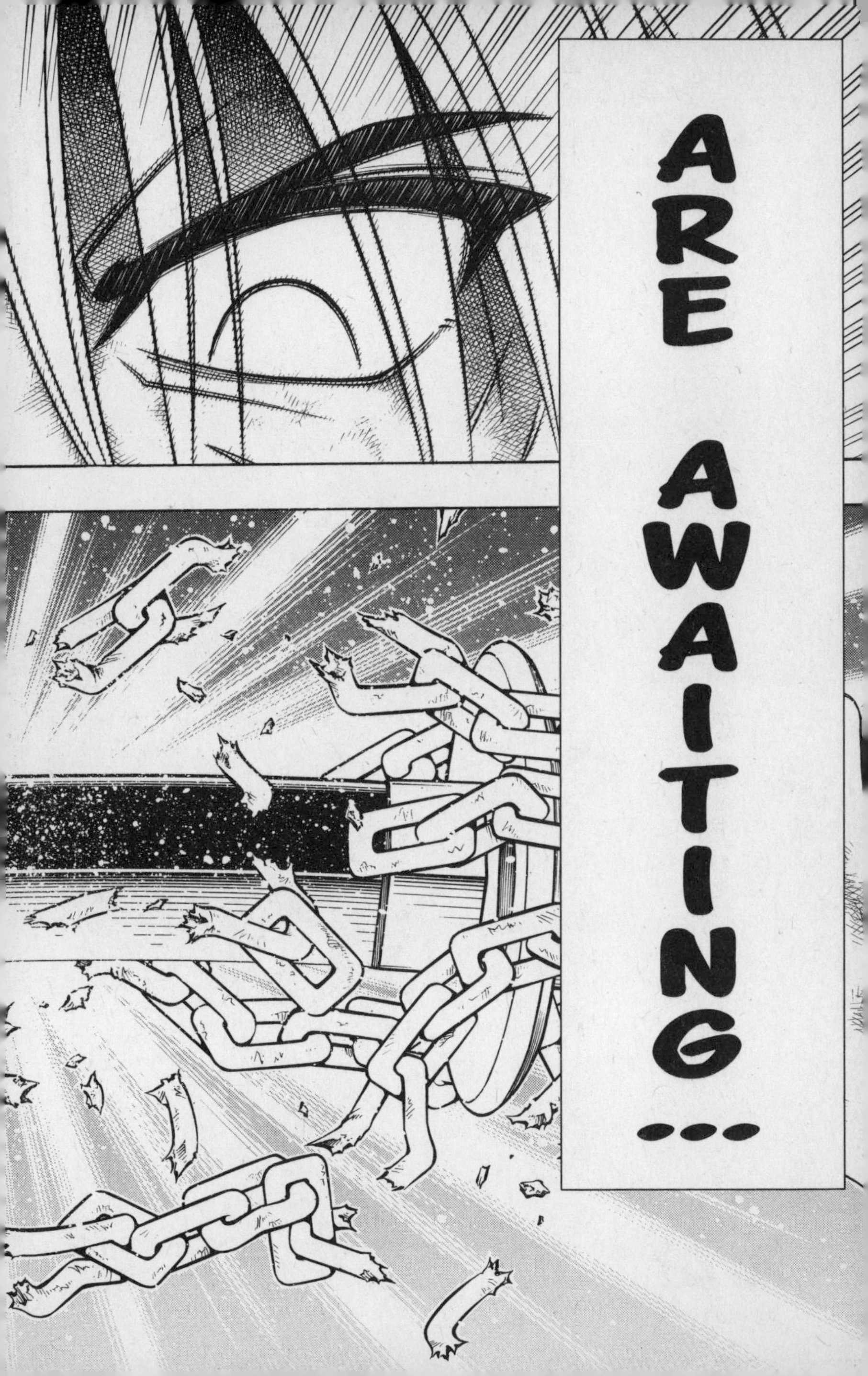
ARE AWAITING...

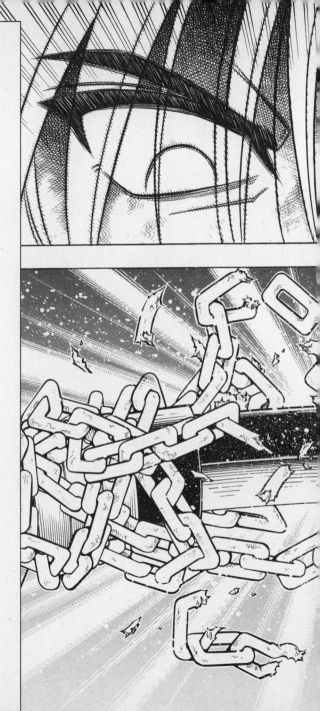

"YOUR RETURN!!!

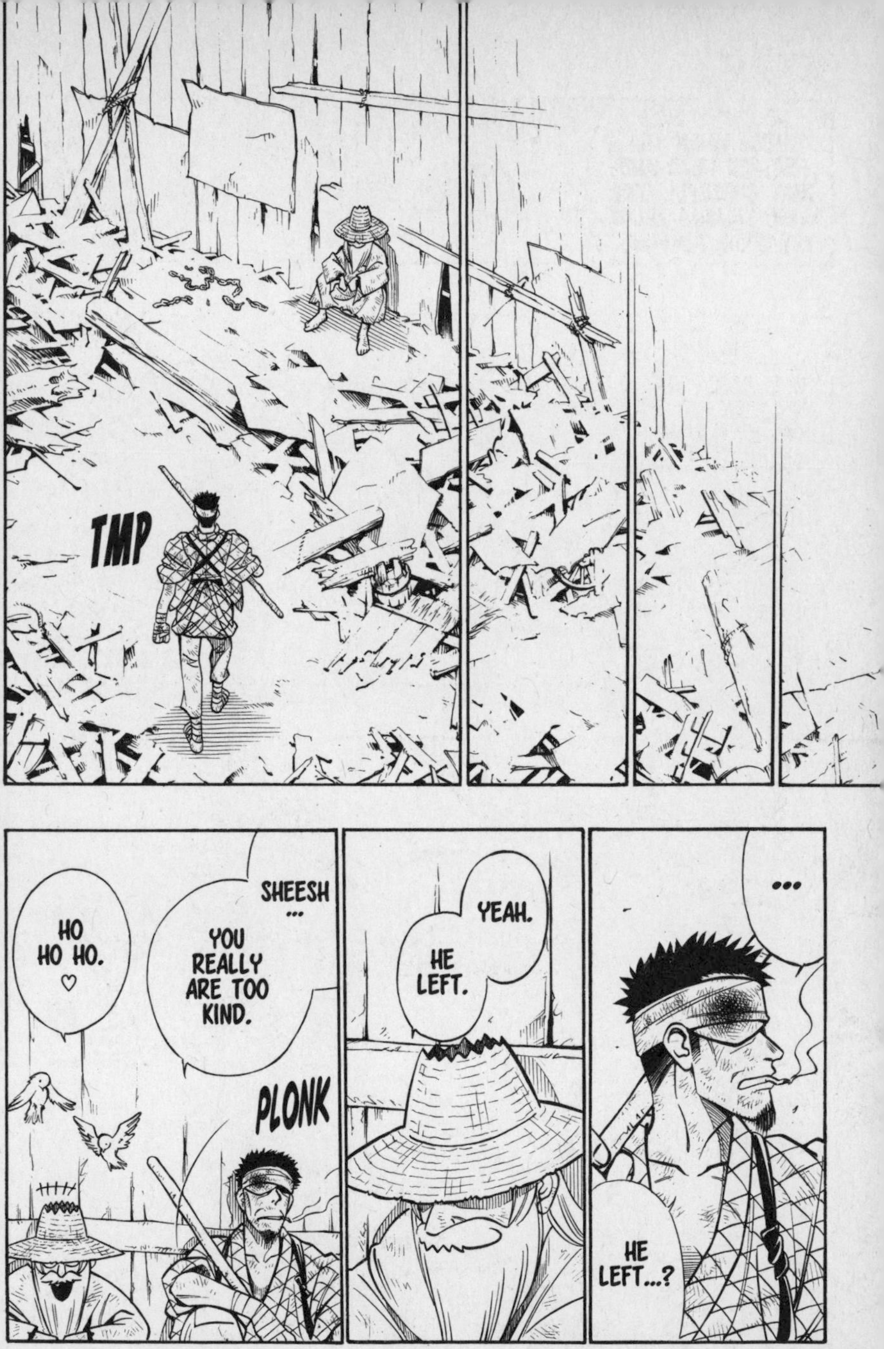
TMP
...
HE LEFT...?
YEAH.
HE LEFT.
SHEESH ...
YOU REALLY ARE TOO KIND.
HO HO HO. ♡
PLONK

READ THIS WAY

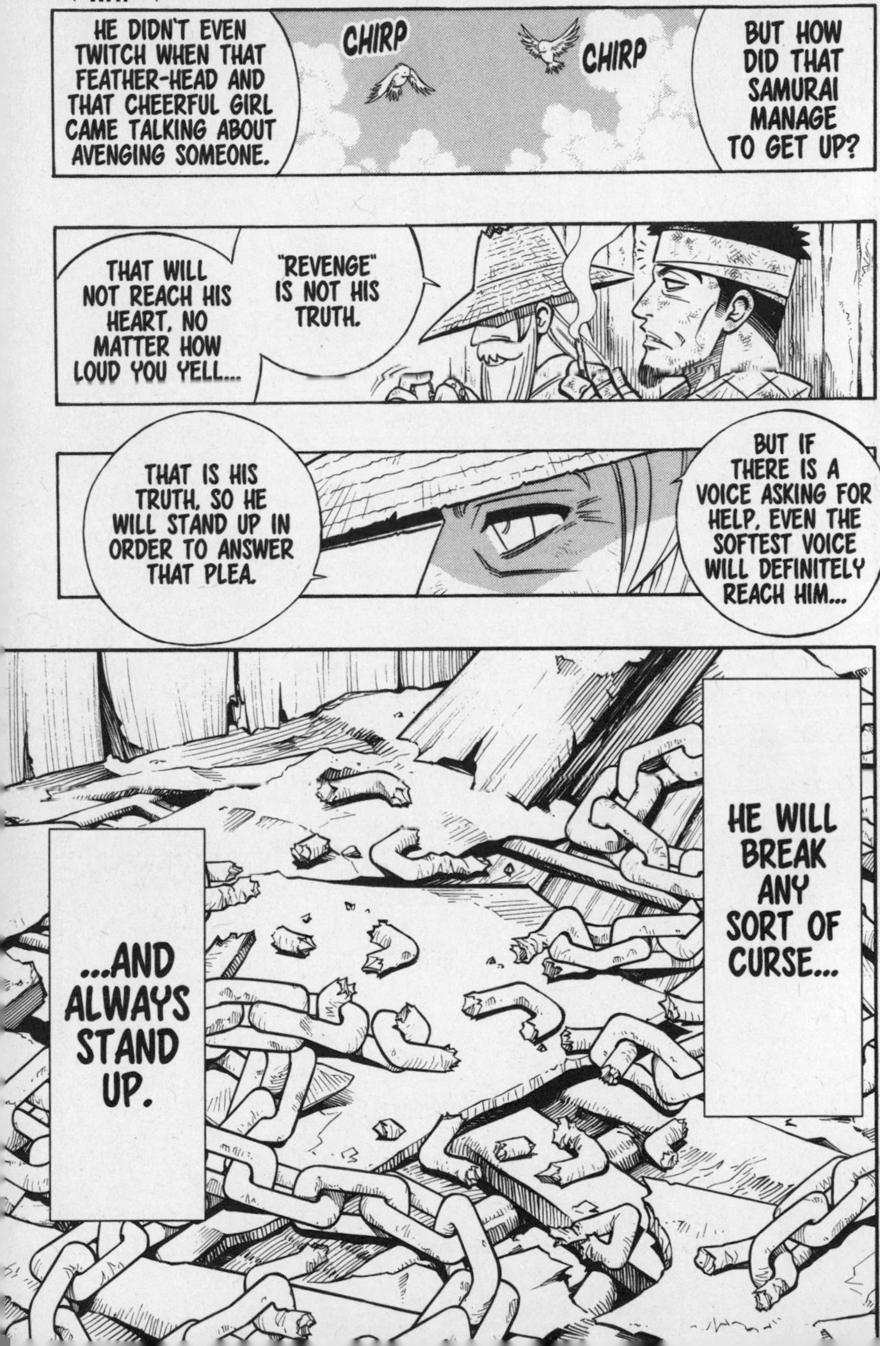
BUT HOW DID THAT SAMURAI MANAGE TO GET UP?
CHIRP
CHIRP
HE DIDN'T EVEN TWITCH WHEN THAT FEATHER-HEAD AND THAT CHEERFUL GIRL CAME TALKING ABOUT AVENGING SOMEONE.
"REVENGE" IS NOT HIS TRUTH.
THAT WILL NOT REACH HIS HEART, NO MATTER HOW LOUD YOU YELL...
BUT IF THERE IS A VOICE ASKING FOR HELP, EVEN THE SOFTEST VOICE WILL DEFINITELY REACH HIM...
THAT IS HIS TRUTH, SO HE WILL STAND UP IN ORDER TO ANSWER THAT PLEA.
HE WILL BREAK ANY SORT OF CURSE...
...AND ALWAYS STAND UP.

"FREE TALK"

Gyaaaaa!! I make a sudden appearance screaming like Fujiko Fujio A-*sensei* (aka Motō Abiko). Long time no see, this is Watsuki. *Manga Michi* by Fukiko Fukio A is always a must read for a manga artist with self-doubt. I read it over just now, and have recharged myself with power. One more time, Gyaaaaaa!!

We'll start with the usual talk about figures and games. In terms of European figures, the *X-Men* series from Toy Biz has ended, and the McFarlane toys are heading more and more in a creature direction, and I am a bit disappointed. The Japanese figures tend to be very well made, but have few movable parts or gimmicks. Or they are the complete opposite with too many attachments and things. Watsuki feels action figures should be both good for displaying and good for playing with, so though I can see the makers' effort, I would like one more try. I'll stop here. Wait, who do I think I am? I'm sorry! I'm looking forward to them! Please keep working hard! So, the "Gachapon" I said I might get hooked on, I've most definitely gotten hooked on. Also, I really like the Gufu and B-3 Gufu of *Gundam* from Bandai's HG (high grade), and Neo Getter Robo (I love the second series of the OAV version of the original *Getter*). *Samurai Spirits* (Nanase Aoi-*sensei* version!) from the Yujin SR (Super Real), "Natsu Robo Museum" (Machine Blaster and Atlanger!) have all got me so hooked I think, "Is there someone out there reading my mind and coming up with the line-up?" Good!

In terms of games, I've gotten further away from the arcade recently, and haven't played much there at all. I did acquire a Dreamcast, so I've played a bit of *Power Stone* from CAPCOM. But I keep getting thoroughly beat by my assistants, making me think, "Are you releasing all of your daily grudges against me here?" Of course, I am still limited in my time, but there are two titles I am interested in, and am contemplating buying them. At the time this volume is published in Japan, I will probably have already made a decision and have taken action, so I will write the results in the next volume. One of the two is a girly game. Watsuki has finally fallen! More like, have you crossed the line, Nobuhiro?! Is there any hope for a humanity that keeps crumbling as I approach 30? Please tune in to the next volume.

Change in topics. As I touched on in my author's note, it is the cherry blossom season. Last year I was so busy I had to forgo it, but I plan to go see evening blossoms this year. Viewing parties are not bad, but possibly due to my age, I feel like being quietly charmed by the evening blossoms. I will shave so that I will not get questioned by the police (happened before), and I'll have a canned coffee in my hand because I can't drink alcohol. I will watch the petals falling, remembering the days when I had just started the series, building up the tension, cranking up the voltage, advancing myself further on the manga road. Therefore, the closing will be, for the third time, the scream of my soul. GYAAAA!!

See you in the next volume.

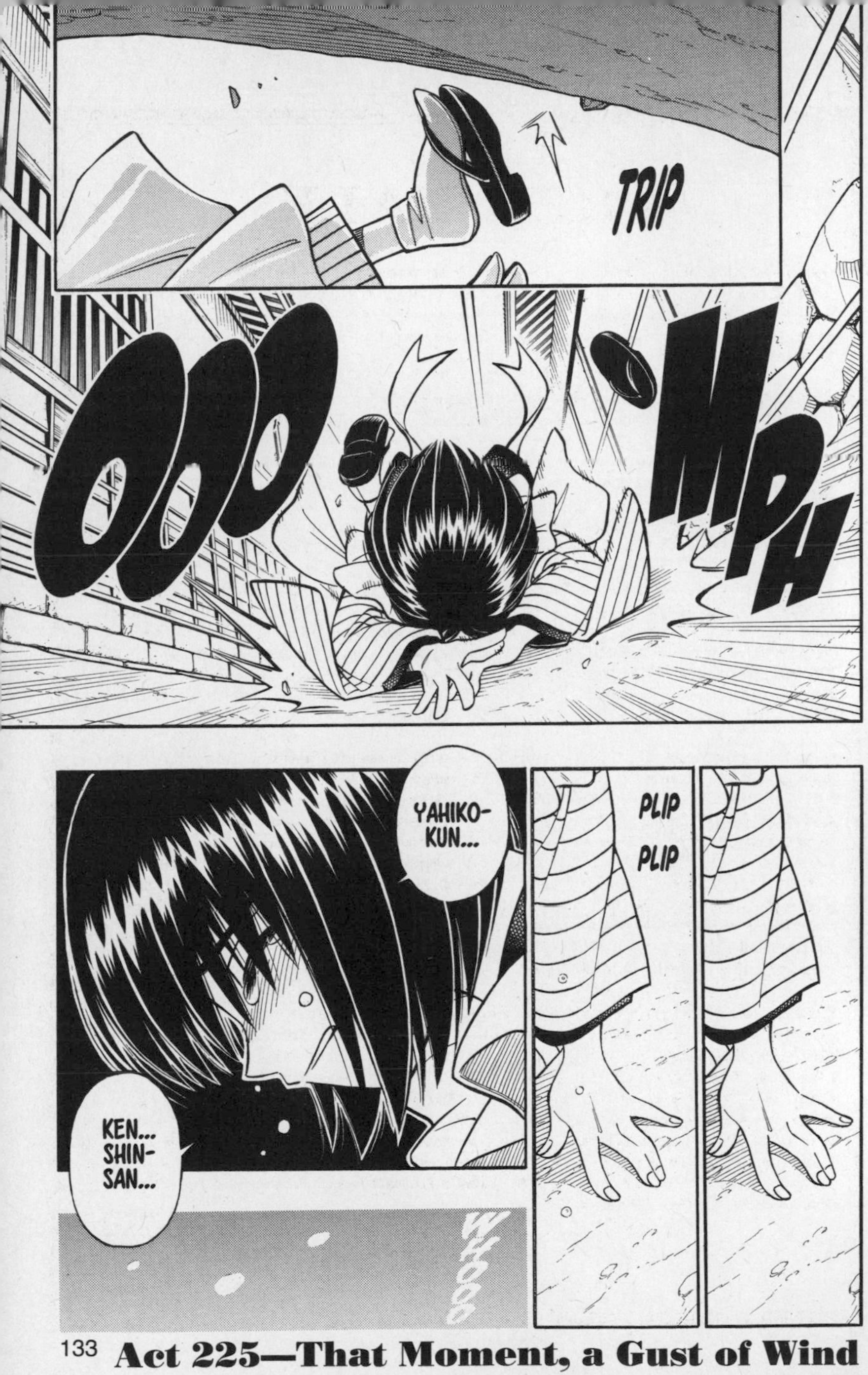
TRIP
OOOMPH
PLIP
PLIP
YAHIKO-KUN...
KEN... SHIN-SAN...
WHOOOO

Act 225—That Moment, a Gust of Wind

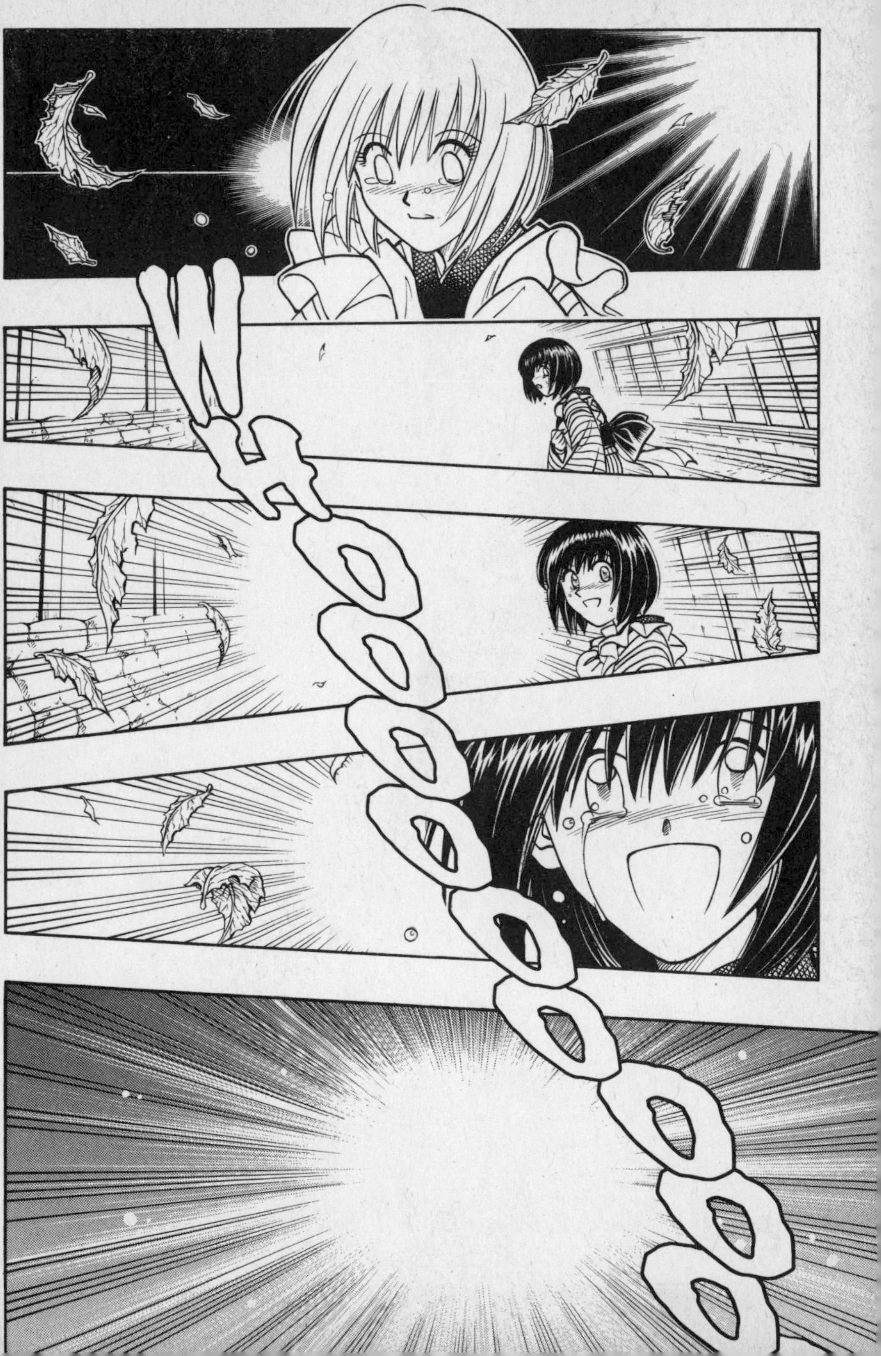
WHOOOOOOOOO

Act 225
That Moment, a Gust of Wind

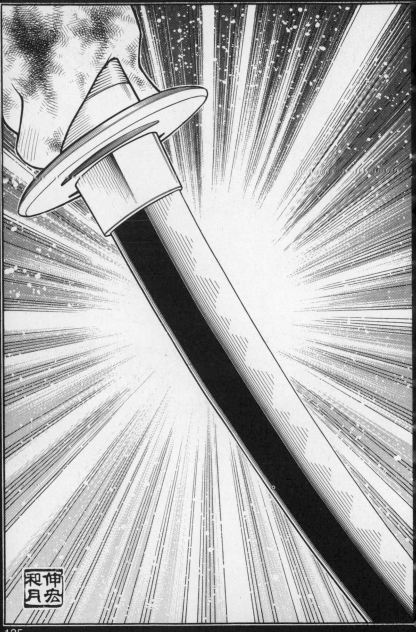

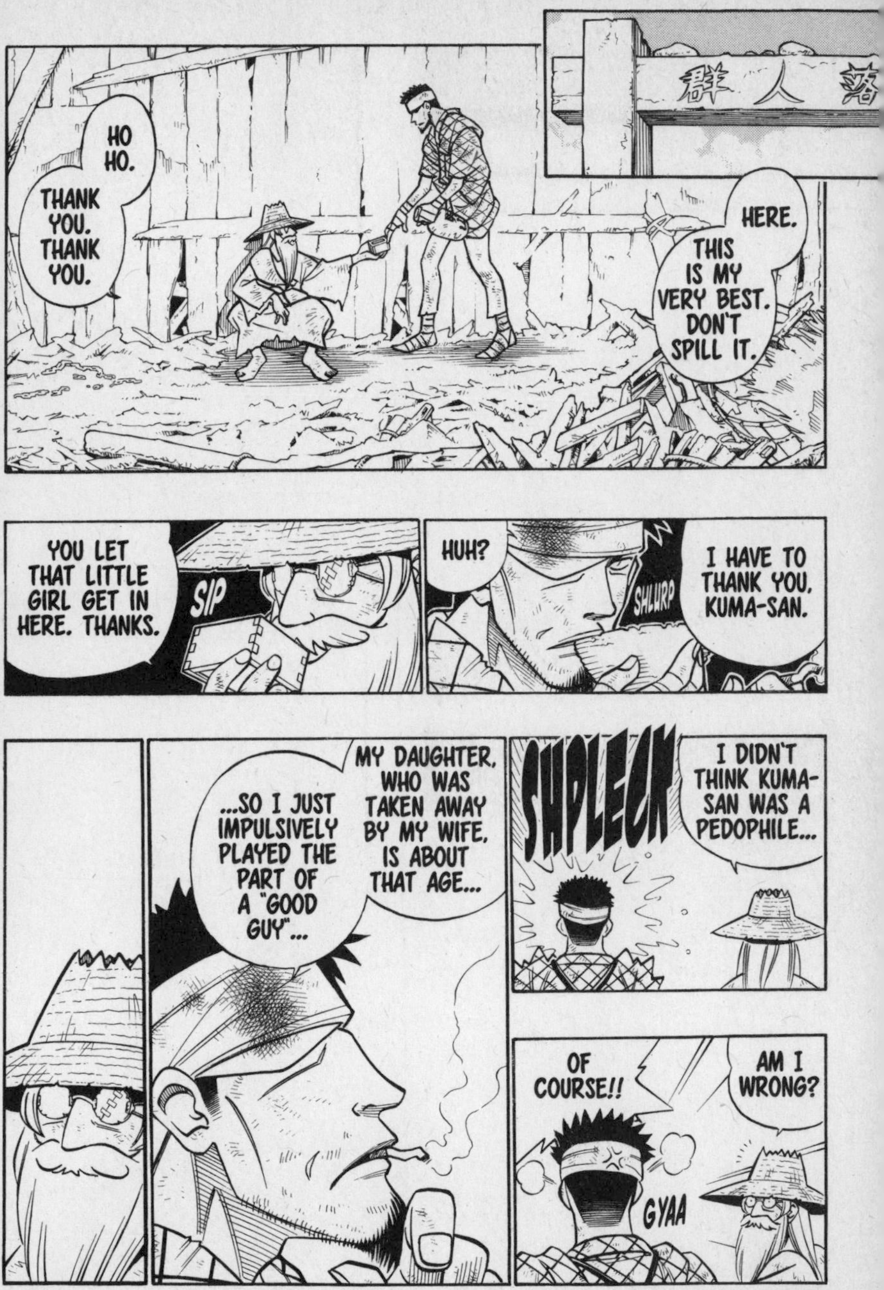
落人群
HERE. THIS IS MY VERY BEST. DON'T SPILL IT.
HO HO. THANK YOU. THANK YOU.
I HAVE TO THANK YOU, KUMA-SAN.
SHLURP
HUH?
YOU LET THAT LITTLE GIRL GET IN HERE. THANKS.
SIP
I DIDN'T THINK KUMA-SAN WAS A PEDOPHILE...
SHPLECH
AM I WRONG?
OF COURSE!!
GYAA
MY DAUGHTER, WHO WAS TAKEN AWAY BY MY WIFE, IS ABOUT THAT AGE...
...SO I JUST IMPULSIVELY PLAYED THE PART OF A "GOOD GUY"...

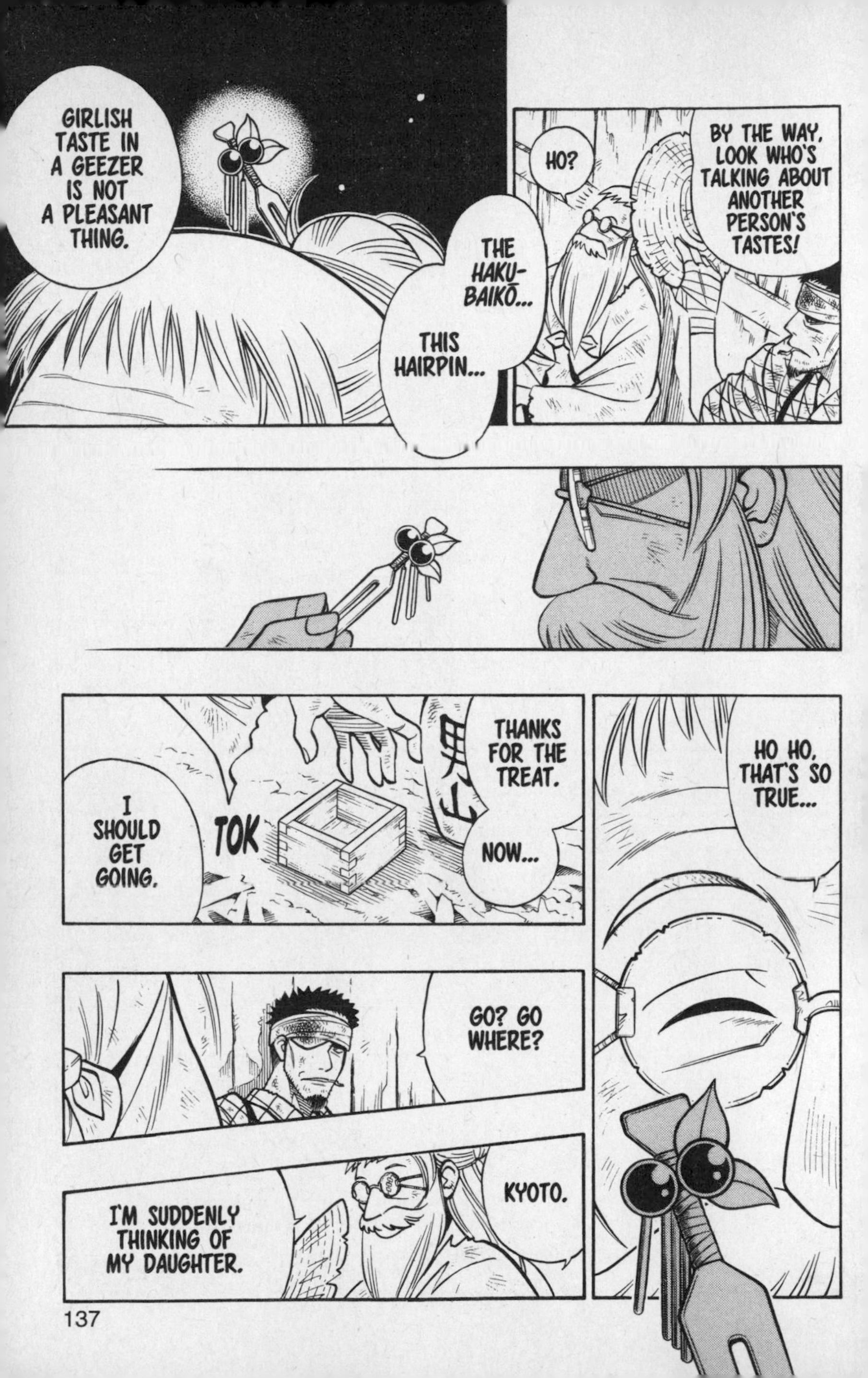
BY THE WAY, LOOK WHO'S TALKING ABOUT ANOTHER PERSON'S TASTES!
HO?
THE HAKU-BAIKŌ...
THIS HAIRPIN...
GIRLISH TASTE IN A GEEZER IS NOT A PLEASANT THING.
HO HO, THAT'S SO TRUE...
THANKS FOR THE TREAT.
男山
NOW...
TOK
I SHOULD GET GOING.
GO? GO WHERE?
KYOTO.
I'M SUDDENLY THINKING OF MY DAUGHTER.

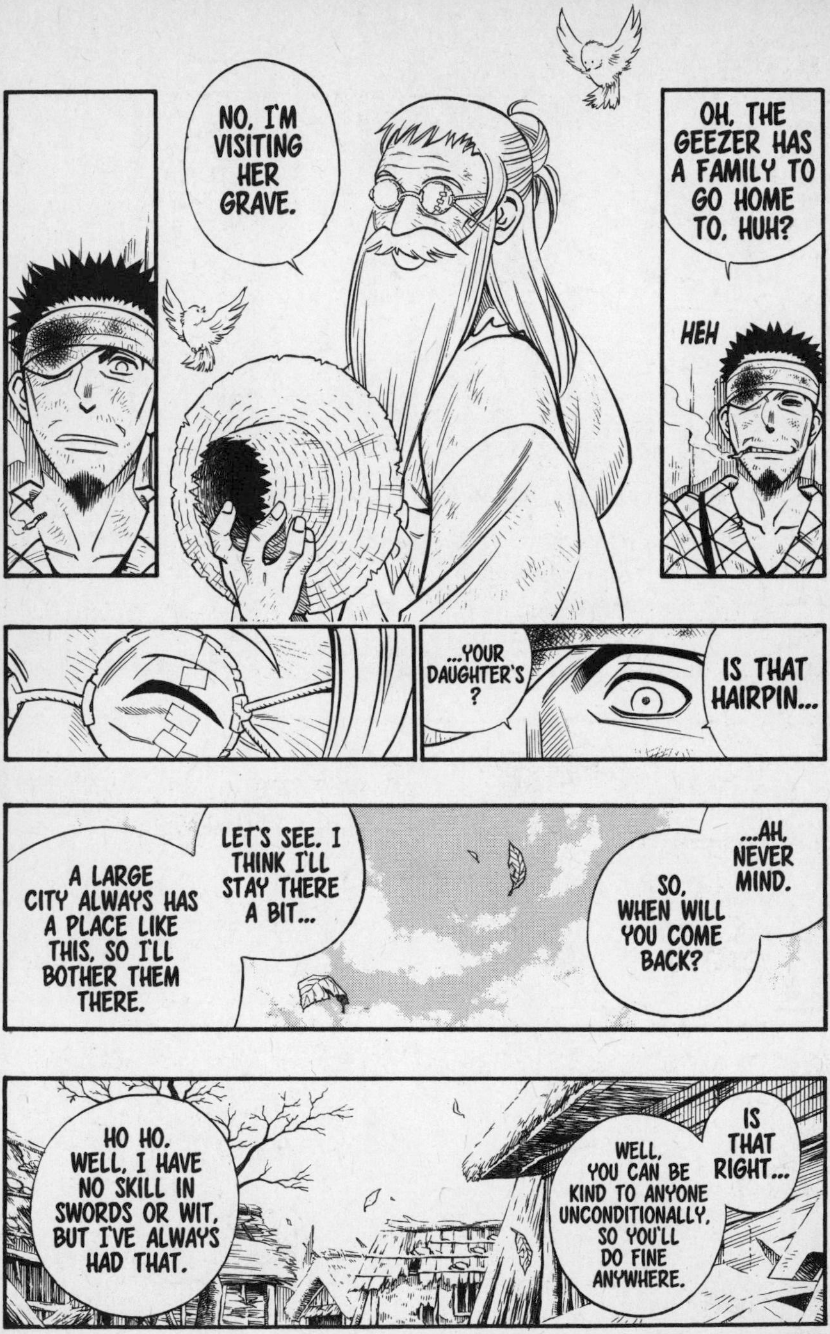
OH, THE GEEZER HAS A FAMILY TO GO HOME TO, HUH?
HEH
NO, I'M VISITING HER GRAVE.
IS THAT HAIRPIN...
...YOUR DAUGHTER'S?
...AH, NEVER MIND.
SO, WHEN WILL YOU COME BACK?
LET'S SEE. I THINK I'LL STAY THERE A BIT...
A LARGE CITY ALWAYS HAS A PLACE LIKE THIS, SO I'LL BOTHER THEM THERE.
IS THAT RIGHT...
WELL, YOU CAN BE KIND TO ANYONE UNCONDITIONALLY, SO YOU'LL DO FINE ANYWHERE.
HO HO. WELL, I HAVE NO SKILL IN SWORDS OR WIT, BUT I'VE ALWAYS HAD THAT.

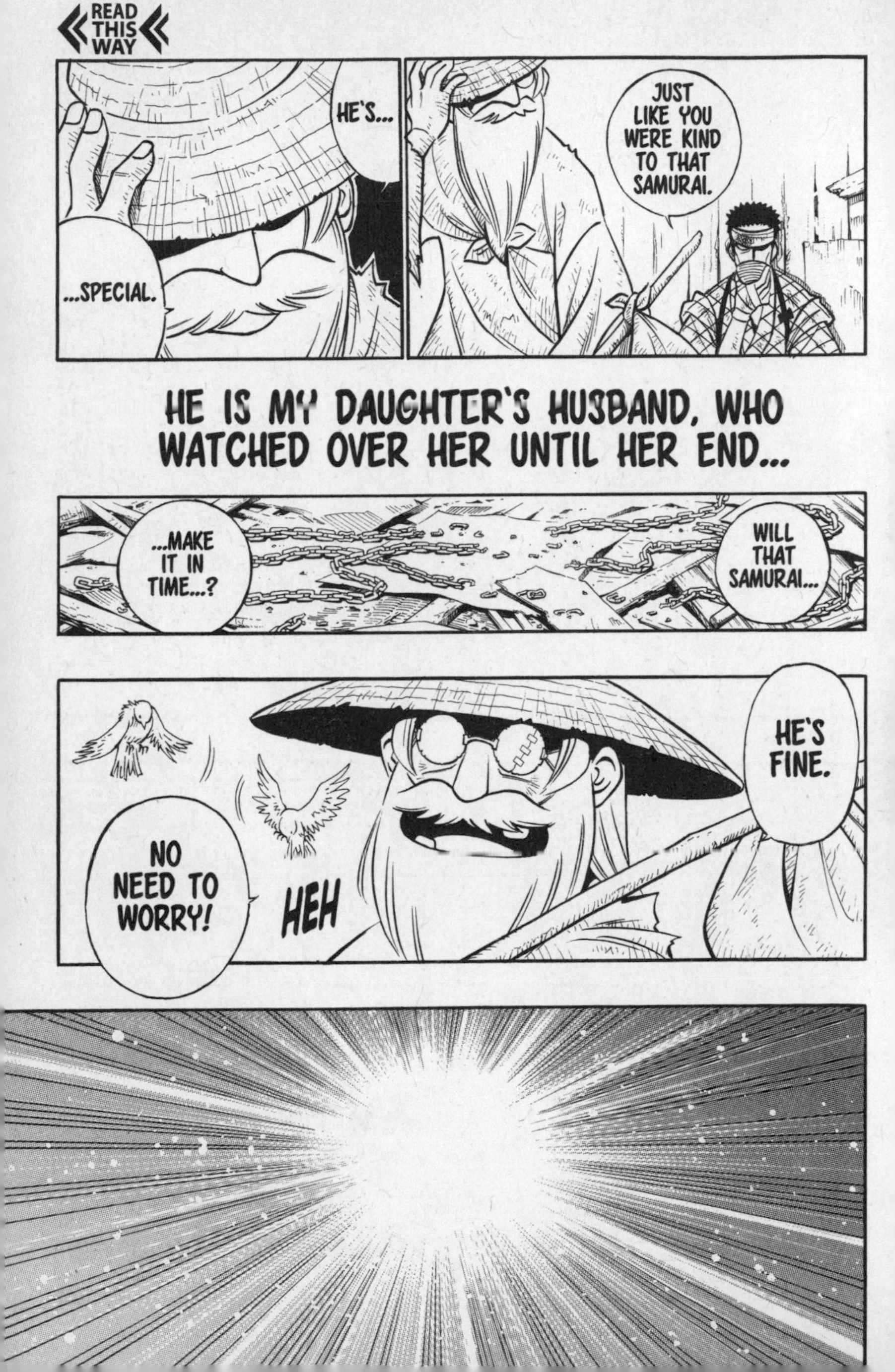
READ THIS WAY
JUST LIKE YOU WERE KIND TO THAT SAMURAI.
HE'S...
...SPECIAL.
HE IS MY DAUGHTER'S HUSBAND, WHO WATCHED OVER HER UNTIL HER END...
WILL THAT SAMURAI...
...MAKE IT IN TIME...?
HE'S FINE.
HEH
NO NEED TO WORRY!

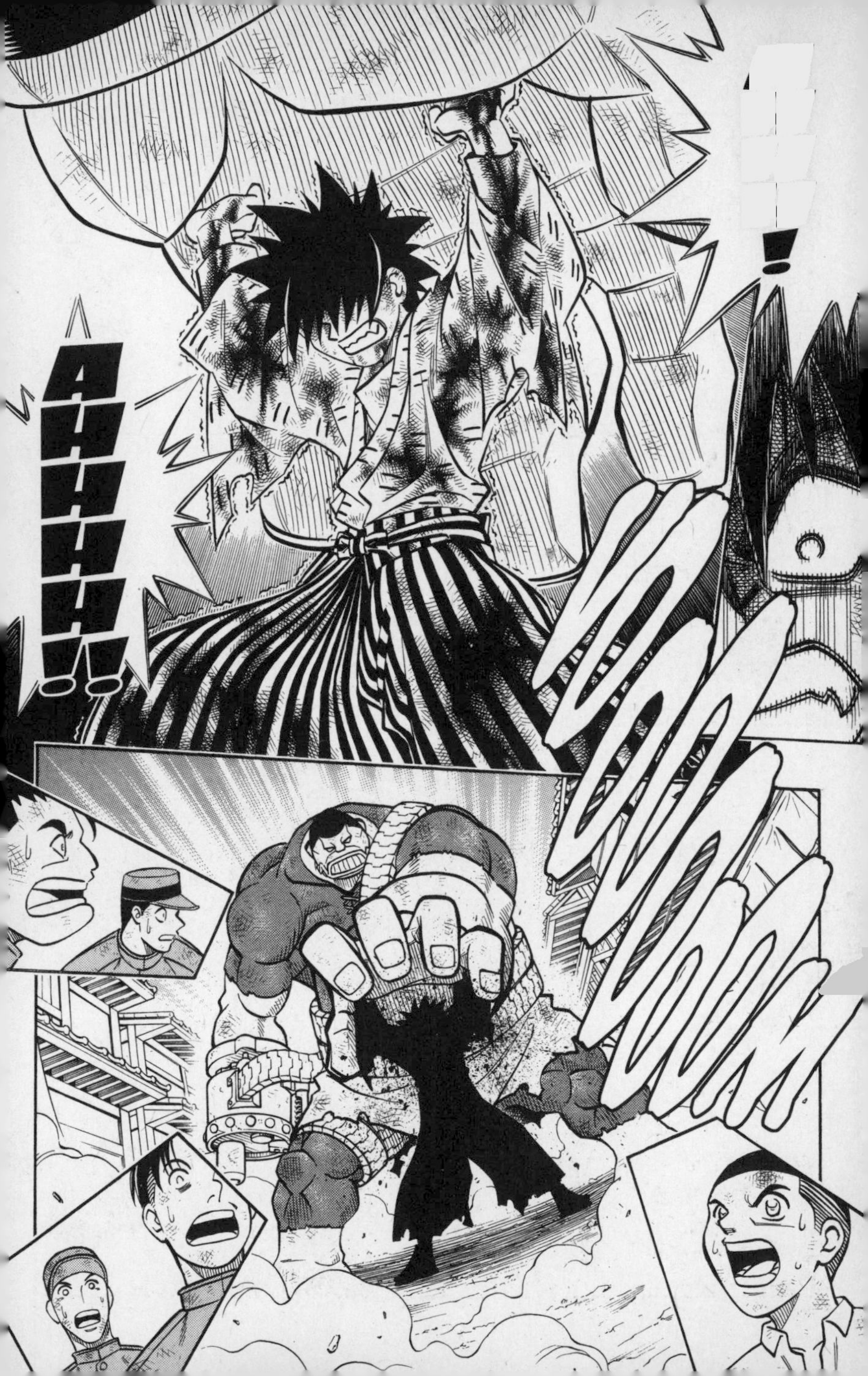
AHHHH!!

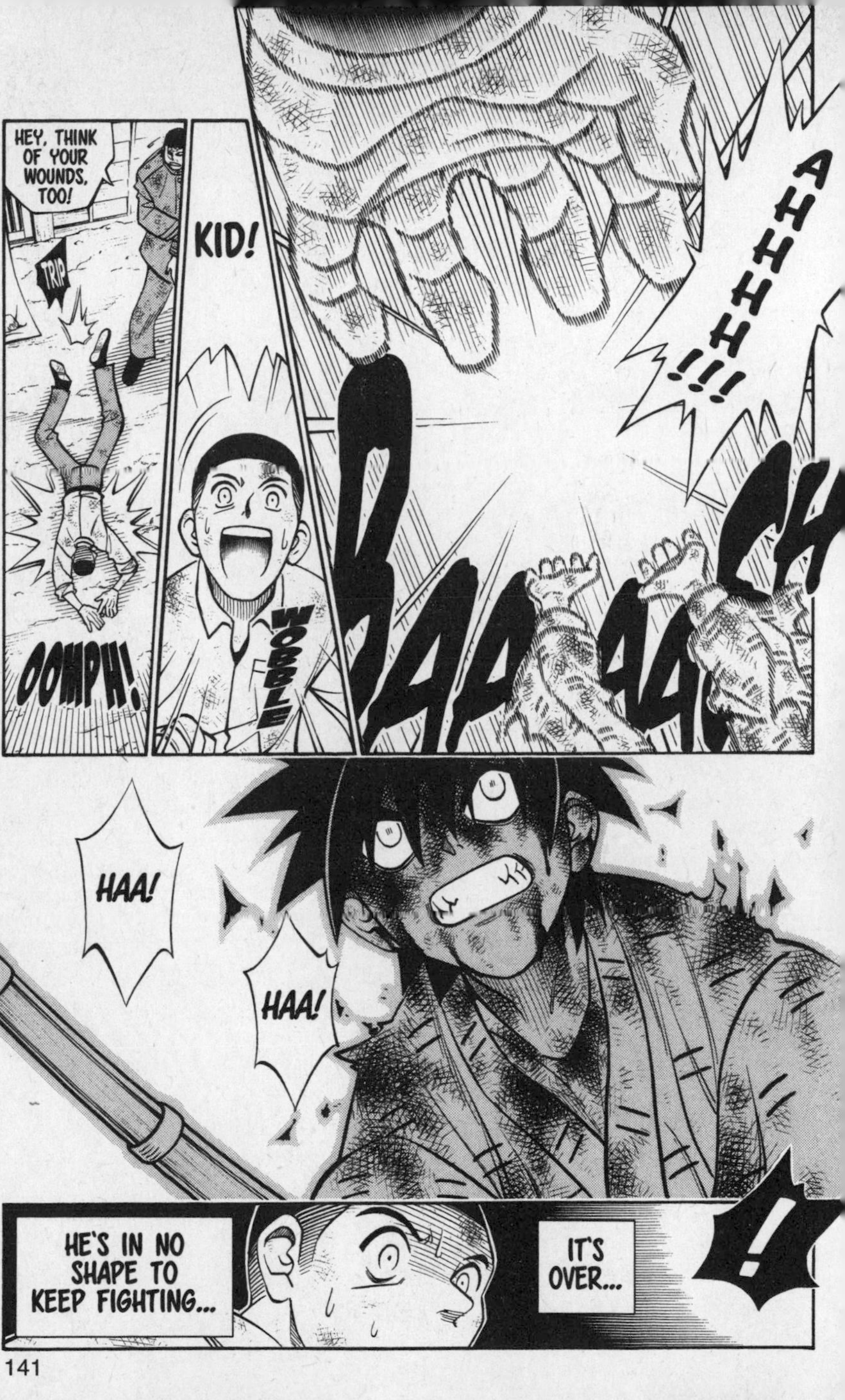
AHHHHH!!!!
BAAAACH
KID!
WOBBLE
HEY, THINK OF YOUR WOUNDS, TOO!
TRIP
OOMPH!
HAA!
HAA!
!
IT'S OVER...
HE'S IN NO SHAPE TO KEEP FIGHTING...

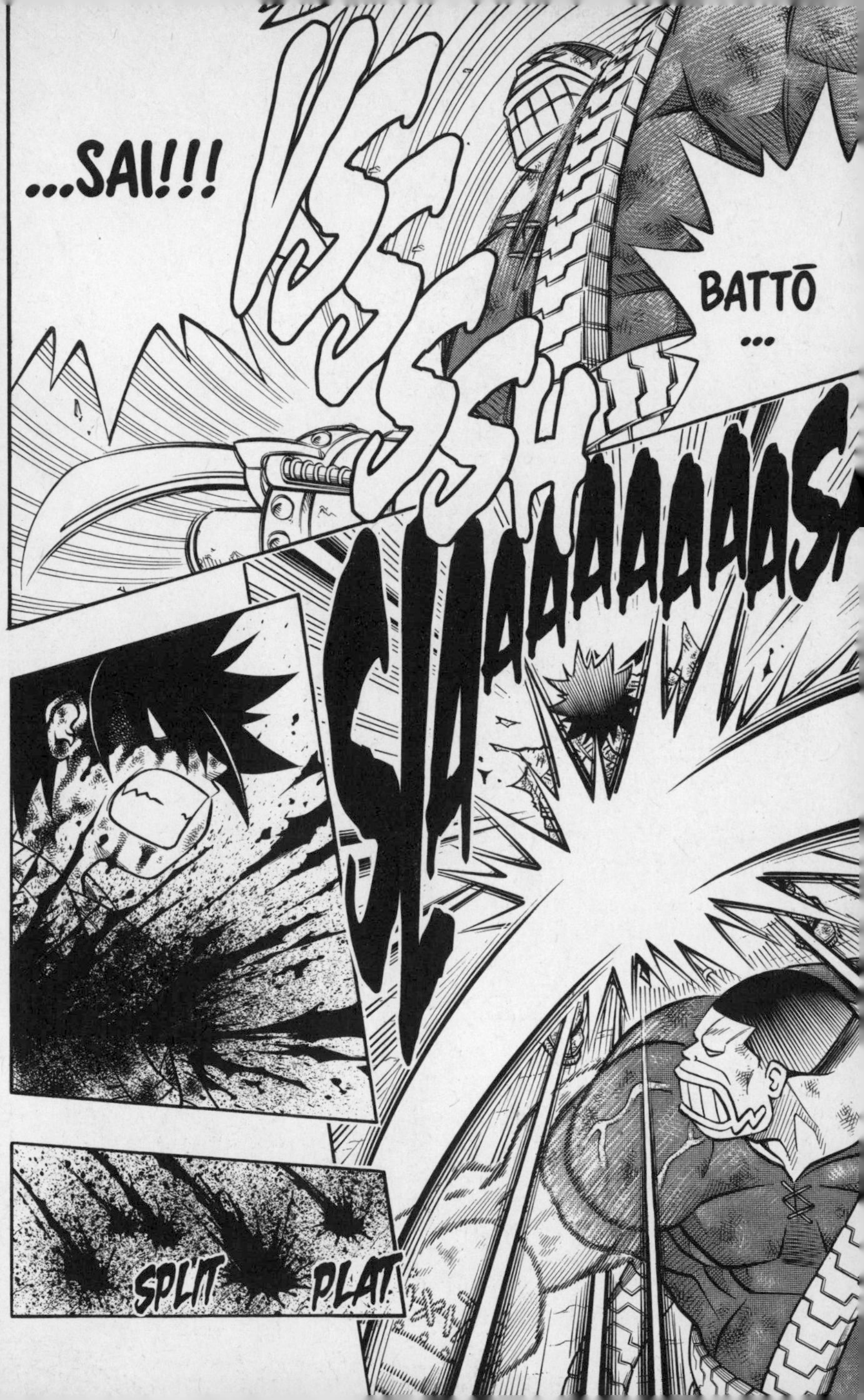
BATTŌ
...
...SAI!!!
PLAT
SPLIT

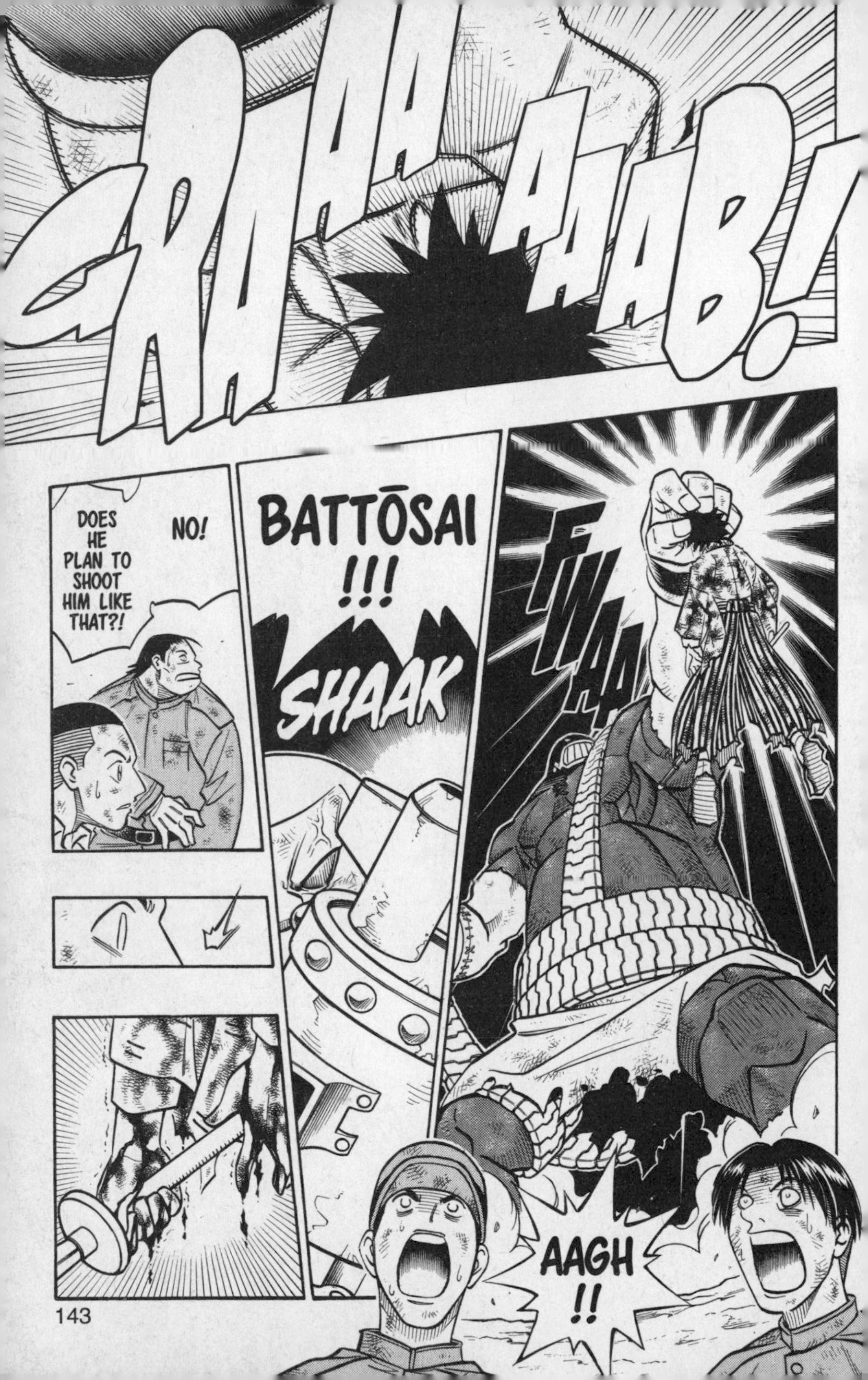
GRAAAAAB!
FWAA
AAGH!!
BATTŌSAI!!!
SHAAK
NO!
DOES HE PLAN TO SHOOT HIM LIKE THAT?!

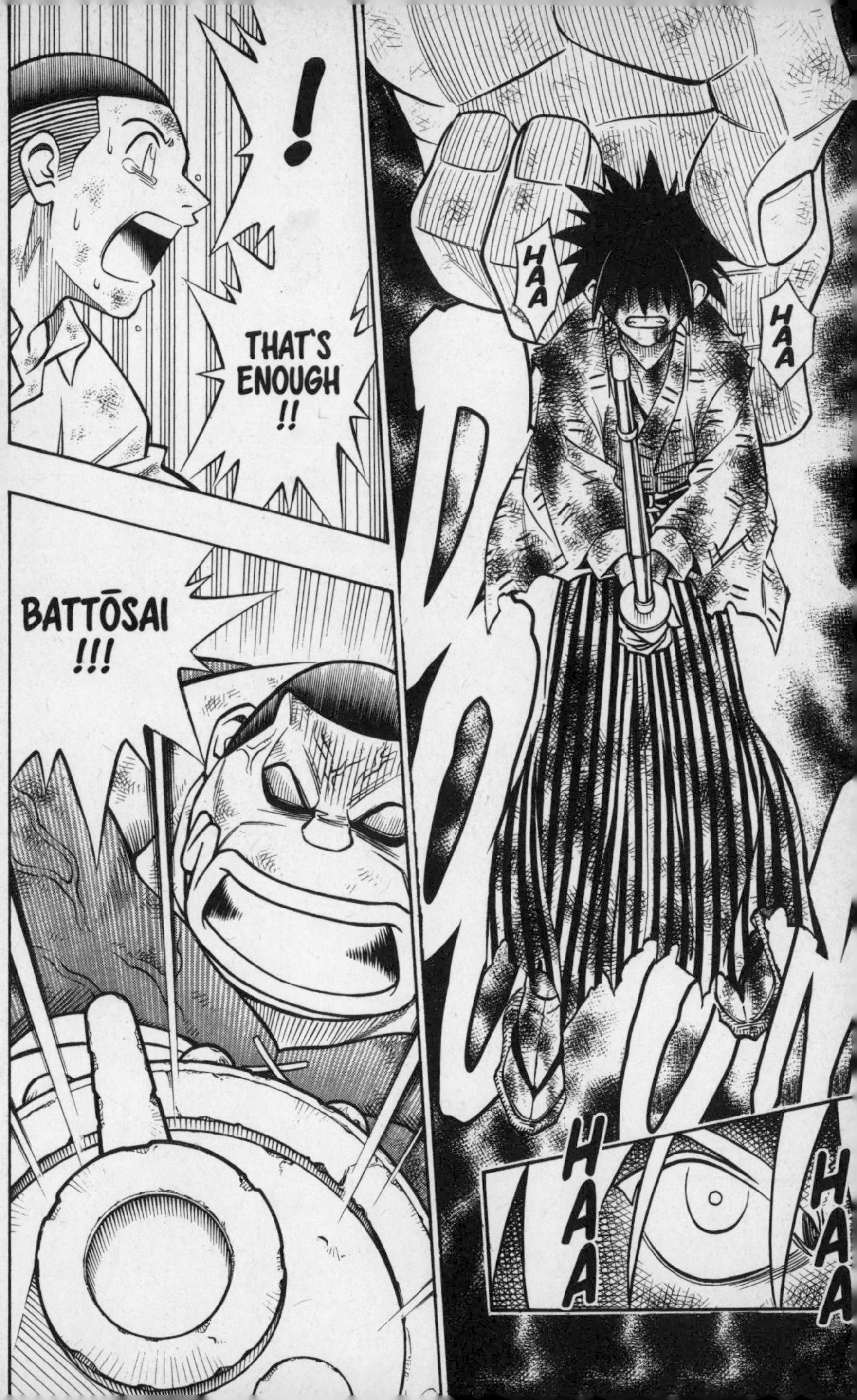
HAA
HAA
HAA
HAA
!
THAT'S ENOUGH !!
BATTŌSAI !!!

READ THIS WAY

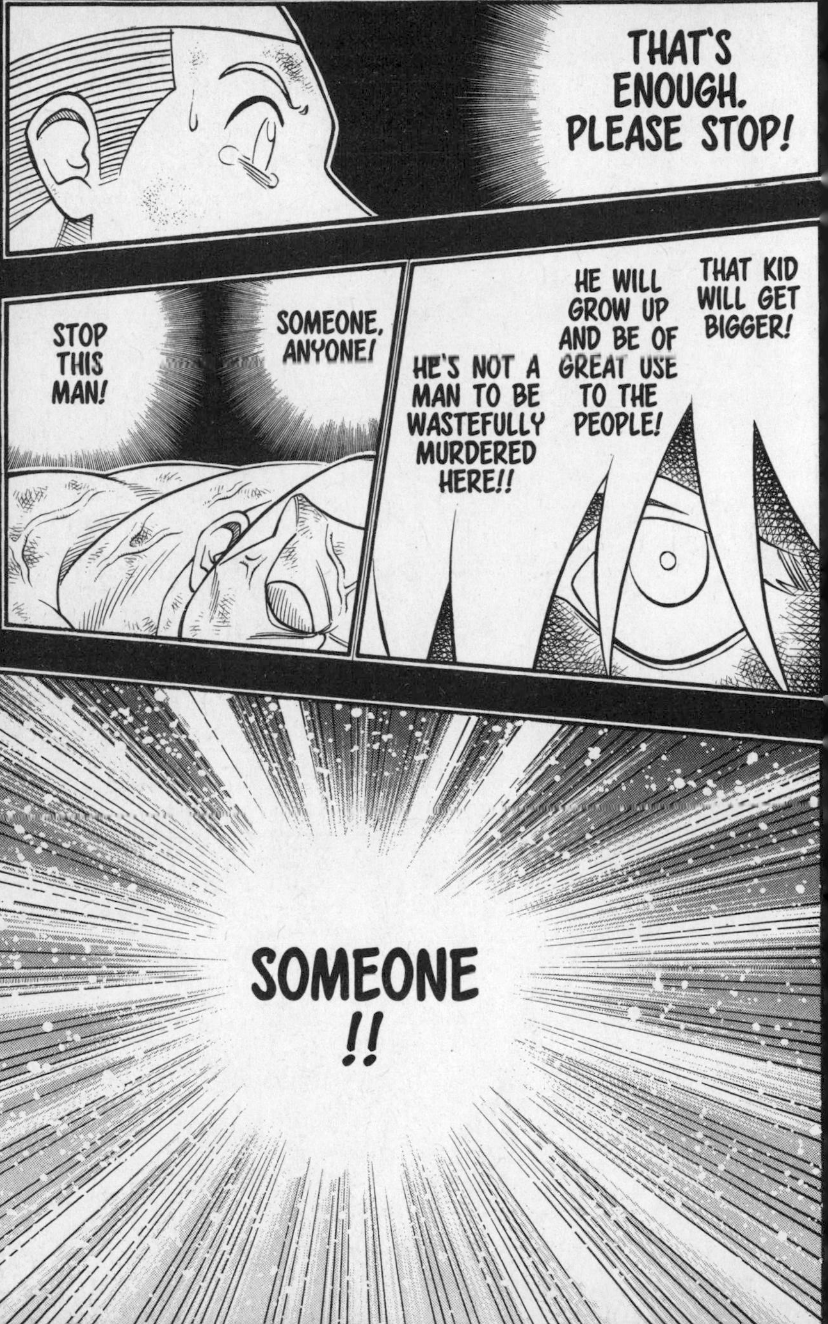
THAT'S ENOUGH. PLEASE STOP!
THAT KID WILL GET BIGGER!
HE WILL GROW UP AND BE OF GREAT USE TO THE PEOPLE!
HE'S NOT A MAN TO BE WASTEFULLY MURDERED HERE!!
SOMEONE, ANYONE!
STOP THIS MAN!
SOMEONE !!

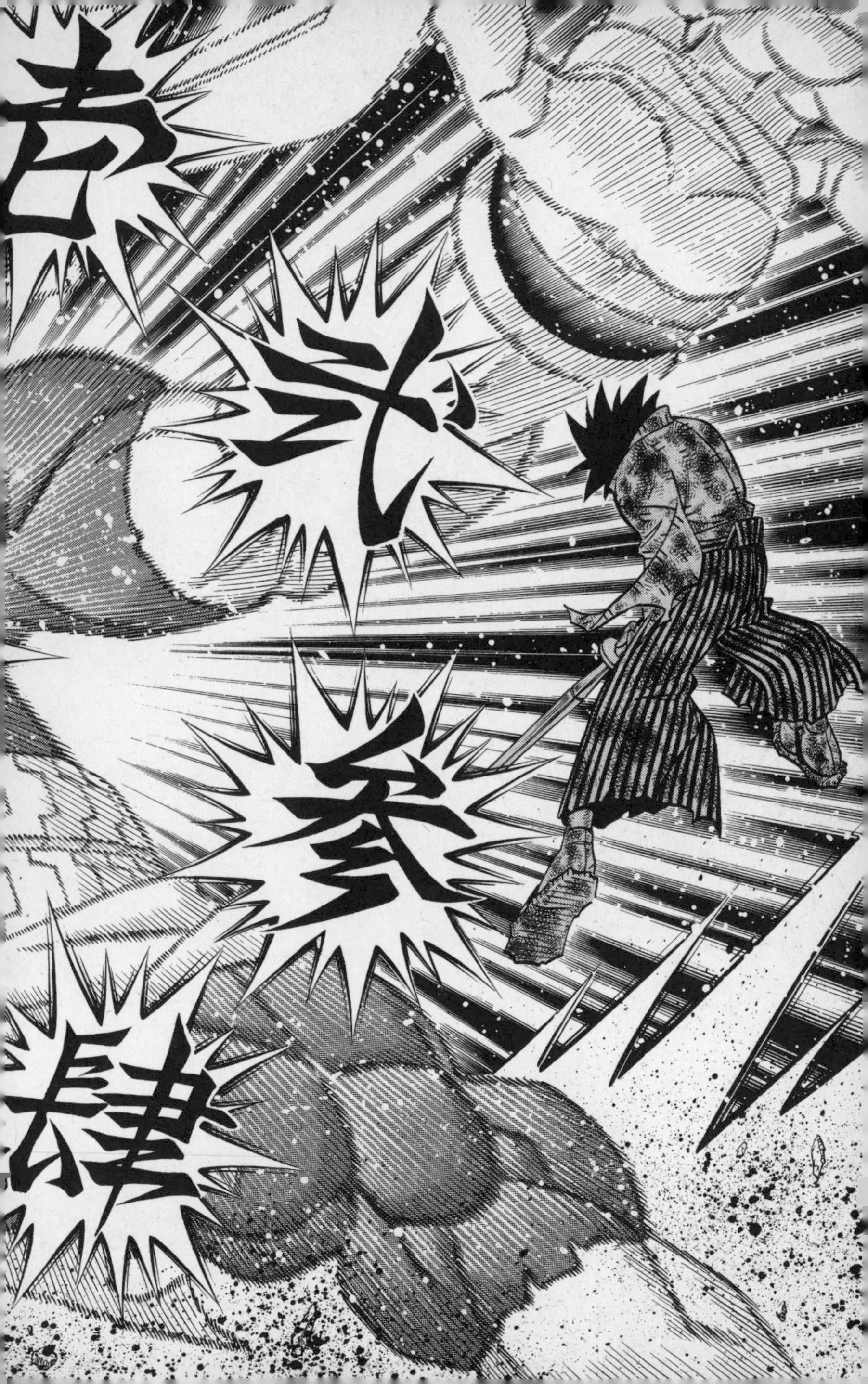
壱
弐
参
肆

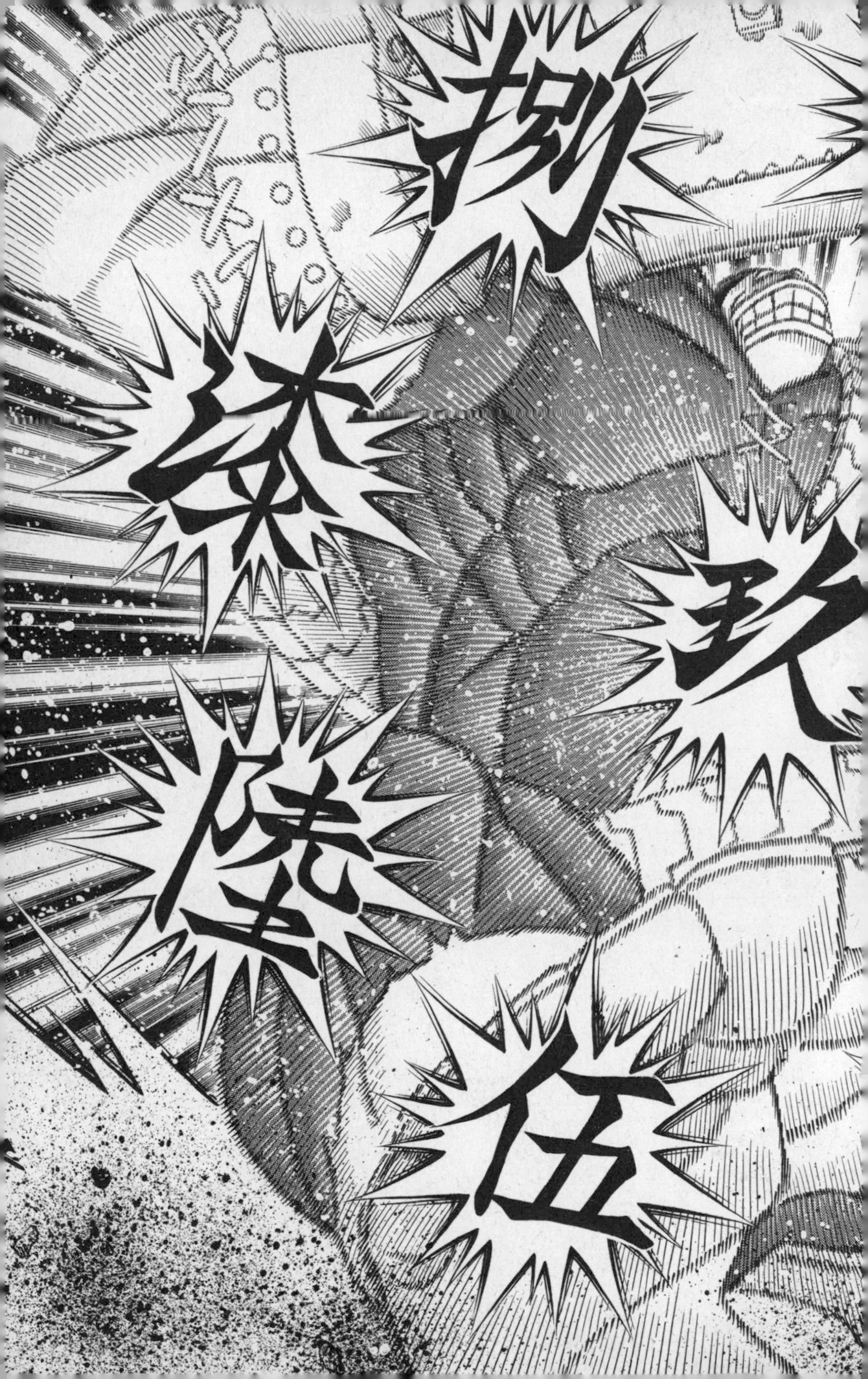
捌
玖
柒
陸
伍

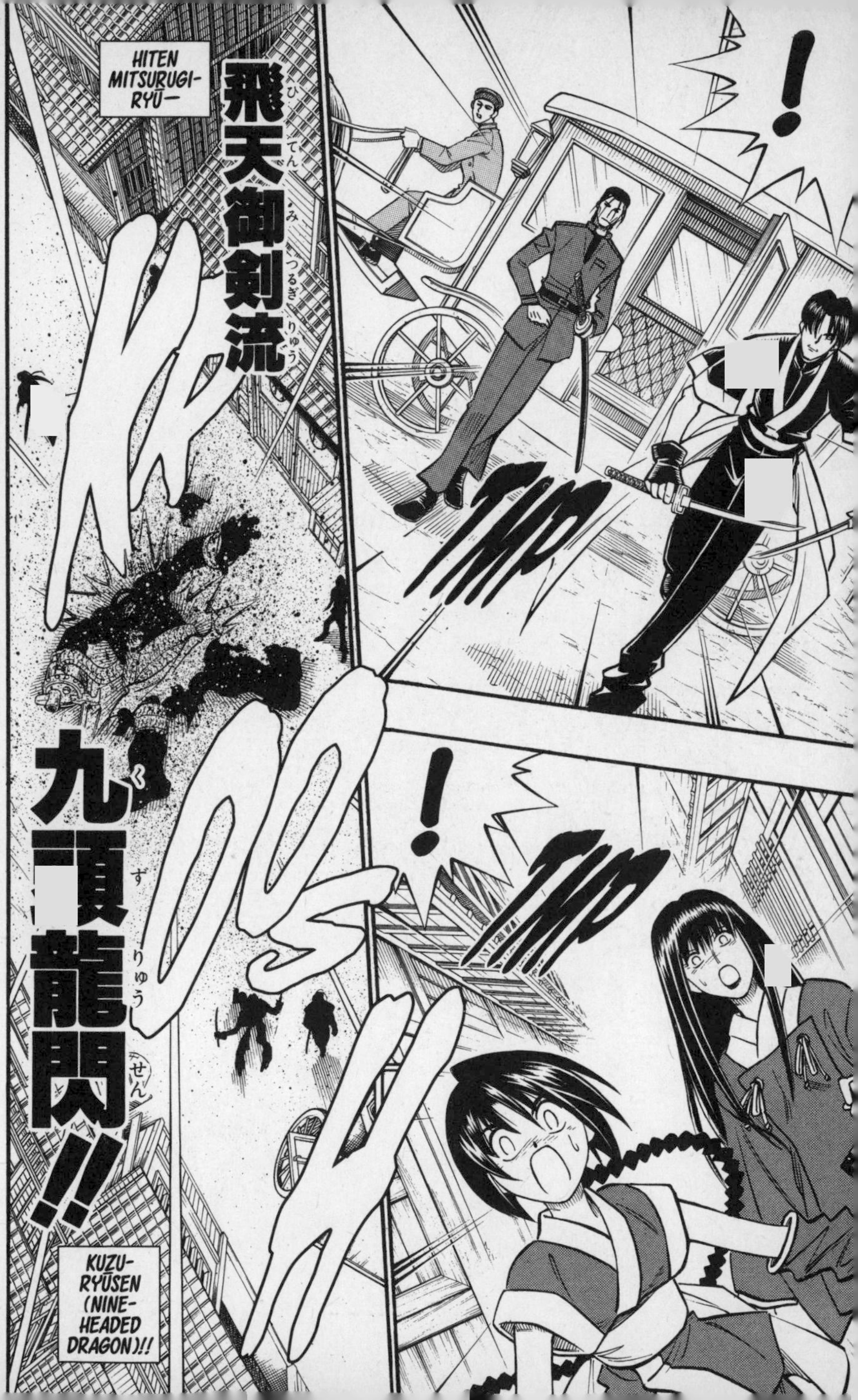
!
TMP
!
TMP
HITEN MITSURUGI-RYŪ—
飛天御剣流
九頭龍閃!!
KUZU-RYŪSEN (NINE-HEADED DRAGON)!!

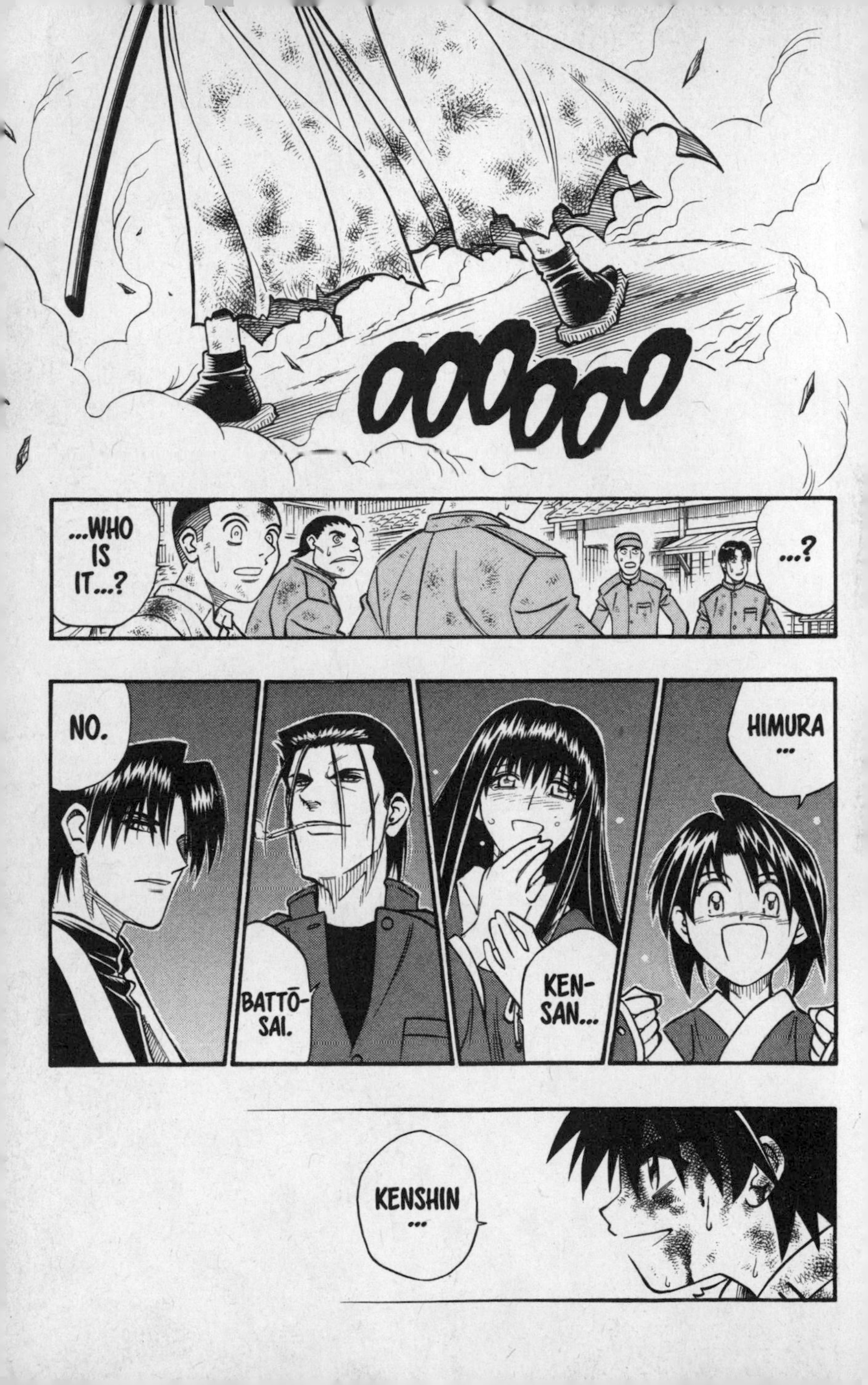
OOOOOO
...?
...WHO IS IT...?
HIMURA ...
KEN-SAN...
BATTŌSAI.
NO.
KENSHIN ...

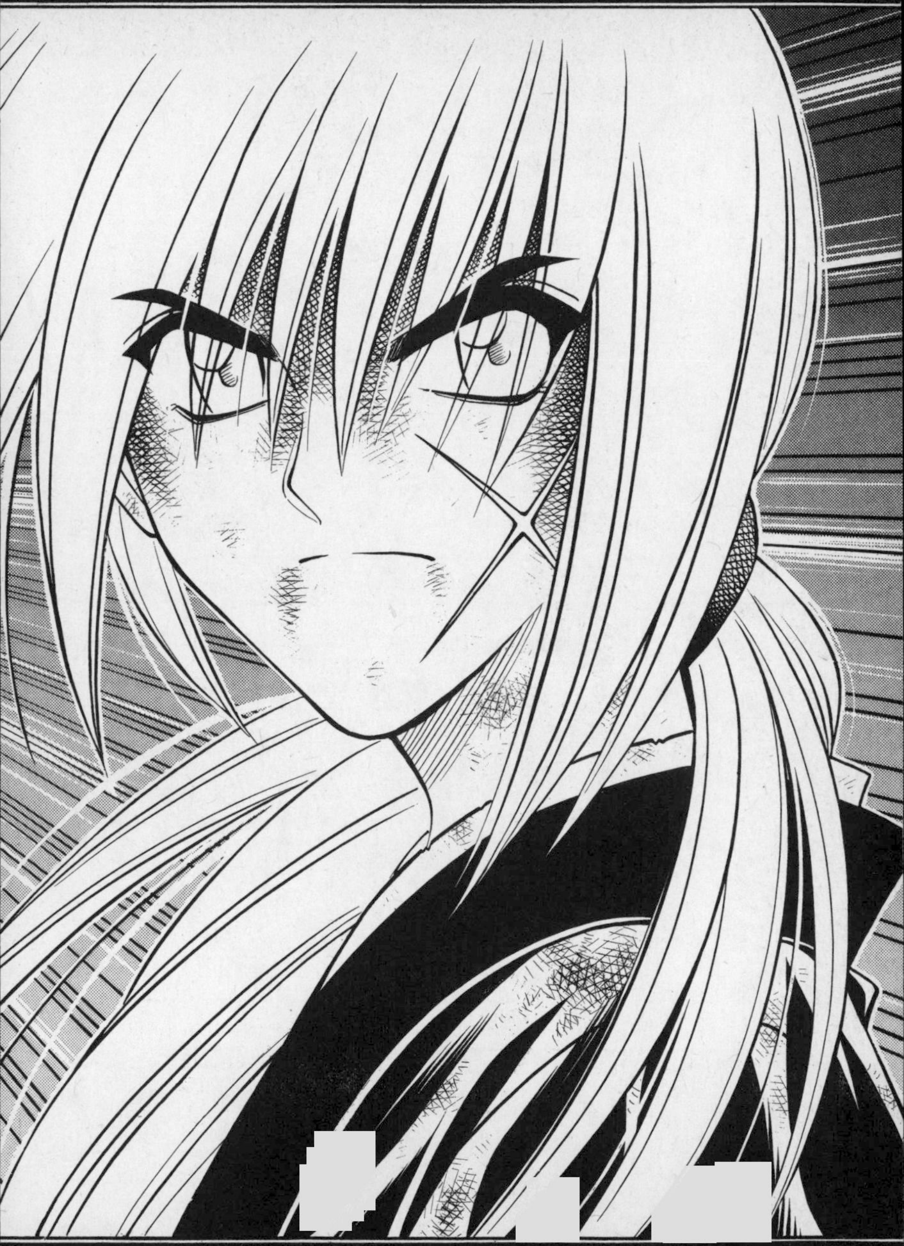

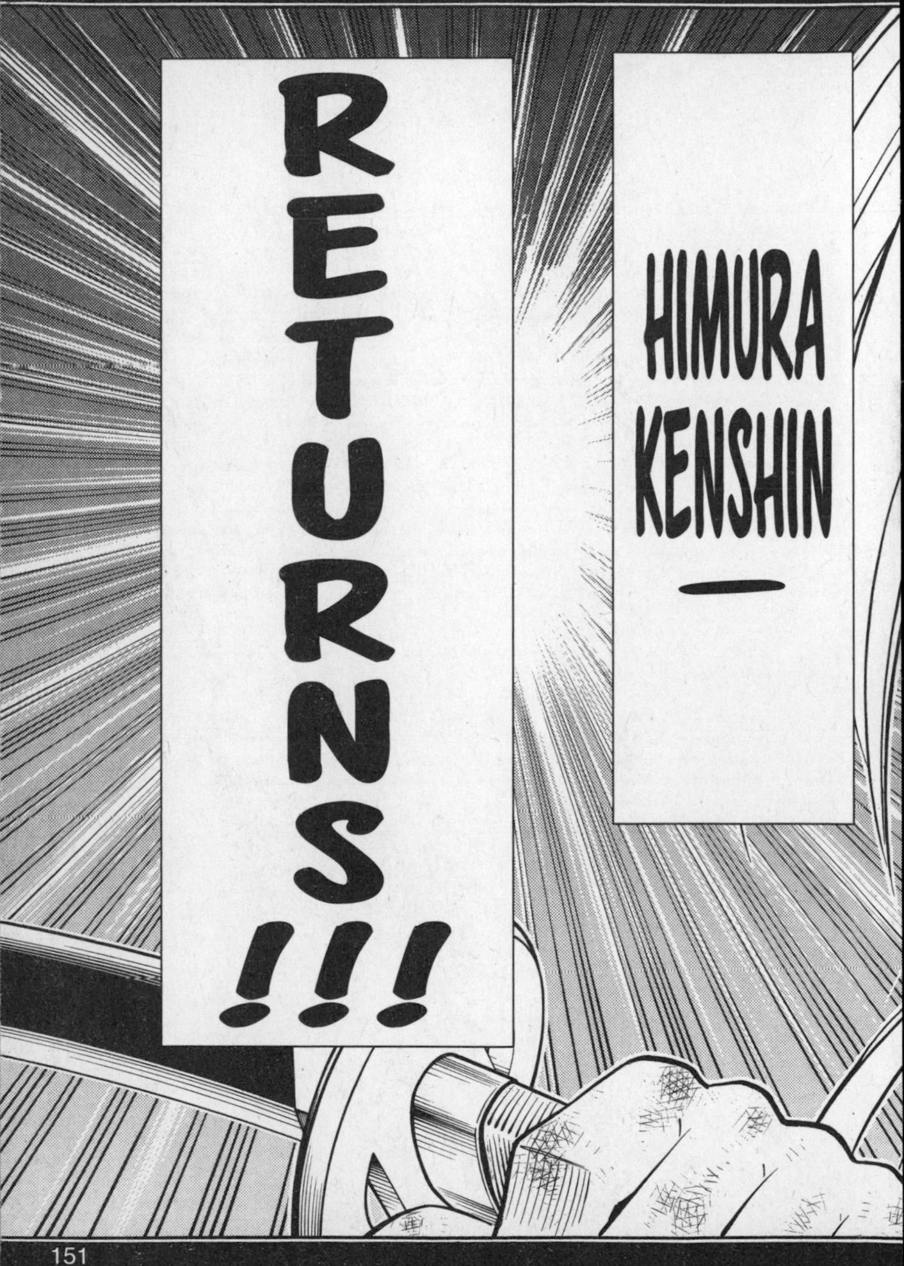
HIMURA KENSHIN —
RETURNS!!!

The Secret Life of Characters (48)
—Geezer—

The episodes with the Geezer where "the main character sits amongst the homeless" could at one glance be seen as being influenced by *Spawn*. So then, the popular theory is that Geezer is the mysterious old man, Cagliostro, who gives advice to Spawn. But this is dead wrong. The actual American comic it is influenced by is *Silver Surfer* by Moebius. So then, the motif (especially concerning the return of the main character) is actually "Now go, Robot!," a story by Ōishi Makoto-*sensei*, targeted at younger elementary school kids. In this story, a toy robot falls off a moving truck, and starts a journey to find its owner. The robot that gets dirty and damaged is Kenshin, and the dump he gets thrown into is the Fallen village, and the empty milk can he meets there is the Geezer. (By the way, the stuffed teddy bear missing one eye is Kuma). "Now go, Robot!" was recommended to Watsuki by my older brother, and I was in high school when I read it. Honestly speaking, I was moved to tears. There also is "A Witch in the Classroom" (this one is so sad, I cried) and the like, all wonderful works by Ōishi Makoto-*sensei*, that do not allow me to discount children's books. Kenshin's return, in the end, can only be accomplished by himself. My intention from the beginning was to have Geezer just give a light shove forward, but did it go well...? As I wrote in the Tomoe piece, lack of time, willpower, and endurance is a big problem for me.

Geezer shows up once more in this series. He happens to have quite an important role.

There is no real model in terms of design. When I considered that he is homeless, that he has an unusual personality, and that he does not show his true thoughts easily, he turned out like this. I did realize that he is very similar to Grandpa Bob in *BØY—Boy—* by Umezawa Haruto-*sensei*, but that was only after I finished. I thought to myself, I should broaden my creative scope a bit more.

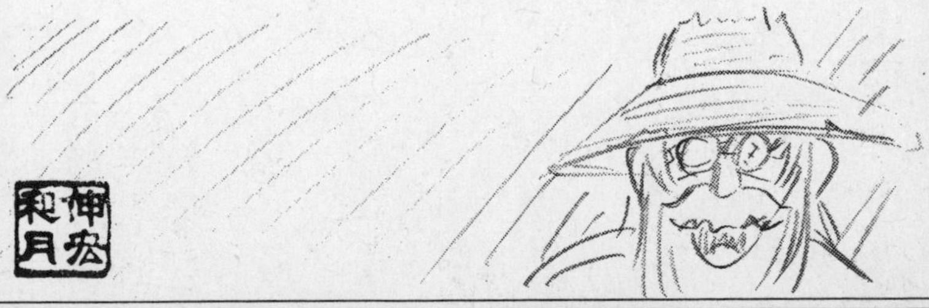

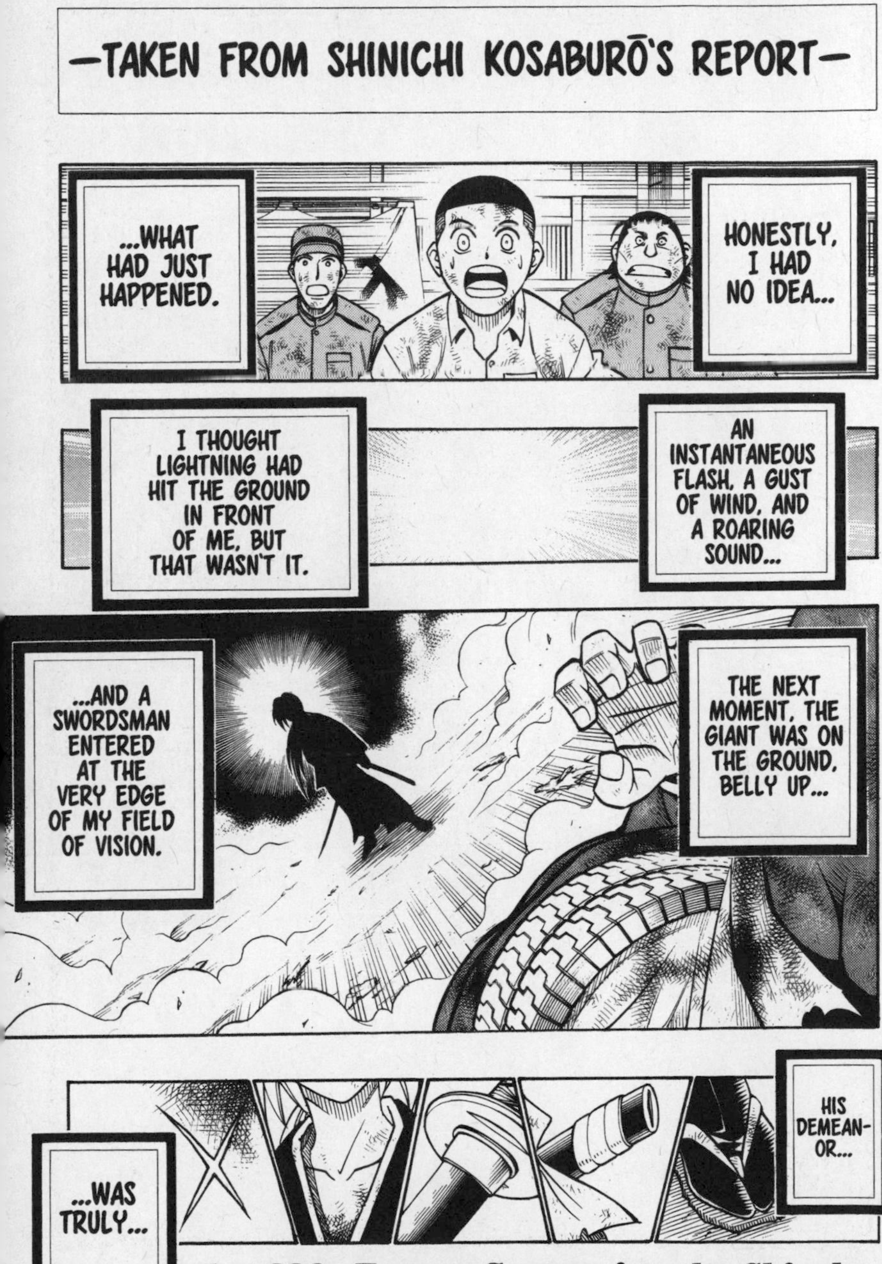
—TAKEN FROM SHINICHI KOSABURŌ'S REPORT—
HONESTLY, I HAD NO IDEA...
...WHAT HAD JUST HAPPENED.
AN INSTANTANEOUS FLASH, A GUST OF WIND, AND A ROARING SOUND...
I THOUGHT LIGHTNING HAD HIT THE GROUND IN FRONT OF ME, BUT THAT WASN'T IT.
THE NEXT MOMENT, THE GIANT WAS ON THE GROUND, BELLY UP...
...AND A SWORDSMAN ENTERED AT THE VERY EDGE OF MY FIELD OF VISION.
HIS DEMEAN-OR...
...WAS TRULY...

Act 226—From a Samurai to the *Shizoku*

Act 226
From a Samurai to the *Shizoku*

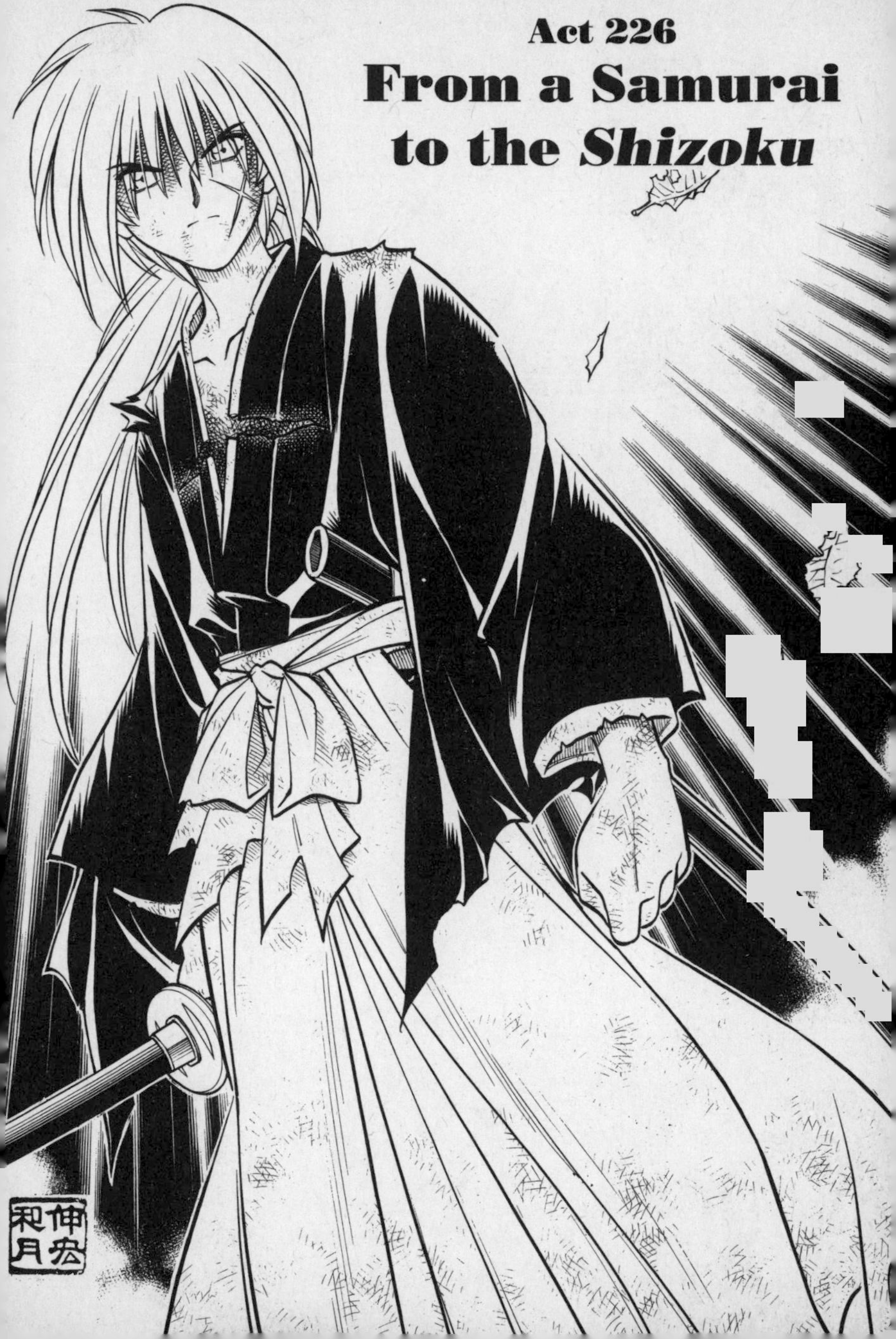

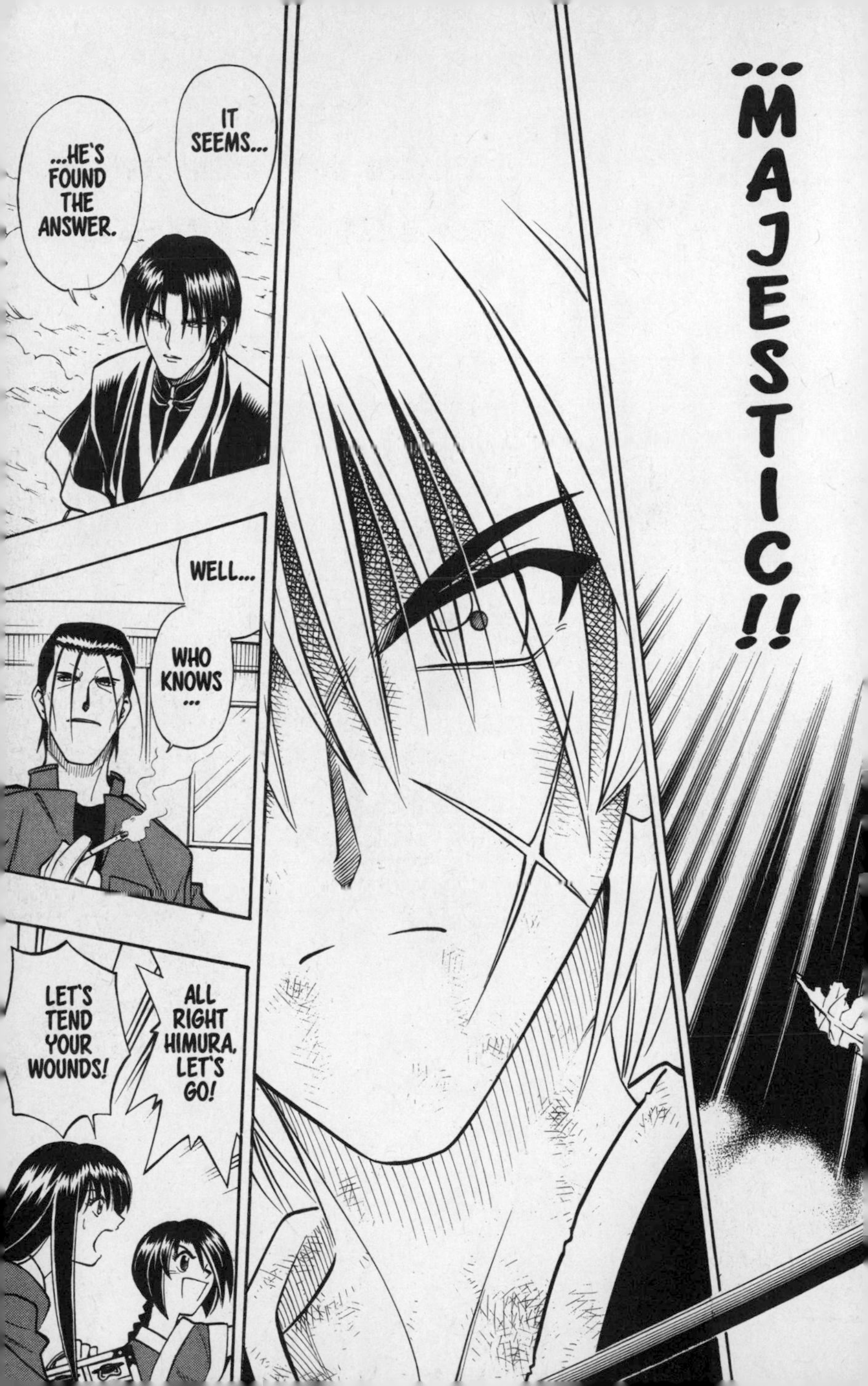
...MAJESTIC!!
IT SEEMS...
...HE'S FOUND THE ANSWER.
WELL...
WHO KNOWS...
ALL RIGHT HIMURA, LET'S GO!
LET'S TEND YOUR WOUNDS!

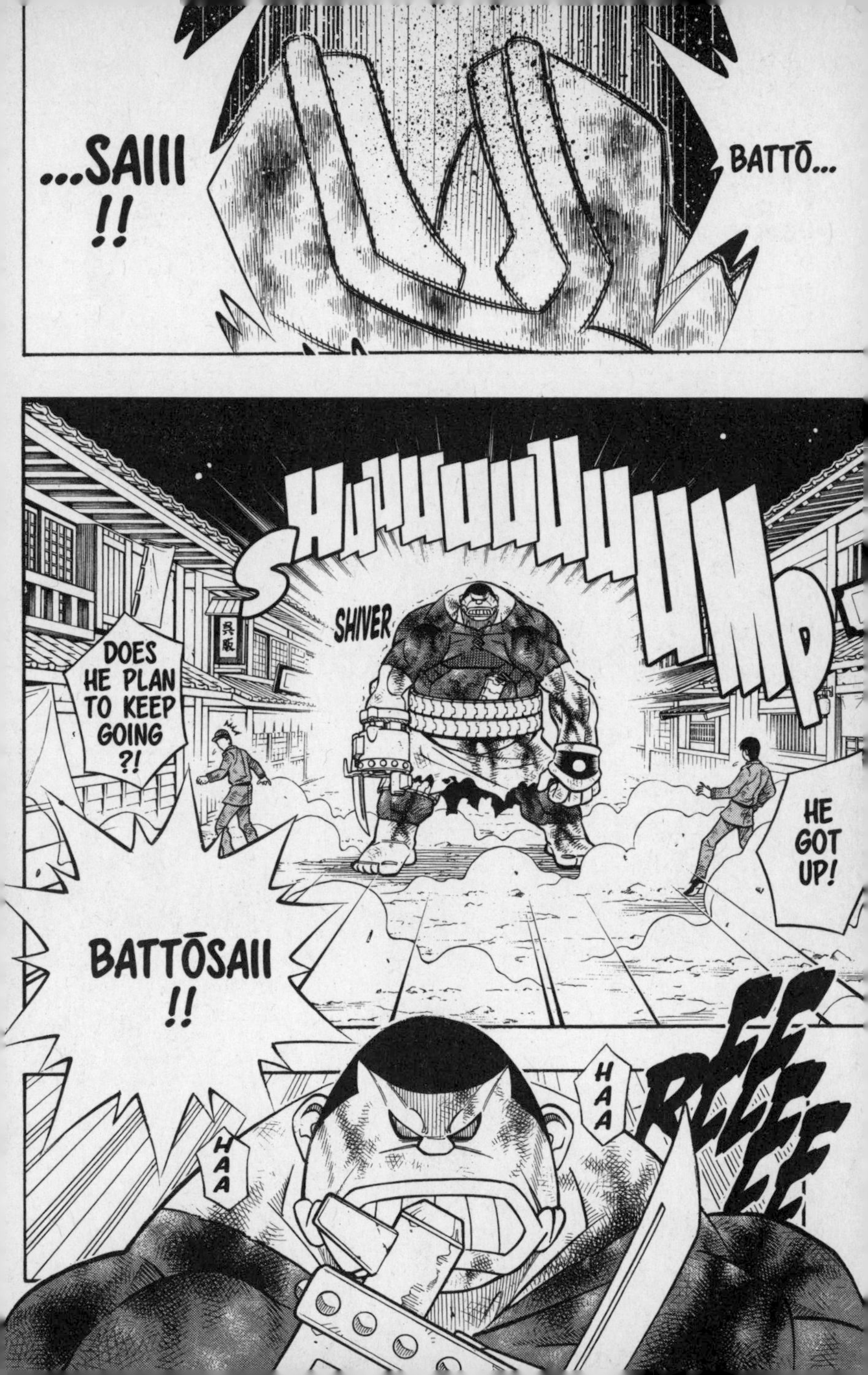
BATTŌ...
...SAIII !!
HE GOT UP!
SHIVER
DOES HE PLAN TO KEEP GOING ?!
BATTŌSAIII !!
HAA HAA
HAA HAA

READ THIS WAY

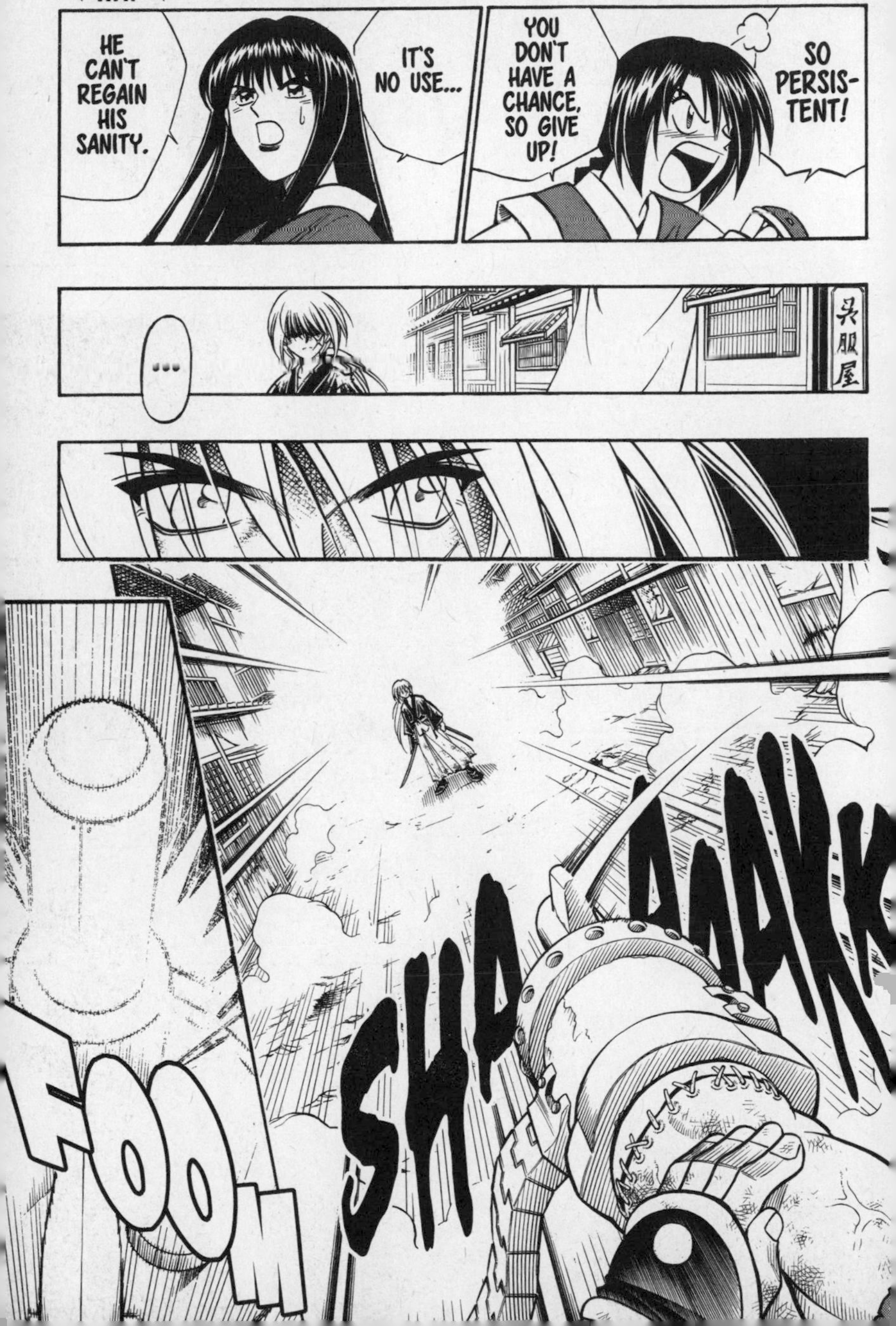

SO PERSIS-TENT!
YOU DON'T HAVE A CHANCE, SO GIVE UP!
IT'S NO USE...
HE CAN'T REGAIN HIS SANITY.
呉服屋
...
SHAAAAK
FOOOM

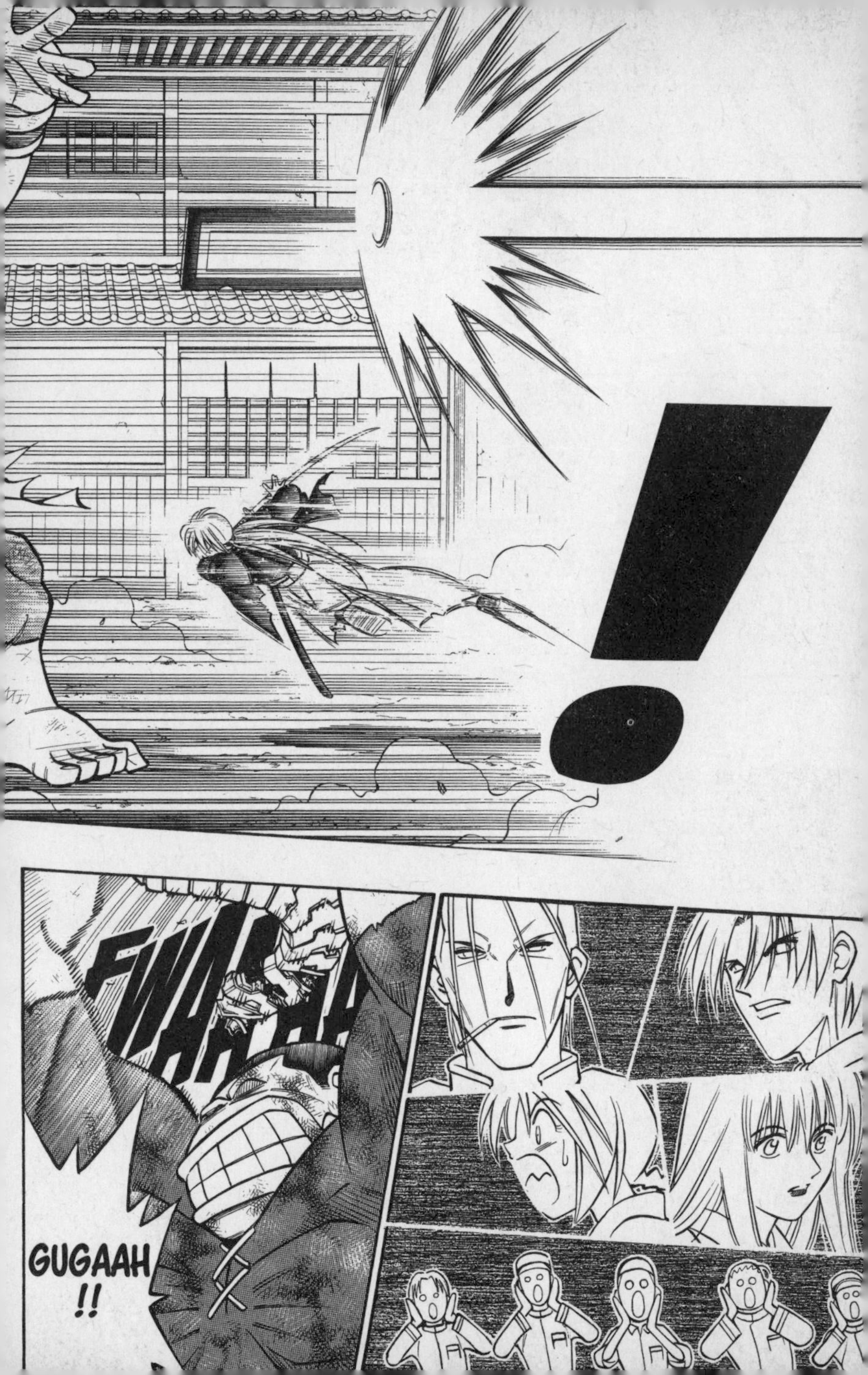
!
GUGAAH !!

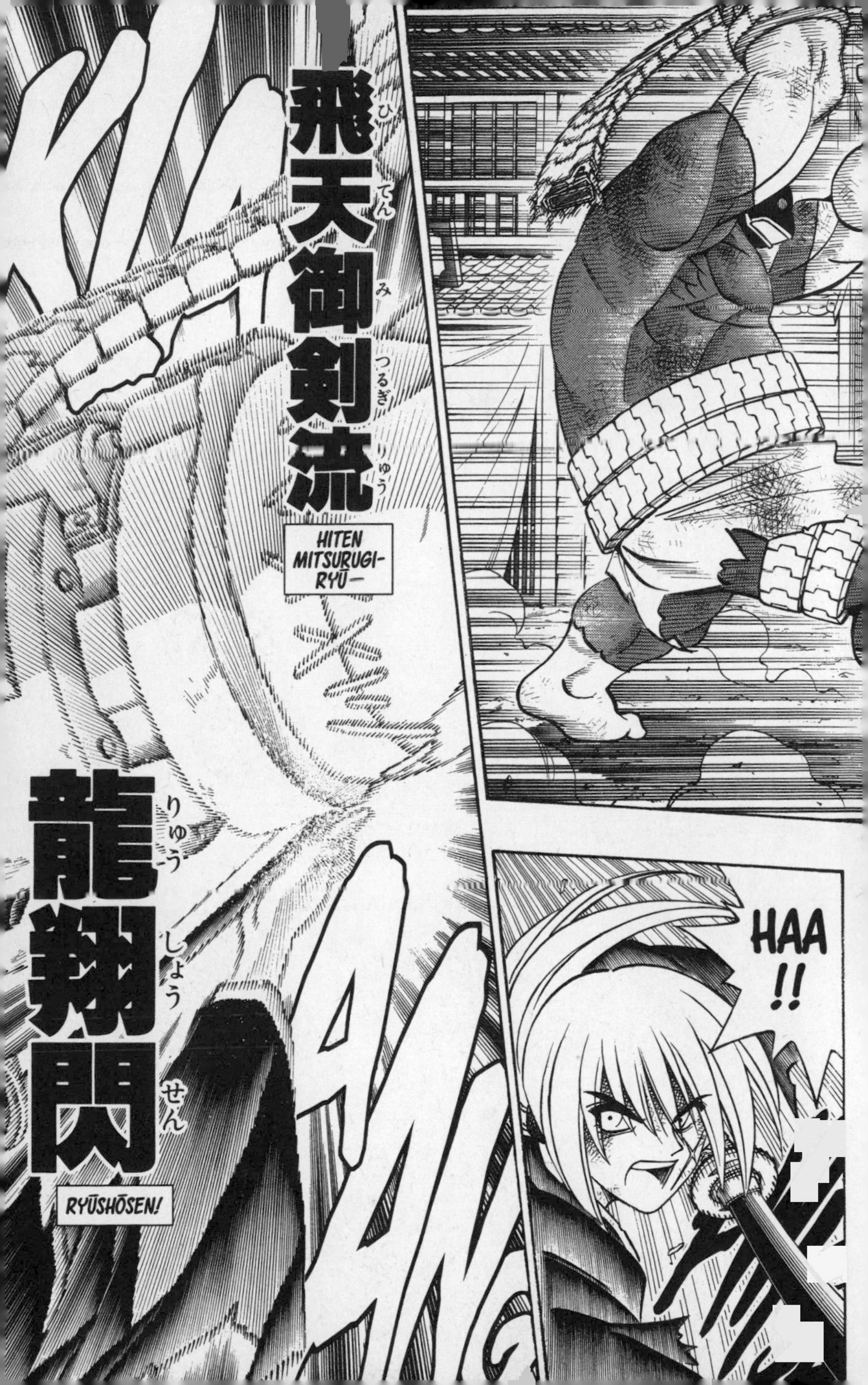
HAA!!
飛天御剣流
HITEN MITSURUGI-RYŪ—
龍翔閃
RYŪSHŌSEN!

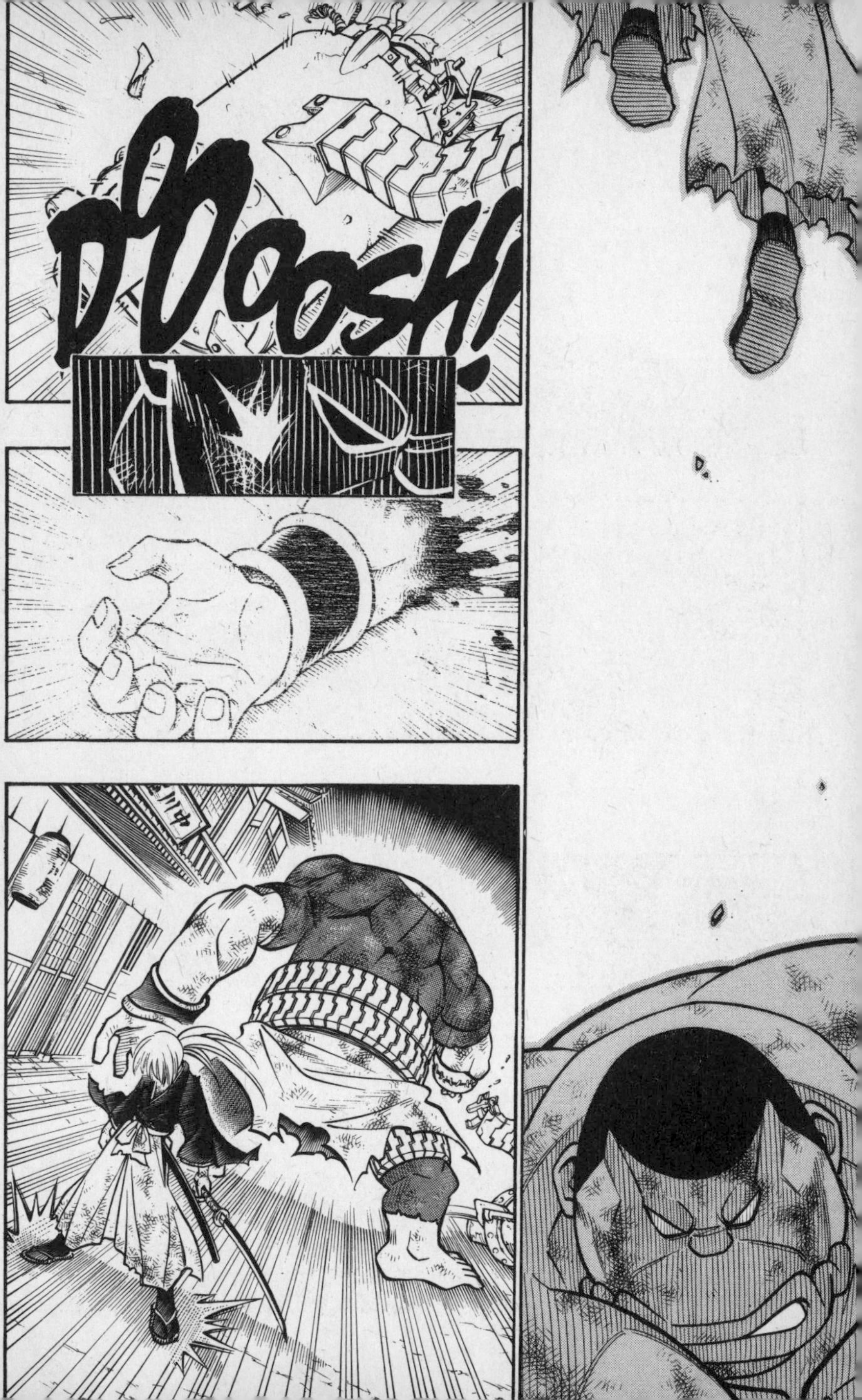
DOOOSH!

READ THIS WAY

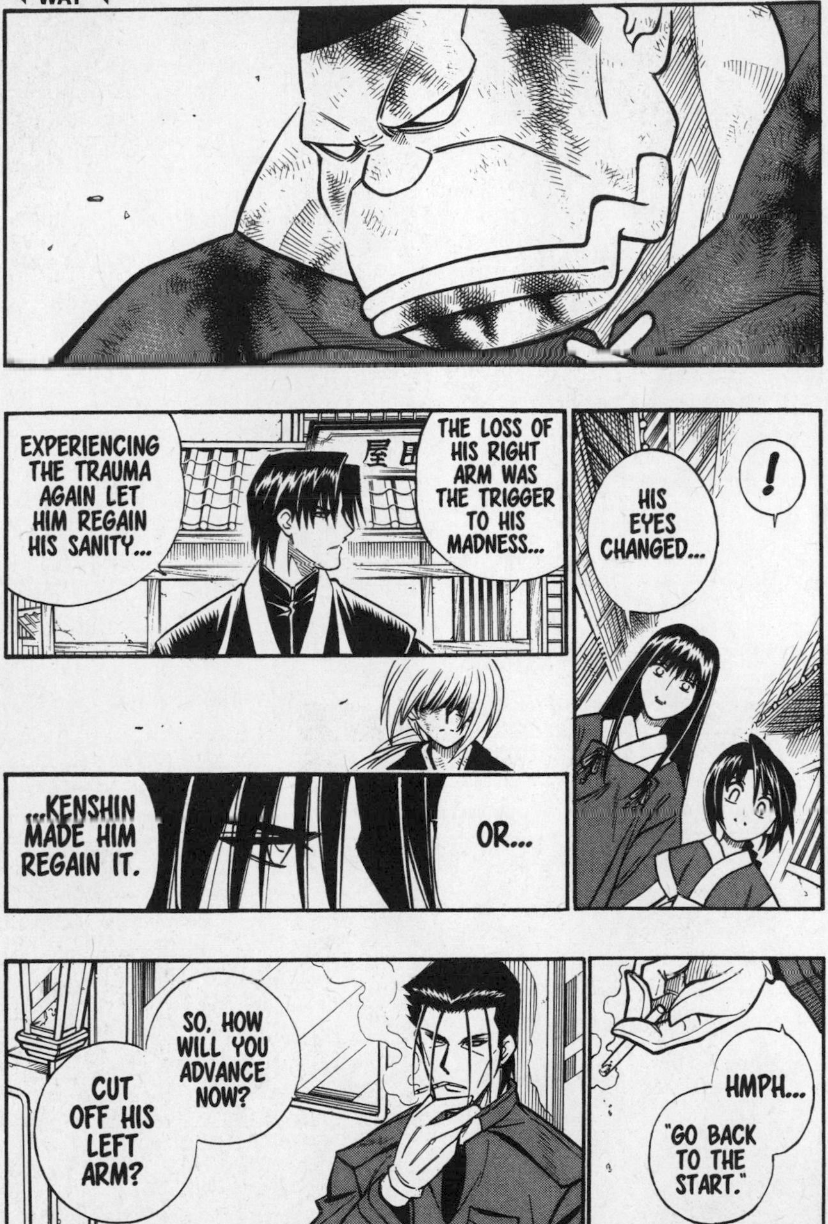

!
HIS EYES CHANGED...
THE LOSS OF HIS RIGHT ARM WAS THE TRIGGER TO HIS MADNESS...
EXPERIENCING THE TRAUMA AGAIN LET HIM REGAIN HIS SANITY...
OR...
...KENSHIN MADE HIM REGAIN IT.
HMPH...
"GO BACK TO THE START."
SO, HOW WILL YOU ADVANCE NOW?
CUT OFF HIS LEFT ARM?

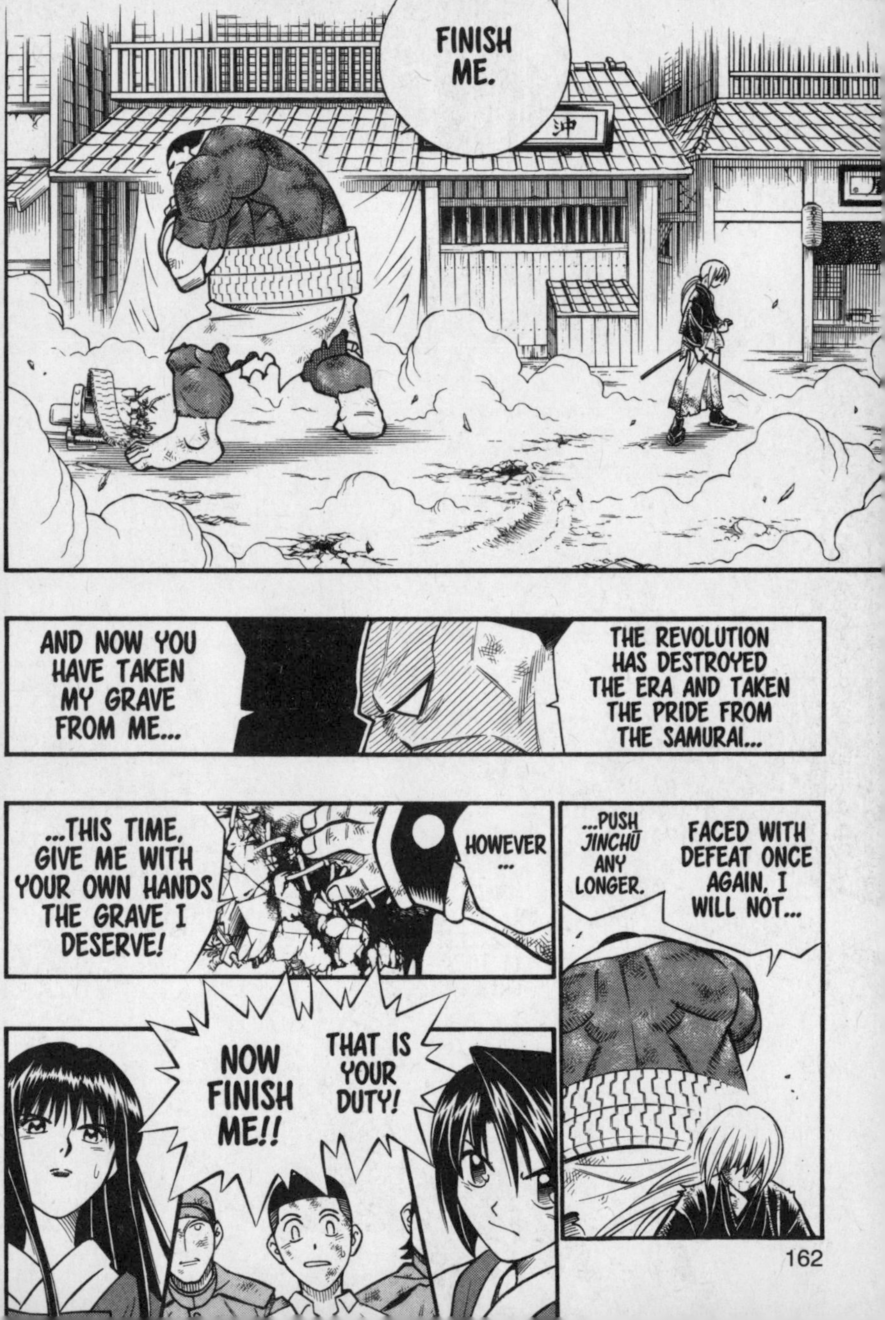
FINISH ME.
THE REVOLUTION HAS DESTROYED THE ERA AND TAKEN THE PRIDE FROM THE SAMURAI...
AND NOW YOU HAVE TAKEN MY GRAVE FROM ME...
FACED WITH DEFEAT ONCE AGAIN, I WILL NOT...
...PUSH JINCHŪ ANY LONGER.
HOWEVER...
...THIS TIME, GIVE ME WITH YOUR OWN HANDS THE GRAVE I DESERVE!
THAT IS YOUR DUTY!
NOW FINISH ME!!

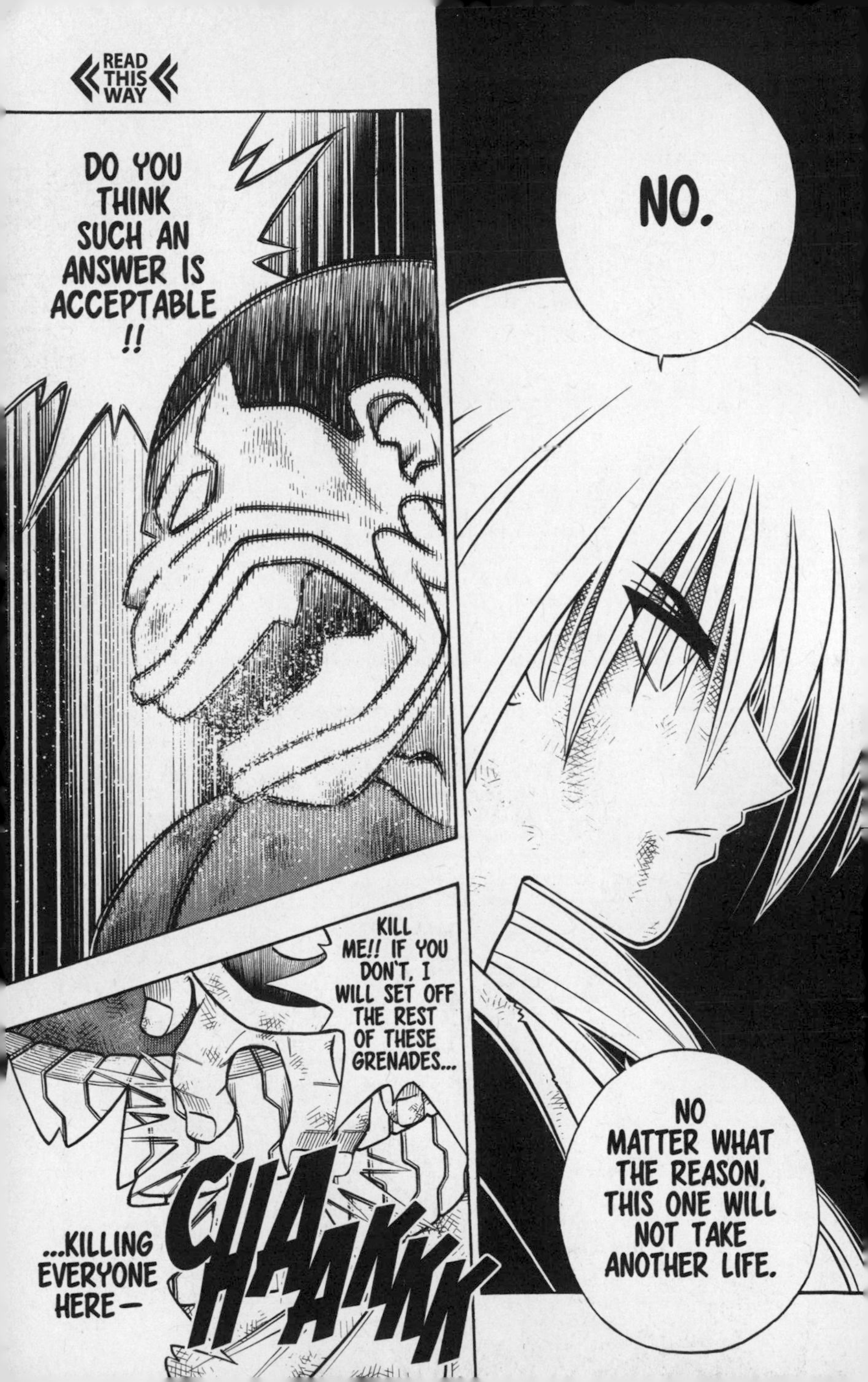
READ THIS WAY
NO.
NO MATTER WHAT THE REASON, THIS ONE WILL NOT TAKE ANOTHER LIFE.
DO YOU THINK SUCH AN ANSWER IS ACCEPTABLE !!
KILL ME!! IF YOU DON'T, I WILL SET OFF THE REST OF THESE GRENADES...
...KILLING EVERYONE HERE—
CHAMM

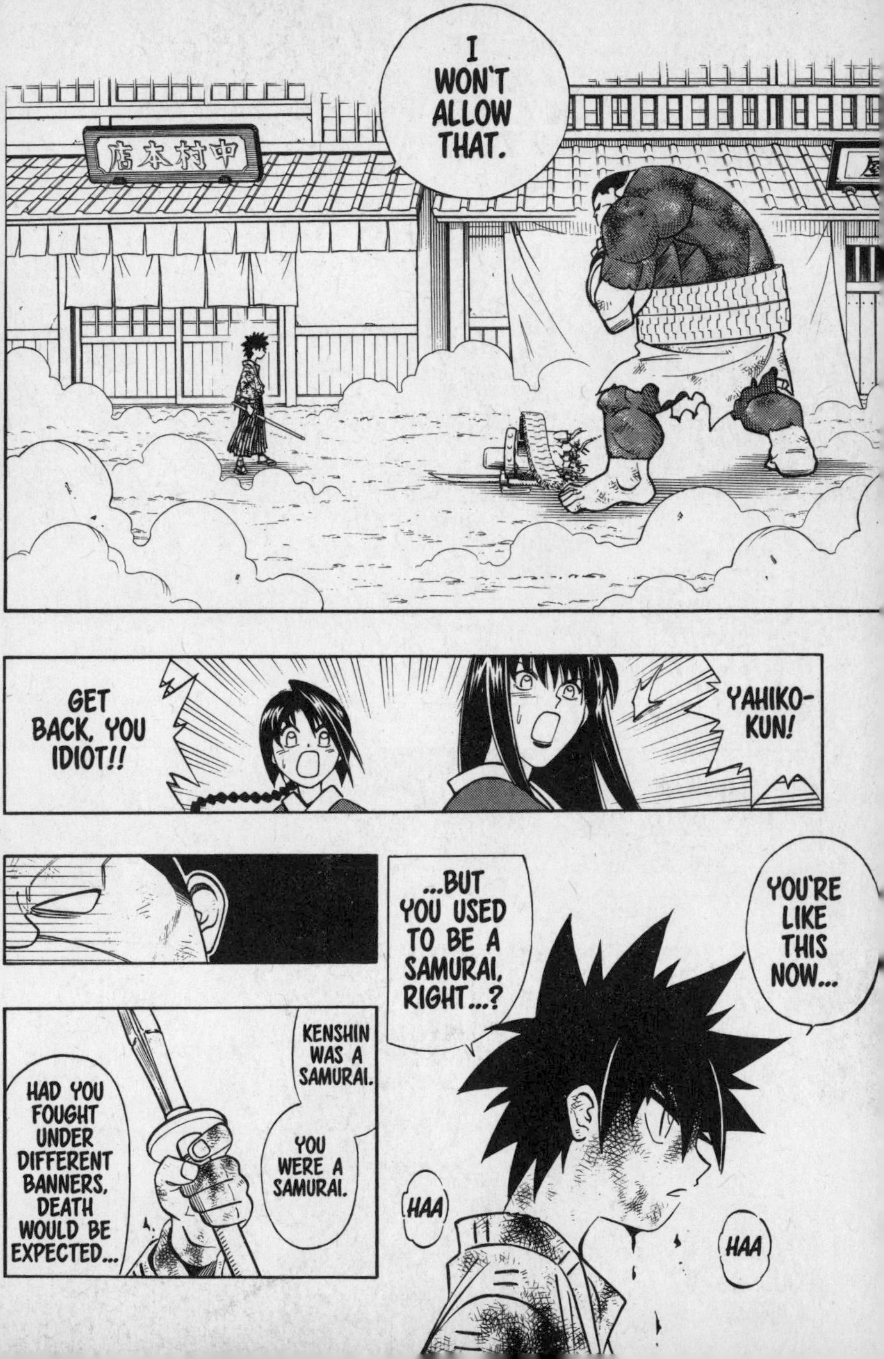
I WON'T ALLOW THAT.
中村本店
YAHIKO-KUN!
GET BACK, YOU IDIOT!!
YOU'RE LIKE THIS NOW...
...BUT YOU USED TO BE A SAMURAI, RIGHT...?
HAA
HAA
KENSHIN WAS A SAMURAI.
YOU WERE A SAMURAI.
HAD YOU FOUGHT UNDER DIFFERENT BANNERS, DEATH WOULD BE EXPECTED...

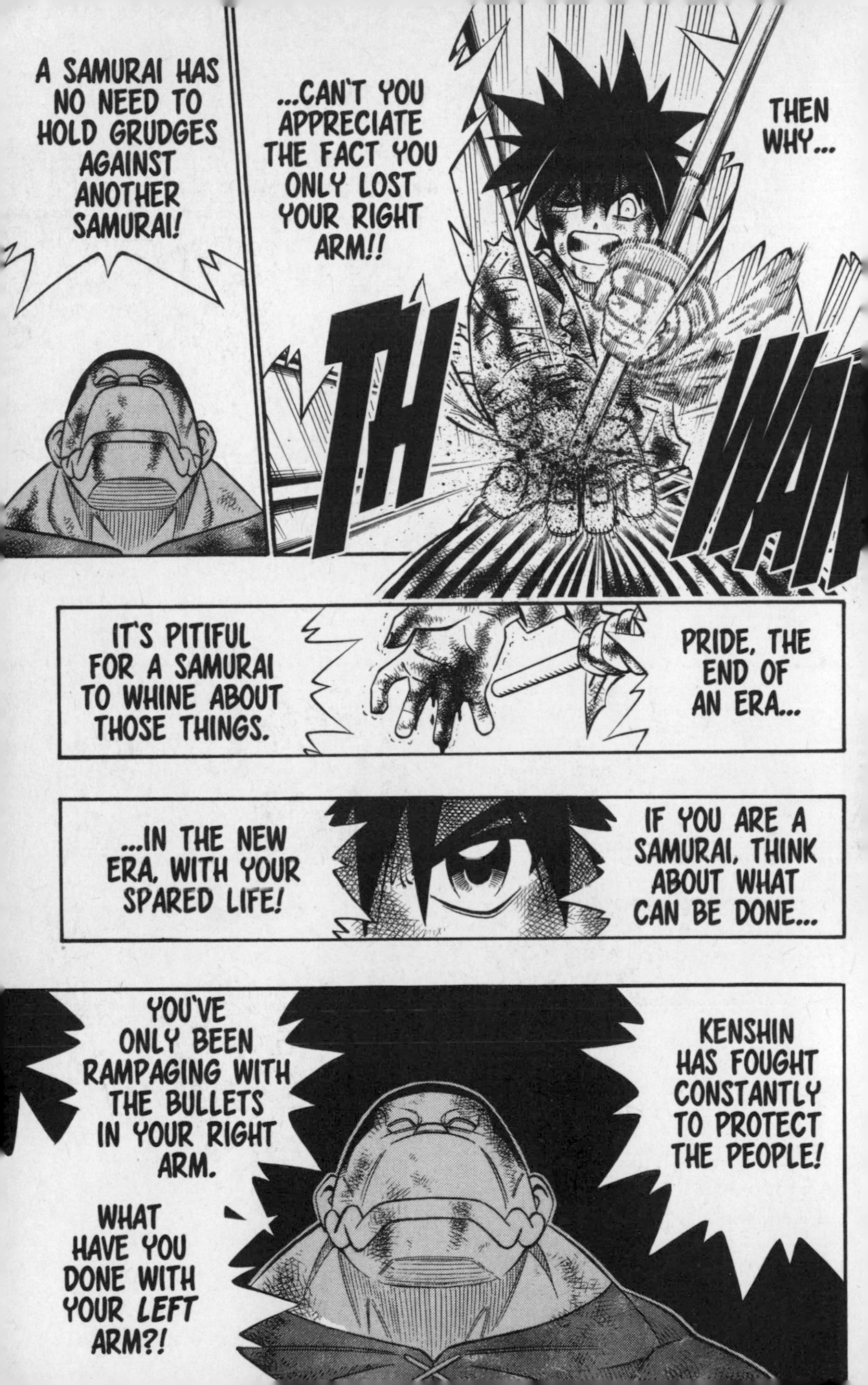
THEN WHY...
...CAN'T YOU APPRECIATE THE FACT YOU ONLY LOST YOUR RIGHT ARM!!
TH
WA
A SAMURAI HAS NO NEED TO HOLD GRUDGES AGAINST ANOTHER SAMURAI!
PRIDE, THE END OF AN ERA...
IT'S PITIFUL FOR A SAMURAI TO WHINE ABOUT THOSE THINGS.
IF YOU ARE A SAMURAI, THINK ABOUT WHAT CAN BE DONE...
...IN THE NEW ERA, WITH YOUR SPARED LIFE!
KENSHIN HAS FOUGHT CONSTANTLY TO PROTECT THE PEOPLE!
YOU'VE ONLY BEEN RAMPAGING WITH THE BULLETS IN YOUR RIGHT ARM.
WHAT HAVE YOU DONE WITH YOUR *LEFT* ARM?!

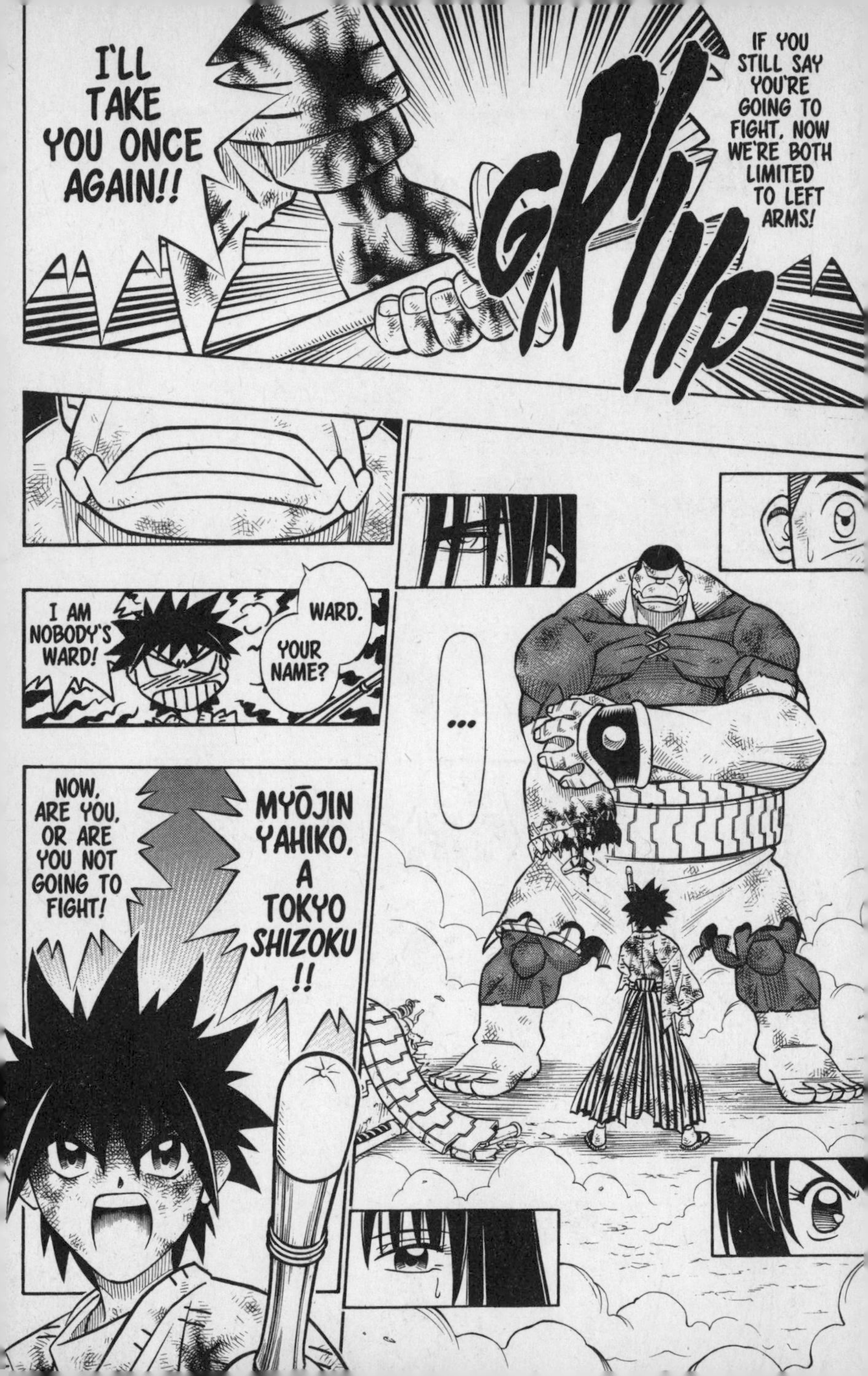
IF YOU STILL SAY YOU'RE GOING TO FIGHT, NOW WE'RE BOTH LIMITED TO LEFT ARMS!
GRIIP
I'LL TAKE YOU ONCE AGAIN!!
...
WARD.
YOUR NAME?
I AM NOBODY'S WARD!
MYŌJIN YAHIKO, A TOKYO SHIZOKU!!
NOW, ARE YOU, OR ARE YOU NOT GOING TO FIGHT!

READ THIS WAY

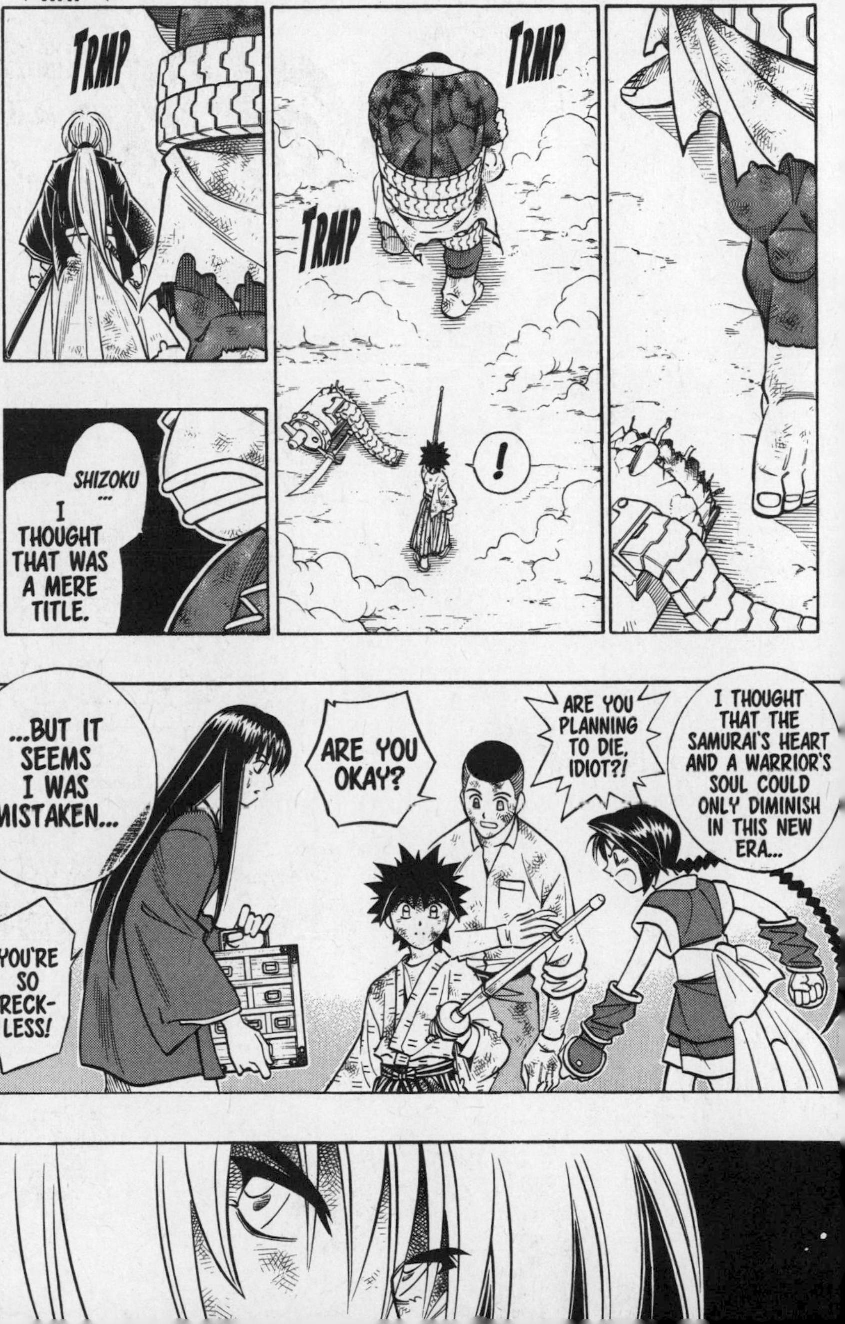
TRMP
TRMP
!
TRMP
SHIZOKU...
I THOUGHT THAT WAS A MERE TITLE.
I THOUGHT THAT THE SAMURAI'S HEART AND A WARRIOR'S SOUL COULD ONLY DIMINISH IN THIS NEW ERA...
ARE YOU PLANNING TO DIE, IDIOT?!
ARE YOU OKAY?
...BUT IT SEEMS I WAS MISTAKEN...
YOU'RE SO RECK-LESS!

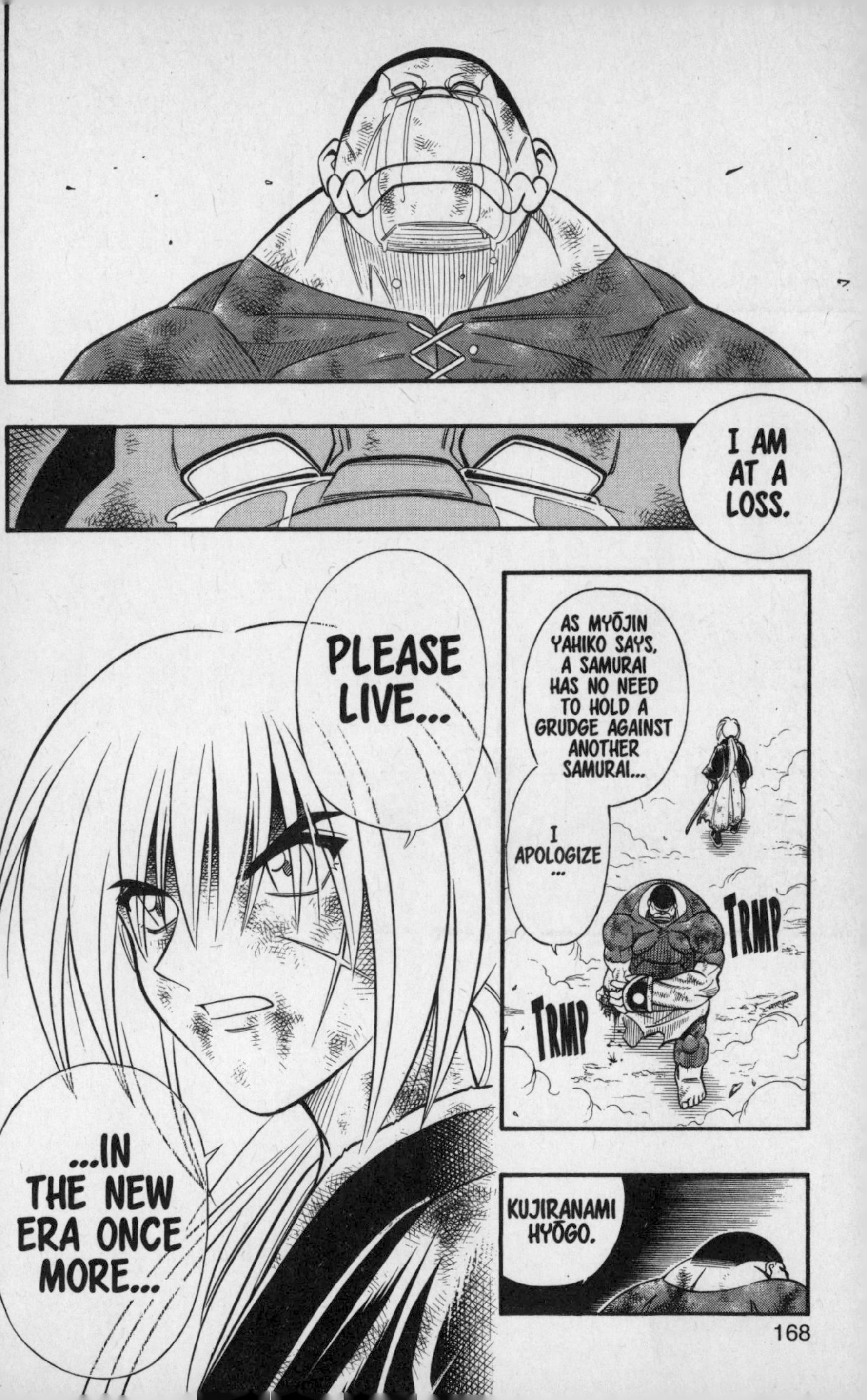
I AM AT A LOSS.
AS MYŌJIN YAHIKO SAYS, A SAMURAI HAS NO NEED TO HOLD A GRUDGE AGAINST ANOTHER SAMURAI...
I APOLOGIZE...
TRMP
TRMP
KUJIRANAMI HYŌGO.
PLEASE LIVE...
...IN THE NEW ERA ONCE MORE...

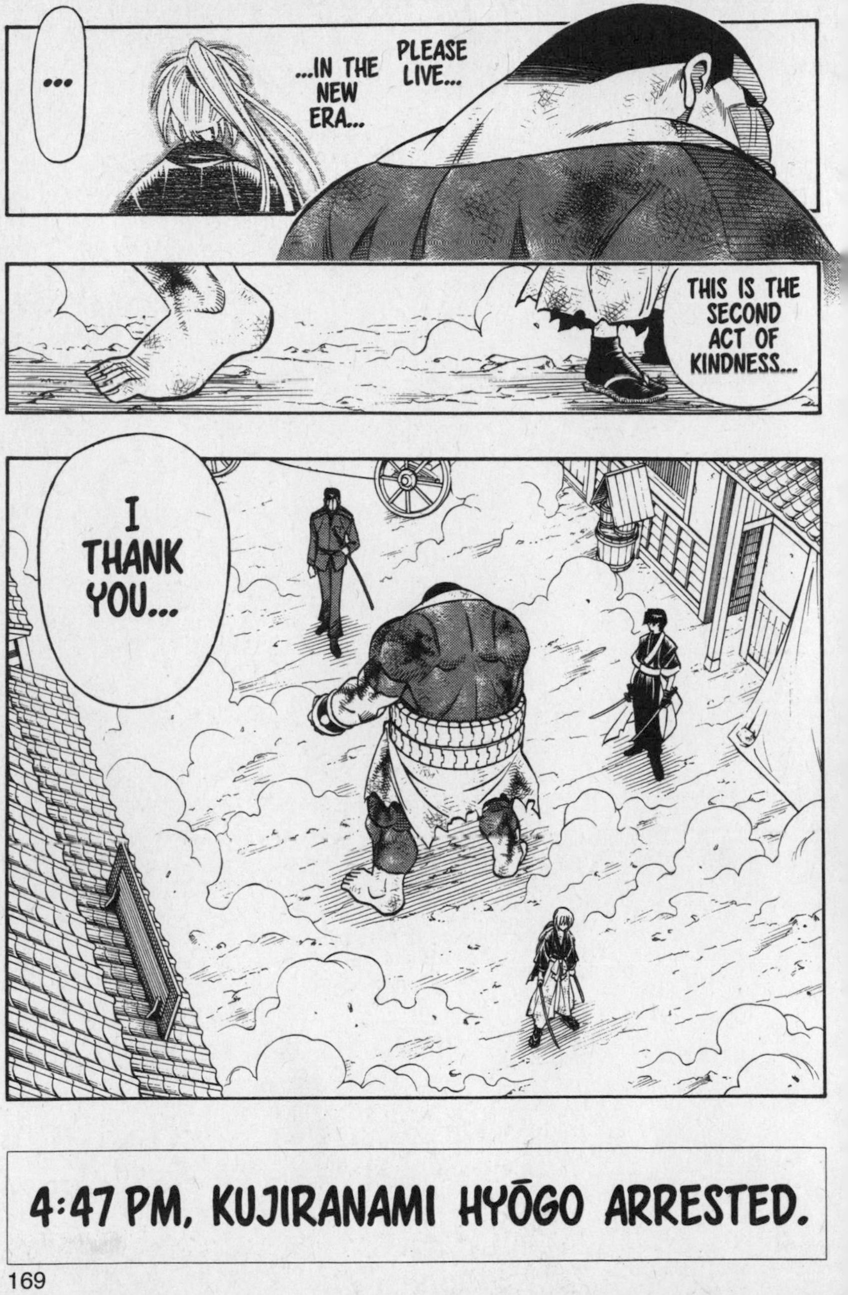
PLEASE LIVE...
...IN THE NEW ERA...
...
THIS IS THE SECOND ACT OF KINDNESS...
I THANK YOU...
4:47 PM, KUJIRANAMI HYŌGO ARRESTED.

Act 227

Four More Days, One More Person

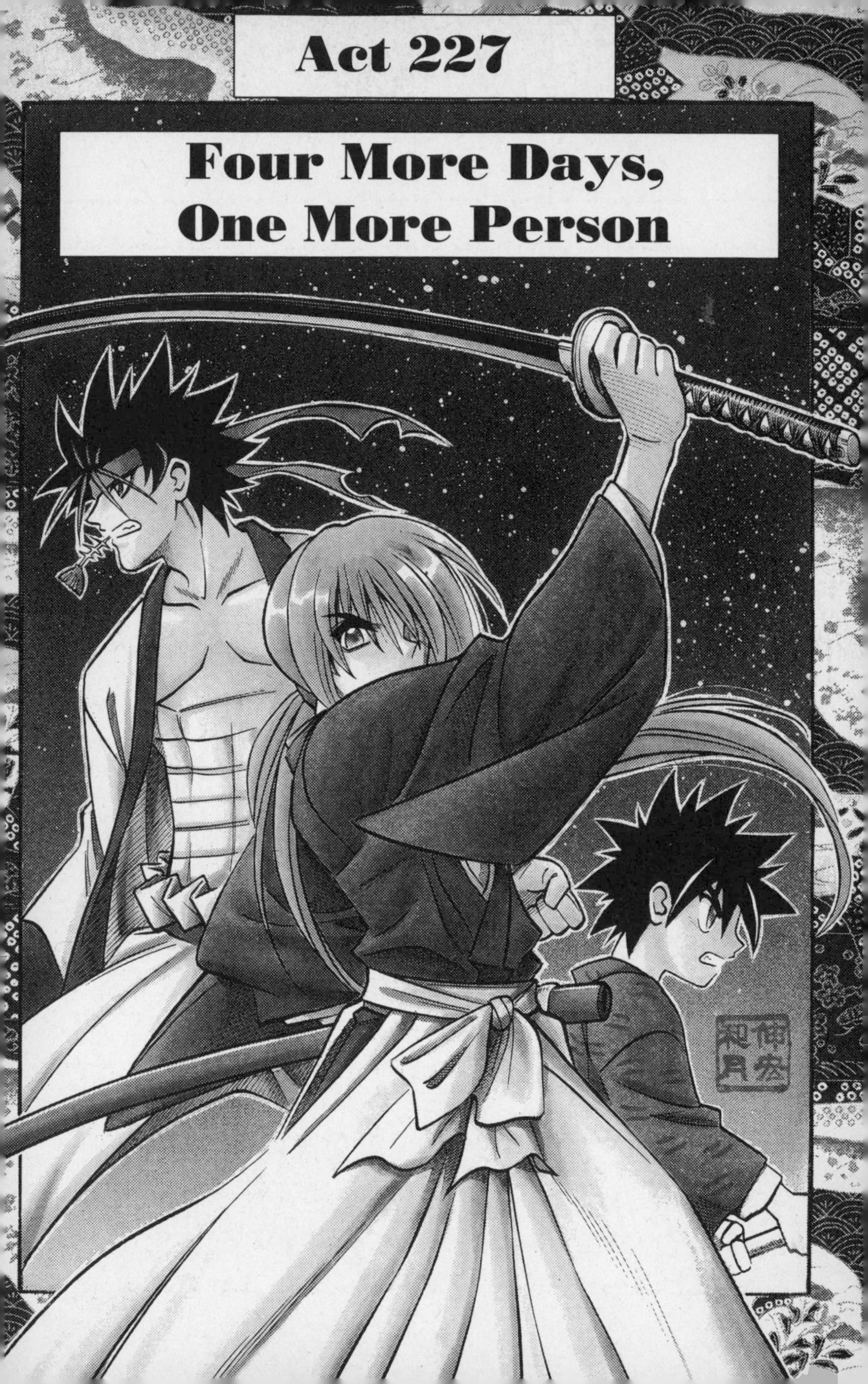

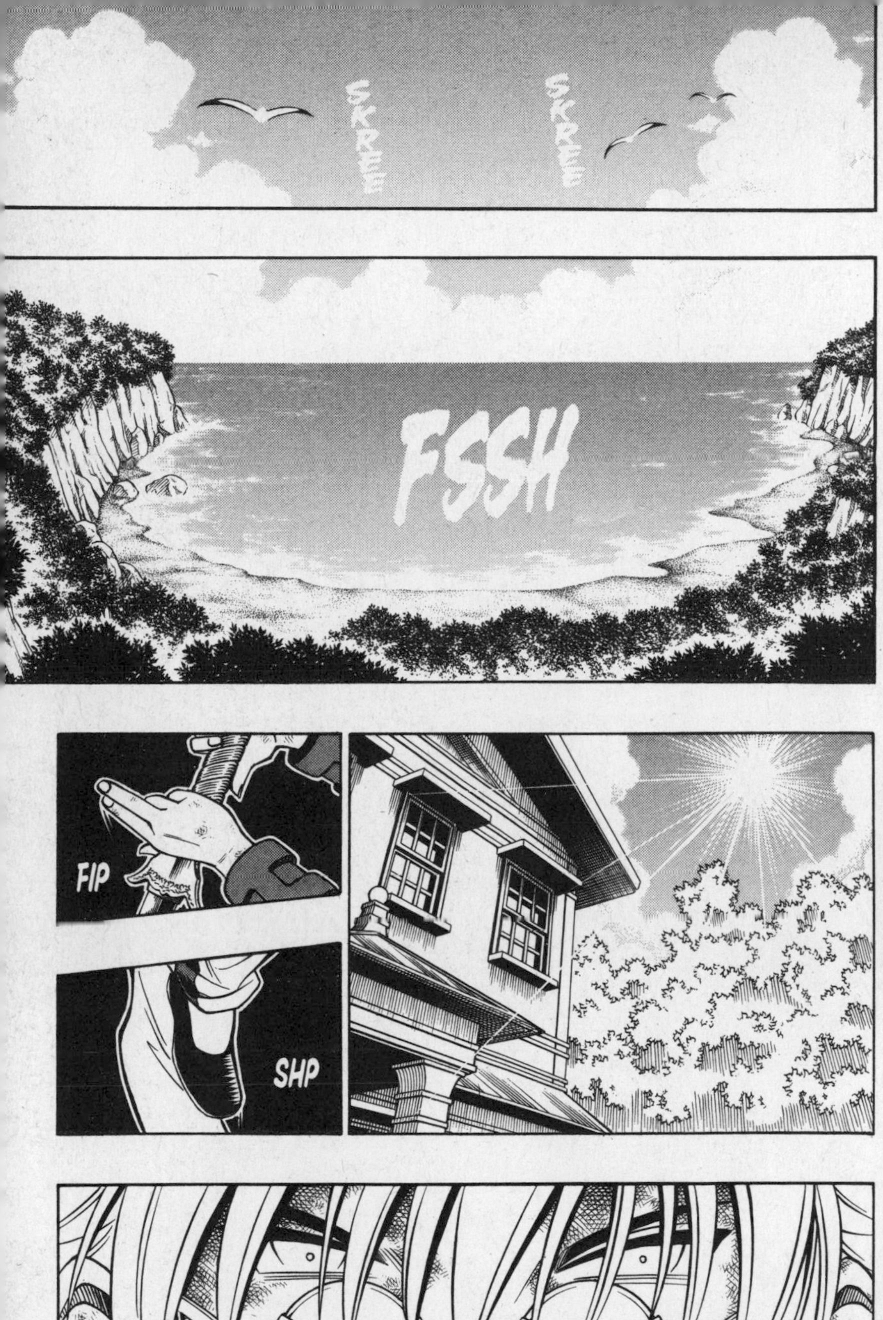
SKREE
SKREE
FSSH
FIP
SHP

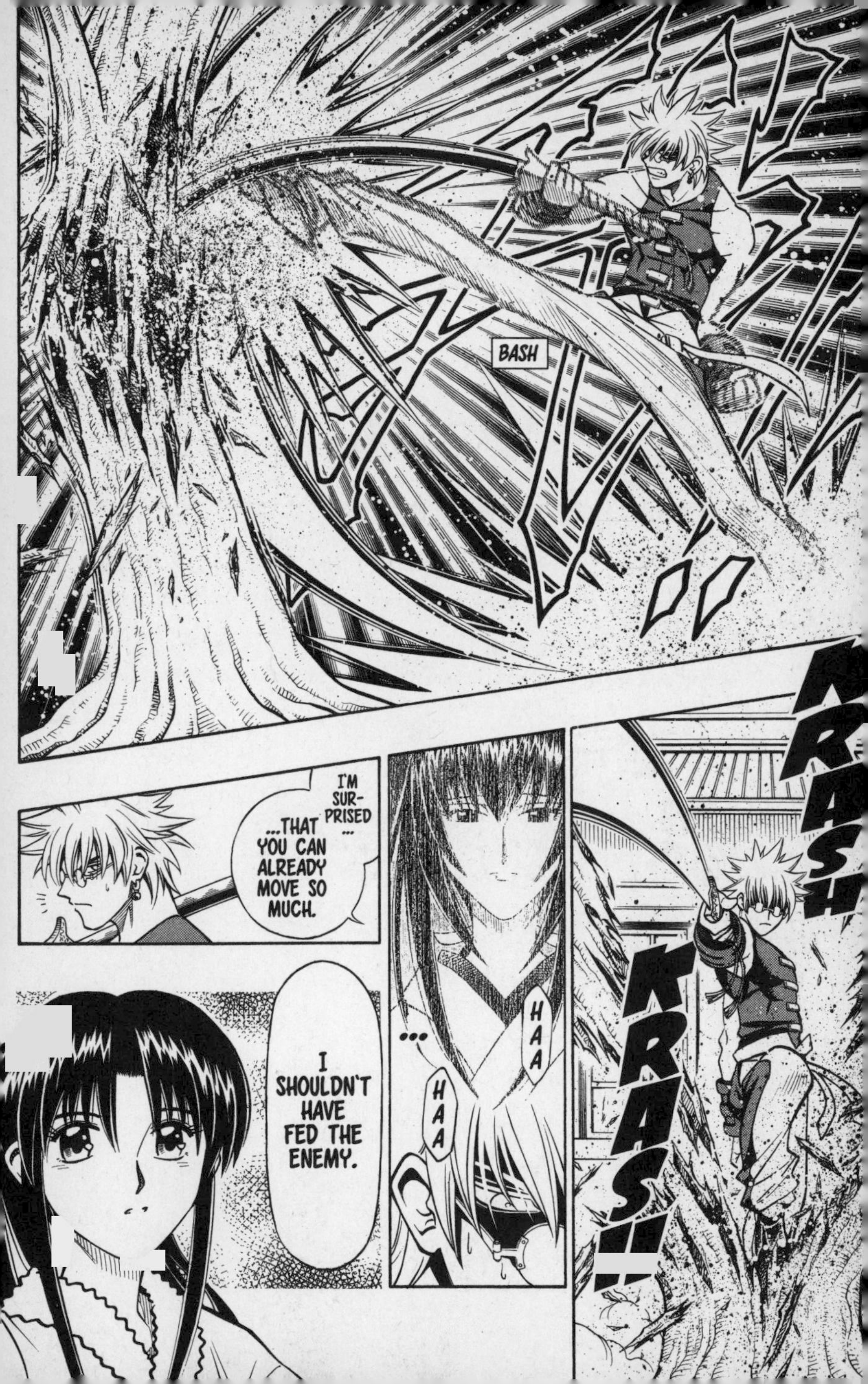
BASH
KRASH
KRASH!!
HAA
HAA
...
I'M SURPRISED...
...THAT YOU CAN ALREADY MOVE SO MUCH.
I SHOULDN'T HAVE FED THE ENEMY.

READ THIS WAY

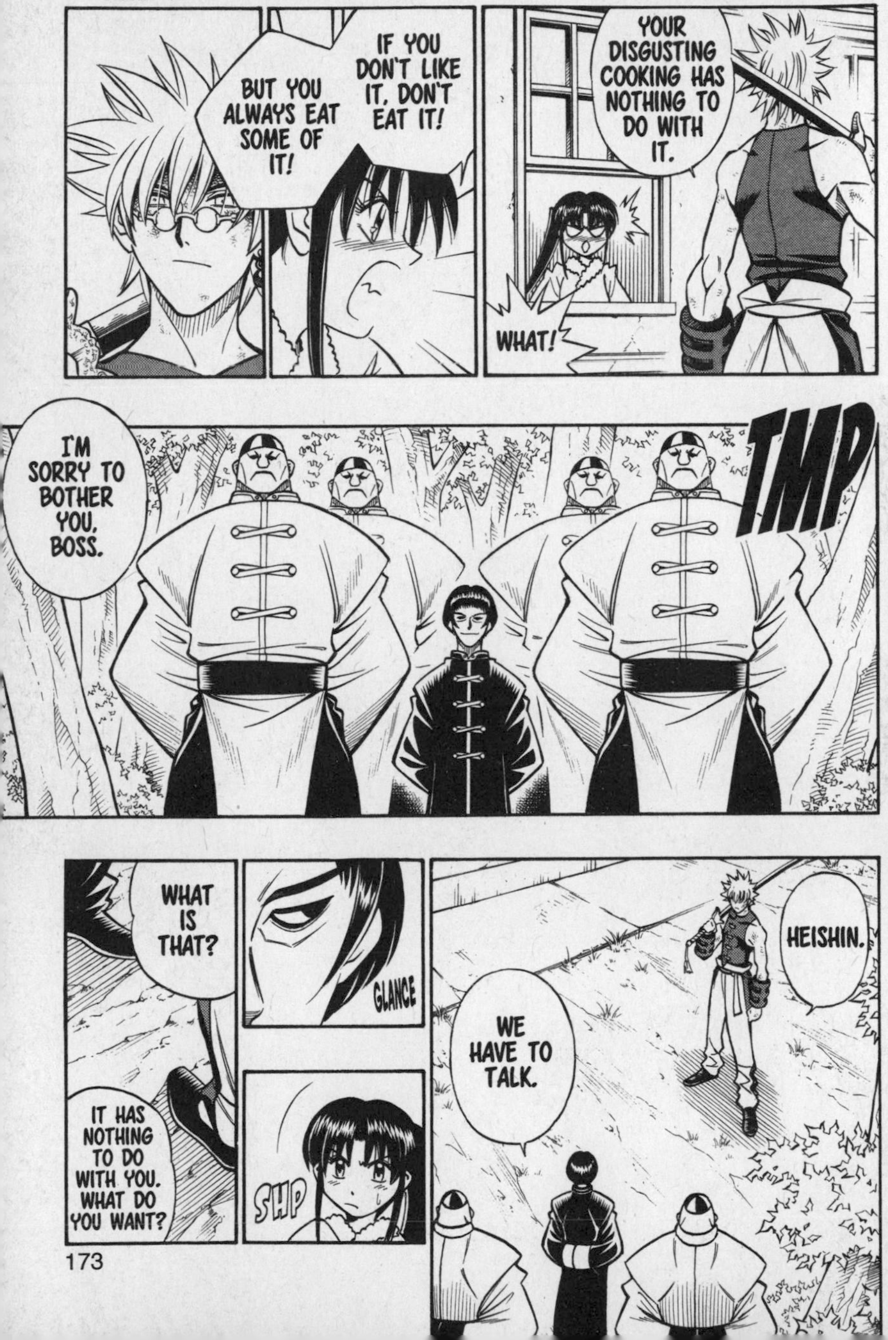
YOUR DISGUSTING COOKING HAS NOTHING TO DO WITH IT.
WHAT!
IF YOU DON'T LIKE IT, DON'T EAT IT!
BUT YOU ALWAYS EAT SOME OF IT!
TMP
I'M SORRY TO BOTHER YOU, BOSS.
HEISHIN.
WE HAVE TO TALK.
GLANCE
SHP
WHAT IS THAT?
IT HAS NOTHING TO DO WITH YOU. WHAT DO YOU WANT?

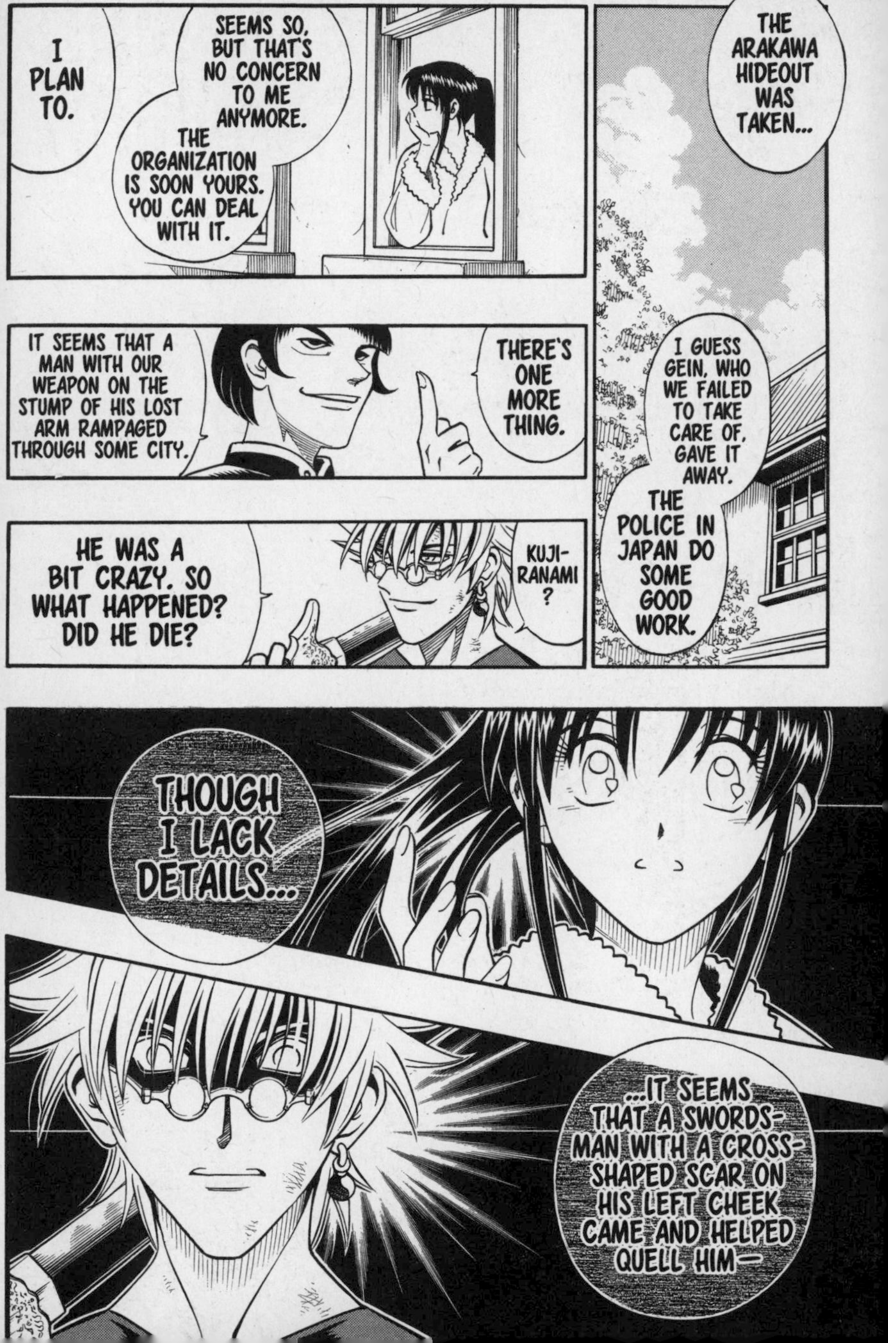
THE ARAKAWA HIDEOUT WAS TAKEN...
I GUESS GEIN, WHO WE FAILED TO TAKE CARE OF, GAVE IT AWAY.
THE POLICE IN JAPAN DO SOME GOOD WORK.
SEEMS SO, BUT THAT'S NO CONCERN TO ME ANYMORE.
THE ORGANIZATION IS SOON YOURS. YOU CAN DEAL WITH IT.
I PLAN TO.
THERE'S ONE MORE THING.
IT SEEMS THAT A MAN WITH OUR WEAPON ON THE STUMP OF HIS LOST ARM RAMPAGED THROUGH SOME CITY.
KUJI-RANAMI?
HE WAS A BIT CRAZY. SO WHAT HAPPENED? DID HE DIE?
THOUGH I LACK DETAILS...
...IT SEEMS THAT A SWORDS-MAN WITH A CROSS-SHAPED SCAR ON HIS LEFT CHEEK CAME AND HELPED QUELL HIM—

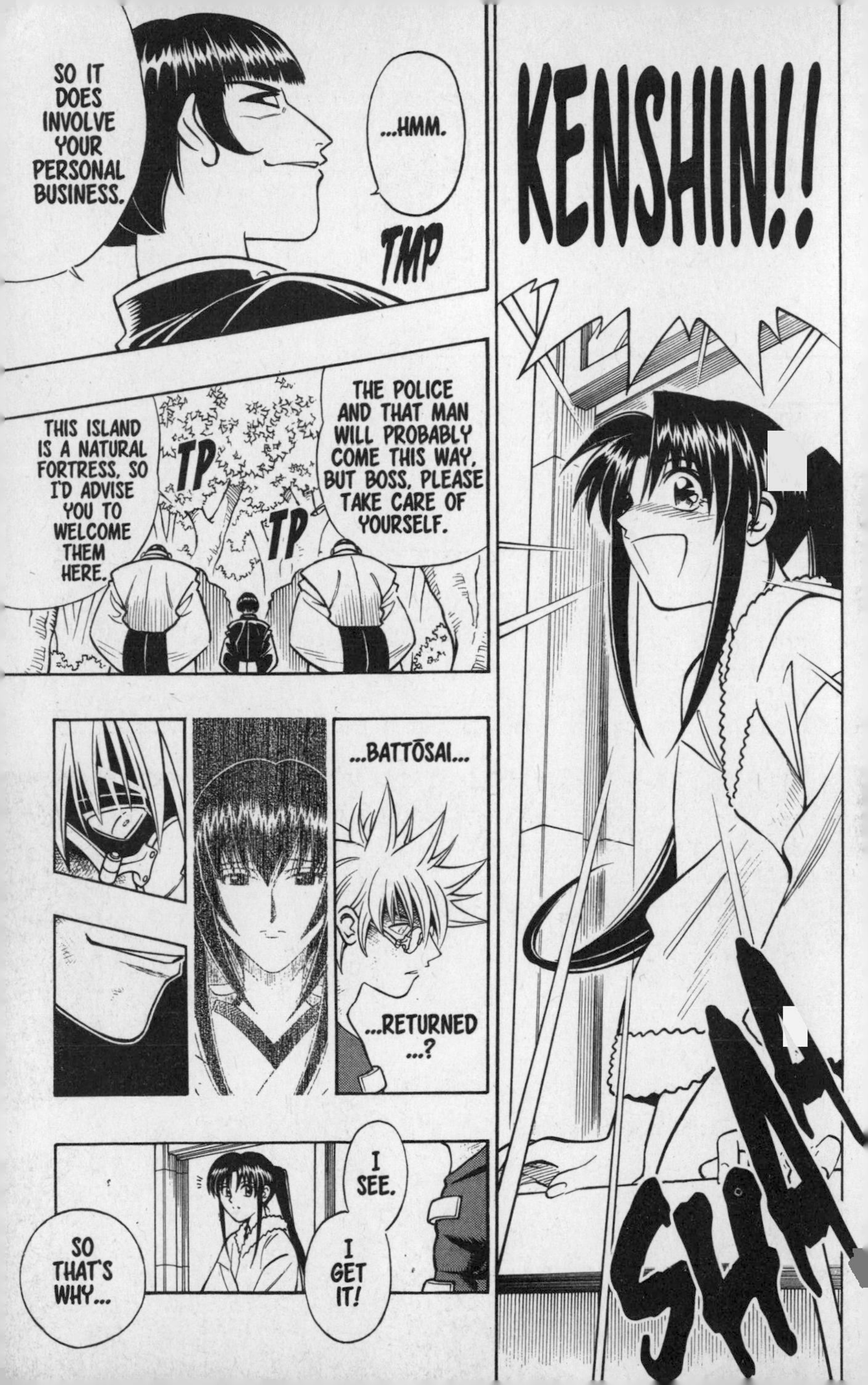
KENSHIN!!
SHA
...HMM.
TMP
SO IT DOES INVOLVE YOUR PERSONAL BUSINESS.
THE POLICE AND THAT MAN WILL PROBABLY COME THIS WAY, BUT BOSS, PLEASE TAKE CARE OF YOURSELF.
TP
TP
THIS ISLAND IS A NATURAL FORTRESS, SO I'D ADVISE YOU TO WELCOME THEM HERE.
...BATTŌSAI...
...RETURNED ...?
I SEE.
I GET IT!
SO THAT'S WHY...

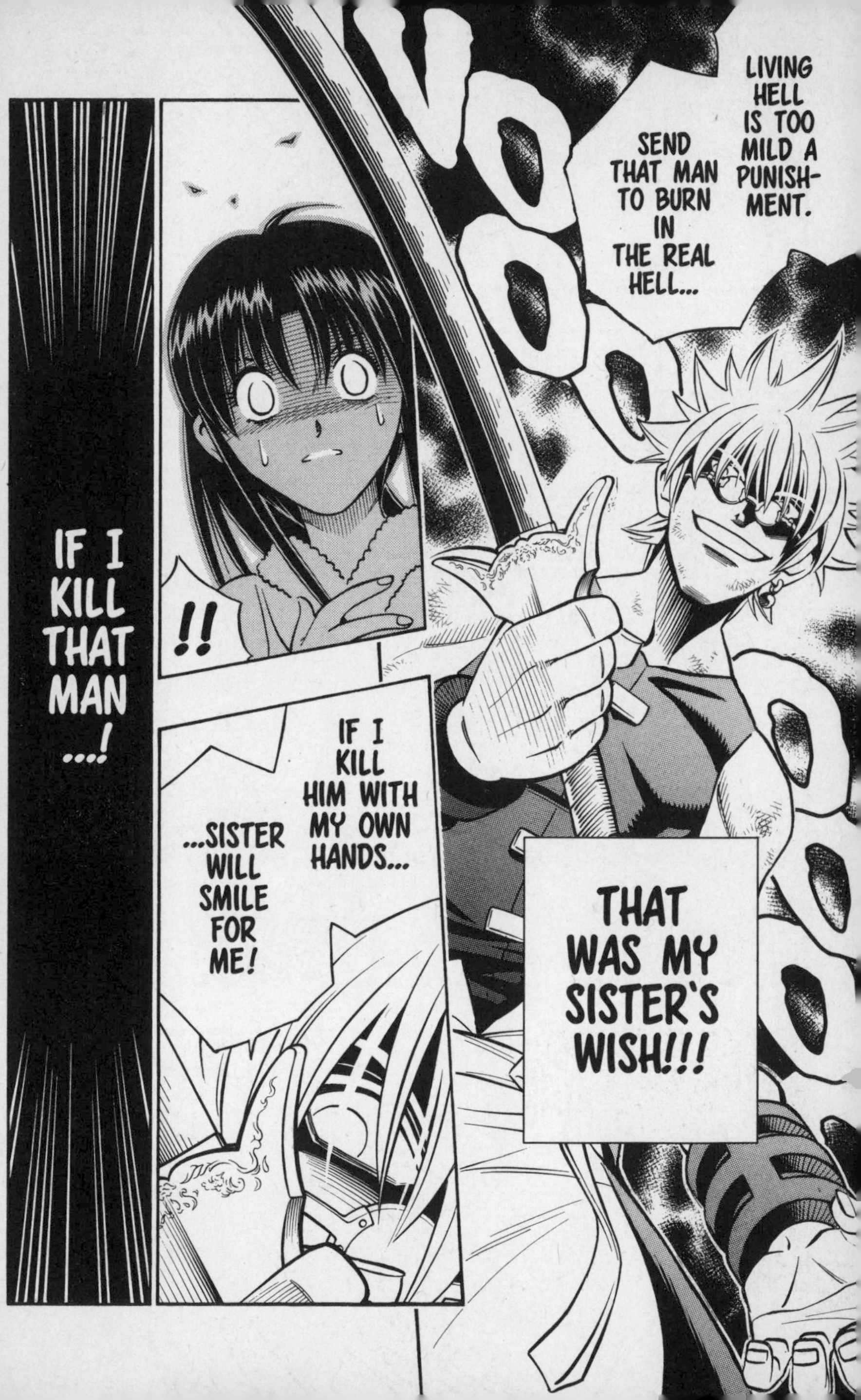
LIVING HELL IS TOO MILD A PUNISHMENT.
SEND THAT MAN TO BURN IN THE REAL HELL...
THAT WAS MY SISTER'S WISH!!!
!!
IF I KILL HIM WITH MY OWN HANDS...
...SISTER WILL SMILE FOR ME!
IF I KILL THAT MAN...!

READ THIS WAY

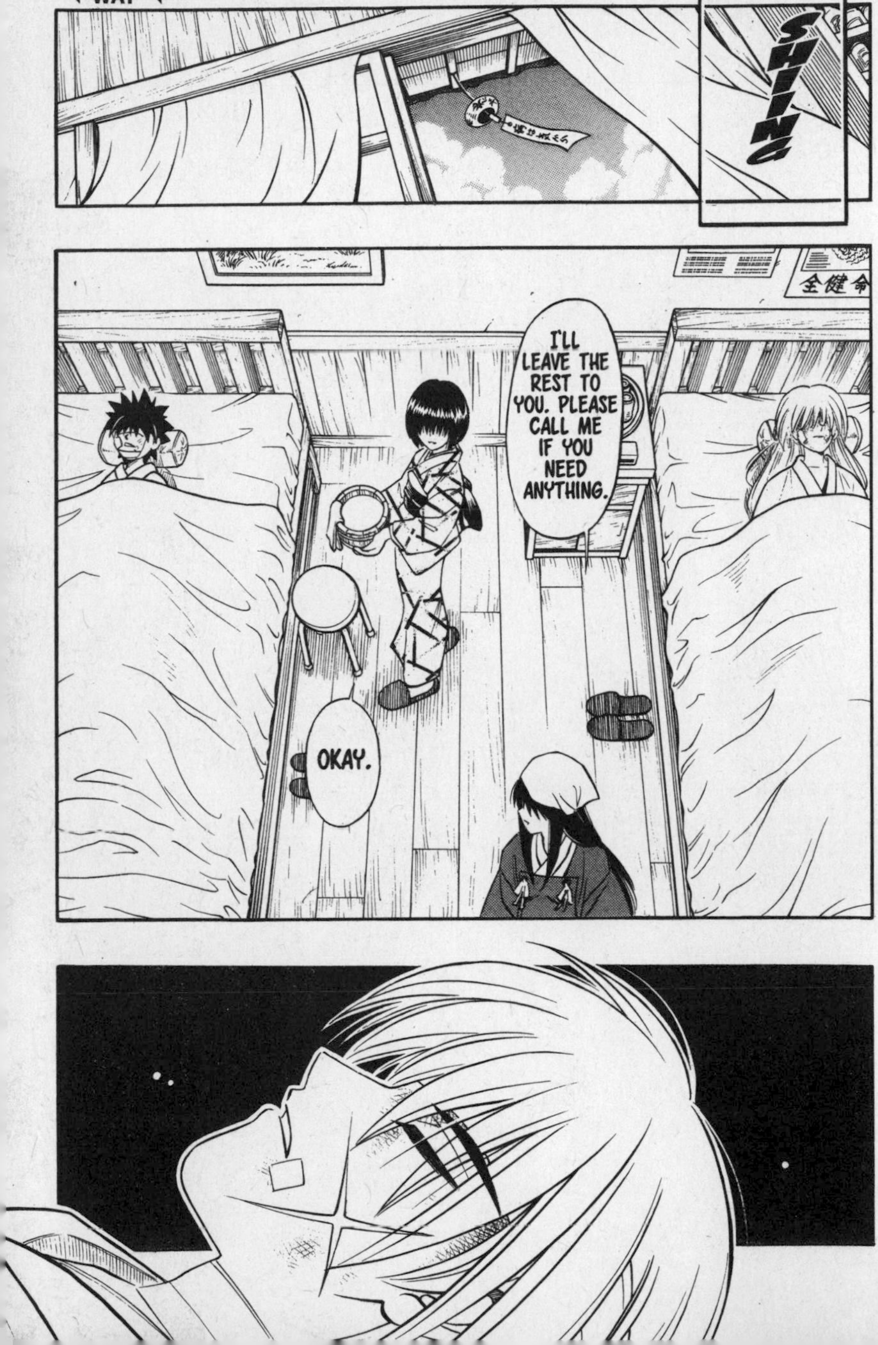
SHING
全健命
I'LL LEAVE THE REST TO YOU. PLEASE CALL ME IF YOU NEED ANYTHING.
OKAY.

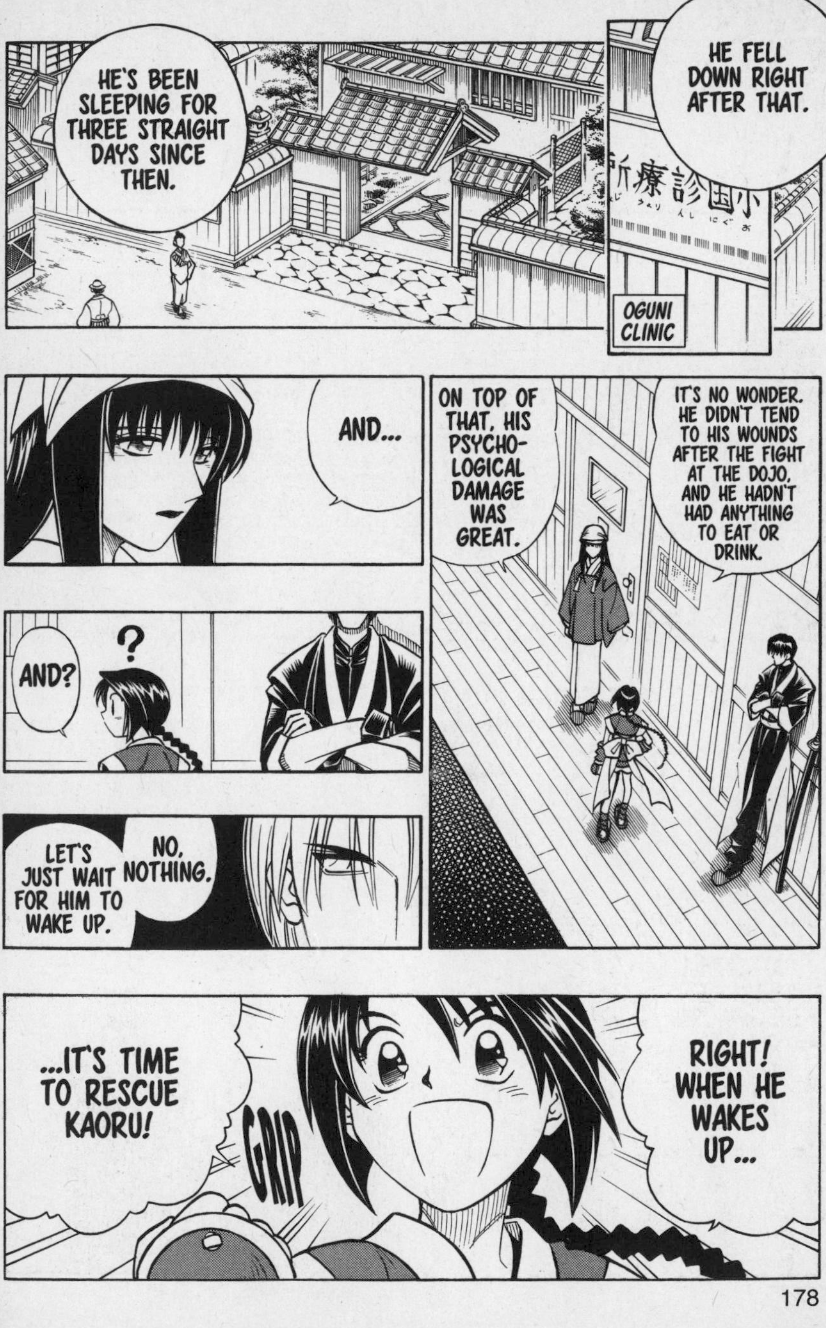
HE FELL DOWN RIGHT AFTER THAT.
小国診療所
OGUNI CLINIC
HE'S BEEN SLEEPING FOR THREE STRAIGHT DAYS SINCE THEN.
IT'S NO WONDER. HE DIDN'T TEND TO HIS WOUNDS AFTER THE FIGHT AT THE DOJO, AND HE HADN'T HAD ANYTHING TO EAT OR DRINK.
ON TOP OF THAT, HIS PSYCHOLOGICAL DAMAGE WAS GREAT.
AND...
AND?
?
NO, NOTHING.
LET'S JUST WAIT FOR HIM TO WAKE UP.
RIGHT! WHEN HE WAKES UP...
GRIP
...IT'S TIME TO RESCUE KAORU!

READ THIS WAY

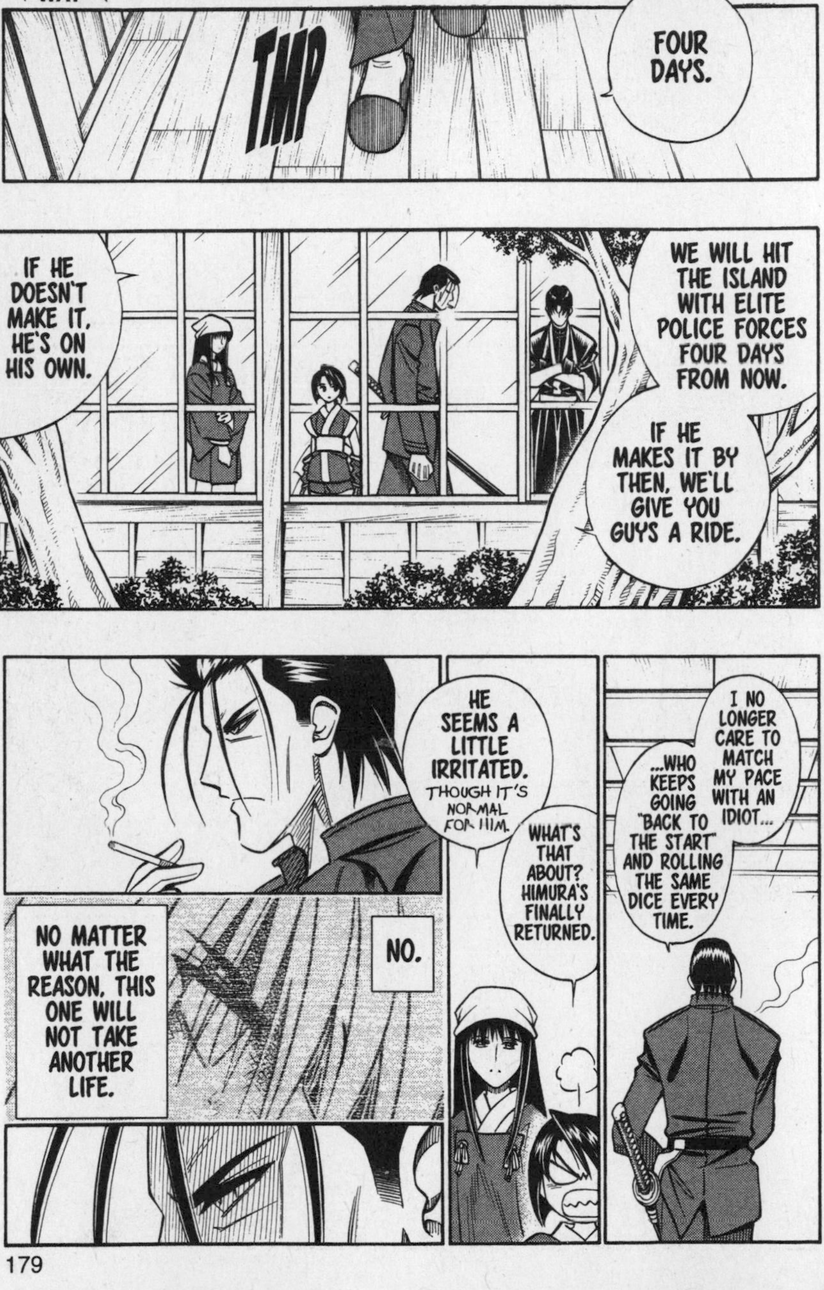

FOUR DAYS.
TMP
WE WILL HIT THE ISLAND WITH ELITE POLICE FORCES FOUR DAYS FROM NOW.
IF HE MAKES IT BY THEN, WE'LL GIVE YOU GUYS A RIDE.
IF HE DOESN'T MAKE IT, HE'S ON HIS OWN.
I NO LONGER CARE TO MATCH MY PACE WITH AN IDIOT...
...WHO KEEPS GOING "BACK TO THE START" AND ROLLING THE SAME DICE EVERY TIME.
HE SEEMS A LITTLE IRRITATED.
THOUGH IT'S NORMAL FOR HIM.
WHAT'S THAT ABOUT? HIMURA'S FINALLY RETURNED.
NO.
NO MATTER WHAT THE REASON, THIS ONE WILL NOT TAKE ANOTHER LIFE.

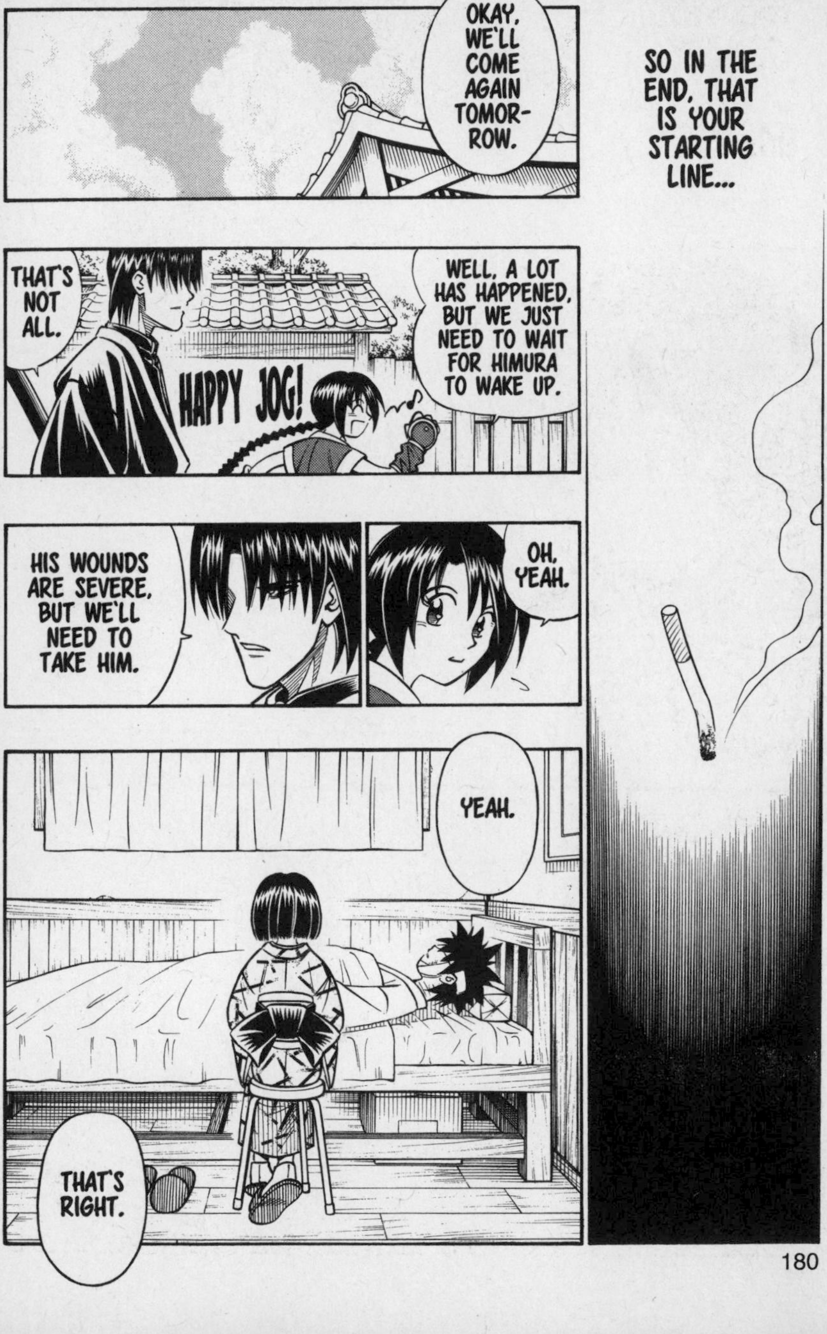
SO IN THE END, THAT IS YOUR STARTING LINE...
OKAY, WE'LL COME AGAIN TOMORROW.
WELL, A LOT HAS HAPPENED, BUT WE JUST NEED TO WAIT FOR HIMURA TO WAKE UP.
HAPPY JOG!
THAT'S NOT ALL.
OH, YEAH.
HIS WOUNDS ARE SEVERE, BUT WE'LL NEED TO TAKE HIM.
YEAH.
THAT'S RIGHT.

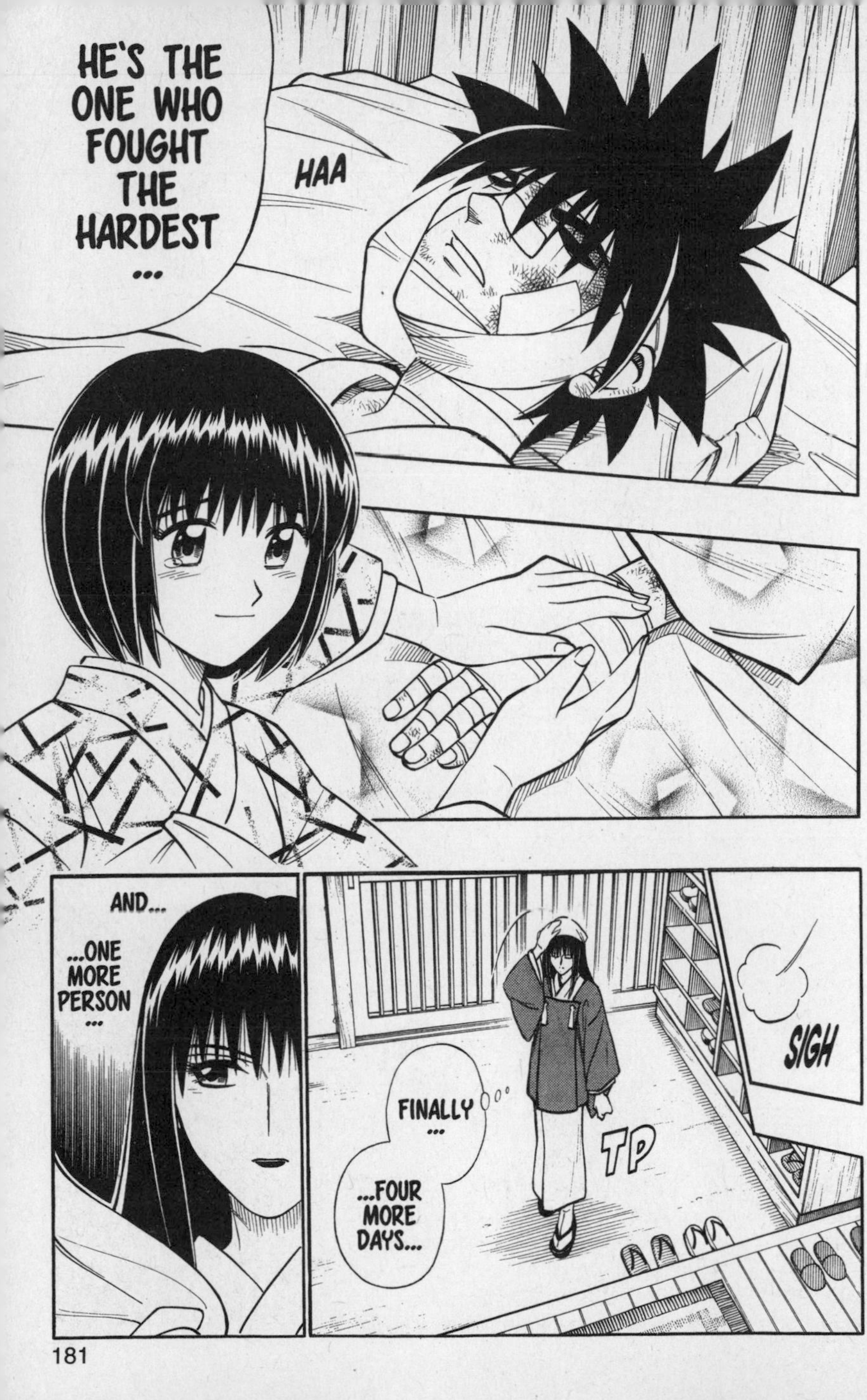
HE'S THE ONE WHO FOUGHT THE HARDEST ...
HAA
SIGH
FINALLY ...
TP
...FOUR MORE DAYS...
AND...
...ONE MORE PERSON ...

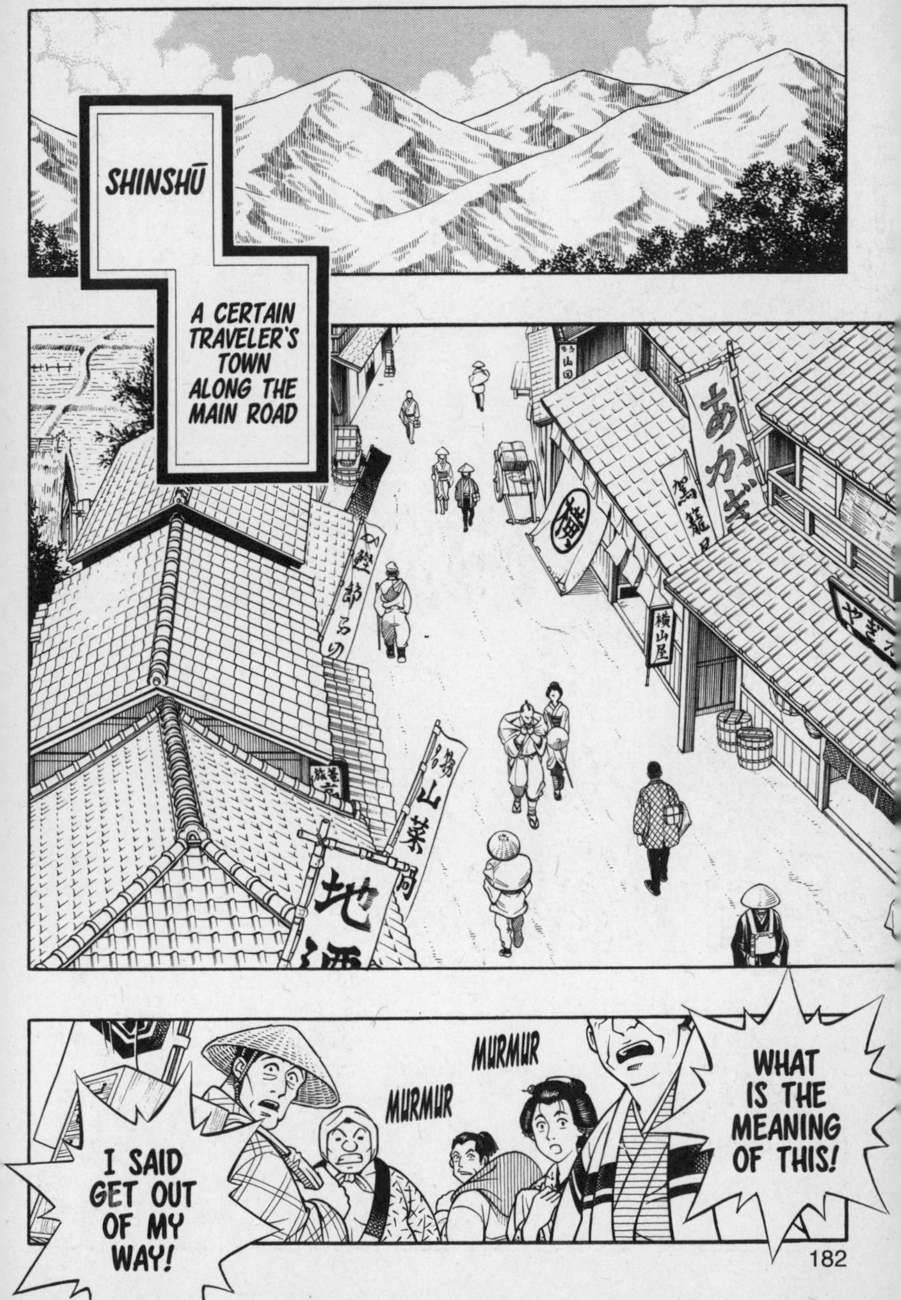
SHINSHŪ
A CERTAIN TRAVELER'S TOWN ALONG THE MAIN ROAD
WHAT IS THE MEANING OF THIS!
MURMUR
MURMUR
I SAID GET OUT OF MY WAY!

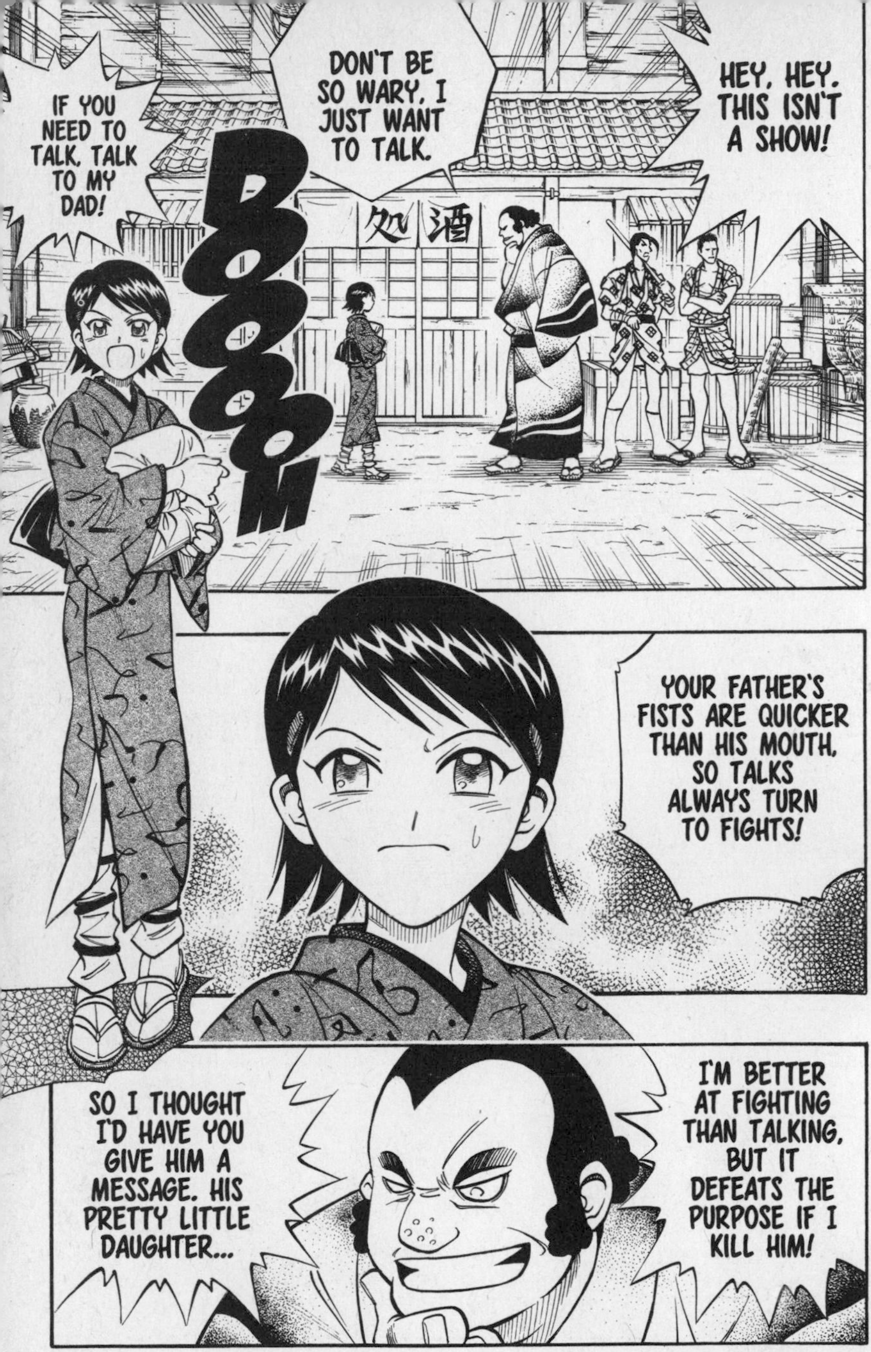
HEY, HEY. THIS ISN'T A SHOW!
DON'T BE SO WARY, I JUST WANT TO TALK.
IF YOU NEED TO TALK, TALK TO MY DAD!
BOOOOM
YOUR FATHER'S FISTS ARE QUICKER THAN HIS MOUTH, SO TALKS ALWAYS TURN TO FIGHTS!
I'M BETTER AT FIGHTING THAN TALKING, BUT IT DEFEATS THE PURPOSE IF I KILL HIM!
SO I THOUGHT I'D HAVE YOU GIVE HIM A MESSAGE. HIS PRETTY LITTLE DAUGHTER...

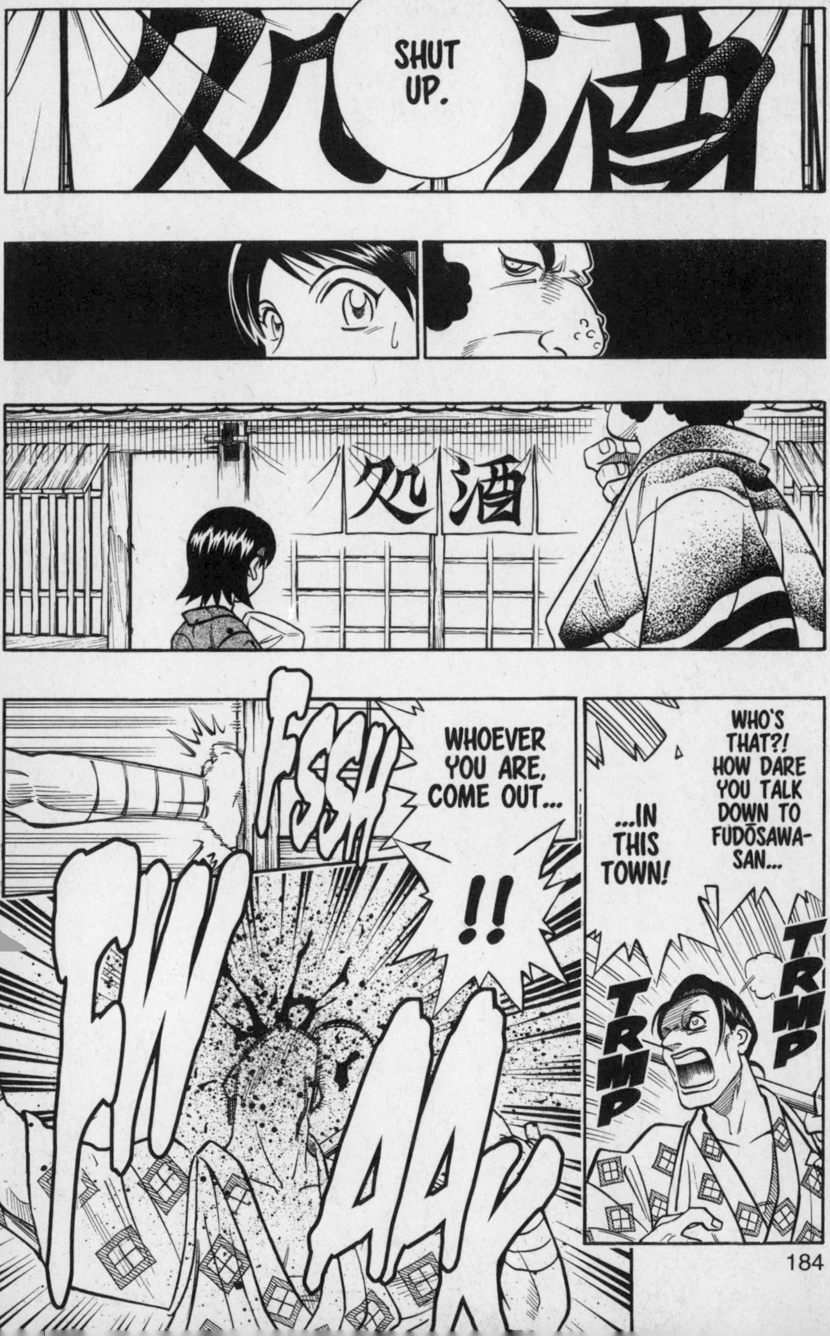
SHUT UP.
WHO'S THAT?! HOW DARE YOU TALK DOWN TO FUDŌSAWA-SAN...
...IN THIS TOWN!
TRMP
TRMP
WHOEVER YOU ARE, COME OUT...
!!

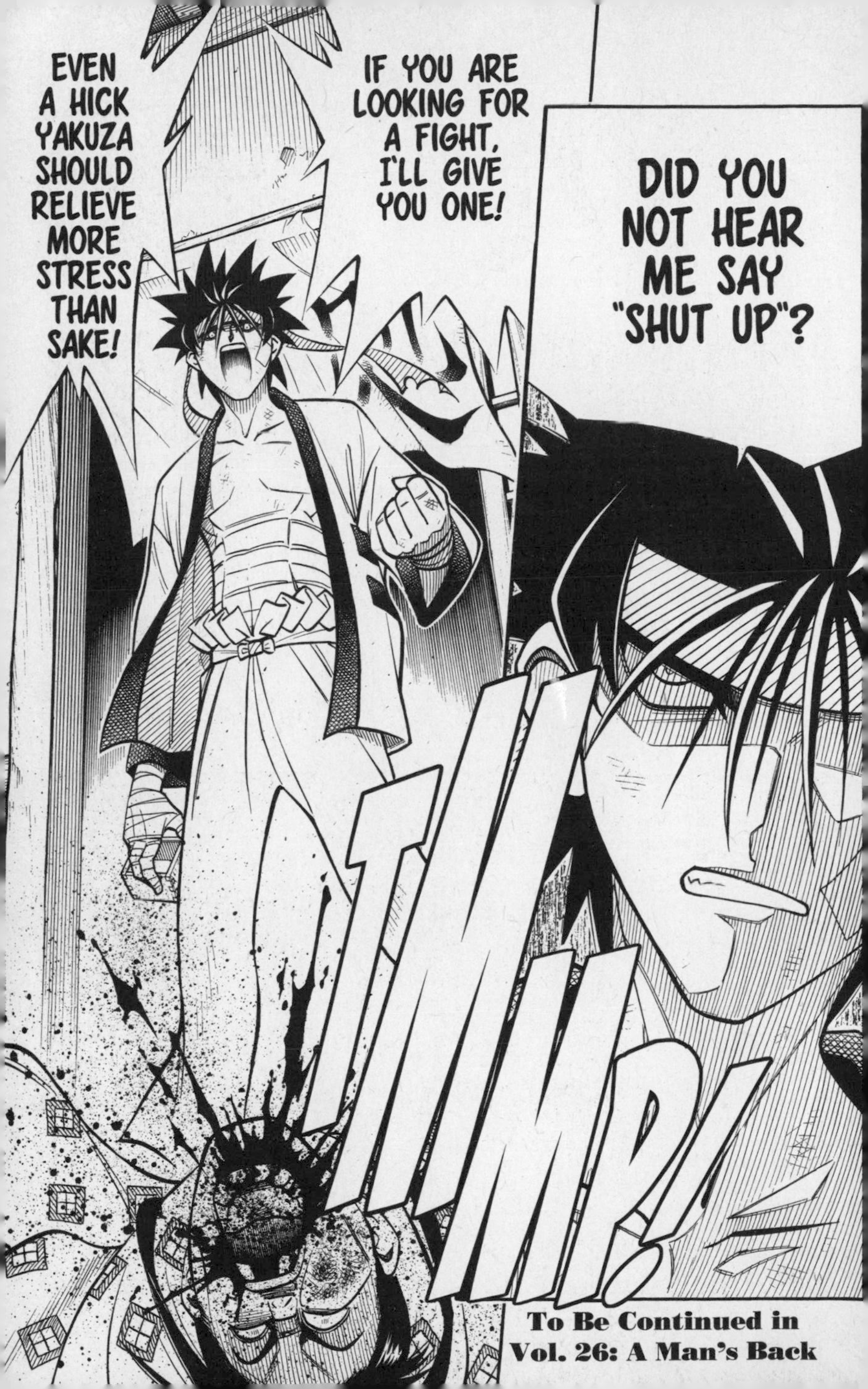
DID YOU NOT HEAR ME SAY "SHUT UP"?
THMP!
IF YOU ARE LOOKING FOR A FIGHT, I'LL GIVE YOU ONE!
EVEN A HICK YAKUZA SHOULD RELIEVE MORE STRESS THAN SAKE!

To Be Continued in Vol. 26: A Man's Back

The Secret Life of Characters (49)

—Kujiranami Hyōgo—

The origin of his one-handedness is the handsome swordsman Iba Hachirō from the Bakumatsu. But there was not originally a direct link from Iba Hachirō to Kujiranami. The one-hand idea was originally reserved for Yukishiro Enishi, but I thought, "Could a one-armed man fight equally against Kenshin, who's mastered Hiten Mitsurugi-ryū?" and "Boss fights should be simple, sword vs. sword." So that was rejected. As a result, we had Iba Hachirō→Yukishiro Enishi→Kujiranami. Kujiranami was supposed to be the Terminator-like character I couldn't depict with Usui, but as the story progressed, he just turned out the way he did. When the story was being worked out, we planned on having a Terminator-like Kujiranami fight Yahiko in the city. But during this time, Watsuki's exhaustion was at its peak, and the assistants were also in the same state, so I thought, "If we do this, someone WILL die! (Destruction of buildings and people scrambling are tiring things)," so I gave up on the Terminator idea. Third time's the charm! I'll create a Terminator character next time!!

Yagyū Hanma from *Samu-Supi*, or Barrett from *FFVII* (I haven't played *FFVII* yet!) have been suggested as models in terms of design. But if you see him, you'll easily realize that the model is Apocalypse from *X-Men*. The lips are quite interesting on this guy, but since nobody would understand it, I used it here. Apocalypse in *X-Men* is Watsuki's favorite villain, equaling even the archrival Magneto. I feel true manliness in his absolute belief in the survival of the fittest, making me want to be like that as a man and as a manga artist, and be able to create characters like him.

Another theme for Kujiranami is "macho middle age fatness," which I enjoyed depicting. No matter what we say, muscles are a symbol of strength. This is a point I must master if I plan on drawing battles, so I plan to keep challenging different types of muscles.

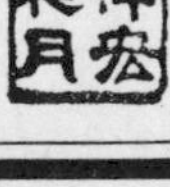

伸宏
和月

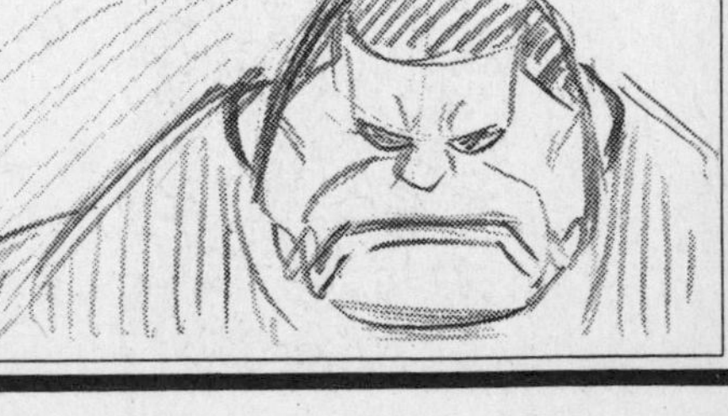

Rurouni Kenshin

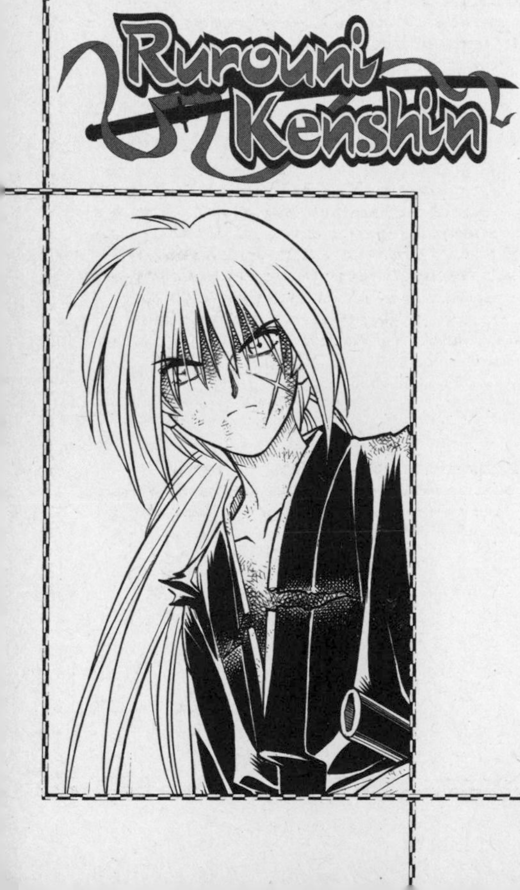

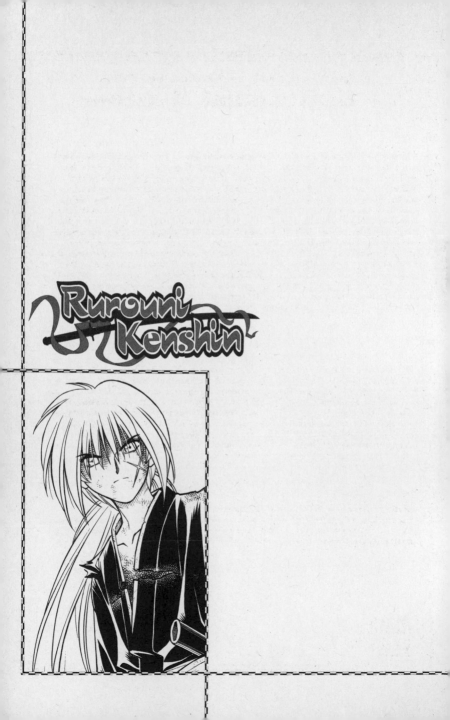

GLOSSARY of the RESTORATION

A brief guide to select Japanese terms used in **Rurouni Kenshin***. Note that, both here and within the story itself, all names are Japanese style—i.e., last or "family" name first, with personal or "given" name following. This is both because* **Kenshin** *is a "period" story, as well as to decrease confusion—if we were to take the example of Kenshin's* sakabatô *and "reverse" the format of the historically established assassin-name "Hitokiri Battôsai," for example, it would make little sense to then call him "Battôsai Himura."*

Hiten Mitsurugi-ryû
Kenshin's sword technique, used more for defense than offense. An "ancient style that pits one against many," it requires exceptional speed and agility to master.

hitokiri
An assassin. Famous swordsmen of the period were sometimes thus known to adopt "professional" names—**Kawakami Gensai**, for example, was also known as "Hitokiri Gensai."

Ishin Shishi
Loyalist or pro-Imperialist **patriots** who fought to restore the Emperor to his ancient seat of power

jinchû
Hitokiri were fond of the word *tenchû*, or "judgment from the heavens," which expressed their belief that judgment lay in their hands. Enishi calls his form of revenge *jinchû*, meaning that if the heavens won't cast judgment on Kenshin, he will with his own brand of justice.

Kawakami Gensai
Real-life, historical inspiration for the character of **Himura Kenshin**

Bakumatsu
Final, chaotic days of the Tokugawa regime

-chan
Honorific. Can be used either as a diminutive (e.g., with a small child—"Little Hanako or Kentarô"), or with those who are grown, to indicate affection ("My dear...").

-dono
Honorific. Even more respectful than *-san*; the effect in modern-day Japanese conversation would be along the lines of "Milord So-and-So." As used by Kenshin, it indicates both respect and humility.

Edo
Capital city of the **Tokugawa Bakufu**; renamed **Tokyo** ("Eastern Capital") after the Meiji Restoration

hakubaikô
The fragrance of white plum blossoms

Himura Kenshin
Kenshin's "real" name, revealed to Kaoru only at her urging

-sama

Honorific. The respectful equivalent of **-san**, **-sama** is used primarily in addressing persons of much higher rank than one's self...or, in a romantic sense, in addressing those upon whom one is crushing, wicked hard.

-san

Honorific. Carries the meaning of "Mr.," "Ms.," "Miss," etc., but used more extensively in Japanese than its English equivalent (note that even an enemy may be addressed as "**-san**").

shizoku

Replaced the term "samurai" in the new era. Made up of ex-samurai and military families, it came to be the gentry class.

shôgun

Feudal military ruler of Japan

shôgunate

See **Tokugawa Bakufu**

Tokugawa Bakufu

Military feudal government which dominated Japan from 1603 to 1867

Tokyo

The renaming of "**Edo**" to "**Tokyo**" is a marker of the start of the **Meiji Restoration**

-kun

Honorific. Used in the modern day among male students, or those who grew up together, but another usage—the one you're more likely to find in *Rurouni Kenshin*—is the "superior-to-inferior" form, intended as a way to emphasize a difference in status or rank, as well as to indicate familiarity or affection.

Kyoto

Home of the Emperor and imperial court from A.D. 794 until shortly after the **Meiji Restoration** in 1868

loyalists

Those who supported the return of the Emperor to power; **Ishin Shishi**

Meiji Restoration

1853-1868; culminated in the collapse of the **Tokugawa Bakufu** and the restoration of imperial rule. So called after Emperor Meiji, whose chosen name was written with the characters for "culture and enlightenment."

patriots

Another term for **Ishin Shishi**... and, when used by Sano, not a flattering one

rurouni

Wanderer, vagabond

sakabatô

Reversed-edge sword (the dull edge on the side the sharp should be, and vice versa); carried by Kenshin as a symbol of his resolution never to kill again

IN THE NEXT VOLUME...

While it appears that Kenshin has regained his senses and is now ready to continue his fight with Enishi, what has become of surly street brawler Sanosuke? Taking a break from Tokyo (and a once-comatose Kenshin), Sano departs to a small farming village that holds special memories for him. It doesn't take Sano long, though, to get caught up in a local land squabble, and he returns to his former "fight merchant" days as a hired fist. But his would-be opponent turns out to be the last person on earth Sano ever expected he'd be paid to fight...his father!

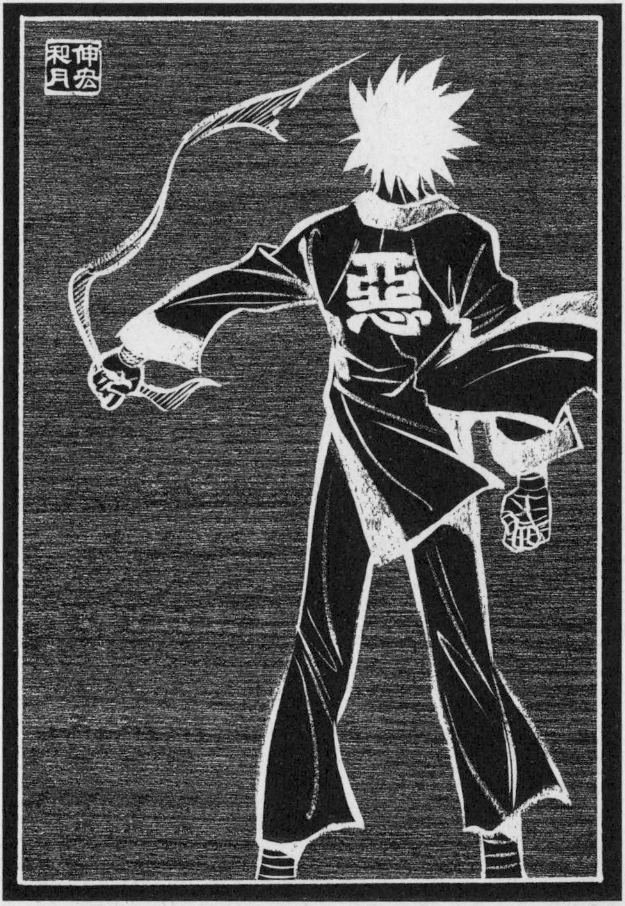
伸宏
和月
悪

Available in May 2006

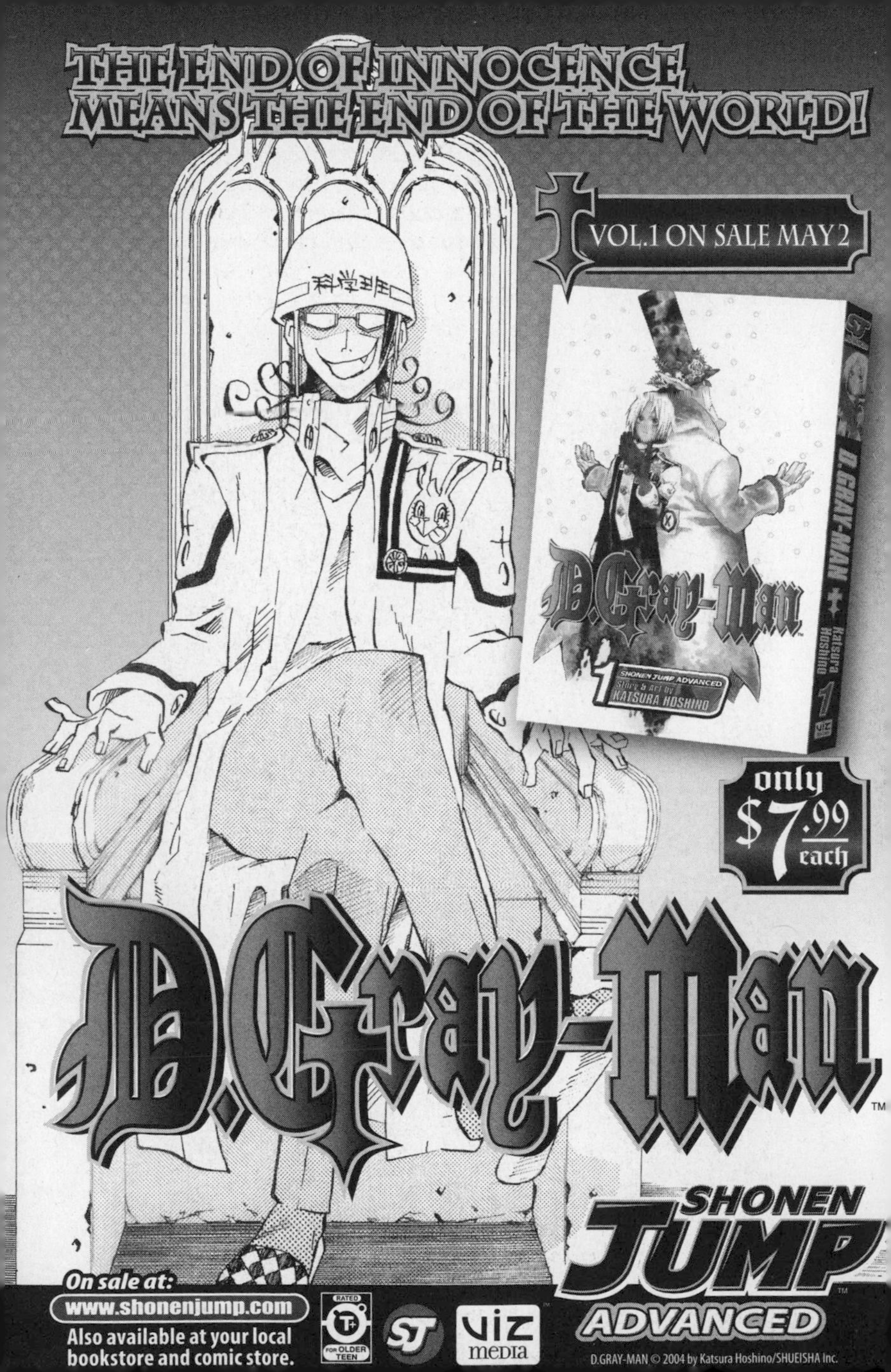
THE END OF INNOCENCE
MEANS THE END OF THE WORLD!
VOL.1 ON SALE MAY 2
D.GRAY-MAN
SHONEN JUMP ADVANCED
Story & Art by KATSURA HOSHINO
only $7.99 each
D.Gray-man™
SHONEN JUMP ADVANCED
On sale at:
www.shonenjump.com
Also available at your local bookstore and comic store.
RATED T+ FOR OLDER TEEN
viz media
D.GRAY-MAN © 2004 by Katsura Hoshino/SHUEISHA Inc.

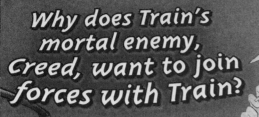

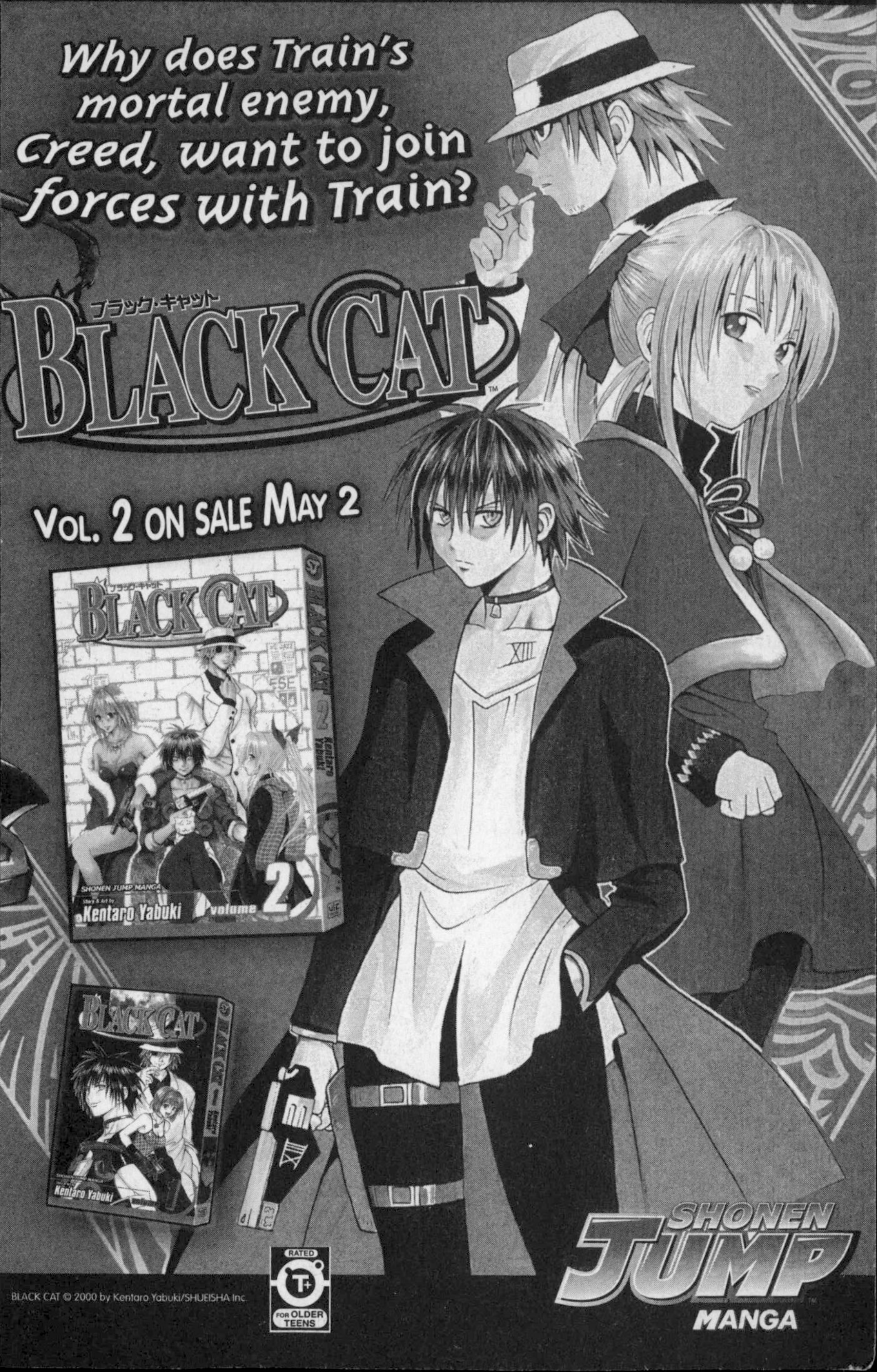

Why does Train's mortal enemy, Creed, want to join forces with Train?
ブラック・キャット
BLACK CAT
VOL. 2 ON SALE MAY 2
BLACK CAT
SHONEN JUMP MANGA
Kentaro Yabuki
volume 2
BLACK CAT
Kentaro Yabuki
RATED T+ FOR OLDER TEENS
BLACK CAT © 2000 by Kentaro Yabuki/SHUEISHA Inc.
SHONEN JUMP MANGA

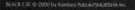

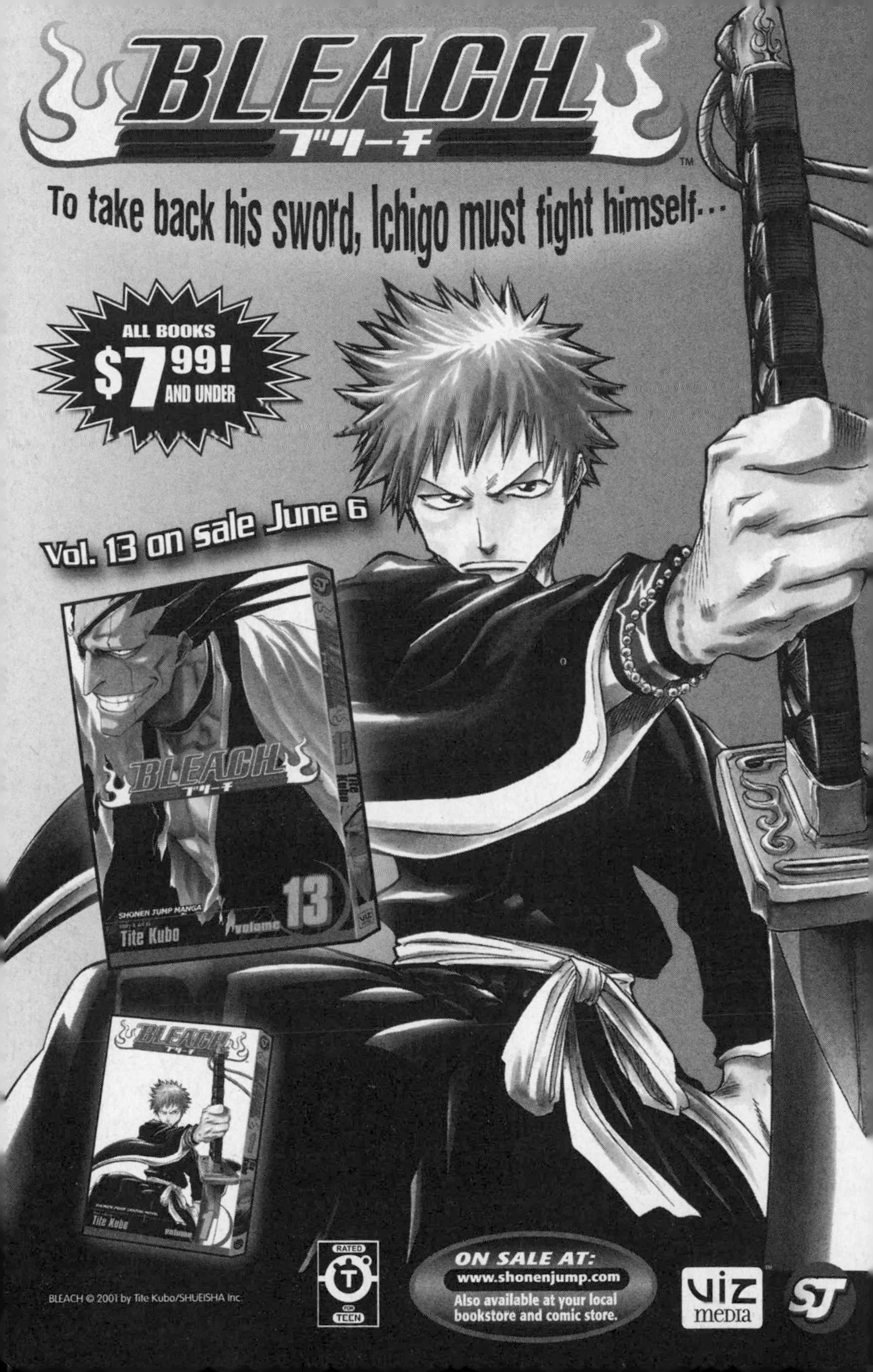

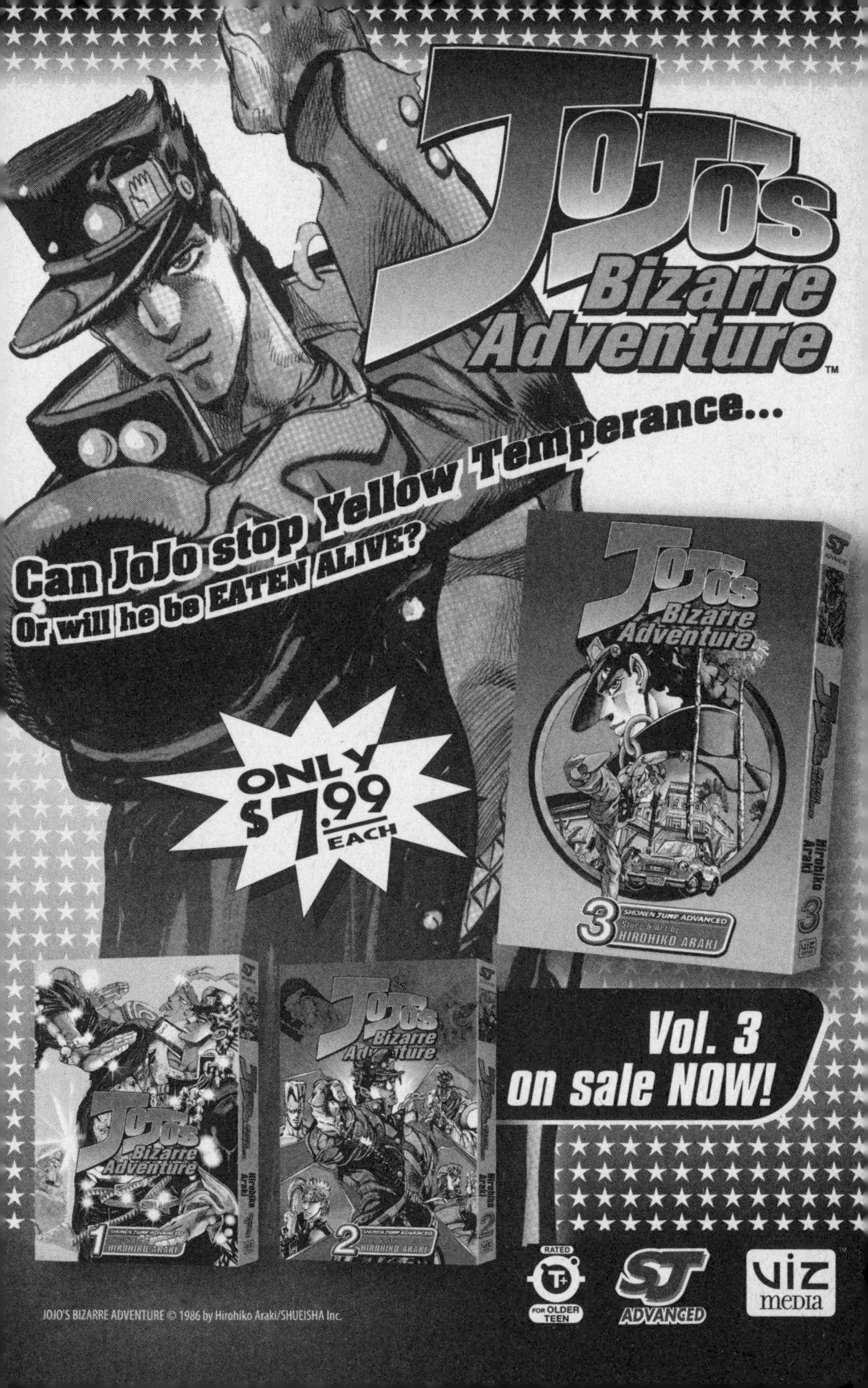
JoJo's Bizarre Adventure™
Can JoJo stop Yellow Temperance...
Or will he be EATEN ALIVE?
ONLY $7.99 EACH
Vol. 3 on sale NOW!
RATED T+ FOR OLDER TEEN
SJ ADVANCED
VIZ media
JOJO'S BIZARRE ADVENTURE © 1986 by Hirohiko Araki/SHUEISHA Inc.

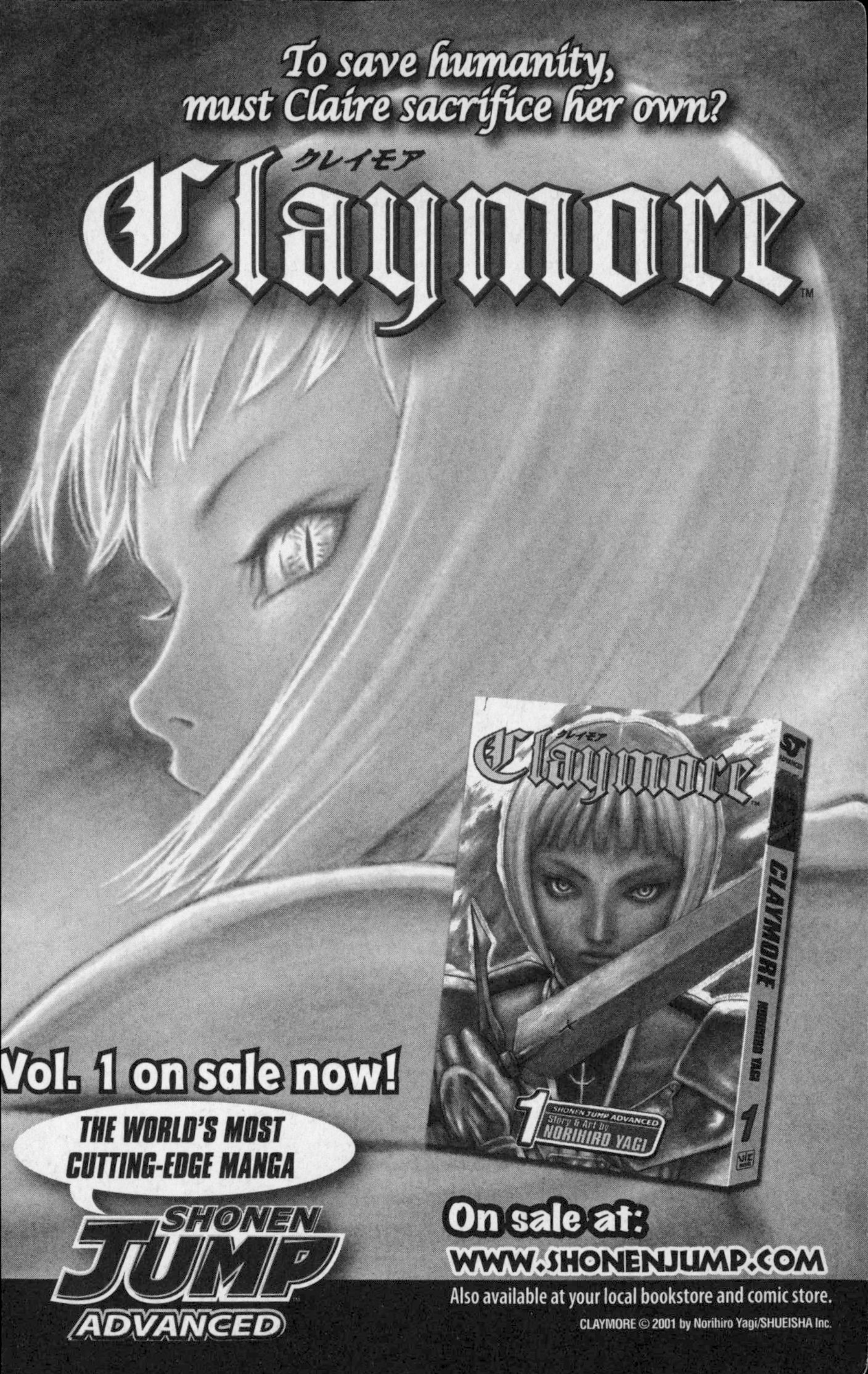
To save humanity,
must Claire sacrifice her own?
クレイモア
Claymore™
Claymore
CLAYMORE
NORIHIRO YAGI
SHONEN JUMP ADVANCED
Story & Art by
NORIHIRO YAGI
Vol. 1 on sale now!
THE WORLD'S MOST CUTTING-EDGE MANGA
SHONEN JUMP ADVANCED
On sale at:
WWW.SHONENJUMP.COM
Also available at your local bookstore and comic store.
CLAYMORE © 2001 by Norihiro Yagi/SHUEISHA Inc.

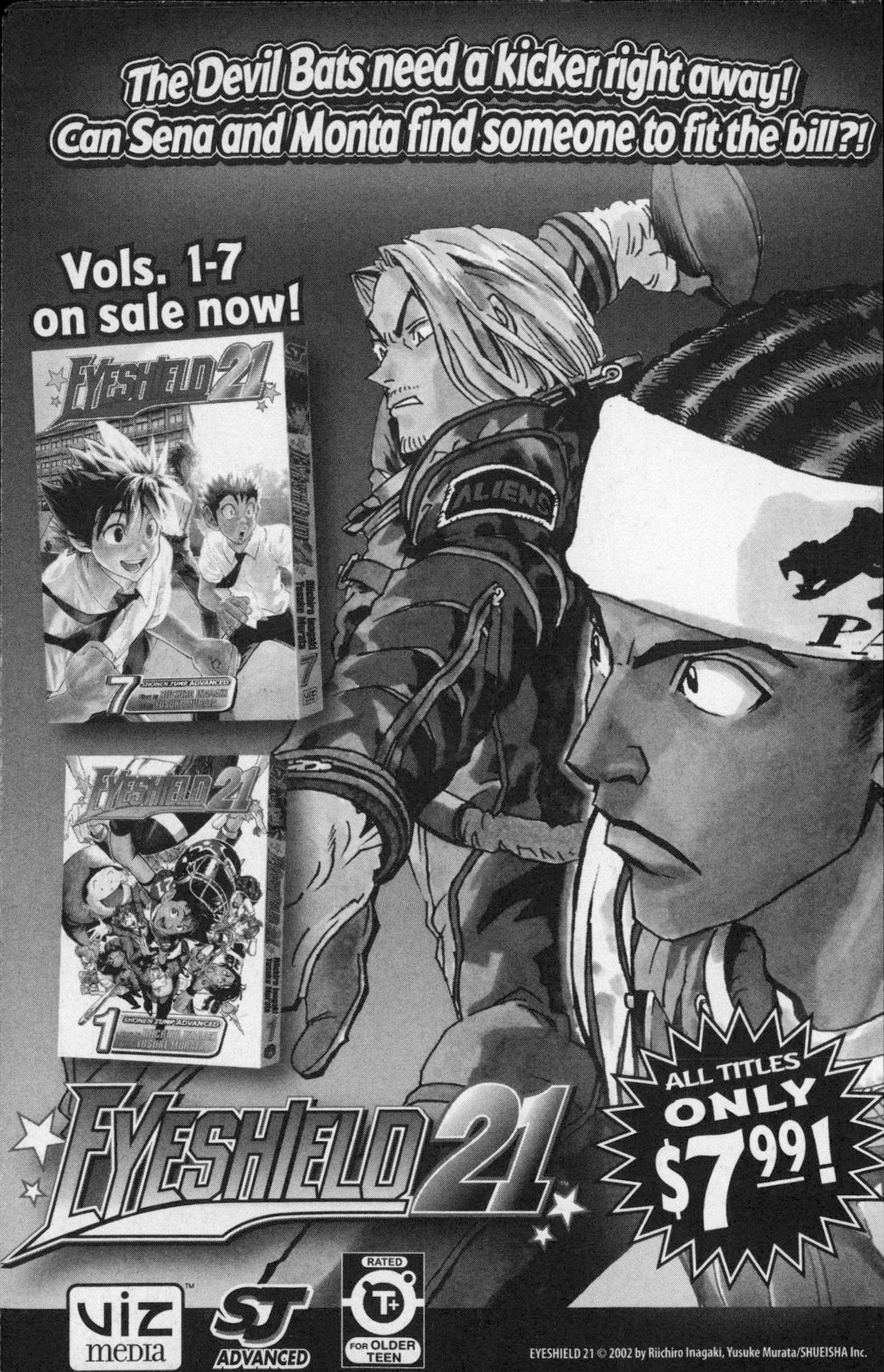

The Devil Bats need a kicker right away!
Can Sena and Monta find someone to fit the bill?!
Vols. 1-7
on sale now!
EYESHIELD 21
7
SHONEN JUMP ADVANCED
EYESHIELD 21
1
SHONEN JUMP ADVANCED
ALIENS
EYESHIELD 21™
ALL TITLES
ONLY
$7.99!
viz media™
SJ ADVANCED
RATED T+ FOR OLDER TEEN
EYESHIELD 21 © 2002 by Riichiro Inagaki, Yusuke Murata/SHUEISHA Inc.

Tell us what you think about SHONEN JUMP manga!

Our survey is now available online.
Go to: www.SHONENJUMP.com/mangasurvey

Help us make our product offering better!

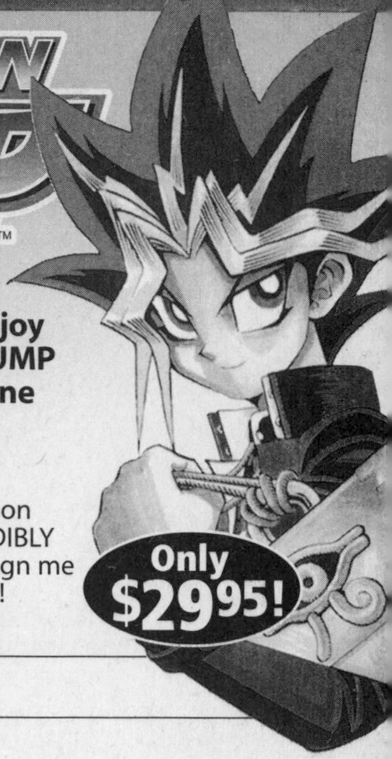